D1784018

FOUR RENAISSANCE COMEDIES

Also published by Palgrave Macmillan:

Colin Gibson (ed.), *Six Renaissance Tragedies*
David Thomas (ed.), *Six Restoration and French Neoclassic Plays*
David Thomas (ed.), *Four Georgian and Pre-Revolutionary Plays*

Four Renaissance Comedies

The Old Wives Tale
The Shoemakers Holiday
The Alchemist
A New Way to Pay Old Debts

Edited by

ROBERT SHAUGHNESSY

Introduction, selection and editorial matter
© Robert Shaughnessy 2004

All rights reserved. No reproduction, copy or transmission of this publication may be made without written permission.

No paragraph of this publication may be reproduced, copied or transmitted save with written permission or in accordance with the provisions of the Copyright, Designs and Patents Act 1988, or under the terms of any licence permitting limited copying issued by the Copyright Licensing Agency, 90 Tottenham Court Road, London W1T 4LP.

Any person who does any unauthorised act in relation to this publication may be liable to criminal prosecution and civil claims for damages.

The author has asserted his right to be identified as the author of this work in accordance with the Copyright, Designs and Patents Act 1988.

First published 2004 by
PALGRAVE MACMILLAN
Houndmills, Basingstoke, Hampshire RG21 6XS and
175 Fifth Avenue, New York, N.Y. 10010
Companies and representatives throughout the world

PALGRAVE MACMILLAN is the global academic imprint of the Palgrave Macmillan division of St. Martin's Press, LLC and of Palgrave Macmillan Ltd. Macmillan® is a registered trademark in the United States, United Kingdom and other countries. Palgrave is a registered trademark in the European Union and other countries.

ISBN 0–333–97365–8 hardback
ISBN 0–333–97366–6 paperback

This book is printed on paper suitable for recycling and made from fully managed and sustained forest sources.

A catalogue record for this book is available from the British Library.

Library of Congress Cataloging-in-Publication Data
    Four Renaissance comedies / edited by Robert Shaughnessy.
        p. cm.
    Includes bibliographical references and index.
    Contents: The old wives tale / George Peele—The shoemakers' holiday / Thomas Dekker—The alchemist / Ben Jonson—A new way to pay old debts / Philip Massinger.
        ISBN 0–333–97365–8—ISBN 0–333–97366–6 (pbk.)
    1. English drama (Comedy) 2. English drama—Early modern and Elizabethan, 1500–1600. 3. English drama—17th century. I. Shaughnessy, Robert, 1962–

PR1248.F68 2003
822'.05230803—dc22   2003053655

10 9 8 7 6 5 4 3 2 1
13 12 11 10 09 08 07 06 05 04

Printed in China

For Jacqueline

Contents

Acknowledgements	viii
General Introduction	ix
A Note on the Texts	xxvii
The Old Wives Tale	1
Introductory Note	1
Text	6
Notes to the Play	29
The Shoemakers Holiday	33
Introductory Note	33
Text	41
Notes to the Play	95
The Alchemist	105
Introductory Note	105
Text	113
Notes to the Play	213
A New Way to Pay Old Debts	231
Introductory Note	231
Text	238
Notes to the Play	308
Further Reading	313

Acknowledgements

Thanks are due to all those at Palgrave Macmillan who have supported this edition, especially Sonya Barker, Felicity Noble, Beverley Tarquini and Anna Sandeman; to the anonymous readers who offered constructive criticism and saved me from a number of egregious errors; to my students at the University of Surrey Roehampton, whose enthusiastic engagement with the plays has confirmed for me their enduring comic life; and to my family, for offering the space in which I could make it happen.

General Introduction

For many contemporary readers, theatre practitioners and theatregoers, there is one basic problem with the plays that are found under the generic umbrella of comedy during the late sixteenth and early seventeenth centuries: they are not, on the face of it, very funny. Indeed, at the turn of the twenty-first century, when the global template of comedy is defined by the uniquely brilliant combination of domestic soap opera, everyday surrealism, sly media references and social satire of *The Simpsons*, the sense of humour that informs the comic drama of the English Renaissance can often seem misguided, objectionable or incomprehensible, and the plays themselves contrived and artificial. The theatre director Sam Mendes recalled a particularly dispiriting experience of this kind during the first reading of *The Alchemist* for the RSC in 1991: 'the first day in rehearsal, it was like the actors were reading a sort of Swahili text. I've never had such a terrible run-through in my life, and such an appallingly depressed group of actors'.[1] Jonson, like most if not all of his contemporaries (other than Shakespeare for some; including Shakespeare for others), is perceived as opaque, deadly and alien; and no doubt a major component of the actors' despondency was the dread that they were not only going to have to make the text work, but, even more terrifyingly, actually provoke audiences to laughter. Mendes and his team quickly realised that the most effective route into the play was to abandon preconceptions about motivation and character psychology and to focus instead upon the rhythm and shape of the action, which meant 'doing a very early run-through just to see what doors people had to come in and out of'; 'we had to sort of decode it as a series of moves, a series of journeys, a series of stage shapes'.[2] It seems a sensible way of approaching not only Jonsonian comedy but comic drama in general (and one not without precedent in

original stage practice, where the work of rehearsal would of
necessity be limited to the orchestration of entrances and exits,
set-pieces and group scenes[3]), and the result was a brilliantly
energetic, intelligent and genuinely laugh-filled production.
Nonetheless, the adjustment of perception that was needed
in order to negotiate the difference between modern and early
modern comic expectations was quite considerable, and prompts
not only the theoretical and practical question of whether renaissance comedy can still be funny, but also the more historical
question of what 'comedy', in this setting and in subsequent
ones, actually means.

Kings and Clowns

We can address this question, initially, by considering two very
different views of the comic drama in the early modern period.
The first is taken from a work of literary theory, Sir Philip
Sidney's *The Defence of Poesie* (written 1582; published 1595).
Sidney wrote within the context of the literary culture of the
court, and the *Defence*, is accordingly, coloured by disdain for
the products of the popular entertainment industry. Noting that
the comic was something that 'naughty play-makers and stage
keepers have justly made odious', the poet Sidney castigates the
lowly hacks of the popular stage (whom he characterises as arti-
san 'play-makers' rather than 'poets') for corrupting a genre
which, after its particular fashion, has both a formal and generic
coherence, and an ethical purpose. Comedy, Sidney proposes, 'is
an imitation of the common errors of our life, which he represen-
teth in the most ridiculous and scornful sort that may be; so as it
is impossible that any beholder can be content to be such a one'.[4]
Sidney's conviction that comedy should be sternly corrective
rests upon an austerely classical understanding of the purpose of
comic satire, and thus furnishes the rationale for comedy that
was unaccountably omitted from Aristotle's *Poetics*, in which the
philosopher had observed that 'comedy aims at representing
men as worse than they are nowadays, tragedy as better'; according to Aristotle, 'worse' is used 'in the sense that the ridiculous is
a species of ugliness or badness', and thus is amenable to exposure and correction.[5] For Sidney, comedy presents the grotesque,
the excessive and the disordered to mirror the spectator's own
deficiencies (primarily greed, lust and vanity), and to prompt

him to mend his ways accordingly: 'nothing can more open his eyes than to see his own actions contemptibly set forth'.[6]

According to this scheme, proper comedy proceeds appropriately and decorously in its chosen task, and Sidney illustrates its basic sobriety (indeed, its legitimacy) by comparing the relation of comic vice to virtue to the kind of reciprocity found in geometry, where 'the oblique must be known as well as the right, and in arithmetic the odd as well as the even'; similarly, 'the actions of our life, who seeth not the filthiness of evil, wanteth a great foil to perceive the beauty of virtue'.[7] Comedy, moreover, balances tragedy by dealing with 'our private and domestical matters',[8] whereas its generic partner addresses the larger issues of politics and statecraft. The difficulty, unsurprisingly, is that few if any sixteenth-century plays come anywhere near to living up to the strictures Sidney prescribes. Sidney is hard pressed throughout the *Defence* to sustain the case for the high purpose and political orthodoxy of the drama with contemporary examples (although he does cite Sackville and Norton's *Gorboduc* as one instance of a tragedy 'full of stately speeches and well sounding phrases ... full of notably morality'[9]); all the more because, as he sees it, the popular drama is in a scandalous state of generic fluidity and hybridity. In an often-quoted passage, Sidney lampoons the extravagances of a performance practice that wantonly ignores the Aristotlean unities of time, place and action:

> ... you shall have Asia of the one side, and Afric of the other, and so many other under kingdoms, that the player, when he comes in must ever begin with telling where he is, or else the tale will not be conceived. Now you shall have three ladies walk to gather flowers, and then we must believe the stage to be a garden. By and by we hear news of a shipwreck in the same place, then we are to blame if we accept it not for a rock. Upon the back of that comes out a hideous monster with fire and smoke, and then the miserable beholders are bound to take it for a cave; while in the meantime two armies fly in, represented with swords and bucklers, and then what hard heart will not receive it for a pitched field?[10]

Sidney evokes a drama that is episodic, picaresque, given to extravagant spectacle and cheerfully accommodating the everyday alongside the materials of romance and fantasy. This is the style of plays such as Robert Greene's *Friar Bacon and Friar Bungay*

(1589), in which Prince Edward swaps roles with his Fool to pursue love in the countryside, encountering magicians and the devil; and, as represented in this volume, George Peele's *The Old Wives Tale* (1592). Nor that this eclecticism was confined to the works that advertised themselves as comedies. The new and experimental genre of the history play, in particular, was particularly energetic in its assimilation of legendary and folklore material into the process of national myth-making (as in Robert Greene's *Scottish History of James IV* [1590], Shakespeare's *Henry VI* plays [c. 1590]); and in the hands of a writer such as Christopher Marlowe, plays nominally designated as tragedies made extensive use of burlesque, black comedy and clowning (e.g., *The Jew of Malta* [1589] and *Doctor Faustus* [1592]). At the end of stage performances, even of tragedies, it was customary for the players to dance a jig.[11]

For some Renaissance theorists, as Stephen Orgel points out, comedy was not just tragedy's corollary but 'the largest condition of drama',[12] in that the comic both encompassed the tragic and permeated it. For Sidney, however, the mixture of modes and styles in the drama was a serious moral concern, in that both tragedy and comedy were, as a consequence of this mixing, denied their appropriate functions:

> But besides these gross absurdities, how all their plays be neither right tragedies nor right comedies, mingling kings and clowns, not because the matter so carrieth it, but thrust in the clown by head and shoulders to play a part in majestical matters, with neither decency nor discretion; so as neither the admiration and commiseration, nor the right sportfulness, is by their mongrel tragicomedy obtained.[13]

If 'right sportfulness' is proper to comedy, it is not the same thing as laughter; and the distinction between 'laughter' and 'delight' forms the basis for a further refinement of Sidney's definition of the genuinely comic. 'Our comedians' (i.e. players), Sidney gloomily notes, 'think there is no delight without laughter, which is very wrong … delight hath a joy in it either permanent or present. Laughter hath only a scornful tickling'.[14] Delight resides in the contemplation of truth and beauty, whereas laughter is provoked by the sorry spectacle of deformity and misfortune. Here, then, is one Elizabethan view of comedy in which raising a laugh is not the primary imperative; indeed, it may even be detrimental to the purpose.

Although it is impossible to determine whether Sidney's 'thrust in the clown by head and shoulders' is intended to refer to actual performance practice, it is reminiscent of the stage antics of his contemporary, the celebrated clown Richard Tarlton, whose exploits articulate a radically different account of the comic. According to one writer, Tarlton had only to show his memorably grotesque face onstage to reduce audiences to helplessness:

> As Tarlton when his head was only seen,
> The Tire-house and the tapestry between,
> Set all the multitude in such a laughter,
> They could not hold for scarce an hour after.[15]

Gratuitous, senseless and uncontrolled, this is the kind of laughter that Sidney deplored; nonetheless, Tarlton's skill in soliciting it earned him the kind of favour that the poet might well have envied, in that the monarch herself was reportedly one of his admirers: 'when Queen Elizabeth was serious, I dare not say sullen, and out of good humour, he could *un-dumpish* her at his pleasure … he told the Queen more of her faults than most of her chaplains, and cured her melancholy better than all of her physicians'.[16] The idea that laughter had a quasi-medicinal function, perhaps analogous to purging or laxatives, in addition to an ethical one, can be traced back to Aristotle, and it is echoed in theoretical pronouncements on comedy elsewhere; as Nicholas Udall claimed in the Prologue to one of the earliest printed English-language comedies, *Ralph Roister Doister* (1541), 'Mirth prolongeth life, and causeth health / Mirth recreates our spirits, and voideth pensiveness' (Prologue, 3–4). Tarlton, however, evidently felt no inclination to engage an ethical rationale for his craft. In addition to his ready, often brutal wit, and the singing and dancing skills that were *de rigeur* for the professional clown, he was renowned for his talent for extemporisation. His part in the comic chronicle history *The Famous Victories of Henry V* (c. 1588) afforded one such opportunity:

> At the Bull at Bishopsgate was a play of Henry the fift, wherein the judge was to take a box on the ear; and because he was absent that should take the blow, Tarlton himself, ever forward to please, took upon him to play the same judge, besides his own part of the clown: and Knel then playing Henry the fift, hit Tarlton a sound box indeed, which made

the people laugh the more because it was he, but anon the judge goes in, and immediately Tarlton in his clown's clothes comes out, and asks the actors what news. O, saith one, hadst thou been here, thou shouldest have seen Prince Henry hit the judge a terrible box on the ear. What, man, said Tarlton, strike a judge? It is true, yfaith, said the other. No other like, said Tarlton, and it could not be but terrible to the judge, when the report so terrifies me, that methinks the blow remains still on my cheek, that it burns again. The people laughed at this mightily: and to this day I have heard it commended for rare; but no marvel, for he had many of these.[17]

The anecdote suggests a performer in his element in a theatre that is rowdy, makeshift, iconoclastic and ripe for moments of spontaneous improvisation: if the initial joke resides in the substitution of clown for Lord Chief Justice, Tarlton's subsequent ironic play upon the doubling points to the sustained and sophisticated self-awareness of Elizabethan popular performance. Armed with the levelling scepticism, sardonic wit and direct rapport with the audience inherited from the medieval stage figure of the Vice, the clown is able to move in and out of the dramatic fiction at will; as this incident suggests, moreover, the scope of comic improvisation was not limited to the written script. Although Hamlet was later to warn the players visiting Elsinore to 'let those that play your clowns speak no more than is set down for them' (3.2.34–5), it appears that ad-libbing was the professional clown's stock-in-trade. In a period in which all playscripts had to be submitted to the state censor, the Master of the Revels, for licensing, this was a dangerously unregulated domain of speech, all the more so because the clown's discourse characteristically engages with the profane, the lewd, the scurrilous and the scatological.

An important aspect of the history of comic drama during the late sixteenth and early seventeenth century, then, was the progressive reining-in of the clown, so that Tarlton's successors (including Robert Armin and Will Kemp) found themselves increasingly – although still not entirely – integrated within the dramatic fictions they inhabited. By the time of Jonson's *Bartholomew Fair* (1614), the clown's (and, by extension, the player's) penchant for extra-textual improvisation and horseplay has been drastically curtailed, and thoroughly subordinated to the authority of the dramatic text and its author. In the Induction to this play, the 'Stage-keeper', a figure directly associated with the older tradition, introduces the action with nostalgic recollections of 'Master Tarlton's time', but ruefully reports that the author, one of 'these Master-Poets', has 'kicked me three or four times about the tiring-house' (Induction, 24–5); he is then banished from the stage by his literary- (and legalistically) minded successors, the Book-holder and the Scrivener, whose task is to establish a new contractual relationship between author, text, stage and spectators, whereby 'the Author promiseth to present them by us, with a new sufficient play called *Bartholomew Fair*, merry, and as full of noise, as sport; made to delight all, and to offend none. Provided they have the wit or the honesty to think well of themselves' (Induction, 74–5).[18] As Jonson was at pains to point out (and as *The Alchemist* perfectly demonstrates), the comic dramaturgy that this entailed was one that adhered to the classical precepts which Sidney had regarded as shamefully lacking in the dramas of the previous century; by his own account, 'the laws of time, place, persons he observeth / From no needful rule he swerveth' (*Volpone, or The Fox*, Prologue, 31–2). There may have been no place for clowns like Tarlton in either Sidney's or Jonson's comic worldviews, but audiences continued to remember them with affection well into the seventeenth century.

Money, Sex and the City

The polar positions occupied by Sidney, apologist for a courtly mode of comedy conceived in a spirit of high literary seriousness, and Tarlton, representative and exponent of a clowning tradition that subordinated drama to improvised play and the exigencies of circumstance and popular taste, indicate the spectrum of opinion and activity within which English Renaissance comic theatre operated. In the years before and after the opening of London's (and England's) first permanent playhouse, The Theatre in Shoreditch, in 1576, comedy was characterised by opportunism, eclecticism and diversity; it was a genre – or range of genres – which drew upon a range of comic sources, models and traditions: domestic material such as fairytales and folktales, ballads, mummers' plays, mystery and miracle plays, interludes; and also classical and contemporary European influences such as Roman New Comedy, Italian *commedia erudita* (learned comedy) and the *commedia dell'arte*. The comic genre in this period thus encompassed works of fantasy such as *Clyomon and Clamydes* (1570), *Mucedorus* (1590) and Greene's *Orlando Furioso* (1594), works of erotic intrigue imitating the Roman model such as George Gascoigne's *Supposes* (1566; this was a reworking of the Italian Arisoto's *I Suppositi*), elegant, stylised compliments to Queen Elizabeth such as John Lyly's *Endymion* (1588) and plays written for schoolboys, students and clerics as an extension of their training in the arts of rhetoric and public speech, and as the vernacular became recognised as a legitimate medium for comic drama (*Ralph Roister Doister, Gammer Gurton's Needle* [1575]).

The form and content of early modern comedy was shaped by the material circumstances in which it was produced. The establishment of the playhouses on the outskirts of the city of London (so located in order to elude the regulatory powers of the City of London authorities) during the final decades of the sixteenth century (the Curtain was built in 1577, the Rose in 1587, and the Globe in 1599), and the formation of playing companies under the protective auspices of the nominal aristocratic patronage, marked the beginnings of the professionalisation of the theatre industry, but also an important change in the nature of the conceptual, as well as material, domain of performance: in that its conduct began to be conceived in terms of architecture and fixed location, as well as according to the shifting and contingent circumstances faced by the older itinerant playing troupes. The playhouses continued to operate as one among many of the places in which players could be called to perform (indeed, some maintained that the playhouses were merely the venues in which they rehearsed prior to performances at court), but the increasing identification of playing companies with specific buildings was reflected in the drama itself in the cultivation of a dramaturgy precisely attuned to the rhythms and practices of everyday life in the city of London. The success of the early modern metropolitan theatre industry was to a large extent a result of the expansion and economic success of the capital itself, whose population grew to a quarter of a million during the period, and whose patterns of entrepreneurial activity and business organisation provided the template for those of the playing companies. These were, of the most part, set up as joint stock entities with a core of named sharers (the principal players), surrounded by a support system of apprentices (boy players, who took the female roles until they reached maturity) and hired men, amongst which group were included musicians and writers. Within this system, the craft of playwriting was conducted in a situation in which the dramatist was subordinate to the company that had commissioned him: plays became the property of the playing company, not the author (and were often printed with the former's name on the title page rather than that of the latter), and literary ambitions were decisively secondary to the imperative of catering to the tastes of the heterogeneous popular audiences which, much to the displeasure of the city authorities, the playhouses succeeded in cultivating and sustaining over a quarter of a century of profound social, cultural and economic change. It is this sense of change and mutability that is at the heart of the comic drama of the sixteenth and seventeenth centuries: it is a landscape of gulls and tricksters, in which lovers keep as wary an eye on their chances of financial gain as on the possibility of erotic satisfaction (this is the prevailing mood of plays ranging from Jonson's *Every Man in his Humour* [1598], through Thomas Middleton's *A Trick to Catch the Old One* [1606], to Philip Massinger's *A New Way to Pay Old Debts* [c. 1625]); in which the business of role-playing, disguise and cross-dressing (from Shakespeare's *As You Like It* [1599] to Thomas Middleton and Thomas Dekker's *The Roaring Girl* [1608]), reflects deeper unease about the mutability of class and gender roles; and in which the traditional prerogatives of the aristocracy find themselves vulnerable to the new civic mercantile order.

When the playhouses re-opened in 1594 after two years of closure enforced by the prevalence of plague, it marked the emergence of a small nucleus of companies that would dominate the theatrical market during the last decade of the sixteenth century and into the seventeenth: chief among them the Lord Admiral's Men, based at the Rose and subsequently the Fortune, and the Lord Chamberlain's Men, first at the Theatre and the Curtain and, from 1599, at the Globe. Backed by the theatrical entrepreneur Philip Henslowe, whose ledger of accounts of his financial dealings have provided an invaluable record of the business of playmaking during the period,[19] the Admiral's Men hosted the output of writers such as George Chapman and Thomas Dekker; the Lord Chamberlain's Men (who became the King's Men after the accession of James I in 1603), meanwhile, claimed the talents of Ben Jonson and William Shakespeare. Jonson also supplied material to rival organisations such as the St Paul's Boys, a company of juvenile players located at the Cathedral specialising in satirical drama (*Cynthia's Revels, Poetaster* [both 1601]); and scripted a considerable number of masques staged at James's court. Shakespeare, however, wrote exclusively for the Lord Chamberlain's/King's Men, and, indeed, was one of the company's most profitable assets. From the early 1590s through to 1613, the year of the burning of the Globe playhouse during a performance of Shakespeare and John Fletcher's history play *Henry VIII, or All is True*, Shakespeare supplied a steady stream of works that were sufficiently lucrative for him, as one of the company's principal sharers, to be able to purchase a substantial house in Stratford and, in 1613, property in Blackfriars. Shakespeare may have been a shrewd businessman and author of demonstrably popular plays, but, at least as far as his comic writing went, his success was achieved by going against the grain of his contemporaries, in that the social milieu of the works is primarily aristocratic rather than bourgeois, its geographical setting fabled or romantically foreign (the Forest of Arden, Illyria, Verona, Vienna) rather than localised, its general tenor rural and pastoral rather than civic; unlike Jonson or his occasional collaborator Middleton, Shakespeare rarely foregrounds financial imperatives as the driving forces of plot or characterisation (in part, this explains Shakespeare's longevity as a theatrical presence).

Shakespeare's house in London was close to the Blackfriars playhouse, an indoor venue acquired by the principal members of the King's Men in 1608 as a subsidiary outlet for their work during the winter months, the open-air Globe remaining in use during the summer. The Blackfriars theatre was one of a number of playhouses located within the environs of the city of London that have often been described as 'private' (as distinct from the 'public' playhouses distributed around the city's perimeter, along the South Bank of the Thames and to the North). Smaller, more expensively priced and more socially exclusive, catering for a coterie audience rather than the variegated, volatile crowds drawn to the open-air stages, these indoor theatres housed a theatrical practice subtly differentiated from that of the public playhouses in terms of technical sophistication and formal organisation: in order to allow for the trimming and re-lighting of the candles that provided the sole means of illumination, plays were required to be structured in five acts, with musicians playing during the intervals (the texts of plays designed for the public playhouses were generally published without act divisions). Formidably equipped with machinery for the production of spectacle, contrivance and effect, the Blackfriars could accommodate the late comedies of Shakespeare (featuring, e.g., the appearance and disappearance of a banquet in *The Tempest* [1611] and the descent of Jupiter in *Cymbeline* [1610]); it was equally the perfectly apposite setting for *The Alchemist* (1611), a play confined for four of its five acts to the domestic interior of 'a house in Blackfriars'.

The relative intimacy of the indoor playhouses furnished the circumstances for a progressive narrowing of the social range and theatrical ambition of the stage comedies of the Caroline period (whose beginning was marked by the accession of Charles I in 1625, although the inward-looking trend was already well under way). The primary audience was now the fashionable London elite, and the comedies of the 1620s and 1630s reflected their tastes and preoccupations, as represented, for example, in the plays of James Shirley, whose *Hyde Park* (1632) indicates in its title the limited social and geographical locale inhabited by the work and its intended recipients. As Simon Shepherd and Peter Womack observe, playwriting, at least when operating in the service of the court, was a respectable and well-rewarded activity by the 1630s: 'no longer the preserve of jumped-up craftsmen's sons and traders', it was 'an acceptable demonstration of one's courtly accomplishment'.[20] But as the boundaries of the private-playhouse drama's subject-matter contracted, the numbers of new plays diminished: whereas thirty-six works were commissioned in 1624, a mere nine were in 1630.[21] Meanwhile, the open-air playhouses continued to operate on the fringes of the city, surviving on revivals of Elizabethan and Jacobean scripts, recycled, rewritten and adapted to sustain their appeal to popular tastes, but also mobilising a nostalgia for the drama of a former era that offered an alternative perspective upon the critical period that culminated, in 1642, with the closure of the playhouses and the outbreak of the English Civil War.[22]

New Ways to Play Old Texts

It remains to return to the concerns aired at the beginning of this introduction; and in particular to the question of how far, and in what ways, the comic drama of early modern England remains theatrically viable within a twenty-first-century performance culture which we may suspect to be largely unsympathetic to it. The situation is complicated, of course, by the anomalous position of Shakespeare, a selection of whose plays continue to dominate what is already a fairly restricted and repetitive professional theatrical repertoire. In general, the history of early modern drama on stage from the late seventeenth century (when the theatres were restored along with the monarchy in the person of Charles II) through to the twenty-first has been that of Shakespeare in performance; it is a history that has been well-documented, as have the complex cultural, political and ideological forces which have manufactured and perpetuated Shakespeare's global dominance.[23] As a consequence of the imperialist ventures of the English, then British, empire (and its successor, the United States), Shakespeare has entered into – and has been adapted to – the theatrical repertoires of most cultures worldwide; and this ubiquity has been both celebrated (as proof of the Bard's universality) and condemned (as evidence of cultural colonialism). As far as the consequences for the reception of the works of Shakespeare's contemporaries are concerned, however, the centrality, and singularity, of Shakespeare has meant that these are almost invariably regarded as the master-dramatist's 'others', perpetually defined in terms of what they are not. As Mick Jardine has argued, paying specific attention to the critical pairing of Shakespeare and Jonson (although his analysis could be amplified, adjusted and extended to account for the processing of many other Elizabethan and Jacobean writers), 'Shakespeare's cultural pre-eminence is posited upon Jonson's secondary status as a scapegoating Other to a Shakespearean centre or ideal'.[24] Simon Shepherd makes a similar case in relation to Marlowe, who is, he urges, customarily treated as 'Marlowe-who-isn't-Shakespeare, the leading playwright in what is always called "pre-Shakespearean" drama, but who, in comparison with Shakespeare, is found to be immature'.[25]

In such instances, so the argument runs, the immense gravitational force of Shakespeare has the effect of bending his fellow-travellers out of shape, so that readers, critics and theatregoers find them wanting because they are looking for the wrong kind of pleasures – particular modes of characterisation, of narrative construction, or, perhaps most troublingly, of dramatic ethos.

This problem is further exacerbated by the fact that there has been a long cultural tradition of adjusting Shakespeare to conform to the theatrical norms of the age (sometimes drastically so, as in Nahum Tate's 1681 revisions to *King Lear*, which supplied the play with a romantic subplot and a happy ending; sometimes in the spirit of reclaiming the authentic spirit of the work, as in Peter Brook's modernist/Absurdist 1962 version of the same play); so that Shakespeare can continue to be plausibly claimed as a kind of modern. The result is that the work of his contemporaries can seem even more mired in its own period, its own conventions, and, therefore, its own limitations. Nowhere is this more evident than in the sphere of comedy: cruelly liable to the harsh test of the presence or absence of laughter, the genre is spectacularly exposed to the prospect of failure.

For many advocates of the non-Shakespearean sixteenth- and seventeenth-century drama, this is a risk worth taking, for there is a body of valuable and viable work here which, if it were allowed to escape from Shakespeare's shadow, might prove its worth alongside (and in some instances over and above) that of the tried-and-tested canon. Of the many hundreds of plays that survive from the period between the accession of Elizabeth I in 1588 and the closure of the playhouses in 1642, no more than a few dozen have been revived with any degree of regularity, at least in the professional theatre; and while there are multiple film and television versions of Shakespeare's plays, the screen history of the non-Shakespearean drama is negligible.[26] In a valuable history of stagings of early modern drama on the London stage from the late seventeenth century through to the twentieth, Wendy Griswold demonstrates that the eighteenth-century theatre turned repeatedly to *Bartholomew Fair*, *Epicoene*, *Every Man in His Humour* and *The Alchemist* (the basis for Francis Gentleman's popular adaptation, *The Tobacconist* [1770], which became a successful vehicle for David Garrick), to Jonson, Marston and Chapman's *Eastward Ho!*, and to *A New Way to Pay Old Debts*. By the middle of the nineteenth century, this had narrowed to *Every Man* and *New Way*. From 1848 (when *Every Man* was staged at the Haymarket) to 1899, Jonson disappeared from the English stage, although Massinger's comedy remained popular (it was revived at least seventeen times between 1840 and 1877).[27] In 1899, under the auspices of his amateur group the Elizabethan Stage Society, William Poel produced the first showing of

The Alchemist for over a century at the Apothecaries Hall; committed to 'authentic' stagings of Renaissance plays within reconstructed Elizabethan performance conditions, Poel established an important aspect of the twentieth-century history of Shakespeare's contemporaries in performance.[28] As far as the professional theatre in the British Isles has been concerned, the record has been patchy. Griswold documents the re-establishment of the Jonsonian nucleus, and the sporadic reappearance of *Eastward Ho!* and *New Way*; to these can be added the return (in 1921) of what would prove to be the perennially resilient *Volpone*;[29] and revivals at the Old Vic during the 1920s and 1930s of Beaumont's *The Knight of the Burning Pestle* (1931–32); it was not until 1962 that the Old Vic company returned to early modern comedy with Tyrone Guthrie's rendering of *The Alchemist*. According to the editors of the 1979 Revels edition of the play, *The Shoemakers Holiday* could be fairly claimed as 'the most frequently performed non-Shakespearean play of its period,' with a professional stage history that begins in 1922 with the Birmingham Repertory Theatre (closely followed by an Old Vic revival in 1925); its most recent revival was at the National Theatre in 1981.[30] Outside London, the Shakespeare Memorial Theatre at Stratford-upon-Avon staged *The Knight of the Burning Pestle* (1910), *The Two Angry Women of Abingdon* (1914) and *Volpone* (1944, 1952). During the same period, the Birmingham Repertory Theatre also presented *A New Way to Pay Old Debts* (1914), *The Alchemist* (1916), *The Knight of the Burning Pestle* (1919), *Volpone* (1935), *The Silent Woman* (*Epicoene*) (1947), *The Alchemist* (1957) and, in 1958, a programme of 'Three Elizabethan Rarities,' which included *A Mery Play Between Johan Johan, the Husbande, Tyb, his Wyfe, and Sir Johan, the Preest*. This was a daring experiment: for the most part, the revival of the more obscure aspects of Elizabethan and Jacobean drama has been the provenance of amateur organisations and university drama departments.

In the 1960s, the advent of the National Theatre and the Royal Shakespeare Company saw the non-Shakespearean repertoire extended to incorporate many rarely performed comedies. The only Renaissance comedies to be staged at the National when it was housed at the Old Vic were Marston's *The Dutch Courtesan* in 1964 and *Volpone* in 1968; after the move to the South Bank in 1976 (an event marked by Peter Hall's epic production of Marlowe's *Tamburlaine*), the handful of revivals included

Middleton and Rowley's *A Fair Quarrel* (1979), *Bartholomew Fair* (1989), *Volpone* (1995) and *The Alchemist* (1996). The Royal Shakespeare Company revived only two non-Shakespearean comedies in the first two decades of its existence: *Bartholomew Fair* in 1969 and *The Alchemist* in 1977. However, the 1980s saw a clutch of revivals of non-Shakespearean work: Dekker and Middleton's *The Roaring Girl* was aired on the main stage at Stratford in 1983, whilst the company's studio space, The Other Place, presented *A New Way to Pay Old Debts* (1983) and *Volpone* (1983). A further impetus was given by the opening of the RSC's replica Jacobean auditorium The Swan in 1986, which initially pledged itself to the fostering of the plays of Shakespeare's antecedents, colleagues and successors, 'to provide a context for our Shakespeare productions', by presenting 'the plays that influenced Shakespeare and the plays that Shakespeare influenced'.[31] The Swan has mounted numerous productions of Jonson, including not only the relatively familiar *Every Man in His Humour* (1986), *The Alchemist* (1991), *Bartholomew Fair* (1997) and *Volpone* (1999), but also *The Silent Woman* (1989) and *The Devil is an Ass* (1995); it has also undertaken Heywood's *Fair Maid of the West* (1986) and Shirley's *Hyde Park* (1987), although in recent years the keen winds of commercial viability have whittled down the repertoire to a more mainstream Shakespeare-dominated programme (even so, 2003 saw the RSC mount an unprecedented West End season of Jacobean plays, including John Marston's *The Malcontent*, John Fletcher's *The Island Princess* and Massinger's *The Roman Actor*). A second boost was supplied by the opening of the reconstructed Shakespeare's Globe on Bankside in 1997: its revivals have included *A Chaste Maid in Cheapside* (1997), *A Mad World, My Masters*, Dekker's *The Honest Whore* (both 1998) and Brome's *The Antipodes* (1999). The Globe also hosts a regular programme of rehearsed readings of unperformed early modern plays.

I began by observing how many encounters with non-Shakespearean early modern drama – and with comedy in particular – are initially conducted in a spirit of anxiety and despondency; the experience of theatre history shows that, when negotiated successfully, these forebodings give way to relief, and sometimes astonishment and exhilaration. For some, the first seasons at The Swan not only demonstrated the viability of a neglected and undervalued body of work, but also prompted

questions about the early modern comic canon itself: as Barry
Kyle, The Swan's first Artistic Director put it in 1987 (citing two
of the space's hits): *'Fair Maid of the West* and *Hyde Park* could
now be taken up by other theatres as alternatives to say *Comedy
of Errors* or *Much Ado.'*[32] As ever, Shakespeare remains an issue,
but Shakespeare does not necessarily have the upper hand:
in such experiences of performance, somewhere between the
pleasures of novelty and unfamiliarity, lies the prospect of laughter that has not grown forced and stale through convention and
repetition. Such a hope may be optimistic and, given the dwin-
dling range of Shakespearean drama engaged by the mainstream
theatre, even wilfully naïve, but it articulates something important about our relationship with the early modern comedy and
with Shakespeare's place within it, in that it dreams of a capacity
for spontaneity, surprise and delight that – thanks to the accu-
mulated weight of cultural history – Shakespeare's comedies can
no longer have. Whether this relationship is best explored by presenting the texts more or less as they stand in physical conditions
intended to replicate those of their originating context, or by
subjecting the raw material of early modern drama to the kind
of bold interventions and improvisations that characterised its
writing and performance, is beyond the scope of the present discussion; it is enough here to observe that the centuries of cultural
difference that separate the early modern sense(s) of humour
from their late modern counterparts makes the task a daunting
but potentially rewarding one.[33] It is as well to be realistic:
although full production (preferably by professional actors)
remains for many the ideal, the smaller-scale, but perhaps more
adventurous and open-ended, possibilities afforded by workshop performance may yet yield results that are more achievable,
more productive and, perhaps, genuinely funnier in practice.[34]
Representative as they are of the range and diversity of comic
drama during the period, the plays in this volume are offered in
this understanding that, just as reading alone is unlikely to reveal
their real comic potential, so may the strategies and vocabularies
of comic performance that have served in the past also need
re-imagining for a new century. It is for the reader to discover
how the cues these plays provide may best be answered.

Notes

1 'Interlude 1: Sam Mendes talks to Brian Woolland', in *Ben Jonson and Theatre: Performance, Practice and Theory*, ed. Richard Cave, Elizabeth Schafer and Brian Woolland (London: Routledge, 1999), p. 79.
2 Ibid., p. 80.
3 See Tiffany Stern, *Rehearsal from Shakespeare to Sheridan* (Oxford: Clarendon Press, 2000).
4 Sir Philip Sidney, *The Defence of Poesie*, in *The Prose Works of Sir Philip Sidney*, Vol. 3, ed. Albert Fueillerat (Cambridge: Cambridge University Press, 1962), p. 23.
5 Aristotle, *On the Art of Poetry*, in Aristotle, Horace, Longinus, *Classical Literary Criticism*, trans. and ed. T. S. Dorsch (Harmondsworth: Penguin, 1965), pp. 33–7.
6 Sidney, *Defence*, p. 23.
7 Ibid.
8 Ibid.
9 Ibid., p. 38
10 Ibid.
11 See Richard Wilson, *Will Power: Essays on Shakespearean Authority* (Hemel Hempstead: Harvester Wheatsheaf, 1993), pp. 45–62.
12 Stephen Orgel, 'The Comedian as the Character C', in *English Comedy*, ed. Michael Cordner, Peter Holland and John Kerrigan (Cambridge: Cambridge University Press, 1994), p. 36.
13 Sidney, *Defence*, p. 39.
14 Ibid., p. 40.
15 Peachum, 'Thalia's Banquet' (1620), quoted in *Tarlton's Jests and News Out of Purgatory*, ed. J. O. Halliwell (London: The Shakespeare Society, 1844), pp. xxvi–xxvii. See Peter Thomson, 'The True Physiognomy of a Man: Richard Tarlton and His Legend', in *Shakespeare and His Contemporaries in Performance*, ed. Edward J. Esche (Aldershot: Ashgate, 2000), pp. 191–210.
16 *Fuller's Worthies*, Vol. 2., p. 312, quoted in *Tarlton's Jests*, p. xxvii.
17 *Tarlton's Jests*, pp. 24–5.
18 See Michael D. Bristol, *Carnival and Theater: Plebeian Culture and the Structure of Authority in Renaissance England* (London: Methuen, 1985), pp. 118–19.
19 See *Henslowe's Diary*, ed. R. A. Foakes and R. T. Rickert (Cambridge: Cambridge University Press, 1962).
20 Simon Shepherd and Peter Womack, *English Drama: A Cultural History* (Oxford: Blackwell, 1996), pp. 78–9.
21 James C. Bulman, 'Caroline Drama', in *The Cambridge Companion to English Renaissance Drama*, ed. A. R. Braunmuller and Michael Hattaway (Cambridge: Cambridge University Press, 1990), p. 353.
22 See Martin Butler, *Theatre and Crisis 1632–1642* (Cambridge: Cambridge University Press, 1984); David Kastan, *Shakespeare After Theory* (London: Routledge, 1999), pp. 201–20.
23 See Gary Taylor, *Reinventing Shakespeare: A Cultural History from the Restoration to the Present* (New York: Weidenfeld and Nicholson, 1989); Michael Dobson, *The Making of the National Poet: Shakespeare, Adaptation and Authorship, 1660–1769* (Oxford: Clarendon Press, 1992); Jonathan Bate, *The Genius of Shakespeare* (London: Picador, 1997). For the history of Shakespeare on stage, see Jonathan Bate and Russell Jackson (eds), *Shakespeare: An Illustrated Stage History* (Oxford: Oxford University Press, 1996).
24 Mick Jardine, 'Jonson as Shakespeare's Other', in *Ben Jonson and Theatre*, p. 104.

25 Simon Shepherd, *Marlowe and the Politics of Elizabethan Theatre* (Brighton: Harvester, 1986), p. xiii.
26 Richard Cave observes that there is 'no recording of a Jonson production contained within the archives of the British Film Institute', and the BBC has 'only a truncated version dating back to the early 1950s of Wolfit's *Volpone* in its archive of televised drama' (*Ben Jonson and Theatre*, p. 1). *Volpone* has occasioned one modern screen spin-off, in the shape of Joseph Manciewicz's *The Honey Pot* (1966), which was derived from Frederick Knott's stage play *Mr Fox of Venice*.
27 See Wendy Griswold, *Renaissance Revivals: City Comedy and Revenge Tragedy in the London Theatre, 1576–1980* (Chicago and London: University of Chicago Press, 1986).
28 See Marion O'Connor, *William Poel and the Elizabethan Stage Society* (Cambridge: Chawyck-Healey, 1987); Gabriel Egan, 'Reconstructions of the Globe: A Retrospective', *Shakespeare Survey*, 52 (1999), 1–16; Robert Shaughnessy, *The Shakespeare Effect: A History of Twentieth-Century Performance* (Basingstoke: Palgrave Macmillan, 2002).
29 See Robert Shaughnessy, 'Twentieth-Century Fox: Volpone's Metamorphosis', *Theatre Research International*, 27, 1 (2002), 37–48.
30 R. L. Smallwood and Stanley Wells (eds), *The Shoemaker's Holiday*, The Revels Plays (Manchester: Manchester University Press, 1979), p. 47.
31 Trevor Nunn, 'Flying High', in *Royal Shakespeare Company 1978*, ed. Simon Trussler (RSC/TQ Publications, 1979), p. 5.
32 Barry Kyle, 'Role of the Swan', *Plays International*, September 1987.
33 For a discussion of a range of twentieth-century revisions of Elizabethan and Jacobean texts, see Martin White, *Renaissance Drama in Action* (London: Routledge, 1998), pp. 217–32.
34 Simon Shepherd offers a range of possibilities of intervention in 'Acting Against Bardom: Some Utopian Thoughts on Workshops', in *Shakespeare in Performance: Contemporary Critical Essays*, ed. Robert Shaughnessy (Basingstoke: Palgrave Macmillan, 2000), pp. 218–34.

A Note on the Texts

This anthology is primarily intended for use by general and student readers, interested practitioners and theatregoers, and the texts have been edited with their needs in mind. Accordingly, spelling, punctuation, font styles and capitalisation have been regularised and modernised throughout, act and scene headings translated from Latin to English and speech tags rendered consistent (although this is done in the awareness that variation in speech headings in the original texts may be an significant index of a shift of theatrical status or function). With regard to the identification of speaking parts, I have, where appropriate, opted to follow the lead of the texts by identifying dramatis personae in terms of role rather than personal name (thus Wife rather than Margery). In this respect, only the Jonson and Massinger texts supply castlists of the kind found in modern editions; for the remaining plays in the volume, I have incorporated lists of *parts* (rather than 'persons', or more anachronistically, 'characters'), as this better approximates to the early modern performer's relation with the text. I have refrained from interpolating extensive editorial stage directions (such as asides), in the belief that thoughtful and imaginative reading and rehearsal practice are best geared towards finding creative solutions to any ambiguities, lacunae or apparent contradictions in the texts themselves. Interpolations are clearly marked by square brackets ([...]). In the case of Peele and Dekker, I have made one substantial editorial intervention, in that (largely for the purposes of ease of reference) I have divided the texts into scenes, for the most part according to the principle that a scene ends when the stage is cleared of performers. For the most part, the texts of the five plays present few major headaches for the editor, and in each case I have worked

from the recognised control text of the play: the 1595 Quarto of
The Old Wives Tale, the 1600 Quarto of *The Shoemakers Holiday*, the
version of *The Alchemist* included in Jonson's 1616 Folio edition
of his works and the 1633 Quarto of *A New Way to Pay Old
Debts*. Readers looking for more specialist information about
textual variants and emendations should consult the Revels
Plays editions of Peele, Dekker and Jonson, and the Clarendon
Press edition of the works of Massinger. The present edition is, of
course, extensively indebted to these and other modern scholarly
editions of the plays.

The Old Wives Tale

GEORGE PEELE

In terms of its plot, *The Old Wives Tale* fully confirms the promise of its title, which, besides acting as a marker of the play's implausible and inconsequential quality, is also an accurate definition of what it actually is: a tale of romance, fantasy, magic and adventure told by a old woman to while away a dark winter's night. Three pages, Antic, Frolic and Fantastic, abandoned by their (possibly) newly-wed master and left to wander miserably through a forest, happily stumble into the house of a Smith. Inviting them to taste of the comforts of a barking dog, 'a good fire to sit by' (1.41), pudding and cheese, and hot spiced ale, the Smith introduces them to the Old Woman, the wife of the title; the pages clamour for 'a merry winter's tale' which 'would drive away the time trimly' (1.70). As the Smith coaxes one of the pages offstage to take an 'unnatural rest' in a shared bed, the Old Woman embarks upon a rambling account of 'a king, or a lord, or a duke that had a fair daughter', of 'a conjurer' who 'turned himself into a great dragon and carried the king's daughter away in his mouth' (1.102–3) to a stone castle, and of her two brothers sent in pursuit. Before she can go any further, the brothers themselves materialise onstage; the Old Woman's narrative within drama dissolves into a play within a play. She and the pages become silent spectators of a picaresque, oddly dreamlike sequence of happenings involving, amongst others, the noble brothers, figures from the world of medieval epic romance, who are themselves enslaved by the evil conjurer Sacrapant, a pompous braggart captain, Huanebango, a wandering knight, Eumenides,

1

the friendly ghost of a poor man, Jack, and a mysterious Head that appears from a well, urging young women to 'comb me smooth, and stroke my head' with a lascivious promise of 'cockle-bread' (7.26). Improbable incident is matched by spectacular effect: the source of the conjurer's power is a light in a glass phial secreted 'under a little hill' (6.62. s.d.); the ghost of Jack enters 'invisible' (10.12. s.d.); the Head has pitchers smashed on him but rewards the virtuous maiden with a flood of ears of corn and pieces of gold; old men turn into their younger selves and young men age just as rapidly; a troupe of harvesters occasionally appear to sing and dance. The play ends with the conjurer defeated, lovers united and the ghost laid to rest; and we are returned to the world of the frame that contains the Pages and the Old Woman who, it transpires, has herself succumbed to the sleep that the tale was intended to prevent.

In the context of an Elizabethan comic dramaturgy that drew upon the resources of the classical tradition, the medieval romance, folklore and entertainments such as the mummers' plays, *The Old Wives Tale* is an eclectic mix of the learned and popular, fairytale and parody, contained within the flexible framework of the dream-story. Whether it was a success with its contemporaries can only be guessed at. The title page of the quarto published in 1595 advertised the play as 'a pleasant conceited comedy' which had been 'played by the Queenes Majesties players', and assigned its authorship to 'G. P.'; this was the only one of the handful of plays attributed to George Peele to identify its author on the title page in his own lifetime (*The Arraignement of Paris* and *The Battle of Alcazar* were published anonymously in 1584 and 1594 respectively, *The Famous Chronicle of Edward I* appeared in 1593 bearing the legend 'by George Peele Maister of Arts in Oxenford' on the final page; in 1599, three years after his death, *The Love of King David and Fair Bathsabe* was printed with a full attribution). Peele had been praised by Thomas Nashe in his preface to Robert Greene's *Menaphon* in 1589 as 'the Atlas of poetry, and *primum verborum Artifex'*, and for 'his pregnant dexterity of wit, and manifold variety of invention, wherein...he goeth a step beyond all that write'; a panegyric that was inspired by the classical-pastoral royal entertainment *The Arraignment*; but in common with a number of other poet-playwrights of the time, Peele seemed to prefer to define his significant literary identity through his poetry. Born in 1556 the son of James Peele, an accountant and citizen of London who also scripted city pageants, George Peele had been educated at Christchurch College, Oxford in the 1570s. Among his contemporaries at Oxford was Philip Sidney, whose *Defence of Poesie* was published the same year as *The Old Wives Tale*; the free-ranging eclecticism of Peele's play would not have impressed his sterner literary colleague.

The abruptness of the play's narrative transitions, which afford it an episodic quality, and the carefree fashion in which genres, plotlines, dramatis personae and linguistic idioms are introduced (and abandoned) may be true to the aleatoric and indiscriminate improvisations of dreamwork, but they have not recommended themselves critics and theatre practitioners accustomed to the ordered and rational comic craft of, say, Jonson and Shakespeare. Critical interest has lain in untangling the sources and generic affiliations of the play, the provenance of the text and the metatheatrical ramifications of the dream framework; positive opinion is divided between those prepared to be charmed by the play's wayward and digressive tendencies and those who discern behind them a more subtle, synthetic unity. The theatre has generally concurred with the critics' at best marginal interest in the play. The nature of its putative first performance is unknown: it has been speculated that it was a work commissioned for a wedding celebration, or that it was played by one of the boys' companies. A BBC radio version of the play was broadcast in 1972, but there is no record of a professional production since the sixteenth century, although it was given a rehearsed reading at Shakespeare's Globe (London) on 28 August 2000 as part of the 'Olde Summer's Wakes and Revels' festivities, and there have been amateur stagings at schools and universities. If, as seems likely, the play's future as a performance text will continue to lie outside of the realms of mainstream professional theatre, it may be that the current convergence of postmodern theory and performance practice will provide more fertile ground for a text whose disregard for depth characterisation, stylistic consistency, narrative unity and conventional distinctions between low and high culture makes it well suited to the theatre of the twenty-first century. In such circumstances, *The Old Wives Tale* might once again seem worth re-telling.

Further reading

Ashley, Leonard R. N., *George Peele* (New York: Twayne, 1970).

Binnie, Patricia (ed.), *The Old Wives Tale*, The Revels Plays (Manchester: Manchester University Press, 1980).

Jackson I. Cope, 'Peele's *Old Wives Tale*: Folk Stuff into Ritual Form', *ELH*, 49 (1982), 326–38.

Ewbank, Inga-Stina, ' "What words, what looks, what wonders?": Language and Spectacle in the Theatre of George Peele', *The Elizabethan Theatre*, 5 (ed.) G. R. Hibbard (Toronto: Macmillan, 1975).

Hook, F. S. (ed.), *The Life and Works of George Peele* (New Haven: Yale University Press, 1970).

Marx, Joan C., ' "Soft, Who Have We Here?": The Dramatic Technique of *The Old Wives Tale*', *Renaissance Drama*, New Series, 12 (1981), 117–44.

Viguers, Susan T., 'The Hearth and the Cell: Art in *The Old Wives Tale*', *Studies in English Literature*, 21 (1981), 209–21.

Whitworth, Charles (ed.), *The Old Wife's Tale*, New Mermaids (London: Ernest Benn, 1996).

Parts in the Play

ANTIC
FROLIC } *Pages*
FANTASTIC
Clunch, a SMITH
OLD WOMAN
Calypha, the FIRST BROTHER
Thelea, the SECOND BROTHER
Erestus, the OLD MAN
VENELIA, *his betrothed*
LAMPRISCUS
HUANEBANGO, *a braggart knight*
BOOBY/COREBUS, *a clown**
SACRAPANT, *a conjurer*
DELIA
FRIAR
Two FURIES
EUMENIDES, *the Wandering Knight*
WIGGEN
CHURCHWARDEN
SEXTON
HARVEST-MEN AND WOMEN
ZANTIPPA, *the Curst Daughter* } *daughters to Lampriscus*
CELANTA, *the Foul Wench*
JACK
HOSTESS
HEAD

Scene One

Enter ANTIC, FROLIC *and* FANTASTIC.

ANTIC: How now, fellow Frolic?* What, all amort?* Doth this sadness
    become thy madness? What, though we have lost our way in the
    woods, yet never hang the head as though thou had no hope to live till
    tomorrow; for Fantastic and I will warrant thy life tonight for twenty in
    the hundred.*   5
FROLIC: Antic and Fantastic, as I am frolic franion,* never in all my life was I
    so dead slain. What? To lose our way in the wood, without either fire or
    candle, so uncomfortable? *O coelum! O terra! O maria!** O Neptune!*
FANTASTIC: Why makes thou it so strange, seeing Cupid hath led our young
    master to the fair lady, and she is the only saint that he hath sworn to 10
    serve?
FROLIC: What resteth then but we commit him to his wench, and each of us
    take his stand up in a tree, and sing out our ill fortune to the tune of 'O,
    man in desperation'.
ANTIC: Desperately spoken, fellow Frolic, in the dark; but seeing   15
    it falls out thus, let us rehearse the old proverb [*sings*]:

> *Three merry men, and three merry men,*
> *And three merry men be we.*
> *I in the wood, and thou on the ground,*
> *And Jack sleeps in the tree.*   20

FANTASTIC: Hush, a dog in the wood, or a wooden* dog. O comfortable
    hearing! I had even as live the chamberlain of the White Horse had
    called me up to bed.
FROLIC: Either hath this trotting cur gone out of his circuit, or else we are
    near some village,   25

Enter a SMITH *with a lantern and candle.*

which should not be far off, for I perceive the glimmering of a glow-
    worm, a candle, or a cat's eye; my life for a half-penny. In the name of
    my own father, be thou ox or ass that appearest, tell us what thou art.
SMITH: What am I? Why, I am Clunch the Smith. What are you? What make
    you* in my territories at this time of the night?   30
ANTIC: What do we make, dost thou ask? Why, we make faces for fear, such
    as if thy mortal eyes could behold would make thee water the long
    seams of thy side slops,* Smith.
FROLIC: And in faith, sir, unless your hospitality do relieve us, we are like to
    wander with a sorrowful 'hey ho' among the owlets and hobgoblins   35
    of the forest. Good Vulcan,* for Cupid's sake that hath cozened* us all,

befriend us as thou mayest, and command us howsoever, wheresover,
whensoever, in whatsoever, for ever and ever.

SMITH: Well, masters, it seems to me you have lost your way in the wood; in
consideration whereof, if you will go with Clunch to his cottage, you   40
shall have house room, and a good fire to sit by,
although we have no bedding to put you in.

ALL: O blessed Smith! O bountiful Clunch!

SMITH: For your further entertainment, it shall be as it may be, so and so.

Here a dog barks.

Hark, this is Ball my dog, that bids you all welcome in his own   45
language; come, take heed for stumbling on the threshold. Open door,
Madge, take in guests.

Enter OLD WOMAN.

OLD WOMAN: Welcome, Clunch, and good fellows all that come with
my good man for my good man's sake; come on, sit down: here is a
piece of cheese and a pudding of my own making.   50

ANTIC: Thanks, gammer;* a good example for the wives of our town.

FROLIC: Gammer, thou and thy good man sit lovingly together. We come to
chat and not to eat.

SMITH: Well, masters, if you will eat nothing, take away. Come, what do we
to pass away the time? Lay a crab* in the fire to roast for   55
lambswool?* What, shall we have a game at trump or ruff* to drive
away the time? How say you?

FANTASTIC: This Smith leads a life as merry as a king with Madge his wife.
Sirrah Frolic, I am sure thou art not without some round or other. No
doubt but Clunch can bear his part.   60

FROLIC: Else think you me ill brought up, so set to it when you will.

They sing.
Song.

When as the rye reach to the chin,
And chop cherry, chop cherry ripe within,*
Strawberries swimming in the cream,
And schoolboys playing in the stream;   65
Then O, then O, then O, my true love said,
Till that time come again,
She could not live a maid.

ANTIC: This sport does well, but methinks, gammer, a merry winter's tale
would drive away the time trimly: come, I am sure you are not   70
without a score.

FANTASTIC: I' faith, gammer, a tale of an hour long were as good as an
hour's sleep.

FROLIC: Look you, gammer, of the giant and the king's daughter, and I know
    not what. I have seen the day, when I was a little one, you might   75
    have drawn me a mile after you with such a discourse.

OLD WOMAN: Well, since you be so importunate, my good man shall fill the
    pot and get him to bed. They that ply their work must keep good hours.
    One of you go lie with him; he is a clean-skinned man, I tell you,
    without either spavin or windgall.* So, I am, content to drive   80
    away the time with an old wives winter's tale.

FANTASTIC: No better hay in Devonshire.* A' my word, gammer, I'll be one
    of your audience.

FROLIC: And I another, that's flat.

ANTIC: Then must I to bed with the good man. *Bona nox,** gammer. Good   85
    night, Frolic.

SMITH: Come on, my lad; thou shalt take thy unnatural* rest with me.
                                   Exeunt ANTIC *and the* SMITH.

FROLIC: Yet this vantage shall we have of them in the morning, to be ready
    at the sight thereof extempore.*

OLD WOMAN: Now this bargain, my masters, must I make with you, that   90
    you will say 'hum' and 'ha' to my tale, so shall I know you are awake.

BOTH: Content, gammer, that will we do.

OLD WOMAN: Once upon a time there was a king or a lord, or a duke, that
    had a fair daughter, the fairest that ever was, as white as snow and as
    red as blood, and once upon a time his daughter was stolen away,   95
    and he sent all his men to seek out his daughter, and he sent so long
    that he sent all his men out of his land.

FRANTIC: Who dressed* his dinner then?

OLD WOMAN: Nay, either hear my tale, or kiss my tail.*

FRANTIC: Well said! On with your tale, gammer.   100

OLD WOMAN: O Lord, I quite forgot: there was a conjurer, and this conjurer
    could do anything, and he turned himself into a great dragon, and carried
    the king's daughter away in his mouth to a castle that he made of stone,
    and there he kept her I know not how long, till at last all the king's men
    went out so long that his two brothers went to seek her. O, I forget: 105
    she (he I would say) turned a proper* young man to a bear in the night
    and a man in the day, and keeps* by a cross that parts three several
    ways, and made his lady run mad – Gods me bones, who comes here?

Scene Two

Enter the two BROTHERS.

FROLIC: Soft, gammer, here some come to tell your tale for you.

FANTASTIC: Let them alone, let us hear what they will say.

1 BROTHER: Upon these chalky cliffs of Albion

We are arrived now with tedious toil,
And compassing the wide world round about   5
To seek our sister, to seek fair Delia forth,
Yet cannot we so much as hear of her.
2 BROTHER: O fortune cruel, cruel and unkind!
Unkind in that we cannot find our sister,
Our sister hapless in her cruel chance –   10
Soft, who have we here?

Enter [OLD MAN] *at the cross, stooping to gather.*

Now, father, God be your speed. What do you gather there?
OLD MAN: Hips and haws,* and sticks and straws, and things that I gather
on the ground, my son.
1 BROTHER: Hips and haws, and sticks and straws; why, is that all your   15
food, father?
OLD MAN: Yea, son.
2 BROTHER: Father, here is an alms-penny* for me; and if I speed in that I go
for, I will give thee as good a gown of grey* as ever thou didst wear.
1 BROTHER: And, father, here is another alms-penny for me; and if   20
I speed* in my journey, I will give thee a palmer's* staff of ivory,
and a scallop shell of beaten gold.
OLD MAN: Was she fair?
2 BROTHER: Ay, the fairest for white, and the purest for red, as the blood of
the deer or the driven snow.   25
OLD MAN: Then hark well, and mark well my old spell:
Be not afraid of every stranger,
Start not aside at every danger,
Things that seem are not the same;
Blow a blast at every flame,   30
For when one flame of fire goes out,
Then comes your wishes well about.
If any ask who told you this good,
Say the White Bear of England's wood.
1 BROTHER: Brother, heard you not what the old man said?   35
Be not afraid of every stranger,
Start not aside for every danger:
Things that seem are not the same,
Blow a blast at every flame;
If any ask who told you this good;   40
Say the White Bear of England's wood.
2 BROTHER: Well, if this do us any good,
Well fare the White Bear of England's wood.
                                    Ex[eunt BROTHERS].
OLD MAN: Now sit thee here and tell a heavy tale.

Sad in thy mood, and sober in thy cheer,*   45
Here sit thee now, and to thyself relate
The hard mishap of thy most wretched state.
In Thessaly* I lived in sweet content,
Until that Fortune wrought my overthrow;
For there I wedded was unto a dame,   50
That lived in honour, virtue, love, and fame.
But Sacrapant, that cursed sorcerer,
Being besotted with my beauteous love,
My dearest love, my true betrothed wife,
Did seek the means to rid me of my life.   55
But worse than this, he with his chanting spells
Did turn me straight unto an ugly bear.
And when the sun doth settle in the west,
Then I begin to don my ugly hide
And all the day I sit, as now you see,   60
And speak in riddles all inspired with rage,*
Seeming an old and miserable man.
And yet I am in April of my age.

Enter VENELIA *his lady, mad, and goes in again.*

See where Venelia my betrothed love
Runs madding* all enraged about the woods,   65
All by his cursed and enchanting spells.

Enter LAMPRISCUS *with a pot of honey.*

But here comes Lampriscus, my discontented neighbour. How now,
neighbour, you look toward the ground as well as I. You muse on
something.
LAMPRISCUS: Neighbour, on nothing, but on the matter I so often moved*   70
to you. If you do anything for charity, help me; if for neighbourhood or
brotherhood, help me; never was one so cumbered* as poor Lampriscus.
And to begin, I pray receive this pot of honey to mend your fare.*
OLD MAN: Thanks, neighbour, set it down; honey is always welcome to the
bear. And now, neighbour, let me hear the cause of your coming.   75
LAMPRISCUS: I am – as you know, neighbour – a man unmarried, and lived
so unquietly with my two wives, that I keep every year holy the day
wherein I buried the both; the first was on Saint Andrew's day, the
other on Saint Luke's.*
OLD MAN: And now, neighbour, you of this country say your custom is   80
out* – but on with your tale, neighbour.

LAMPRISCUS: By my first wife, whose tongue wearied me alive, and
    sounded in my ears like the clapper of a great bell, whose talk was a
    continual torment to all that dwelt by her or lived nigh her, you have
    heard me say I had a handsome daughter.   85
OLD MAN: True, neighbour.
LAMPRISCUS: She it is that afflicts me with her continual clamours, and
    hangs on me like a bur. Poor she is, and proud she is:* as poor as a
    sheep new shorn, and as proud of her hopes as a peacock of her tail
    well grown.   90
OLD MAN: Well said, Lampricus, you speak it like an Englishman.
LAMPRISCUS: As curst* as a wasp, and as froward* as a child new taken from
    the mother's teat. She is to my age as smoke to the eyes or as vinegar to
    the teeth.*
OLD MAN: Holily praised, neighbour. As much for the next.   95
LAMPRISCUS: By my other wife I had a daughter so hard-favoured, so foul
    and ill-faced, that I think a grove full of golden trees, and the leaves of
    rubies and diamonds, would not be a dowry answerable to her
    deformity.
OLD MAN: Well, neighbour, now you have spoke, hear me speak.   100
    Send them to the well for the water of life: there shall they find their
    fortunes unlooked for. Neighbour, farewell.   *Exit.*
LAMPRISCUS: Farewell and a thousand.* And now goeth poor Lampriscus to
    put in execution this excellent counsel.   *Exit.*
FROLIC: Why this goes round without a fiddling stick.* But do you hear, 105
    gammer, was this the man that was a bear in the night and a man in the
    day?
OLD WOMAN: Ay, this is he; and this man that came to him was a beggar, and
    dwelt upon a green. But soft, who comes here? O, these are the harvest
    men; ten to one they sing a song of mowing.   110

Enter the HARVEST MEN *a-singing, with this song double repeated.*

> *All ye that lovely lovers be, pray you for me,*
> *Lo here we come a-sowing, a-sowing,*
> *And sow sweet fruits of love.*
> *In your sweet hearts well may it prove.*   *Exeunt.*

Scene Three

Enter HUANEBANGO *with his two-hand sword, and* BOOBY *the Clown.*

FANTASTIC: Gammer, what is he?
OLD WOMAN: O, this is one that is going to the conjurer. Let him alone, hear
    what he says.

HUANEBANGO: Now by Mars and Mercury, Jupiter and Janus, Sol and
Saturnas, Venus and Vesta, Pallas and Proserpina, and by the honour   5
of my house Polimackeroeplacydus, it is a wonder to see what this love
will make silly fellows adventure, even in the wane of their wits and
infancy of their discretion. Alas, my friend, what fortune calls thee forth
to seek thy fortune among brazen gates, enchanted towers, fire and
brimstone, thunder and lightning? Beauty, I tell thee, is peerless,   10
and she precious whom thou affectest.* Do off* these desires, good
countryman; good friend, run away from thyself, and so soon as thou
canst, forget her, whom none must inherit but he that can monsters
tame, labours achieve, riddles absolve*, loose enchantments, murder
magic, and kill conjuring; and that is the great and mighty   15
Huanebango.
BOOBY: Hark you, sir, hark you. First know I have here the flurting* feather,
and have given the parish the start for the long stock.* Now, sir, if it be
no more but running through a little lightning and thunder, and –
riddle me, riddle me, what's this – I'll have the wench from   20
the conjurer if he were ten conjurers.
HUANEBANGO: I have abandoned the court and honourable company, to do
my devoir* against this sore sorcerer and mighty magician. If this lady
be so fair as she is said to be, she is mine, she is mine. *Meus, mea, meum,
in contemptum omnium grammaticorum.**   25
BOOBY: *O falsum Latinum!* The fair maid is *minum, cum apurtinantibus gibletes*
and all.*
HUANEBANGO: If she be mine, as I assure myself the heavens will do
somewhat to reward my worthiness, she shall be allied to none of the
meanest gods, but be invested in the most famous stock of   30
Huanebango Polimackeroeplacydus, my grandfather; my father,
Pergopolyneo; my mother, Dionora de Sardinia, famously descended.
BOOBY: Do you hear, sir? Had not you a cousin that was called
Gustecerydis?
HUANEBANGO: Indeed, I had a cousin that sometime followed the court   35
infortunately, and his name Bustegustecerydis.
BOOBY: O Lord, I know him well. He is the knight of the neat's feet.*
HUANEBANGO: O, he loved no capon better. He hath oftentimes deceived his
boy* of his dinner. That was his fault, good Bustegustecerydis.
BOOBY: Come, shall we go along? Soft, here is an old man at the cross.   40
Let us ask him the way thither. Ho, you gaffer, I pray you tell where
the wise man the conjurer dwells.
HUANEBANGO: Where that earthly goddess keepeth her abode, the
commander of my thoughts and fair mistress of my heart.
OLD MAN: Fair enough, and far enough from thy fingering, son.   45
HUANEBANGO: I will follow my fortune after mine own fancy, and do
according to mine own discretion.
OLD MAN: Yet give something to an old man before you go.

HUANENBANGO: Father, methinks a piece of this cake might serve your turn.
OLD MAN: Yea, son.   50
HUANEBANGO: Huanebango giveth no cakes for alms; ask of them that give
    gifts for poor beggars. Fair lady, if thou wert once shrined in this
    bosom, I would buckler* thee. Harantara!   *Exit.*
BOOBY: Father, do you see this man? You little think he'll run a mile or two
    for such a cake, or pass for* a pudding. I tell you, father, he has kept   55
    such a begging of me for a piece of this cake. Whoo, he comes upon me
    with a superfantial* substance, and the foison* of the earth, that I knew
    not what he means. If he came to me thus and said, 'My friend Booby'
    or so, why, I could spare him a piece with all my heart; but when he tells
    me how God hath enriched me above other fellows with a cake,   60
    why, he makes me blind and deaf at once. Yet, father, here is a piece of
    cake for you, as hard as the world goes.*
OLD MAN: Thanks, son, but list to me:
    He shall be deaf when thou shalt not see.
    Farewell, my son, things may so hit,   65
    Thou mayest have wealth to mend thy wit.
BOOBY: Farewell, father, farewell; for I must make haste after my two-hand
    sword that is gone before.   *Exeunt omnes.*

Scene Four

Enter SACRAPANT *in his study.*

SACRAPANT: The day is clear, the welkin* bright and grey,
    The lark is merry, and records* her notes;
    Each thing rejoiceth underneath the sky,
    But only I whom heaven hath in hate,
    Wretched and miserable Sacrapant.   5
    In Thessaly was I born and brought up,
    My mother Meroe* hight,* a famous witch,
    And by her cunning I of her did learn
    To change and alter shapes of mortal men.
    There did I turn myself into a dragon,   10
    And stole away the daughter to the king,
    Fair Delia, the mistress of my heart,
    And brought her hither to revive the man
    That seemeth young and pleasant to beheld,
    And yet is aged, crooked, weak and numb.   15
    Thus by enchanting spells I do deceive
    Those that behold and look upon my face,
    But well may I bid youthful years adieu.

Enter DELIA *with a pot in her hand.*

See where she comes, from whence my sorrows grow. How now, fair
Delia, where have you been? 20
DELIA: At the foot of the rock for running water, and gathering roots for
your dinner, sir.
SACRAPANT: Ah, Delia, fairer art thou than the running water, yet harder far
than steel or adamant.
DELIA: Will it please you to sit down, sir? 25
SACRAPANT: Ay, Delia, sit and ask me what wilt; thou shalt have it brought
into thy lap.
DELIA: Then I pray you, sir, let me have the best meat from the king of
England's table, and the best wine in all France, brought in by the
veriest* knave in all Spain. 30
SACRAPANT: Delia, I am glad to see you so pleasant. Well, sit thee down.
Spread, table, spread; meat, drink and bread.
Ever may I have,what I ever crave.
When I am spread, for meat for my black cock,
And meat for my red. 35

Enter a FRIAR *with a chine* of beef and a pot of wine.*

Here, Delia, will ye fall to?
DELIA: Is this the best meat in England ?
SACRAPANT: Yea.
DELIA: What is it?
SACRAPANT: A chine of English beef, meat for a king, and a king's followers. 40
DELIA: Is this the best wine in France?
SACRAPANT: Yea.
DELIA: What wine is it?
SACRAPANT: A cup of neat* wine of Orleans, that never came near the
brewers in England. 45
DELIA: Is this the veriest knave in all Spain?
SACRAPANT: Yea.
DELIA: What, is he a friar?
SACRAPANT: Yea, a friar indefinite, and a knave infinite.
DELIA: Then I pray ye, Sir Friar, tell me before you go: which is the most 50
greediest Englishman?
FRIAR: The miserable and most covetous usurer.*
SACRAPANT: Hold thee there,* Friar. *Exit* FRIAR.
But soft, who have we here? Delia, away, begone!

Enter the two BROTHERS.

Delia, away, for beset are we, 55

But heaven or hell shall rescue her for me.

                         [*Exeunt* SACRAPANT *and* DELIA.]

1 BROTHER: Brother, was not that Delia did appear?
   Or was it but her shadow that was here?
2 BROTHER: Sister, where art thou? Delia, come again!
   He calls, that of thy absence doth complain,   60
   Call out, Calypha, that she may hear,
   And cry aloud, for Delia is near.
ECHO: Near.
1 BROTHER: Near? O where? Hast thou any tidings?
ECHO: Tidings.   65
2 BROTHER: Which way is Delia, then? Or that, or this?
ECHO: This.
1 BROTHER: And may we safely come where Delia is?
ECHO: Yes.
2 BROTHER: Brother, remember you the White Bear of England's Wood? 70
   Start not aside for every danger,
   Be not afeared of every stranger;
   Things that seem are not the same.
1 BROTHER: Brother, why do we not then courageously enter?
2 BROTHER: Then, brother, draw thy sword and follow me.   75

       Enter [SACRAPANT] *the conjurer; it lightens and thunders.*
             The second BROTHER *falls down.*

1 BROTHER: What, brother, dost thou fall?
SACRAPANT: Ay, and thou too, Calypha.   *Falls first* BROTHER.

            Enter two FURIES.

*Adeste Daemones!** Away with them!
Go, carry them straight to Sacrapanto's cell,
There in despair and torture for to dwell.   80
              [*Exeunt* FURIES *with the two* BROTHERS.]
These are Thenore's sons of Thessaly,
That come to seek Delia their sister forth.
But with a potion I to her have given,
My arts hath made her to forget herself.
          He removes a turf, and shows a light in a glass.
See here the thing which doth prolong my life.   85
With this enchantment I do anything,
And till this fade, my skill shall still endure,
And never none shall break this little glass,
But she that's neither wife, widow nor maid.

Then cheer thyself; this is thy destiny,   90
Never to die, but by a dead man's hand.   *Exit.*

Scene Five

Enter EUMENIDES, *the Wandering Knight [to] the* OLD MAN *at the cross.*

EUMENIDES: Tell me, Time, tell me, just Time,
    When shall I Delia see?
    When shall I see the lodestar* of my life?
    When shall my wandering course end with her sight,
    Or I but view my hope, my hearts delight?   5
    Father, God speed. If you tell fortunes, I pray, good father, tell me mine.
OLD MAN: Son, I do see in thy face
    Thy blessed fortune work apace.
    I do perceive that thou hast wit;*
    Beg of thy fate to govern it,   10
    For wisdom governed by advice
    Makes many fortunate and wise.
    Bestow thy alms; give more than all,
    Till dead men's bones come at thy call.
    Farewell, my son, dream of no rest   15
    Till thou repent that thou did best.   *Exit.*
EUMENIDES: This man hath left me in a labyrinth.
    He biddeth me give more than all,
    Till dead men's bones come at thy call.
    He biddeth me dream of no rest,   20
    Till I repent that I do best.

Enter WIGGEN, COREBUS, CHURCHWARDEN *and* SEXTON.

WIGGEN: You may be ashamed, you whoreson scald* sexton and
    churchwarden, if you had any shame in those shameless faces of yours,
    to let a poor man lie so long above ground unburied. A rot on you all,
    that have no more compassion of a good fellow when he is gone.   25
CHURCHWARDEN: What, would you have us to bury him, and to answer* it
    ourselves to the parish?
SEXTON: Parish me no parishes; pay me my fees, and let the rest run on in
    the quarter's accounts, and put it down for one your good deeds, a'
    God's name, for I am not one that curiously* stands upon merits.   30
COREBUS: You whoreson sodden-headed sheep's-face, shall a good fellow
    do service and more honesty to the parish, and will you not when he is
    dead let him have Christmas* burial?

WIGGEN: Peace, Corebus! As sure as Jack was Jack, the frolic'st franion
 amongst you, and I Wiggen his sweet sworn brother, Jack shall have 35
 his funerals,* or some of them shall lie on God's dear earth for it,
 that's once.*
CHURCHWARDEN: Wiggen, I hope thou wilt do no more than thou dar'st
 answer.
WIGGEN: Sir, sir, dare or dare not, more or less, answer or not answer, do 40
 this, or have this.
SEXTON: Help, help, help, Wiggen sets upon the parish* with a pikestaff!
      EUMENIDES *awakes and comes to them.*
EUMENIDES: Hold thy hands, good fellow.
COREBUS: Can you blame him, sir, if he take Jack's part against this 45
 shake-rotten* parish that will not bury Jack?
EUMENIDES: Why, what was that Jack?
COREBUS: Who, Jack, sir? Who, our Jack, sir? As good a fellow as ever trod
 upon neat's leather.*
WIGGEN: Look you, sir, he gave four score and nineteen mourning gowns* 50
 to the parish when he died, and because he would not make them up a
 full hundred, they would not bury him. Was not this good dealing?
CHURCHWARDEN: O Lord, sir, how he lies! He was not worth a halfpenny,
 and drunk out every penny, and now his fellows, his drunken
 companions, would have us to bury him at the charge of the parish. 55
 And* we make many such matches, we may pull down the steeple, sell
 the bells, and thatch the chancel.* He shall lie above ground till he
 dance a galliard* about the churchyard, for Steven Loach.*
WIGGEN: *Sic argumentaris Domine Loach:** and we make many such matches,
 we may pull down the steeple, sell the bells, and thatch the 60
 chancel – in good time, sir, and hang yourselves in the bellropes
 when you have done. *Domine, oponens praepono tibi hanc questionem:**
 whether you will have the ground broken, or your pates broken first,
 for one of them shall be done presently*, and to begin mine*, I'll seal
 it upon your coxcomb. 65
EUMENIDES: Hold thy hands, I pray thee, good fellow; be not too hasty.
COREBUS: You capon's face,* we shall have you turned out of the parish one
 of these days, with never a tatter to your arse. Then you are in worse
 taking* than Jack.
EUMENIDES: Faith, and he is bad enough. This fellow does but the part 70
 of a friend to seek to bury his friend; how much will bury him?
WIGGEN: Faith, about some fifteen or sixteen shillings will bestow him
 honestly.*
SEXTON: Ay, even thereabouts, sir.
EUMENIDES: Here, hold it then, and I have left me but one poor three 75
 half-pence.* Now do I remember the words the old man spake at the
 cross: 'Bestow all thou hast', and this is all, 'Till dead men's bones
 comes at the call'. Here, hold it; and so farewell.

WIGGEN: God and all good be with you, sir. Nay, you cormorants,* I'll
    bestow one peal* of Jack at mine own proper costs and charges.   80
COREBUS: You may thank God the long staff and the bilbo-blade* crossed not
    your coxcomb. Well, we'll to the church stile and have a pot,* and so
    trill-lill*.
BOTH: Come, let's go.   *Exeunt.*
FANTASTIC: But, hark you, gammer; methinks this Jack bore a great   85
    sway in the parish.
OLD WOMAN: O, this Jack was a marvellous fellow. He was but a poor man
    but very well beloved; you shall see anon what this Jack will come to.

            Enter the HARVEST MEN *singing, with women in their hands.*

FROLIC: Soft, who have we here? Our amorous harvesters.
FANTASTIC: Ay, ay, let us sit still and let them alone.   90
            Here they begin to sing, the song doubled.

           Lo, here we come a-reaping, a-reaping,
           To reap our harvest fruit,
           And thus we pass the year so long,
           And never we be mute.   *Exeunt the* HARVEST MEN

Scene Six

           Enter HUANEBANGO *and* COREBUS *the clown.*

FROLIC: Soft, who have we here?
OLD WOMAN: O, this is a choleric* gentleman! All you that love your lives,
    keep out of the smell* of his two-hand sword. Now goes he to the
    conjurer.
FANTASTIC: Methinks the conjurer should put the fool into a juggling box*. 5
HUANEBANGO: Fee, fa, fum, here is the Englishman.
    Conquer him that can,
    Came for his lady bright,
    To prove himself a knight,
    And win her love in fight.   10
COREBUS: Hoo, ha, Master Bango, are you here? Hear you, you had best sit
    down here and beg an alms with me.
HUANEBANGO: Hence, base cullion.* Here is he that commandeth ingress
    and egress with his weapon, and will enter at his voluntary,* whosoever
    saith no.   15
           A voice of flame and fire. HUANEBANGO *falleth down.*
VOICE: No.

OLD WOMAN: So with that they kissed, and spoiled the edge of as good a
    two-hand sword as ever God put life in. Now goes Corebus in, spite of
    the conjurer.

        Enter [SACRAPANT] *the conjurer and strike* COREBUS *blind.*

SACRAPANT: Away with him* into the open fields,   20
    To be a ravening prey to crows and kites.
    And for this villain, let him wander up and down
    In nought but darkness and eternal night.
COREBUS: Here hast thou slain Huan, a slashing knight
    And robbed poor Corebus of his sight.   *Exit.*   25
SACRAPANT: Hence, villain, hence.
    Now I have unto Delia given a potion of forgetfulness,
    That when she comes she shall not know her brothers.
    Lo, where they labour like to country* slaves,
    With spade and mattock* on this enchanted ground.   30
    Now will I call her by another name,
    For never shall she know herself again
    Until that Scarapant hath breathed his last.
    See where she comes.

                Enter DELIA.

    Come hither, Delia, take this goad.* Here hard   35
    At hand two slaves do work and dig for gold.
    Gore* them with this and thou shalt have enough.
                               He gives her a goad.
DELIA: Good sir, I know not what you mean.
SACRAPANT: She hath forgotten to be Delia,
    But not forgot the same she should forget.   40
    But I will change her name.
    Fair Berecynthia* – so this country calls you –
    Go ply* these strangers, wench; they dig for gold.   *Exit.*
DELIA: O heavens! How am I beholding* to this fair young man.
    But I must ply these strangers to their work.   45
    See where they come.

      Enter the two BROTHERS *in their shirts with spades digging.*

1 BROTHER: O brother, see where Delia is.
2 BROTHER: O Delia, happy are we to see thee here.
DELIA: What tell you me of Delia, prating swains?*
    I know no Delia nor know I what you mean,   50

Ply you* your work or else you are like to smart.
1 BROTHER: Why, Delia, knowest thou not thy brothers here?
 We come from Thessaly to seek thee forth,
 And thou deceivest thyself, for thou art Delia.
DELIA: Yet more of Delia! Then take this, and smart!   55
 What, feign you shifts* for to defer your labour?
 Work, villains, work; it is for gold you dig.
2 BROTHER: Peace, brother, peace; this vild* enchanter
 Hath ravished Delia of her senses clean,
 And she forgets that she is Delia.   60
1 BROTHER: Leave, cruel thou, to hurt the miserable.
 Dig, brother, dig; for she is as hard as steel.
    Here they dig and descry the light under a little hill.*
2 BROTHER: Stay, brother. What hast thou descried?
DELIA: Away, and touch it not. It is something that my lord hath hidden
 there.   65
       She covers it again.

    Enter SACRAPANT.

SACRAPANT: Well said. Thou pliest these pioneers* well. Go, get you in, you
 labouring slaves.
 Come, Berecynthia, let us in likewise,
 And hear the nightingale record her notes.   *Exeunt omnes.*

Scene Seven

Enter ZANTYPPA, *the Curst Daughter, to the well, with a pot in her hand.*

ZANTYPPA: Now for a husband, house and home! God send a good one, or
 none, I pray God. My father hath sent me to the well for the water of
 life, and tells me if I give fair words I shall have a husband.

 Enter [CELANTA] *the Foul Wench to the well for water, with a pot in her hand.*

 But here comes Celanta, my sweet sister. I'll stand by and hear what she
 says.   5
CELANTA: My father hath sent me to the well for water, and he tells me if I
 speak fair, I shall have a husband and none of the worst. Well, though I
 am black,* I am sure all the world will not forsake me, and, as the old
 proverb is, though I am black, I am not the devil*.
ZANTYPPA: Marry, gup with a murrain!* I know wherefore thou speakest 10
 that, but go thy ways home as wise as thou canst, or I'll set thee home
 with a wanion.*
    Here she strikes her pitcher against her sister's,
      and breaks them both and goes her way.

CELANTA: I think this be the curstest* quean* in the world. You see what she
is: a little fair, but as proud as the devil, and the veriest vixen that
lives upon God's earth. Well, I'll let her alone, and go home and   15
get another pitcher, and for all this get me to the well for water.   *Exit.*

> *Enter two* FURIES *out of the conjurer's cell,*
> *and lays* HUANEBANGO *by the well of life.*
> *Enter* ZANTYPPA *with a pitcher in her hand.*

ZANTYPPA: Once again for a husband and in faith, Celanta, I have got the
start of you. Belike* husbands grow by the well-side. Now my father
says I must rule my tongue; why, alas, what am I then? A woman
without a tongue is as a soldier without his weapon. But I'll have   20
my water and be gone.
> *Here she offers to dip the pitcher in,*
> *and a* HEAD *speaks in the well.*

HEAD: Gently dip, but not too deep,
For fear you make the golden bird* to weep.
Fair maiden, white and red,
Stroke me smooth, and comb my head.   25
And thou shall have some cockle-bread.*
ZANTYPPA: What is this? Fair maiden white and red,
Comb me smooth, and stroke my head,
And thou shalt have some cockle-bread.
Cockle, callest thou it, boy? Faith, I'll give you cockle-bread!   30
> *She breaks her pitcher upon his head, then it*
> *thunders and lightens, and* HUANEBANGO *rises up.*
> HUANEBANGO *is deaf and cannot hear.*

HUANEBANGO: Phylyda phylerydos, Pamphylyda floryda flortos,
Dub dub-a-dub, bounce, quoth the guns, with a sulphurous huff-snuff,
Waked with a wench, pretty peat,* pretty love, and my sweet pretty
pigsnie.*
Just by thy side shall sit surnamed great Huanebango;   35
Safe in my arms will I keep thee, threat Mars, or thunder Olympus.
ZANTYPPA: Foh, what greasy groom* have we here? He looks as though he
crept out of the backside of the well, and speaks like a drum perished at
the west end.*
HUANEBANGO: O that I might but I may not; woe to my destiny therefore.* 40
Kiss that I clasp, but I cannot; tell me my destiny wherefore?
ZANTYPPA: Whoop! Now I have my dream! Did you never hear so great a
wonder as this? Three blue beans in a blue bladder: rattle, bladder,
rattle.*
HUANEBANGO: I'll now set my countenance and to her in prose; it may be   45
this rim-ram-ruff* is too rude an encounter. Let me, fair lady, if you be at

leisure, revel with your sweetness, and rail upon that cowardly conjurer
that hath cast me – or congealed me, rather – into an unkind sleep, and
polluted my carcass.

ZANTYPPA: Laugh, laugh , Zantyppa; thou hast thy fortune – a fool and   50
a husband under one.

HUANEBANGO: Truly, sweetheart as I seem: about some twenty years, the
very April of mine age.

ZANTYPPA: Why, what a prating ass is this!

HUANEBANGO: Her coral lips, her crimson chin,   55
Her silver teeth so white within,
Her golden locks, her rolling eye,
Her pretty parts, let them go by;
Hey ho, hath wounded me,
That I must die this day to see.   60

ZANTYPPA: By Gog's* bones, thou art a flouting knave. Her coral lips, her
crimson chin! Ka, wilshaw!*

HUANEBANGO: True, my own, and my own because mine, and mine because
mine, ha ha! Above a thousand pounds in possibility, and things fitting
thy desire in possession.   65

ZANTYPPA: The sot thinks I ask of his lands. Lob be your comfort,* and
cuckold be your destiny – Hear you, sir: and if you will have us, you
had best say so betime.*

HUANEBANGO: True, sweetheart, and will royalise thy progeny with my
pedigree.   *Exeunt omnes.*   70

Scene Eight

Enter EUMENIDES *the Wandering Knight.*

EUMENIDES: Wretched Eumenides, still unfortunate,
Envied by fortune, and forlorn by fate;
Here pine and die, wretched Eumenides.
Die in the spring, the April of my age?
Here sit thee down, repent what thou hast done.   5
I would to God that it were ne'er begun.
                              Enter JACK.

JACK: You are well overtaken, sir.

EUMENIDES: Who's that?

JACK: You are heartily well met, sir.

EUMENIDES: Forbear, I say. Who is that which pincheth me?   10

JACK: Trusting in God, good master Eumenides, that you are in so good
health as all your friends were at the making hereof. God give you good
morrow, sir. Lack you not a neat, handsome and cleanly young lad,

about the age of fifteen or sixteen years, that can run by your horse,
and for a need* make your mastership's shoes as black as ink? How   15
say you, sir?

EUMENIDES: Alas, pretty lad, I know not how to keep myself, and much less
a servant, my pretty boy, my state is so bad.

JACK: Content yourself, you shall not be so ill a master but I'll be as bad a
servant. Tut, sir, I know you, though you know not me. Are not you   20
the man, sir – deny it if you can, sir – that came from a strange place in
the land of Catita,* where Jackanapes* flies with his tail in his mouth, to
seek out a lady as white as snow, and as red as blood? Ha ha! Have I
touched you now?

EUMENIDES: I think this boy be a spirit – how knowest thou all this?   25

JACK: Tut, are not you the man, sir – deny it if you can, sir – that gave all the
money you had to the burying of a poor man, and but one three half-
pence left in your purse? Content you, sir, I'll serve you, that is flat.

EUMENIDES: Well, my lad, since thou art so importunate,* I am content to
entertain thee, not as a servant, but a copartner in my journey. But   30
whither shall we go? For I have not any money more than one bare
three half-pence.

JACK: Well, master, content yourself; for if my divination* be not out,* that
shall be spent at the next inn or alehouse we come to. For, master, I
know you are passing hungry; therefore I'll go before and provide   35
dinner until that you come. No doubt but you'll come fair and softly
after.

EUMENIDES: Ay, go before; I'll follow thee.

JACK: But do you hear, master? Do you know my name?

EUMENIDES: No, I promise thee, not yet.   40

JACK: Why, I am Jack.   *Exit.*

EUMENIDES: Jack. Why, be it so, then.

Enter the HOSTESS *and* JACK, *setting meat on the table,*
and fiddlers come to play.
EUMENIDES *walketh up and down, and will eat no meat.*

HOSTESS: How say you, sir? Do you please to sit down?

EUMENIDES: Hostess, I thank you. I have no great stomach.*

HOSTESS: Pray, sir, what is the reason your master is so strange? Doth not   45
this meat please him?

JACK: Yes, hostess, but it is my master's fashion to pay before he eats.
Therefore, a reckoning, good hostess.

HOSTESS: Marry, shall you* sir, presently.   *Exit.*

EUMENIDES: Why, Jack, what dost thou mean? Thou knowest I have   50
not any money. Therefore, sweet Jack, tell me: what shall I do?

JACK: Well, master, look in your purse.

EUMENIDES: Why, faith, it is a folly, for I have no money.

JACK: Why, look you, master; do so much for me.

EUMENIDES: Alas, Jack, my purse is full of money.   55

JACK: Alas! Master, does that word belong to this accident? Why, methinks I should have seen you cast away your cloak, and in a bravado* danced a galliard around the chamber. Why, master, your man can teach you more wit than this. Come, hostess, cheer up my master.

[*Enter* HOSTESS.]

HOSTESS: You are heartily welcome; and if it please you to eat of a fat   60
capon, a fairer bird, a finer bird, a sweeter bird, a crisper bird, a neater bird, your worship never eat* of.

EUMENIDES: Thanks, my fine eloquent hostess.

JACK: But hear you, master, one word by the way. Are you content I shall be halves* in all you get in your journey?   65

EUMENIDES: I am, Jack, here is my hand.

JACK: Enough, master, I ask no more.

EUMENIDES: Come, hostess, receive your money, and I thank you for my good entertainment.

HOSTESS: You are heartily welcome, sir.   70

EUMENIDES: Come, Jack, whither go we now?

JACK: Marry, master, to the conjurer's presently.

EUMENIDES: Content, Jack. Hostess, farewell.   *Exe[unt] om[nes].*

Scene Nine

Enter COREBUS *and* [CELANTA] *the foul wench, to the well for water.*

COREBUS: Come, my duck, come. I have now got a wife. Thou art fair, art thou not?

CELANTA: My Corebus, the fairest alive, make no doubt of that.

COREBUS: Come, wench, are we almost at the well?

CELANTA: Ay, Corebus, we are almost at the well now. I'll go fetch some   5
water; sit down while I dip my pitcher in.

HEAD [*off*]: Gently dip, but not too deep,
For fear you make the gold beard to weep.
                              A HEAD *comes up with ears of corn,*
                              and she combs them in her lap.

Fair maiden, white and red,
Comb me smooth, and stroke my head,   10
And thou shall have some cockle-bread.
Gently dip, but not too deep,

For fear thou make the gold beard to weep.
Fair maid, white and red,
Comb me smooth and stroke my head;   15
And every hair a sheaf shall be,
And every sheaf a golden tree.   *A* HEAD *comes up full of gold;*
she combs it into her lap.

CELANTA: O see, Corebus, I have combed a great deal of gold into my lap,
and a great deal of corn!

COREBUS: Well said, wench! Now we shall have just enough. God send us 20
coiners to coin our gold. But come, shall we go home, sweetheart?

CELANTA: Nay, come, Corebus, I will lead you.

COREBUS: So, Corebus, things have well hit,
Thou hast gotten wealth to mend thy wit.   *Exeunt.*

Scene Ten

Enter JACK *and* [EUMENIDES] *the Wandering Knight.*

JACK: Come away, master, come.

EUMENIDES: Go along, Jack, I'll follow thee. Jack, they say it is good to go
cross-legged, and say his prayers backward.* How sayest thou?

JACK: Tut, never fear, master. Let me alone. Here sit you still: speak not a
word. And because you* shall not be enticed with his enchanting   5
speeches, with this same wool I'll stop your ears. And so, master, sit
still, for I must to the conjurer.   *Exit.*

Enter [SACRAPANT] *the Conjurer to* [EUMENIDES] *the Wandering Knight.*

SACRAPANT: How now, what man art thou that sits so sad?
Why dost thou gaze upon these stately trees,
Without the leave and will of Sacrapant?   10
What, not a word but mum*?
Then, Sacrapant, thou art betrayed.

Enter JACK *invisible, and taketh off* SACRAPANT'S
wreath from his head, and his sword out of his hand.

What hand invades the head of Sacrapant?
What hateful fury doth envy my happy state?
Then, Sacrapant, these are thy latest days,   15
Alas, my veins are numbed, my sinews shrink,
My blood is pierced, my breath fleeting away,
And now my timeless date* is come to end.
He in whose life his actions hath been so foul,
Now in his death to hell descends his soul.   *He dieth.*   20

JACK: O sir, are you gone? Now I hope we shall have some other coil.* Now,
master, how like you this? The conjurer he is dead, and vows never to

trouble us more. Now get you to your fair lady and see what you can do
with her. Alas, he heareth me not all this while, but I will help that.
He pulls the wool out of his ears.
EUMENIDES: How now, Jack, what news?   25
JACK: Here, master, take this sword and dig with it at the foot of this hill.
He digs and spies a light.
EUMENIDES: How now, Jack, what is this?
JACK: Master, without this the conjurer could do nothing, and so long as this
light lasts, so long doth his art endure; and this being out, then doth his
art decay.   30
EUMENIDES: Why then, Jack, I will soon put out this light.
JACK: Ay, master, how?
EUMENIDES: Why, with a stone I'll break the glass, and then blow it out.
JACK: No, master, you may as soon break the smith's anvil as this little vial.
Nor the biggest blast that ever Boreas* blew cannot blow out this   35
little light, but she that is neither maid, wife, nor widow. Master, wind*
this horn and see what will happen.   *He winds the horn.*

Here enters VENELIA *and breaks the glass,*
and blows out the light, and goeth in again.

JACK: So, master, how like you this? This is she that ran madding in the
woods, his betrothed love that keeps the cross. And now, this light
being out, all are restored to their former liberty. And now, master, to   40
the lady that you have so long looked for.   *He draweth a curtain, and*
there DELIA *sitteth asleep.*
EUMENIDES: God speed, fair maid sitting alone, there is once;
God speed, fair maid, there is twice;
God speed, fair maid; there is thrice.
DELIA: Not so, good sir, for you are by.   45
JACK: Enough, master. She hath spoke; now I will leave her with you. [*Exit.*]
EUMENIDES: Thou fairest flower of these western parts,
Whose beauty so reflecteth in my sight
As doth a crystal mirror in the sun,   50
For thy sweet sake I have crossed the frozen Rhine,
Leaving fair Po, I sailed up Danuby,
As far as Saba*, whose enchanting streams
Cuts twixt the Tartars and the Russians.*
These have I crossed for thee, fair Delia,
Then grant me that which I have sued for long.   55
DELIA: Thou gentle knight, whose fortune is so good
To find me out, and set my brothers free,
My faith, my heart, my hand, I give to thee.
EUMENIDES: Thanks, gentle madam. But here comes Jack: thank him, for he
is the best friend that we have.   60

Enter JACK *with a head in his hand.*

How now, Jack? What hast thou there?

JACK: Marry, master, the head of the conjurer.

EUMENIDES: Why, Jack, that is impossible. He was a young man.

JACK: Ah, master, so he deceived them that beheld him. But he was a
    miserable, old and crooked man, though to each man's eye he   65
    seemed young and fresh. For, master, this conjurer took the shape of
    the old man that kept the cross, and that old man was in the likeness
    of the conjurer. But now, master, wind your horn.   *He winds his horn.*

Enter VENELIA, *the two* BROTHERS,
and [OLD MAN], *he that was at the cross.*

EUMENIDES: Welcome, Erestus; welcome, fair Venelia;
    Welcome, Thelea, and Calypha both.   70
    Now have I her that I so long have sought,
    So saith fair Delia, if we have your consent.

1 BROTHER: Valiant Eumenides, thou well deservest
    To have our favours; so let us rejoice,
    That by thy means we are at liberty.   75
    Here may we joy each in other's* sight,
    And this fair lady have her wandering knight.

JACK: So, master, now ye think you have have done, but I must have a
    saying to you. You know you and I were partners, I to have half in all
    you got.   80

EUMENIDES: Why, so thou shalt, Jack.

JACK: Why then, master, draw your sword, part your lady; let me have half of
    her presently.

EUMENIDES: Why, I hope, Jack, thou dost but jest. I promised thee half I got,
    but not half my lady.   85

JACK: But what else, master? Have you not gotten her? Therefore divide her
    straight,* for I will have half. There is no remedy.

EUMENIDES: Well, ere I will falsify my word unto my friend, take her all.
    Here, Jack, I'll give her thee.

JACK: Nay, neither more nor less, master, but even just half.   90

EUMENIDES: Before I will falsify my faith to my friend, I will divide her. Jack,
    thou shalt have half.

1 BROTHER: Be not so cruel unto our sister, gentle knight.

2 BROTHER: O spare fair Delia, she deserves no death.

EUMENIDES: Content yourselves; my word is passed to him.* Therefore   95
    prepare thyself, Delia, for thou must die.

DELIA: Then farewell, world! Adieu, Eumenides!   *He offers to strike and* JACK
                                    stays him.

JACK: Stay, master! It is sufficient I have tried your constancy. Do you now
    remember since you paid for the burying of a poor fellow?

EUMENIDES: Ay, very well, Jack.   100

JACK: Then, master, thank thee for that good deed, for this good turn, and so God be with you all.   JACK *leaps down in the ground.*

EUMENIDES: Jack, where art thou gone? Then farewell, Jack.

    Come, brothers, and my beauteous Delia,

    Erestus and thy dear Venelia;   105

    We will to Thessaly with joyful hearts.

ALL: Agreed, we will follow thee and Delia.   *Exeunt omnes.*

Scene Eleven

FANTASTIC: What, gammer, asleep?

OLD WOMAN: By the mass, son, 'tis almost day, and my windows* shuts at the cock's crow.

FROLIC: Do you hear, gammer? Methinks this Jack bore a great sway amongst them.   5

OLD WOMAN: O man, this was the ghost of the poor man that they kept such a coil to bury, and that makes him to help the wandering knight so much. But come, let us in: we will have a cup of ale and a toast this morning, and so depart.

FANTASTIC: Then you have made an end of your tale, gammer?   10

OLD WOMAN: Yes, faith. When this was done, I took my piece of bread and cheese and came my way, and so shall you have too before you go to your breakfast.

Finis

Notes to the Play

Parts in the Play (not in Q)

COREBUS/BOOBY: *there is an ambiguity in Q regarding the nomenclature of the clown(s): Corebus and Booby may represent two parts or a change of name after the first scene in which the clown appears. Many editions conflate the two; I have opted to retain the double nomenclature as a problem to be resolved in performance.*

Scene One

1	Frolic: Q has 'Franticke'
	amort: dejected
4–5	warant … hundred: bet at odds of five to one on your life
6	frolic franion: a joker
8	O coelum … maria!: O heaven! O earth! O sea!
21	wooden: mad
29	what make you: what are you up to
33	side slops: baggy breeches
36	Vulcan: Roman name for Greek god of fire, patron of Smiths
36	cozened: tricked
51	gammer: old woman
55	crab: crab-apple
55	lambswool: sweetened and spiced hot ale mixed with roast apple pulp
56	trump or ruff: card games, similar to whist
63	chop cherry: also known as bob-cherry; a game which involves attempting to catch a cherry on a string by the teeth
80	spavin or windgall: tumours found in horses' legs
82	No … Devonshire: possibly proverbial; this could not be bettered
85	Bona nox: good night
87	unnatural: because the two men are to share a bed
88–9	Yet … extempore: we'll have the advantage of seeing the dawn before they do
98	dressed: prepared

99	kiss my tail: kiss my arse
106	proper: handsome
107	keeps: lives

Scene Two

13	Hips and haws: fruits of the wild rose and hawthorn
18	alms-penny: charitable donation
19	gown of grey: pilgrim's traditional attire
20	speed: succeed
21	palmer's: pilgrim's
45	cheer: face
49	Thessaly: a region of ancient Greece renowned as a place of magic and enchantment
61	rage: prophetic inspiration
65	madding: madly
70	moved: mentioned
72	cumbered: burdened
73	mend your fare: satisfy your need
78–9	Saint Andrew's … Saint Luke's: traditionally favourable days for choosing a lover or spouse
80	custom is out: service is over
88	Poor … proud: proverbial
92	curst: foul-tempered
92	froward: uncooperative
93–4	Smoke … teeth: cf. Proverbs 10:26: 'As vinegar to the teeth, and as smoke to the eyes, so is the sluggard to them that send him.'
103	Farewell … thousand a thousand farewells
105	this … stick this story is moving nicely, like a lively tune played on a fiddle

Scene Three

11	affectest: yearns for
11	do off: leave off
14	absolve: solve
17	flurting: lively waving

18	given ... stock: shocked the entire parish with my fashionable long stockings
23	devoir: chivalric duty
24–5	Meus ... grammaticorum: Mine, mine, mine, is spite of all grammar Huanebango employs male, female and neuter Latin genders (meus, mea, meum) to apply to the lady
26–7	cum apurtinantibus: with its appurtenances (a legal phrase); minum and gibletes are cod-Latin for 'mine' and 'giblets'
37	neat's feet: ox's feet, used for brawn
39	boy: page
53	buckler: defend
55	pass for: wish for
57	superfantial: a nonsense word
57	foison: harvest provision
62	as hard ... goes: in these hard times

Scene Four

1	welkin: sky
2	records: sings
7	Meroe: Thessalonian witch notorious for changing men into beasts
7	hight: named
30	veriest: worst
35	chine: backbone and rib
44	neat: unadulterated
52	usurer: moneylender
53	Hold thee there: stick to that view
79	Adeste Daemones: (Latin) Come forth, spirits

Scene Five

3	lodestar: guiding star
9	wit: intelligence
22	scald: scab-infested, contemptible
26	answer: pay for
30	curiously: fussily
33	Christmas: Christian
36	funerals: funeral obsequies

36–7	that's once: that's for sure
42	parish: parish official
45–6	shake-rotten: utterly corrupt and degraded
48–9	trod ... leather: walked in shoes
50	mourning gowns: black cloth gowns given to the poor to attend the funeral
56	And: if
57	thatch the chancel: substitute a material cheaper than slate or lead
58	galliard: a lively dance
58	Steven Loach: i.e. the churchwarden; 'loach' is a synonym for idiot
59	Sic ... Loach: Thus you argue, Master Loach
62	Domine ... questionem: Sir, in opposition, I propose to you this question
64	presently: immediately
64	to begin mine: to start
67	capon's face: an expression of abuse
69	taking: circumstances
72–3	bestow him honestly: take care of him properly
75–6	three half-pence: a silver coin worth one-and-a-half pence
79	cormorants: scavenging seabirds renowned for their greed
80	bestow one peal: pay for the church bells to ring in memory
81	bilbo-blade: a sword of Spanish steel
82	church-stile ... pot: the alehouse was commonly adjacent to the church
83	trill-lill: imitates the glug ging of ale down the throat

Scene Six

2	choleric: prone to displays of anger
3	smell: range
5	juggling box: obscure; perhaps indicating some kind of conjuring device
13	cullion: rascal
14	at his voluntary: at will

20	away with him: evidently some kind of intervention is required to remove Huanebango from the stage, presumably by the Furies who lay him out by the well in Scene Seven
29	country: crude, ignorant
30	mattock: a kind of pick
35	goad: cattle prod
37	Gore: wound
42	Berecynthia: one of the names of Cybele, ancient Greek goddess of the earth
43	ply: harass
44	beholding: beholden
49	swains: rural labourers
51	Ply you: apply yourself to
56	feign you shifts: are you practising tricks
58	vild: vile
62	descry: see
66	pioneers: diggers

Scene Seven

8	black: dark-complexioned
9	though ... devil: proverbial
10	Marry ... murrain: an expression of contempt and impatience; 'marry' derives from Mary, 'murrain' means plague
12	with a wanion: with a vengeance
13	curstest: most accursed
13	quean: hussy
18	Belike: perhaps
23	bird: many editors emend to 'beard' as more consistent with Head's subsequent appearance at lines xxx–xxx.
26	cockle-bread: corn-bread; cockle is a weed found in cornfields. In his Remaines of *Gentilisme and Judaisme* (1697), the late-seventeenth-century writer John Aubrey unpacks the significance of this phrase: 'Young wenches have a wanton sport, which they call moulding of Cocklebread; viz. they get upon a Table-board, and then gather up their knees and their coats with their hands as high as they can, and then they

wabble to and fro with their Buttocks as if they were kneading of Dough with their Arses.'

33	peat: pet
34	pigsnie: pig's eye (a term of endearment)
37	groom: fellow
38–9	drum ... end: a drum with a skin broken
40	O ... therefore: quoted from Gabriel Harvey's *Encomium Lauri* (1580)
43–4	Three ... rattle: proverbial
46	rim, ram, ruff: refers to Huanebango's ornate discourse
61	Gog's: God's
62	Ka, wilshaw: obscure; an expression of derision
66	Lob ... comfort your: stupidity may be a comfort to you in that it will prevent you from realising your destiny as a cuckold
68	betime: speedily

Scene Eight

15	for a need: as you need
22	Catita: an imagined land evidently invented by Peele
22	Jackanapes: a nickname for someone who makes a monkey of himself
29	importunate: insistent
33	divination: suspicion
33	out: mistaken
44	stomach: appetite
49	shall you: you shall have it
57	in a bravado: with brio
62	eat: ate
64–5	be halves: go halves

Scene Ten

3	go ... backward: ritual actions associated both with the conjuring of evil and wishing for good luck
3	his: one's
5	because you: so that you
11	not ... mum: proverbial

18   timeless date: eternal life
21   some other coil: some more
       mischief
35   Boreas: god of the north wind
36   wind: blow
50–4   For ... Russians: cf. Robert
       Greene, Orlando Furioso (1594),
       ll.72–6

I furrowed Neptune's seas
Northeast as far as is the frozen Rhene;
Leaving fair Voya, crossed up Danuby,
As high as Saba, whose enhancing
       streams

Cut twixt the Tartares and the
       Russians.

52   Saba: Sheba
76   joy each in other's: enjoy each
       other's
87   straight: straight away
95   my word ... him: I have
       promised him

Scene Eleven

2   windows: also refers to the Old
       Woman's eyes

The Shoemakers Holiday or The Gentle Craft

THOMAS DEKKER

Although he was involved in the making of at least 50 plays between 1598 – when his name was mentioned in Henslowe's Diary in connection with the lost play *Phaeton* – and 1603, little is known of Thomas Dekker, other than that he appears to have been born in the early 1570s and that he spent most of his life working in London, the city which features centrally in most of his dramatic writing. A key member of Henslowe's stable of journeyman writers, supplying material for the Lord Admiral's and the Lord Chamberlain's Men, Dekker evidently spent his time in and out of debtors' prison, working meanwhile according to the customary pattern of early modern playmaking, as a collaborator with, amongst others, Thomas Middleton, John Webster, William Rowley and John Ford; he also turned his hand to pamphlet-writing and to scripting civic pageants. *The Shoemakers Holiday* was the first play associated with Dekker to incorporate his name on the title page of its Quarto publication; as this announced, it had enjoyed a successful performance at Court in 1600.

As its title indicates, its appeal lay in a fusion of the materials of romance, popular festivity and civic legend: derived from stories contained in Thomas Deloney's prose collection, *The Gentle Craft* (1597), the main action of the play operates within an established narrative and dramatic tradition of celebrating the heroic history which had become one of London's key industries in the late years of the sixteenth century: shoemaking. In Deloney's tales, cobblers are ascribed an innate nobility that is manifested through the dignity of labour rather than the precedent of rank; in Dekker's play, this is rendered in Simon Eyre's reiterated claim, 'Prince am I none, yet am I princely born'. The play, however, is careful to mind existing social hierarchies, presenting an optimistic, even idealistic, picture of the London scene during a period of rapid and, for many, disconcerting social and economic change. Its dramatis personae ranges across the social scale, incorporating the volunteer soldier, Rafe, who returns wounded from the military campaign in France to be spared, according to the play's charitable scheme, the destitution that would have been his likely fate in historical reality; as well as the monarch himself, whose *deus ex machina* intervention in the final scenes resolves the apparently intractable conflicts between love, social status and financial gain upon which the romance plot hinges. Importantly, in view of the play's advertised royal audience, the message is that regal intervention can ensure that love conquers all, enabling the coupling of Rose and Lacy, and the reunion of Rafe and Jane, who succeeds in rebutting Hammon's tactics of coercion; it is a nominally happy ending within which the Earl of Lincoln and the former Lord Mayor are left silent, truculently acquiescent to a dispensation secured by monarchical *fiat*. The play is offered as escapist entertainment, not social realism, but nonetheless engages with the tensions and conflicts of a social order riven by the competing claims of an aristocracy whose traditional claims to privilege are rooted in land and the those of an emergent manufacturing class which is still partially implicated within the working practices of the late medieval guild system, and which threatens to accelerate social mobility even as it embraces and appropriates traditional civic rites and ceremonies.

The historical figure of Simon Eyre, the fifteenth-century tradesman who rose to the position of Lord Mayor of London, is pivotal: in Dekker's play this bourgeois shoemaker becomes a fairly sober and industrious Lord of Misrule, presiding over a cheery, beery crew of conscientious prentices and journeymen, united in the gentle craft under Eyre's benevolent gaze. Amongst their number is Firk (pronounced, usually, as 'fuck'), a figure directly derived from the medieval Vice, who acts as a conduit for the licensed disorder which the holiday ethos of the play as a whole celebrates on a larger scale. Both Eyre and Firk are, in a sense, timeless figures, in that they, like the events of the play's narrative, and like the popular theatre for which it was designed, simultaneously straddle past and present, the Londons of the fifteenth and late sixteenth centuries, and of myth, legend and folklore. The person of the King (who would historically have been Henry VI, but who is dramatically closer to his more successful father, the legendary 'bully king', Henry V) is imagined in terms of a mythic combination of charismatic authority and the common touch that is able to transcend the hierarchies to which both the aspirant middle classes and insecure aristocracy continue to subscribe.

If the overall mood of the play is one of holiday, it is one in which the rhythms of work and the pressures of social conformity have been seamlessly incorporated into the potentially anarchic time of time off: as the narrative moves towards its happy closure, the energies which feed the pleasures of feasting and indulgence, eating and drinking, harness the potential disorder of the cudgel-wielding prentices who take to the streets to ambush the would-be seducer, Hammon, so that, even as he harmlessly evaporates from the play, he salutes the 'good fellows of the gentle trade', whose 'morning's mirth my mourning day hath made' (18. 92–93). Imagining how the new Lord Mayor's largesse will supply the gargantuan appetites of the prentices, Firk extols his fellow prentices with visions of unlimited satiety:

> There's cheer for the heavens – venison pasties
> walk up and down, piping hot like sergeants; beef
> and brewis comes marching in dry fats; fritters
> and pancakes comes trolling in in wheelbarrows,
> hens and oranges hopping in porters' baskets,
> collops and eggs in scuttles, and tarts and
> custards comes quavering in in malt shovels.
>
> (Scene 18, 183–88)

Such vistas of plenty are the dream-fodder of the starved and the dispossessed, but the latent violence within the play suggests that it is, at another level, aware of the potential for trouble that lies within the period of holiday (it was on such holiday moments as Shrove Tuesday that London's prentices would mark their temporary freedom from work through rioting, sometimes in the playhouses themselves).

Such undercurrents have generally gone unnoticed in modern productions of the play, of which there have been a considerable number. There are no records of performances after the 1600 Court appearance, although the fact that the play was reprinted five times between this date and 1657 may indicate a degree of theatrical popularity; the play was absent from the English stage from the Restoration until the beginning of the twentieth century. Once it had been retrieved by a series of amateur performances in the first decades of the century, *The Shoemakers Holiday* was afforded a professional production in 1922 at the Birmingham Repertory Theatre; it was then seen at the Old Vic in 1926, and then in a succession of London stagings up until the National Theatre version of 1981.

Further reading

Bevington, David, 'Theatre as Holiday', in *The Theatrical City: Culture, Theatre and Politics in London, 1576–1649*, ed. David L. Smith, Richard Strier and David Bevington (Cambridge: Cambridge University Press, 1995).

Bowers, Fredson (ed.), *The Dramatic Works of Thomas Dekker* (Cambridge: Cambridge University Press, 1953).

Gasper, Julia, *The Dragon and the Dove: The Plays of Thomas Dekker* (Oxford: Clarendon Press, 1990).

Kastan, David Scott, 'Workshop and/as Playhouse: *The Shoemaker's Holiday* (1599)', in *Staging the Renaissance: Reinterpretations of Elizabethan and Jacobean Drama*, ed. David Scott Kastan and Peter Stallybrass (London and New York: Routledge, 1991).

McLuskie, Kathleen E., *Dekker and Heywood: Professional Dramatists*, English Dramatists (Basingstoke: Macmillan, 1994).

Palmer, D. J. (ed.), *The Shoemakers' Holiday*, New Mermaids (London: Ernest Benn, 1975).

Seaver, Paul S., 'The Artisanal World', in *The Theatrical City*, ed. Smith, Strier and Bevington.

Smallwood, R. L. and Stanley Wells (ed.), *The Shoemaker's Holiday*, The Revels Plays (Manchester: Manchester University Press, 1979).

Parts in the Play

Sir Roger Oatley, LORD MAYOR *of London*
Earl of LINCOLN
LOVELL
LACY, *Lincoln's nephew*
ASKEW
Simon EYRE, *a Master Shoemaker*
Margery, his WIFE
HODGE, *his foreman*
FIRK, *Eyre's journeyman*
RAFE, *Eyre's journeyman*
JANE, *his wife*
DODGER, *the Earl of Lincoln's parasite*
ROSE, *Roger Oatley's daughter*
SYBIL, *Rose's maid*
A BOY, *working for Eyre*
HAMMON, *a city gentleman*
WARNER, *his brother-in-law*
A BOY, *with the huntsmen*
A Dutch SKIPPER
A PRENTICE, *working for Roger Oatley*
Master SCOTT, *an associate of Oatley*
KING *of England*

Huntsmen, Soldiers, Servants, Shoemakers, Prentices

To all good fellows, professors of the Gentle Craft, of what degree soever.

Kind gentlemen and honest boon companions, I present you here with a
merry conceited comedy called *The Shoemakers Holiday*, acted by my Lord
Admiral's Players this present Christmas before the Queen's most excellent
Majesty; for the mirth and pleasant matter by her Highness graciously
accepted, being indeed in no way offensive. The argument of the play   5
I will set down in this epistle: Sir Hugh Lacy, Earl of Lincoln, had a young
gentleman of his own name, his near kinsman, that loved the Lord Mayor's
daughter of London; to prevent and cross which love the Earl caused his
kinsman to be sent colonel of a company into France, who resigned his
place to another gentleman his friend, and came disguised his place like 10
a Dutch shoemaker to the house of Simon Eyre in Tower Street, who served
the Mayor and his household with shoes: the merriments that passed in
Eyre's house, his coming to be Lord Mayor of London, Lacy's getting his
love, and other accidents; with two merry three-men's songs.* Take all in
good worth that is well intended, for nothing is purposed but mirth.   15
Mirth lengtheneth long life, which with all other blessings I heartily wish
you.

Farewell.

The First Three-Man's Song

O the month of May, the merry month of May,
So frolic, so gay, and so green, so green, so green;
O and then did I unto my true love say,
Sweet Peg, thou shalt be my summer's queen.

Now the nightingale, the pretty nightingale,   5
The sweetest singer in all the forest's choir,
Entreats thee, sweet Peggy, to hear thy true love's tale:
Lo, yonder she sitteth, her breast against a briar.*

But O, I spy the cuckoo, the cuckoo, the cuckoo;*
See where she sitteth, come away, my joy: 10
Come away, I prithee, I do not like the cuckoo
Should sing where my Peggy and I kiss and toy.

O the month of May, the merry month of May,
So frolic, so gay, and so green, so green, so green;
And then I did unto my true love say,   15
Sweet Peg, thou shalt be my summer's queen.

The Second Three-Man's Song
(This is to be sung at the latter end)

Cold's the wind, and wet's the rain,
Saint Hugh* be our good speed.
Ill is the weather that bringeth no gain,
Nor helps good hearts in need.

Troll* the bowl, the jolly nut-brown bowl,   5
And here, kind mate, to thee.
Let's sing a dirge for Saint Hugh's soul,
And down it merrily.

Down-a-down, hey down-a-down,
Hey-derry-derry down-a-down   10
Close with the tenor boy.

Ho, well done, to me let come,
Ring compass, gentle joy.*

Troll the bowl, the nut-brown bowl,
And here, kind etc.   *as often as there be men to drink*

At last, when all have drunk, this verse:

Cold's the wind, and wet's the rain,   15
Saint Hugh be our good speed.
Ill is the weather that bringeth no gain,
Nor helps good hearts in need.

The Prologue as it was pronounced before the Queen's Majesty

As wretches in a storm, expecting day,
With trembling hands and eyes cast up to heaven,
Make prayers the anchor of their conquered hopes,
So we, dear goddess,* wonder of all eyes,
Your meanest vassals (through mistrust and fear,   5
To sink into the bottom of disgrace
By our imperfect pastimes) prostrate thus
On bended knees; our sails of hope do strike,*
Dreading the bitter storms of your dislike.
Since then – unhappy men – our hap* is such   10
That to ourselves, ourselves no help can bring,
But needs must perish, if your saint-like ears,
Locking the temple where all mercy sits,
Refuse the tribute of our begging tongues.
O grant, bright mirror of true chastity,
From those life-breathing stars your sun-like eyes   15
One gracious smile; for your celestial breath
Must send us life, or sentence us to death.

Scene One

Enter LORD MAYOR [*and*] LINCOLN.

LINCOLN: My Lord Mayor, you have sundry times
    Feasted myself, and many courtiers more;
    Seldom, or never, can we be so kind
    To make requital of your courtesy.
    But leaving this, I hear my cousin* Lacy   5
    Is much affected* to your daughter Rose.
LORD MAYOR: True, my good lord, and she loves him so well
    That I mislike her boldness in the chase.
LINCOLN: Why, my Lord Mayor, think you it then a shame
    To join a Lacy with an Oatley's name?
LORD MAYOR: Too mean is my poor girl for his high birth.
    Poor citizens must not with courtiers wed,
    Who will in silks and gay apparel spend
    More in one year than I am worth by far.
    Therefore your honour need not doubt* my girl.   15
LINCOLN: Take heed, my lord, advise you what you do.
    A verier unthrift lives not in the world
    Than is my cousin; for, I'll tell you what,
    'Tis now almost a year since he requested
    To travel countries for experience.   20
    I furnished him with coin, bills of exchange,*
    Letters of credit, men to wait on him;
    Solicited my friends in Italy
    Well to respect him. But, to see the end,
    Scant had he journeyed through half Germany   25
    But all his coin was spent, his men cast off,
    His bills embezzled;* and my jolly coz,
    Ashamed to show his bankrupt presence here,
    Became a shoemaker in Wittenberg.
    A goodly science for a gentleman   30
    Of such descent! Now judge the rest by this.
    Suppose your daughter have a thousand pound:
    He did consume me more in one half year,
    And make him heir to all the wealth you have.
    One twelve-month's rioting will waste it all.   35
    Then seek, my lord, some honest citizen
    To wed your daughter to.
LORD MAYOR: I thank your lordship.
    Well, fox, I understand your subtlety;*
    As for your nephew, let your lordship's eye

But watch his actions, and you need not fear,   40
For I have sent my daughter far enough.
And yet your cousin Roland might do well
Now he hath learned an occupation –
And yet I scorn to call him son-in-law.
LINCOLN: Ay, but I have a better trade for him.   45
I thank his Grace,* he hath appointed him
Chief colonel of all those companies
Mustered in London and the shires about,
To serve his Highness in those wars of France.*
See where he comes. Lovell, what news with you?   50

Enter LOVELL, LACY *and* ASKEW.

LOVELL: My lord of Lincoln, 'tis his Highness' will
That presently your cousin ship for France
With all his powers;* he would not for a million
But that they should land at Dieppe within four days.
LINCOLN: Go, certify his grace it shall be done.   *Exit* LOVELL. 55
Now, cousin Lacy, in what forwardness*
Are all your companies?
LACY: All well prepared.
The men of Hertfordshire lie at Mile End;
Suffolk and Essex train in Tothill Fields;
The Londoners and those of Middlesex,   60
All gallantly prepared in Finsbury,*
With frolic spirits long for their parting hour.
LORD MAYOR: They have their imprest,* coats and furniture,*
And, if it please your cousin Lacy come
To the Guildhall,* he shall receive his pay,   65
And twenty pounds besides my brethren*
Will freely give him, to approve* our loves
We bear unto my lord your uncle here.
LACY: I thank your honour.
LINCOLN: Thanks, my good Lord Mayor.
LORD MAYOR: At the Guildhall we will expect your coming.   *Exit.* 70
LINCOLN: To approve your loves to me? No, subtlety!
Nephew, that twenty pound he doth bestow
For joy, to rid you from his daughter Rose.
But, cousins both, now here are none but friends;
I would not have you cast an amorous eye   75
Upon so mean a project as the love
Of a gay, wanton, painted* citizen.
I know this churl, even in the height of scorn,

Doth hate the mixture of his blood with thine.
I pray thee do thou so; remember, coz,   80
What honourable fortunes wait on thee;
Increase the King's love, which so brightly shines,
And gilds my hopes. I have no heir but thee –
And yet not thee if, with a wayward spirit,
Thou start from the true bias* of my love.   85
LACY: My lord, I will – for honour, not desire
Of land or livings, or to be your heir –
So guide my actions in pursuit of France
As shall add glory to the Lacys' name.
LINCOLN: Coz, for those words here's thirty portagues.*   90
And, nephew Askew, there's a few for you.
Fair honour in her loftiest eminence
Stays in France for till you fetch her thence.
Then, nephews, clap swift wings on your designs:
Be gone, be gone; make haste to the Guildhall.   95
There presently I'll meet you. Do not stay;
Where honour beckons, shame attends delay.   *Exit.*
ASKEW: How gladly would your uncle have you gone!
LACY: True, coz, but I'll o'er-reach his policies.*
I have some serious business for three days   100
Which nothing but my presence can dispatch.
You therefore, cousin, with the companies
Shall haste to Dover; there I'll meet with you.
Or if I stay past my prefixed time,
Away to France; we'll meet in Normandy.   105
The twenty pounds my Lord Mayor gives to me
You shall receive, and these ten portagues,
Part of my uncle's thirty. Gentle coz,
Have care to our great charge; I know your wisdom
Hath tried itself in higher consequence.*   110
ASKEW: Coz, all myself am yours. Yet have this care:
To lodge in London with all secrecy.
Our uncle Lincoln hath – besides his own –
Many a jealous* eye, that in your face
Stares only to watch means for your disgrace.   115
LACY: Stay, cousin, who be these?

Enter SIMON EYRE, *his* WIFE,
HODGE, FIRK, JANE *and* RAFE, *with a piece.*

EYRE: Leave whining, leave whining; away with this whimpering, this
puling,* these blubbering tears and these wet eyes. I'll get thy
husband discharged, I warrant thee, sweet Jane. Go to.

HODGE: Master, here be the captains.   120
EYRE: Peace, Hodge! Hush, ye knave, hush.
FIRK: Here be the cavaliers and the colonels,* master.
EYRE: Peace, Firk; peace, my fine Firk. Stand by with your
    pishery-pashery.* Away! I am a man of the best presence.* I'll
    speak to them and they were Popes. Gentlemen, captains, colonels,   125
    commanders! Brave men, brave leaders, may it please you to give
    me audience? I am Simon Eyre, the mad* shoemaker of Tower
    Street; this wench with the mealy mouth that will never tire is my
    wife, I can tell you. Here's Hodge, my man and my foreman. Here's
    Firk, my fine firking* journeyman, and this is blubbered Jane. All   130
    we come to be suitors for this honest Rafe. Keep him at home and,
    as I am a true shoemaker and a gentleman of the gentle craft, buy
    spurs yourself; and I'll find ye boots these seven years.
WIFE: Seven years, husband?
EYRE: Peace, midriff, peace; I know what I do – peace.   135
FIRK: Truly, master cormorant,* you shall do God good service to let
    Rafe and his wife stay together. She's a young new-married woman;
    if you take her husband away from her a-night, you undo her. She
    may beg in the daytime, for he's as good a workman at a prick and
    an awl* as any is in our trade.   140
JANE: O let him stay, else I shall be undone.*
FIRK: Ay, truly; she shall be laid at one side like a pair of old shoes else,
    and be occupied* for no use.
LACY: Truly, my friends, it lies not in my power.
    The Londoners are pressed,* paid and set forth   145
    By the Lord Mayor. I cannot change a man.
HODGE: Why, then you were as good be a corporal as a colonel if you
    cannot discharge one good fellow! And, I tell you true, I think you
    do more than you can answer to press a man within a year and a
    day of his marriage.*   150
EYRE: Well said, melancholy* Hodge! Grammercy,* my fine foreman.
WIFE: Truly, gentlemen, it were ill done for such as you to stand so
    stiffly* against a poor young wife. Considering her case,* she is new
    married – but let that pass. I pray, deal not roughly with her; her
    husband is a young man and but newly entered – but let that pass.   155
EYRE: Away with your pishery-pashery, your polls and your edipolls!*
    Peace, midriff! Silence, Cicely Bumtrinket!* Let your head speak.
FIRK: Yea, and the horns* too, master.
EYRE: Too soon, my fine Firk, too soon; peace, scoundrels! See you this
    man, captains? You will not release him; well, let him go. He's a   160
    proper shot. Let him vanish. Peace, Jane, dry up thy tears; they'll
    make his powder dankish.* Take him, brave men. Hector of Troy
    was a hackney* to him, Hercules and Termagant* scoundrels; Prince

Arthur's round table, by the lord of Ludgate,* ne'er fed such a tall,*
such a dapper* swordman – by the life of Pharoah, a brave, resolute 165
swordman. Peace, Jane. I say no more, mad knaves.

FIRK: See, see, Hodge, how my master raves in commendation of Rafe.

HODGE: Rafe, th'art a gull* by this hand, and thou goest not.

ASKEW: I am glad, good Master Eyre, it is my hap
    To meet so resolute a soldier.   170
    Trust me, for your report and love to him
    A common slight regard shall not respect him.

LACY: Is thy name Rafe?

RAFE: Yes, sir.

LACY: Give me thy hand.
    Thou shalt not want, as I am a gentleman.
    Woman, be patient. God, no doubt, will send   175
    Thy husband safe again, but he must go;
    His country's quarrel says it shall be so.

HODGE: Th'art a gull, by my stirrup, if thou dost not go. I will not
    have thee strike thy gimlet* into these weak vessels;* prick thine
    enemies, Rafe.   180

Enter DODGER.

DODGER: My lord, your uncle on the Tower Hill
    Stays* with the Lord Mayor and the Aldermen,
    And doth request you with all speed you may
    To hasten thither.

ASKEW: Cousin, let us go.

LACY: Dodger, run you before; tell them we come.   *Exit* DODGER.   185
    This Dodger is mine uncle's parasite,*
    The arrant'st* varlet that e'er breathed on earth.
    He sets more discord in a noble house
    By one day's broaching of his pickthank* tales
    Than can be salved again in twenty years.   190
    And he, I fear, shall go with us to France
    To pry into our actions.

ASKEW: Therefore, coz
    It shall behove you to be circumspect.

LACY: Fear not, good cousin. Rafe, hie to your colours.*
                                [*Exeunt* LACY *and* ASKEW.]

RAFE: I must, because there is no remedy.   195
    But, gentle master and my loving dame,
    As you have always been a friend to me,
    So in mine absence think upon my wife.

JANE: Alas, my Rafe!

WIFE: She cannot speak for weeping.   200
EYRE: Peace, you cracked groats, you mustard tokens.* Disquiet not the
    brave soldier. Go thy ways, Rafe.
JANE: Ay, ay, you bid him go. What shall I do when he is gone?
FIRK: Why, be doing with me, or my fellow Hodge; be not idle.
EYRE: Let me see thy hand, Jane. This fine hand, this white hand,   205
    these pretty fingers must spin, must card, must work; work, you
    bombast cotton-candle-quean,* work for your living with a pox to
    you! Hold thee, Rafe; here's five sixpences for thee: fight for the
    honour of the gentle craft, for the gentleman shoemakers, the
    courageous cordwainers,* the flower of Saint Martin's, the mad   210
    knaves of Bedlam, Fleet Street, Tower Street and Whitechapel.*
    Crack me the crowns* of the French knaves; a pox on them!
    Crack them! Fight, by the lord of Ludgate, fight, my fine boy!
FIRK: Here, Rafe, here's three twopences. Two carry into France, the
    third shall wash our souls at parting, for sorrow is dry.* For my   215
    sake, firk the *basa mon cues.**
HODGE: Rafe, I am heavy* at parting, but here's a shilling for thee.
    God send thee to cram thy slops* with French crowns,* and
    thy enemy's bellies with bullets.
RAFE: I thank you, master, and I thank you all.   220
    Now, gentle wife, my loving lovely Jane,
    Rich men at their parting give their wives rich gifts,
    Jewels and rings to grace their lily hands.
    Thou know'st our trade makes rings for women's heels;
    Here, take this pair of shoes cut out by Hodge,   225
    Stitched by my fellow Firk, seamed by myself,
    Made up and pinked with letters for thy name.
    Wear them, dear Jane, for thy husband's sake,
    And every morning when thou pull'st them on
    Remember me, and pray for my return.   230
    Make much of them, for I have made them so
    That I can know them from a thousand moe.*

> *Sound drum, enter* LORD MAYOR, LINCOLN, LACY, ASKEW, DODGER *and*
> *soldiers. They pass over the stage;* RAFE *falls in amongst them.* FIRK *and*
> *the rest cry farewell, etc., and so exeunt.*

Scene Two

Enter ROSE *alone, making a garland.*

ROSE: Here sit thou down on this flowery bank,
    And make a garland for thy Lacy's head.

These pinks, these roses, and these violets,
These blushing gilliflowers,* these marigolds,
The fair embroidery of his coronet,   5
Carry not half such beauty in their cheeks
As the sweet countenance of my Lacy doth.
O my most unkind father! O my stars!
Why loured* you so at my nativity
To make me love, yet live robbed of my love?   10
Here as a thief am I imprisoned
For my dear Lacy's sake within these walls,
Which by my father's cost were builded up
For better purposes. Here must I languish
For him that doth as much lament, I know,   15

Enter SYBIL.

    Mine absence, as for him I pine in woe.
SYBIL: Good morrow, young mistress. I am sure that you
    make that garland for me, against* I shall be Lady of the
    Harvest.*
ROSE: Sybil, what news at London?   20
SYBIL: None but good. My Lord Mayor your father, and Master Philpot
    your uncle, and Master Scot your cousin, and Mistress Frigbottom
    by Doctors' Commons,* do all, by my troth, send you most hearty
    commendations.
ROSE: Did Lacy send kind greetings to his love?   25
SYBIL: O yes. Out of cry,* by my troth; I scant knew him. Here 'a wore
    a scarf,* and here a scarf, and here a bunch of feathers, and here
    precious stones and jewels; and a pair of garters – O monstrous! –
    like one of your yellow silk curtains at home here in Old Ford*
    House, here in Master Bellymount's chamber. I stood at our door   30
    in Cornhill,* looked at him; he at me, indeed; spake to him, but he
    not to me, not a word. Marry, gup, thought I with a wanion,* he
    passed by me as proud – marry, foh! Are you grown humorous,*
    thought I? And so shut the door, and in I came.
ROSE: O Sybil, how dost thou my Lacy wrong!   35
    My Roland is as gentle as a lamb,
    No dove was ever half so mild as he.
SYBIL: Mild? Yea, as a bushel of stamped crabs!* He looked upon as
    me as sour as verjuice.* Go thy ways, thought I, thou mayest be
    much in my gaskins, but nothing in my netherstocks.* This is your   40
    fault, mistress, to love him that loves not you. He thinks scorn to do
    as he's done to, but, if I were you, I'd cry 'go by, Hieronimo, go by',*
    I'd set mine old debts against my new driblets,*

And the hare's foot against the goose giblets.
For if ever I sigh when sleep I should take,   45
Pray God I may lose my maidenhead when I wake.
ROSE: Will my love leave me then and go to France?
SYBIL: I know not that, but I am sure I see him stalk before the
     soldiers. By my troth, he is a proper man; but he is proper that
     proper doth: let him go, snick-up,* young mistress.   50
ROSE: Get thee to London, and learn perfectly
     Whether my Lacy go to France or no.
     Do this, and I will give thee for thy pains
     My cambric* apron and my Romish* gloves,
     My purple stockings and a stomacher.*   55
     Say, wilt thou do this, Sybil, for my sake?
SYBIL: Will I, quoth 'a? At whose suit?* By my troth, yes, I'll go:
     a cambric apron, gloves, a pair of purple stockings and a stomacher!
     I'll sweat in purple,* mistress, for you; I'll take anything that comes,
     'a God's name.* O rich! A cambric apron! Faith, then have at 60
     up-tails all.* I'll go jiggy-joggy* to London and be here in a trice,
     young mistress.   *Exit.*
ROSE: Do so, good Sybil. Meantime, wretched I
     Will sit and sigh for his lost company.   *Exit.*

Scene Three

Enter LACY *like a Dutch shoemaker.*

LACY: How many shapes have gods and kings devised
     Thereby to compass their desired loves?
     It is no shame for Roland Lacy then
     To clothe his cunning with the gentle craft.
     That thus disguised, I may unknown possess   5
     The only happy presence* of my Rose.
     For her have I forsook my charge in France,
     Incurred the king's displeasure, and stirred up
     Rough hatred in mine uncle Lincoln's breast.
     O love, how powerful art thou, that canst change   10
     High birth to bareness,* and to a noble mind
     To the mean semblance of a shoemaker!
     But thus is must be, for her cruel father,
     Hating the single union of our souls,
     Hath secretly conveyed my Rose from London   15
     To bar me of her presence. But I trust
     Fortune and this disguise will further me

Once more to view her beauty, gain her sight.
Here in Tower Street, with Eyre the shoemaker
Mean I a while to work. I know the trade;   20
I learned it when I was in Wittenberg.
Then cheer thy hoping sprites;* be not dismayed,
Thou canst not want, do fortune what she can,
The gentle craft is living for a man.   *Exit.*

Scene Four

Enter EYRE, *making himself ready.*

EYRE: Where be these boys, these girls, these drabs, these scoundrels?
They wallow in the fat brewis* of my bounty and lick up the crumbs
of my table, yet will not rise to see my walks cleansed. Come out,
you powder-beef queans!* What, Nan! What, Madge Mumblecrust!*
Come out, you fat midriff-swag-belly whores, and sweep me these   5
kennels, that noisome stench offend not the nose of my neighbours.
What, Firk, I say! What, Hodge! Open my shop windows. What,
Firk, I say!

Enter FIRK.

FIRK: O master, is 't you that speak bandog and bedlam* this morning?
I was in a dream, and mused what madman was got into the street   10
so early. Have you drunk this morning that your throat is so clear?
EYRE: Ah, well said, Firk; well said, Firk. To work, my fine knave; to work.
Wash thy face, and thou'lt be more blessed.*
FIRK: Let them wash my face that will eat it. Good master, send for a
souse-wife* if you'll have my face cleaner.   15

Enter HODGE.

EYRE: Away, sloven! Avaunt, scroundrel! Good morrow, Hodge; good
morrow, my fine foreman.
HODGE: O master, good morrow. Y'are an early stirrer; here's a fair
morning. Good morrow, Firk. I could have slept this hour; here's a
brave* day towards.*   20
EYRE: O haste to work, my fine foreman, haste to work.
FIRK: Master, I am dry as dust to hear my fellow Roger talk of fair
weather. Let us pray for good leather and let clowns and ploughboys
and those that work in the fields pray for brave days. We work in
a dry shop, what care I if it rains?   25

Enter EYRE'S WIFE.

EYRE: How now, Dame Margery, can you see to rise? Trip and go, call
    up the drabs, your maids.
WIFE: See to rise? I hope 'tis time enough; 'tis early enough for any
    woman to be seen abroad. I marvel how many wives in Tower
    Street are up so soon! God's me, 'tis not noon; here's a yawling.*   30
EYRE: Peace, Margery, peace. Where's Cicely Bumtrinket, your maid?
    She has a privy fault: she farts in her sleep. Call the quean up; if
    my men want shoe-thread, I'll swing her in a stirrup.
FIRK: Yet that's but a dry beating. Here's still a sign of drought.

Enter LACY *singing.*

LACY: *Der was een bore van Gelderland,*   35
    Frolic si byen,
He was als dronck he cold nyet stand,
    Upsolce se byen,
Tap eens de canneken,
    *Drincke, schone mannekin.**   40
FIRK: Master, for my life, yonder's a brother of the gentle craft. If he
    bear not Saint Hugh's bones,* I'll forfeit my bones. He's some
    uplandish* workman; hire him, good master, that I may learn
    some gibble-gabble.* 'Twill make us work the faster.
EYRE: Peace, Firk. A hard world: let him pass, let him vanish. We have   45
    journeymen enow.* Peace, my fine Firk.
WIFE: Nay, nay, y'are best follow your man's counsel. You shall see
    what will come on't. We have not men enow, but we must entertain
    every butterbox!* But let that pass.
HODGE: Dame, 'fore God, if my master follow your counsel he'll   50
    consume little beef. He shall be glad of men and he can catch them.
FIRK: Ay, that he shall.
HODGE: 'Fore God, a proper man and, I warrant, a fine workman.
    Master, farewell! Dame, adieu! If such a man as he cannot find
    work, Hodge is not for you.   *Offers to go.*   55
FIRK: Stay, my fine Hodge.
FIRK: Faith, and your foreman go, dame, you must take a journey to
    seek a new journeyman. If Roger remove, Firk follows. If Saint
    Hugh's bones shall not be set a-work, I may prick mine awl in the
    walls* and go play. Fare ye well, master; God buy, dame.   60
EYRE: Tarry, my fine Hodge, my brisk foreman; stay, Firk. Peace,
    pudding-broth;* by the lord of Ludgate, I love my men as my life.
    Peace, you gallimaufry.* Hodge, if he want work, I'll hire him.
    One of you to him – stay, he comes to us.

LACY: *Goeden dach, meester; ende u vro auch.** 65
FIRK: Nails,* if I should speak after him without drinking, I should choke.
    And you, friend Oak, are you of the gentle craft?
LACY: *Yaw, yaw, ik bin den skomaker.**
FIRK: Den skomaker, quoth 'a. And hark you, skomaker, have you all
    your tools? A good rubbing-pin, a good stopper, a good dresser, 70
    your four sorts of awls and your two balls of wax, your paring knife,
    your hand and thumb-leathers,* and good Saint Hugh's bones to
    smooth up your work?
LACY: *Yaw, yaw, be niet vorveard; ik hab all de dingen voour mack skoes groot*
    *and clean.** 75
FIRK: Ha ha, good master, hire him. He'll make me laugh so that I shall
    work more in mirth than I can in earnest.
EYRE: Hear ye, friend, have ye any skill in the mystery* of cordwainers?
LACY: *Ik weet niet wat yow seg. Ik verstaw you niet.**
FIRK: Why thus, man; 'Ik verste u niet', quoth 'a. 80
LACY: *Yaw, yaw, yaw; ik can dat well done.**
FIRK: Yaw, yaw; he speaks yawing like a jackdaw that gapes to be fed
    with cheese curds. O, he'll give a villainous pull at a can of double*
    beer, but Hodge and I have the vantage. We must drink first because
    we are the eldest journeymen. 85
EYRE: What is thy name?
LACY: Hans. Hans Meulter.
EYRE: Give me thy hand. Th'art welcome. Hodge, entertain him; Firk,
    bid him welcome. Come, Hans. Run, wife, bid your maids, your
    trullibubs,* make ready my fine men's breakfasts. To him, Hodge. 90
HODGE: Hans, th'art welcome. Use thyself friendly, for we are good
    fellows. If not, thou shalt be fought with, wert thou bigger than a giant.
FIRK: Yea, and drunk with, wert thou Gargantua.* My master keeps no
    cowards, I tell thee. Ho boy, bring him an heel-block; here's a new
    journeyman. 95

Enter BOY.

LACY: *O, ik wersto you, ik moet een halve dossen cans betaelen. Here boy,*
    *nempt dis skilling, tap eens freelick.** *Exit* BOY.
EYRE: Quick, snipper-snapper,* away! Firk, scour thy throat; thou
    shalt wash it with Castilian liquor. Come, my last of the fives,*

Enter BOY.

give me a can. Have to thee,* Hans! Here, Hodge! Here, Firk! 100
Drink, you mad Greeks, and work like true Trojans,* and pray for
Simon Eyre the shoemaker. Here, Hans, and th'art most welcome.

FIRK: Lo, dame, you would have lost a good fellow that will teach us to
    laugh – this beer came hopping in well.
WIFE: Simon, it is almost seven.   105
EYRE: Is't so, Dame Clapper Dudgeon?* Is't seven a-clock, and my
    men's breakfast not ready? Trip and go, you soused conger,* away.
    Come, you mad Hyperboreans!* Follow me, Hodge; follow me,
    Hans; come after, my fine Firk. To work, to work a while, and
    then to breakfast.   110
FIRK: Soft, yaw, yaw, good Hans. Though my master have no more
    wit but to call you before me, I am not so foolish to go behind
    you – I being the elder journeyman.   *Exeunt.*

Scene Five

Hollowing within. Enter WARNER *and* HAMMON, *like hunters.*

HAMMON: Cousin, beat every brake;* the game's not far.
    This way with winged feet he fled from death
    Whilst the pursuing hounds, scenting his steps,
    Find out his highway to destruction;
    Besides, the miller's boy told me even now   5
    He saw him take soil,* and he hallowed him,
    Affirming him so embossed*
    That long he could not hold.
WARNER: If it be so,
    'Tis best we trace these meadows by Old Ford.

A noise of hunters within; enter a BOY.

HAMMON: How now, boy, where's the deer? Speak, saw'st thou him?   10
BOY: O, yea, I saw him leap through a hedge, and then over a ditch,
    then at my Lord Mayor's pale; over he skipped me and in he went
    me; and 'Holla!' the hunters cried, and 'There, boy! There, boy!',
    but there he is, 'a mine honesty.
HAMMON: Boy, Godamercy; cousin, let's away.   15
    I hope we shall find better sport today.   *Exeunt.*

Scene Six

Hunting within; enter ROSE *and* SYBIL.

ROSE: Why, Sybil, wilt thou prove* a forester?

SYBIL: Upon some,* no; forester, go by.* No, faith, mistress; the deer
    came running into the barn, through the orchard, and over the pale.
    I wot* well, I looked as pale as a new cheese to see him, but 'Whip!'
    says goodman Pinclose, up with his flail, and our Nick with a prong,   5
    and down he fell, and they upon him, and I upon them; by my troth,
    we had such sport, and in the end we ended him: his throat we cut,
    flayed him, unhorned him, and my Lord mayor shall eat of him
    anon when he comes.
Horns sound within.

ROSE: Hark, hark: the hunters come. Y'are best take heed;   10
    They'll have a saying to you* for this deed.

Enter HAMMON, WARNER, huntsmen and BOY.

HAMMON: God save you, fair ladies.
SYBIL: Ladies! O gross!*
WARNER: Came not a buck this way?
ROSE: No, but two does.
HAMMON: And which way went they? Faith, we'll hunt at those.
SYBIL: At those? Upon some, no; when, can you tell?   15
WARNER: Upon some, aye.
SYBIL: Good Lord!
WARNER: Wounds!* Then farewell.
HAMMON: Boy, which way went he?
BOY: This way, sir, he ran.
HAMMON: This was he ran indeed, fair mistress Rose;
    Our game was lately in your orchard seen.
WARNER: Can you advise which way he took his flight?   20
SYBIL: Follow your nose: his horns* will guide you right.
WARNER: Th'art a mad wench.
SYBIL: O rich!
ROSE: Trust me, not I;
    It is not like that the wild forest deer
    Would come so near to places of resort;
    You are deceived: he fled some other way.   25
WARNER: Which way, my sugar-candy? Can you show?
SYBIL: Come up,* good honeysops!* Upon some, no.
ROSE: Why do you stay, and not pursue your game?
SYBIL: I'll hold my life their hunting nags be lame.
HAMMON: A deer more dear is found within this place.   30
SYBIL: But not the deer, sir, which you had in chase.
HAMMON: I chased the deer, but this dear chaseth me.
ROSE: The strangest hunting that ever I see.
    But where's your park?   *She offers to go away.*

HAMMON: 'Tis here. O stay.
ROSE: Impale me,* and then I will not stray.   25
WARNER: They wrangle, wench; we are more kind than they.
SYBIL: What kind of hart is that, dear heart, you seek?
WARNER: A hart, dear heart.
SYBIL: Who ever saw the like?
ROSE: To lose your heart – is't possible you can?
HAMMON: My heart is lost.
ROSE: Alack, good gentleman.   30
HAMMON: This poor lost hart would I wish you might find.
ROSE: You by such luck might prove your hart a hind.
HAMMON: Why, luck hath horns, so have I heard some say.
ROSE: Now God, and't be his will, send luck your way.

Enter LORD MAYOR *and servants.*

LORD MAYOR: What, master Hammon! Welcome to Old Ford.   35
SYBIL: God's pittikins, hands off, sir; here's my lord.
LORD MAYOR: I hear you had ill luck, and lost your game.
HAMMON: 'Tis true, my lord.
LORD MAYOR: I am sorry for the same.
   What gentleman is this?
HAMMON: My brother-in-law.
LORD MAYOR: Y'are welcome both. Sith* fortune offers you   40
   Into my hands, you shall not part from hence
   Until you have refreshed your wearied limbs.
   Go, Sybil, cover the board; you shall be guest
   To no good cheer, but even a hunter's feast.
HAMMON: I thank your lordship. Cousin, on my life,   45
   For our lost venison I shall find a wife.

Exeunt [ALL *but* LORD MAYOR].

LORD MAYOR: In, gentlemen; I'll not be absent long.
   This Hammon is a proper gentleman:
   A citizen by birth, fairly allied;
   How fit an husband were he for my girl!   50
   Well, I will in, and do the best I can
   To match my daughter to this gentleman.   *Exit.*

Scene Seven

Enter LACY, SKIPPER, HODGE *and* FIRK.

SKIPPER: *Ik sal yow wat, seggen Hans, dis skip dat comen from Candy is al wol, by Got's sacrament, van sugar, civet, almonds, cambric, end all*

dingen tousand tousand ding; nempt it, Hans, nempt it vor ve meester:
daer be de bills van laden, your Meester Simon Eyre sal hae good copen.
*Wat seggen yow, Hans?** 5
FIRK: Wat seggen de reggen de copen, slopen; laugh, Hodge, laugh.
LACY: *Mine liever broder Firk, bringt Meester Eyre tot den sign un swanekin;*
daer sal yow find dis skipper end me. Wat seggen yow, broder Firk?
*Doot it, Hodge;** come, skipper.* *Exeunt* [LACY *and* SKIPPER].
FIRK: Bring him, quoth you? Here's no knavery, to bring my master to 10
buy a ship worth the lading of* two or three thousand pounds!*
Alas, that's nothing: a trifle, a bauble, Hodge.
HODGE: The truth is, Firk, that the merchant owner of the ship dares
not show his head; and therefore this skipper that deals for him,
for the love he bears to Hans, offers my master Eyre a bargain in 15
the commodities. He shall have a reasonable day of payment; he
may well sell the wares by that time, and be an huge gainer himself.
FIRK: Yea, but can my fellow Hans lend my master twenty
porpentines* as an earnest penny?* 20
HODGE: Portagues, thou wouldst say. Here they be, Firk; hark, they
jingle in my pocket like Saint Mary Overy's* bells.

Enter EYRE *and his* WIFE [*and a* BOY].

FIRK: Mum, here comes my dame and my master. She'll scold, on my
life, for loitering this Monday; but all's one, let them all say what
they can: Monday's our holiday.* 25
WIFE: You sing, sir sauce, but I beshrew* your heart;
I fear for this your singing we shall smart.
FIRK: Smart for me, dame? Why, dame, why?
HODGE: Master, I hope you'll not suffer my dame to take down* your
journeymen. 30
FIRK: If she take me down, I'll take her up; yea, and take her down too,
a buttonhole lower.*
EYRE: Peace, Firk! Not I, Hodge. By the life of Pharaoh, by the
Lord of Ludgate, by this beard, every hair whereof I value at
a king's ransom, she shall not meddle with* you. Peace, you 35
bombast-cotton-candle quean; away, Queen of Clubs,* quarrel
not with me and my men, with me and my fine Firk; I'll firk
you if you do.
WIFE: Yea, yea, man, you may use* me as you please; but let that pass.
EYRE: Let it pass, let it vanish away; peace, am I not Simon Eyre? Are 40
these not my brave men? Brave shoemakers, all gentlemen of the
gentle craft? Prince am I none, yet am I nobly born, as being the
sole son of a shoemaker. Away, rubbish, vanish, melt like
kitchen-stuff.*

WIFE: Yea, yea, 'tis well: I must be called rubbish, kitchen-stuff, for a   45
    sort* of knaves.

FIRK: Nay, dame, you shall not weep and wail in woe for me. Master,
    I'll stay no longer; here's a venentory* of my shop tools. Adieu,
    master; Hodge, farewell.

HODGE: Nay, stay, Firk; thou shalt not go alone.   50

WIFE: I pray let them go: there be more maids than Malkin,* more men
    than Hodge, and more fools than Firk.

FIRK: Fools? Nails, if I tarry now, I would my guts might be turned to
    shoe-thread.*

HODGE: And if I stay, I pray God I may be turned to a Turk and set in   55
    Finsbury* for boys to shoot at. Come, Firk.

EYRE: Stay, my fine knaves, you arms of my trade, you pillars of my
    profession. What, shall a tittle-tattle's words make you forsake
    Simon Eyre? Avaunt, kitchen-stuff! Rip,* you brown bread
    tannikin!* Out of my sight, move me not! Have I not ta'en you   60
    from selling tripes in Eastcheap* and set you in my shop, and
    made you hail-fellow with Simon Eyre the shoemaker? And do
    you now deal thus with my journeymen? Look, you powder-beef
    quean, on the face of Hodge: here's a face for a lord.

FIRK: And here's a face for any lady in Christendom.   65

EYRE: Rip, you chitterling;* avaunt, boy: bid the tapster of the Boar's
    Head* fill me a dozen cans of beer for my journeymen.

FIRK: A dozen cans? O brave, Hodge; now I'll stay.   [*Exit* BOY.]

EYRE: And the knave fills any more than two, he pays for them.
    A dozen cans of beer for my journeymen!   70

[*Enter* BOY *with two cans, and exit.*]

Hear, you mad Mesopotamians,* wash your livers with this
    liquor. Where be the odd ten? No more, Madge, no more. Well said:
    drink, and to work! What work dost thou, Hodge? What work?

HODGE: I am making a pair of shoes for my Lord Mayor's daughter,
    Mistress Rose.   75

FIRK: And I a pair of shoes for Sybil, my lord's maid; I deal with* her.

EYRE: Sybil? Fie, defile not thy fine workmanly fingers with the feet of
    kitchen-stuff and basting ladles. Ladies of the Court, fine ladies, my
    lads, commit their feet to our apparelling; put gross work to Hans.
    Yark* and seam, yark and seam.   80

FIRK: For yarking and seaming let me alone, and I come to't.

HODGE: Well, master, all this is from the bias;* do you remember the
    ship my fellow Hans told you of? The skipper and he are both
    drinking at the Swan. Here be the portagues to give earnest;* if
    you go through with it, you cannot choose but be a lord at least.   85

FIRK: Nay, dame; if my master prove not a lord, and you a lady, hang me.

WIFE: Yea, like enough, if you may loiter and tipple thus.

FIRK: Tipple, dame? No, we have been bargaining with Skellum
    Skanderbag – can you Dutch spreaken – for a ship of silk cypress*
    laden with sugar candy.   90

Enter the BOY *with a velvet coat and an Alderman's gown;* EYRE *puts it on.*

EYRE: Peace, Firk; silence, tittle-tattle! Hodge, I'll go through with it.
    Here's a seal-ring, and I have sent for a guarded gown and a
    damask cassock:* see where it comes. Look here, Maggy; help me,
    Firk; apparel me, Hodge. Silk and satin, you mad Philistines,* silk
    and satin.   95

FIRK: Ha, ha; my master will be as proud as a dog in a doublet,* all in
    beaten* damask and velvet.

EYRE: Softly, Firk, for rearing of* the nap, and wearing threadbare my
    garments! How dost thou like me, Firk? How do I look, my fine
    Hodge?   100

HODGE: Why, now you look like yourself, master, I warrant you.
    There's few in the city but will give you the wall,* and come upon
    you with the right worshipful.*

FIRK: Nails, my master looks like a threadbare cloak new turned and
    dressed.* Lord, Lord, to see what good raiment doth! Dame,   105
    dame, are you not enamoured?

EYRE: How sayest thou, Maggy? Am I not brisk?* Am I not fine?

WIFE: Fine? By my troth, sweetheart, very fine; by my troth, I never
    liked thee so well in my life, sweetheart. But let that pass:
    I warrant there be many women in the city have not such   110
    handsome husbands, but only for* their apparel – but let that
    pass too.

Enter [LACY *as*] HANS *and* SKIPPER.

LACY: *Godden day, mester; dis be de skipper dat heb skip van marchandise; de
    commodity ben good: nempt it, master, nempt it.**

EYRE: Godamercy,* Hans; welcome, skipper. Where lies this ship of   115
    merchandise?

SKIPPER: *De skip ben in revere; dor be van sugar, civet, almonds, cambric,
    and a tousand tousand tings. Got's sacrament, nempt it mester: yo sal
    heb good copen.**

FIRK: To him, master: O sweet, master! O sweet wares, prunes, almonds, 120
    sugar-candy, carrot roots, turnips! O brave fatting meat;* let not a
    man buy a nutmeg but yourself.

EYRE: Peace, Firk. Come, skipper, I'll go aboard with you. Hans, have
    you made him drink?

SKIPPER: *Yaw, yaw, Ik heb veale ge drunck.**   125

EYRE: Come, Hans, follow me: skipper, thou shalt have my
    countenance* in the city.   *Exeunt* [EYRE, LACY *and* SKIPPER].
FIRK: Yaw heb veale ge drunck, quoth 'a!* They may well be called
    butter-boxes when they drink fat veal,* and thick* beer too! But
    come, dame, I hope you'll chide us no more.   130
WIFE: No, faith, Firk; no, perdie, Hodge; I do feel honour creep upon me,
    and which is more, a certain rising in my flesh* – but let that pass.
FIRK: Rising in your flesh do you feel, say you? Ay, you may be with
    child, but why should not my master feel a rising in his flesh,
    having a gown and a ring on? But you are such a shrew, you'll   135
    soon pull him down.*
WIFE: Ha, ha, prithee peace; thou mak'st my worship laugh, but let that
    pass. I'll go in: Hodge, prithee go before me; Firk, follow me.
FIRK: Firk doth follow; Hodge, pass out in state.   *Exeunt.*

Scene Eight

Enter LINCOLN *and* DODGER.

LINCOLN: How now, good Dodger, what's the news in France?
DODGER: My lord, upon the eighteenth day of May
    The French and English were prepared to fight;
    Each side with eager fury gave the sign
    Of a most hot encounter. Five long hours   5
    Both armies fought together; at the length,
    The lot of victory fell on our sides.
    Twelve thousand of the Frenchmen that day died,
    Four thousand English, and no man of name*
    But Captain Hyam and young Ardington.*   10
LINCOLN: Two gallant gentlemen: I knew them well.
    But Dodger, prithee tell me, in this fight
    How did my cousin Lacy bear himself?
DODGER: My lord, your cousin Lacy was not there.
LINCOLN: Not there?
DODGER: No, my good lord.
LINCOLN: Sure thou mistakest: 15
    I saw him shipped, and a thousand eyes beside
    Were witnesses of the farewells which he gave
    When I with weeping eyes bid him adieu.
    Dodger, take heed.
DODGER: My lord, I am advised*
    That what I spake is true. To prove it so,   20
    His cousin Askew that supplied his place
    Sent me for him from France, that secretly

He might convey himself hither.
LINCOLN: Is't even so?
    Dares he so carelessly venture his life
    Upon the indignation of a king?   25
    Hath he despised my love, and spurned those favours
    Which I with prodigal hand poured on his head?
    He shall repent his rashness with his soul,
    Since of my love he makes no estimate;*
    I'll make him wish he had not known my hate.   30
    Thou hast no other news?
DODGER: None else, my lord.
LINCOLN: None worse I know thou hast. Procure the king
    To crown his giddy brows with ample honours,
    Send him chief colonel, and all my hope
    Thus to be dashed? But 'tis in vain to grieve: 35
    One evil cannot a worse relieve.
    Upon my life, I have found out his plot.
    That old dog Love, that fawned upon him so,
    Love to that puling girl, his fair-cheeked Rose,
    The Lord Mayor's daughter, hath distracted him;   40
    And in the fire of that love's lunacy
    Hath he burnt up himself, consumed his credit,*
    Lost the king's love, yea, and I fear, his life,
    Only to get a wanton to his* wife!
    Dodger, it is so.
DODGER: I fear so, my good lord.   45
LINCOLN: It is so; nay, sure, it cannot be.
    I am at my wit's end. Dodger –
DODGER: Yea, my lord?
LINCOLN: Thou art acquainted with my nephew's haunts:
    Spend this gold for thy pains, go seek him out.
    Watch at my Lord Mayor's; there, if he live,   50
    Dodger, thou shalt be sure to meet with him;
    Prithee, be diligent. Lacy, thy name
    Lived once in honour, now dead in shame!
    Be circumspect.   *Exit.*
DODGER: I warrant you, my lord.   *Exit.*

Scene Nine

Enter LORD MAYOR *and* MASTER SCOTT.

LORD MAYOR: Good Master Scott, I have been bold with you,
    To be a witness to a wedding knot

Betwixt young master Hammon and my daughter;
O stand aside, see where the lovers come.

Enter HAMMON *and* ROSE.

ROSE: Can it be possible you love me so?   5
   No, no, within those eyeballs I espy
   Apparent likelihoods of flattery.
   Pray now, let go my hand.
HAMMON: Sweet Mistress Rose,
   Misconstrue not my words, nor misconceive
   Of my affection, whose devoted soul   10
   Swears that I love thee dearer than my heart.
ROSE: As dear as your own heart? I judge it right.
   Men love their hearts best when th'are out of sight.
HAMMON: I love you, by this hand.
ROSE: Yet hands off, now:
   If flesh be frail,* how weak and frail's your vow?   15
HAMMON: Then by my life I swear.
ROSE: Then do not brawl;
   One quarrel loseth wife and life and all.
   Is not your meaning thus?
HAMMON: In faith, you jest.
ROSE: Love loves to sport;* therefore leave love, y'are best.
LORD MAYOR: What? Square* they, Master Scott?
SCOTT: Sir, never doubt,   20
   Lovers are quickly in, and quickly out.
HAMMON: Sweet Rose, be not so strange in fancying* me;
   Nay, never turn aside: shun not my sight.
   I am not grown so fond,* to found my love
   On any that shall quit* it with disdain.   25
   If you will love me, so; if not, farewell.
LORD MAYOR: Why, how now, lovers, are you both agreed?
HAMMON: Yes, faith, my lord.
LORD MAYOR: 'Tis well: give me your hand.
   Give me yours, daughter. How now, both pull back?
   What means this, girl?
ROSE: I mean to live a maid.   30
HAMMON: But not to die one; pause ere that be said.   *Aside.*
LORD MAYOR: Will you still cross me? Still be obstinate?
HAMMON: Nay, chide her not, my lord, for doing well.
   If she can live an happy virgin's life,
   'Tis far more blessed than to be a wife.*   35
ROSE: Say, sir, I cannot; I have made a vow,

Whoever be my husband, 'tis not you.
LORD MAYOR: Your tongue is quick; but, Master Hammon, know
    I bade you welcome to another end.*
HAMMON: What, would you have me pule,* and pine, and pray, 40
    With lovely lady, mistress of my heart,
    Pardon your servant, and the rhymer play,
    Railing on Cupid, and his tyrant's dart?
    Or shall I undertake some martial spoil,*
    Wearing your glove at tourney, and at tilt, 45
    And tell how many gallants I unhorsed?
    Sweet, will this pleasure you?
ROSE: Yea, when wilt thou begin?
    What, love-rhymes, man? Fie on that deadly sin.
LORD MAYOR: If you will have her, I'll make her agree.
HAMMON: Enforced love is worse than hate to me. 50
    There is a wench keeps shop in the Old 'Change;*
    To her will I. It is not wealth I seek;
    I have enough, and will prefer her love
    Before the world. My good Lord Mayor, adieu;
    Old love for me, I have no luck with new.   *Exit.* 55
LORD MAYOR: Now, mammet,* you have well behaved yourself,
    But you shall curse your coyness* if I live.
    Who's within there? See you convey your mistress
    Straight to th' Old Ford. I'll keep you strait* enough.
    'Fore God, I would have sworn the puling girl 60
    Would willingly have accepted Hammon's love.
    But banish him my thoughts; go, minion, in.   *Exit* ROSE.
    Now tell me, Master Scott, would you have thought
    That Master Simon Eyre the shoemaker
    Had been of wealth to buy such merchandise? 65
SCOTT: 'Twas well, my lord, your honour and myself
    Grew partners with him, for your bills of lading
    Show that Eyre's gains in one commodity
    Rise at the least to full three thousand pound,
    Beside like gain in other merchandise. 70
LORD MAYOR: Well, he shall spend some of his thousands now,
    For I have sent for him to the Guildhall.

Enter EYRE.

See where he comes. Good morrow, Master Eyre.
EYRE: Poor Simon Eyre, my lord, your shoemaker.
LORD MAYOR: Well, well; it likes yourself to term you so. 75

Enter DODGER.

Now, Master Dodger, what's the news with you?
DODGER: I'd gladly speak in private with your honour.
LORD MAYOR: You shall, you shall. Master Eyre and Master Scott,
    I have some business with this gentleman.
    I pray let me entreat you to walk before   80
    To the Guildhall. I'll follow presently.
    Master Eyre, I hope ere noon to call you Sheriff.
EYRE: I would not care, my lord, if you might call me King of Spain.
    Come, Master Scott.   *Exeunt* [EYRE and SCOTT].
LORD MAYOR: Now, Master Dodger, what's the news you bring?   85
DODGER: The Earl of Lincoln by me greets your lordship
    And earnestly requests you, if you can,
    Inform him where his nephew Lacy keeps.*
LORD MAYOR: Is not his nephew Lacy now in France?
DODGER: No, I assure your lordship, but disguised;   90
    Lurks here in London.
LORD MAYOR: London? Is't even so?
    It may be, but upon my faith and soul,
    I know not where he lives, or whether he lives.
    So tell my Lord of Lincoln. Lurk in London?
    Well, Master Dodger, you perhaps may start him:*   95
    Be but the means to rid him into France.
    I'll give you a dozen angels* for thy pains;
    So much I love his honour, hate his nephew,
    So prithee so inform thy lord from me.
DODGER: I take my leave.
LORD MAYOR: Farewell, Master Dodger.   *Exit* DODGER. 100
    Lacy in London? I dare pawn my life
    My daughter knows thereof, and for that cause
    Denied young Master Hammon in his love.
    Well, I am glad I sent her to Old Ford.
    God's Lord, 'tis late! To Guildhall I must hie;   105
    I know my brethren stay* my company.   *Exit.*

Scene Ten

Enter FIRK, EYRE'S WIFE, [LACY *as*] HANS *and* ROGER.

WIFE: Thou goest too fast for me, Roger. O, Firk!
FIRK: Ay, forsooth?

WIFE: I pray thee run, do you hear, run to Guildhall, and learn if my
    husband Master Eyre will take that worshipful vocation of Master
    Sheriff upon him. Hie thee, good Firk.   5
FIRK: Take it? Well, I go; and he should not take it, Firk swears to forswear*
    him. Yes, forsooth, I go to Guildhall.
WIFE: Nay, when? Thou art too compendious* and tedious.
FIRK: O rare: your excellence is full of eloquence. How like a new
    cartwheel* my dame speaks, and she looks like an old musty   10
    ale-bottle going to scalding.*
WIFE: Nay, when? Thou wilt make me melancholy.
FIRK: God forbid your worship should fall into that humour. I run.   *Exit.*
WIFE: Let me see now, Roger and Hans.
HODGE: Ay, forsooth, dame – mistress,* I should say, but the old term so   15
    sticks to the roof of my mouth, I can hardly lick it off.
WIFE: Even what thou wilt, good Roger. Dame is a fair name for any
    honest Christian, but let that pass. How dost thou, Hans?
LACY: *Mee tanck you vro.**
WIFE: Well, Hans and Roger, you see God hath blessed your master;   20
    and, perdie,* it he ever comes to be Master Sheriff of London – as
    we are all mortal – you shall see I will have some odd thing or other
    in a corner for you. I will not be your back friend* – but let that pass.
    Hans, pray thee tie my shoe.
LACY: *Yaw, ik sal vro.**   25
WIFE: Roger, thou knowest the length of my foot,* as it is none of the
    biggest, so I thank God it is handsome enough. Prithee let me have a
    pair of shoes made, cork, good Roger, wooden heel* too.
HODGE: You shall.
WIFE: Art thou acquainted with never a farthingale*-maker, nor a   30
    French-hood* maker? I must enlarge my bum, ha, ha. How shall I
    look in a hood, I wonder? Perdie, oddly, I think.
HODGE: As a cat out of a pillory.* Very well, I warrant you, mistress.
WIFE: Indeed, all flesh is grass,* and, Roger, canst thou tell where I may
    buy a good hair?*   35
HODGE: Yes, forsooth, at the poulterers in Gracious Street.*
WIFE: Thou art an ungracious wag. Perdie, I mean a false hair for my
    periwig.
HODGE: Why, mistress, the next time I cut my beard, you shall have the
    shavings of it; but they are all true hairs.   40
WIFE: It is very hot: I must get me a fan or else a mask.*
HODGE: So had you need, to hide your wicked face.
WIFE: Fie upon it! How costly this world's calling is, perdie. But that it
    is one of the wonderful works of God, I would not deal with it. Is
    not Firk come yet? Hans, be not so sad: let it pass and vanish, as   45
    my husband's worship says.

LACY: *Ik bin vrolick, lot see yow so.**
HODGE: Mistress, will you drink* a pipe of tobacco?
WIFE: O fie upon it, Roger! Perdie, these filthy tobacco pipes are the
    most idle* slavering baubles* that ever I felt; out upon it, God bless   50
    us, men look not like men that use them.

Enter RAFE being lame.

HODGE: What, fellow Rafe? Mistress, look here: Jane's husband! Why,
    how now, lame? Hans, make much of him; he's a brother of our
    trade, a good workman, and a tall* soldier.
LACY: You be welcome, broder.*   55
WIFE: Perdie, I knew him not; how dost thou, good Rafe? I am glad to
    see thee well.
RAFE: I would God you saw me, dame, as well
    As when I went from London into France.
WIFE: Trust me, I am sorry, Rafe, to see thee impotent.* Lord, how the   60
    wars have made him sunburnt!* The left leg is not well; 'twas a
    fair gift of God the infirmity took not hold a little higher,
    considering thou camest from France,* but let that pass.
RAFE: I am glad to see you well, and I rejoice
    To hear that God hath blessed my master so   65
    Since my departure.
WIFE: Yea, truly, Rafe, but let that pass.
HODGE: And, sirrah Rafe, what news, what news in France?
RAFE: Tell me, good Roger, first: what news in England?
    How does my Jane? When didst thou see my wife?   70
    Where lives my poor heart? She'll be poor indeed,
    Now I want limbs to get whereon to feed.
HODGE: Limbs? Has thou not hands, man? Thou shalt never see a
    shoemaker want bread, though he have but three fingers on a hand.
RAFE: Yet all this while I hear not of my Jane.   75
WIFE: O Rafe, your wife! Perdie, we know not what's become of her.
    She was here a while and, because she was married, grew more
    stately* than became her. I checked her, and so forth; away she
    flung, never returned nor said bye or bah. And, Rafe, you know,
    ka me, ka thee.* And so as I tell ye. Roger, is not Firk come yet?   80
HODGE: No, forsooth.
WIFE: And so, indeed, we heard not of her; but I hear she lives in
    London – but let that pass. If she had wanted, she might have
    opened her case* to me or my husband, or to any of my men. I am
    sure there's not any of them, perdie, but would have done her   85
    good to his power. Hans, look if Firk be come.
LACY: *Yaw, ik sal vro.**   *Exit.*

WIFE: And so as I said – but Rafe, why dost thou weep? Thou knowest
    that naked we came out of our mother's womb, and naked we
    must return;* and therefore thank God for all things.   90
HODGE: No, faith, Jane is a stranger here. But, Rafe, pull up a good
    heart* – I know thou hast one. Thy wife, man, is in London; one
    told me he saw her a while ago very brave* and neat. We'll ferret
    her out, and London hold her.
WIFE: Alas, poor soul: he's overcome with sorrow; he does but as I do,   95
    weep for the loss of any good thing. But, Rafe, get thee in; call for
    some meat and drink. Thou shalt find me worshipful* towards thee.
RAFE: I thank you, dame. Since I want limbs and lands,
    I'll to God, my good friends, and to these my hands.   100

Enter [LACY AS] HANS *and* FIRK *running.*

FIRK: Run, good Hans! O Hodge, O mistress! Hodge, heave up thine
    ears; mistress, smug* up your looks; on with your best apparel!
    My master is chosen, my master is called – nay, condemned – by
    the cry of the country* to be Sheriff of the City for this famous
    year now to come, and time now being. A great many men in   105
    black gowns were asked for their voices* and their hands, and my
    master had all their fists about his ears presently;* and they cried
    Ay, ay, ay, ay – and so I came away.
    Wherefore without all other grieve
    I do salute you, Mistress Shrieve.*   110
LACY: *Yaw, my mester is de groot man, de shrieve.**
HODGE: Did I not tell you, mistress? Now I may boldly say: good
    morrow to your worship.
WIFE: Good morrow, good Roger. I thank you, my good people all.
    Firk, hold up thy hand. Here's a threepenny piece for thy tidings.   115
FIRK: 'Tis but three half-pence, I think. Yes, 'tis three pence! I smell
    the rose.*
HODGE: But, mistress, be ruled by me, and do not speak so pulingly.*
FIRK: 'Tis her worship speaks so, and not she. No, faith, mistress,
    speak to me in the old key: to it, Firk; there, good Firk; ply your   120
    business, Hodge; Hodge, with a full mouth; I'll fill your bellies
    with good cheer 'til they cry twang.*

Enter Simon EYRE *wearing a gold chain.*

LACY: *See, myn liever broder, here compt my meester.*
WIFE: Welcome home, Master Shrieve. I pray God you continue in
    health and wealth.   125

EYRE: See here, my Maggy, a chain, a gold chain for Simon Eyre!
I shall make thee a lady. Here's a French hood for thee; on with it,
on with it. Dress thy brows with this flap of a shoulder of mutton*
to make thee look lovely. Where be my fine men? Roger, I'll make
over my shop and tools to thee. Firk, thou shalt be the foreman.   130
Hans, thou shalt have a hundred for twenty.* Be as mad knaves as
your master Simon Eyre hath been, and you shall live to be
sheriffs of London! How dost thou like me, Margery? Prince am
I none, yet am I princely borne, Firk, Hodge and Hans.
ALL THREE: Ay, forsooth! What says your worship, Mistress Sheriff?   135
EYRE: Worship and honour, you Babylonian knaves, for the gentle
craft. But I forget myself: I am bidden by my Lord Mayor to
dinner to Old Ford. He's gone before, I must after. Come, Madge,
on with your trinkets. Now, my true Trojans, my fine Firk, my
dapper Hodge, my honest Hans, some device, some odd   140
crotchets,* some morris or suchlike, for the honour of the gentle
shoemakers. Meet me at Old Ford. You know my mind.
Come, Madge, away:
Shut up the shop, knaves, and make holiday.   *Exeunt* [EYRE *and* WIFE].
FIRK: O rare! O brave! Come, Hodge; follow me, Hans;   145
We'll be with them for a morris dance.   *Exeunt.*

Scene Eleven

Enter LORD MAYOR, EYRE, *his* WIFE *in a French hood,* [ROSE,]
SYBIL *and other servants.*

LORD MAYOR: Trust me, you are as welcome to Old Ford
As I myself.
WIFE: Truly, I thank your lordship.
LORD MAYOR: Would our bad cheer were worth the pains you give.
EYRE: Good cheer, my Lord Mayor; fine cheer, a fine house, fine walls, all   5
fine and neat.
LORD MAYOR: Now, by my troth, I'll tell thee, Master Eyre,
It does me good and all my brethren
That such a madcap fellow as thyself
Is entered into our society.   10
WIFE: Ay, but, my lord, he must learn how to put on gravity.
EYRE: Peace, Maggy! A fig for* gravity! When I go to Guildhall in my
scarlet gown,* I'll look as demurely as a saint and speak as
gravely as a justice of peace; but now I am here at Old Ford, at my
good Lord Mayor's house, let it go by. Vanish, Maggy: I'll be   15
merry! Away with flip-flap,* these fooleries, these gulleries!*

What, honey? Prince am I none, yet am I princely born. What says
    my Lord Mayor?
LORD MAYOR: Ha, ha, ha! I had rather than a thousand pound,
    I had a heart but half so light as yours. 20
EYRE: Why, what should I do, my lord? A pound of care pays not a dram
    of debt.* Hum, let's be merry whiles we are young; old age, sack
    and sugar* will steal upon us ere we be aware.
LORD MAYOR: It's well done. Mistress Eyre, pray give good counsel to
    my daughter. 25
WIFE: I hope Mistress Rose will have the grace to take nothing that's bad.
LORD MAYOR: Pray God she do, for i'faith, Mistress Eyre,
    I would bestow upon that peevish girl
    A thousand marks more than I mean to give her;
    Upon condition she'd be ruled by me. 30
    The ape* still crosseth me! There came of late
    A proper gentleman of fair revenues
    Whom gladly I would call son-in-law;
    But my fine cockney* would have none of him.
    You'll prove a coxcomb* for it ere you die; 35
    A courtier, or no man, must please your eye.
EYRE: Be ruled, sweet Rose. Th'art ripe for a man; marry not with a boy
    that has no more hair on his face than thou hast on thy cheeks.
    A courtier! Wash,* go by; stand not upon pishery-pashery!* Those
    silken fellows are but painted images: outsides, outsides. Rose, 40
    their inner linings are torn. No, my fine mouse, marry me* with a
    gentleman grocer like my Lord Mayor your father. A grocer is a
    sweet trade: plums, plums! Had I a son or daughter should marry
    out of the generation and blood of the shoemakers, he should
    pack.* What, the gentle trade is a living for a man through Europe, 45
    through the world.
              A noise within of a tabor and a pipe.*
LORD MAYOR: What noise is this?
EYRE: O, my Lord Mayor, a crew of good fellows that for love to your
    honour are come hither with a morris dance. Come in, my
    Mesopotamians, cheerily. 50

       Enter HODGE, [LACY AS] HANS, RAFE, FIRK *and other*
              shoemakers in a morris.
      After a little dancing the LORD MAYOR *speaks.*

LORD MAYOR: Master Eyre, are all these shoemakers?
EYRE: All cordwainers, my good Lord Mayor.
ROSE: How like my Lacy looks yond shoemaker!
LACY: O that I durst but speak unto my love!

LORD MAYOR: Sybil, go fetch some wine to make these drink.   55
    You are all welcome.
ALL: We thank your lordship.
            ROSE *takes a cup of wine and goes to* [LACY].
ROSE: For his sake whose fair shape thou represent'st,
    Good friend, I drink to thee.
LACY: *Ik be dancke, good frister.**   60
WIFE: I see, Mistress Rose, you do not want judgement. You have drunk
    to the properest* man I keep.
FIRK: Here be some have done their parts* to be as proper as he.
LORD MAYOR: Well, urgent business calls me back to London.
    Good fellows, first go in and taste our cheer   65
    And, to make merry as you homeward go,
    Spend these two angels in beer at Stratford Bow.*
EYRE: To these two, my mad lads, Simon Eyre adds another. Then cheerily,
    Firk; tickle it,* Hans; and all for the honour of the shoemakers!
            All go dancing out.
LORD MAYOR: Come, Master Eyre, let's have your company.   70
            Exeunt [LORD MAYOR *and* EYRE].
ROSE: Sybil, what shall I do?
SYBIL: Why, what's the matter?
ROSE: That Hans the shoemaker is my love Lacy,
    Disguised in that attire to find me out;
    How should I find the means to speak with him?   75
SYBIL: What, mistress! Never fear, I dare venture my maidenhead to
    nothing – and that's great odds – that Hans the Dutchman, when
    we come to London, shall not only see and speak with you but, in
    spite of all your father's policies*, steal you away and marry you.
    Will this not please you?   80
ROSE: Do this, and ever be assured of my love.
SYBIL: Away, then, and follow your father to London, lest your absence
    cause him to suspect something.
    Tomorrow, if my counsel be obeyed,   85
    I'll bind you prentice to the gentle trade.   *Exeunt.*

Scene Twelve

Enter JANE *in a seamster's shop, working, and* HAMMON *muffled**
*at another door; he stands aloof.**

HAMMON: Yonder's the shop, and there my fair love sits.
    She's fair and lovely, but she is not mine.
    O would that she were! Thrice have I courted her,

Thrice hath my hand been moistened with her hand
Whilst my poor famished eyes do feed on that   5
Which made them famish. I am infortunate;
I still love one,* yet nobody loves me.
I muse in other men what women see
That I so want? Fine Mistress Rose was coy
And this too curious* – O no, she is chaste,   10
And for she thinks me wanton, she denies
To cheer my cold heart with her sunny eyes.
How prettily she works, O pretty hand!
O happy work,* it doth me good to stand
Unseen to see her. Thus I oft have stood,   15
In frosty evenings, a light burning by her,
Enduring biting cold, only to eye her.
One only look hath seemed as rich to me
As a king's crown, such is love's lunacy.
Muffled, I'll pass along, and by that try   20
Whether she know me.
JANE: Sir, what is't you buy?
  What is't you lack, sir? Calico or lawn,
  Fine cambric shirts, or bands;* what will you buy?
HAMMON: That which thou wilt not sell; faith, yet I'll try –
  How do you sell* this handkercher?
JANE: Good cheap.   25
HAMMON: And how these ruffs?
JANE: Cheap too.
HAMMON: And how this band?
JANE: Cheap too.
HAMMON: All cheap; how sell you then this hand?
JANE: My hands are not to be sold.
HAMMON: To be given then?
  No, faith, I come to buy.
JANE: But none knows when.
HAMMON: Good sweet, leave work a little while; let's play.   30
JANE: I cannot live by keeping holiday.
HAMMON: I'll pay you for the time which shall be lost.
JANE: With me you shall not be at so much cost.
HAMMON: Look how you wound this cloth:* so you wound me.
JANE: It may be so.
HAMMON: 'Tis so.
JANE: What remedy?   35
HAMMON: Nay, faith, you are too coy.
JANE: Let go my hand.
HAMMON: I will do any task at your command.

I would let go this beauty, were I not
Enjoined to disobey you by a power
That controls kings. I love you.
JANE: So; now part.   40
HAMMON: With hands I may, but never with my heart.
    In faith, I love you.
JANE: I believe you do.
HAMMON: Shall a true love in me breed hate in you?
JANE: I hate you not.
HAMMON: Then you must love.
JANE: I do.
    What, are you better now? I love not you.   45
HAMMON: All this, I hope, is but a woman's fray*
    That means 'come to me' when she cries 'away'.
    In earnest, mistress, I do not jest;
    A true chaste love hath entered my breast.
    I love you dearly as I love my life,   50
    I love you as a husband loves a wife.
    That, and no other love, my love requires;
    Thy wealth I know is little, my desires
    Thirst not for gold. Sweet, bounteous Jane, what's mine
    Shall, if thou make myself thine, all be thine.   55
    Say, judge, what is thy sentence: life, or death?
    Mercy or cruelty lies in thy breath.
JANE: Good sir, I do believe you love me well.
    For 'tis a silly conquest, silly pride,
    For one like you – I mean a gentleman –   60
    To boast that by his love tricks he hath brought
    Such and such women to his amorous lure.
    I think you do not so, yet many do,
    And make it even a very trade* to woo.
    I could be coy, as many women be,   65
    Feed you with sunshine smiles and wanton looks,
    But I detest witchcraft. Say that I
    Do constantly believe you constant have –
HAMMON: Why dost thou not believe me?
JANE: I believe you.
    But, good sir, because I will not grieve you   70
    With hopes to taste fruit which will never fall,*
    In simple truth this is the sum of all:
    My husband lives. At least, I hope he lives;
    Pressed was he to these bitter wars in France.
    Bitter they are to me by wanting* him.   75
    I have but one heart, and that heart's his due;
    How then can I bestow the same on you?

Whilst he lives, his I live, be it ne'er so poor,
And rather be his wife than a king's whore.
HAMMON: Chaste and dear woman, I will not abuse thee,   80
Although it cost my life if thou refuse me.
Thy husband pressed for France: what was his name?
JANE: Rafe Damport.
HAMMON: Damport. Here's a letter sent
From France to me, from a dear friend of mine;
A gentleman of place,* here he doth write   85
Their names that have been slain in every fight.
JANE: I hope death's scroll contains not my love's name.
HAMMON: Cannot you read?
JANE: I can.
HAMMON: Peruse the same.
To my remembrance such a name I read
Amongst the rest. See here.
JANE: Ay me, he's dead.   90
He's dead; if this be true, my dear heart's slain.
HAMMON: Have patience, dear love.
JANE: Hence, hence!
HAMMON: Nay, sweet Jane:
Make not poor sorrow proud with these rich tears.
I mourn thy husband's death because thou mourn'st.
JANE: That bill* is forged; 'tis signed by forgery.   95
HAMMON: I'll bring thee letters sent besides to many
Carrying the like report. Jane, 'tis too true.
Come, weep not; mourning, though it rise from love,
Helps not the mourned, yet hurts them that mourn.
JANE: For God's sake, leave me!
HAMMON: Wither dost thou turn?   100
Forget the dead: love them that are alive;
His love is faded, try how mine will thrive.
JANE: 'Tis now no time for me to think on love.
HAMMON: 'Tis now best time for you to think on love,
Because your love lives not.
JANE: Though he be dead,   105
My love to him shall not be buried.
For God's sake, leave me to myself alone.
HAMMON: 'Twould kill my soul to lave thee drowned in moan.
Answer me to my suit, and I am gone.
Say to me: yea or no.
JANE: No.
HAMMON: Then farewell.   110
One farewell will not serve. I come again.
Come, dry those cheeks. Tell me, sweet Jane,

Yea, or no: once more.
JANE: Once more I say no.
    Once more, be gone, I pray; else will I go.
HAMMON: Nay then, I will grow rude,* by this white hand.   115
    Until you change that cold no, here I'll stand,
    Till by your hard heart –
JANE: Nay, for God's love, peace!
    My sorrows by your presence more increase.
    Not that you thus are present, but all grief
    Desires to be alone; therefore, in brief,   120
    Thus much I say and, saying, bid adieu:
    If ever I wed a man, it shall be you.
HAMMON: O blessed voice! Dear Jane, I'll urge no more;
    Thy breath had made me rich.
JANE: Death makes me poor.   *Exeunt.*

Scene Thirteen

Enter HODGE *at his shop board,** RAFE, FIRK, [LACY *as*] HANS,
and a boy at work.

ALL: Hey down, a-down, down derry.*
HODGE: Well said, my hearts. Ply your work today; we loitered
    yesterday. To it, pell-mell, that we may live to be lord mayors, or
    aldermen at least.
FIRK: Hey down, a-down derry.   5
HODGE: Well said, i'faith. How sayest thou, Hans: doth not Firk tickle it?
LACY: *Yaw, mester.**
FIRK: Not so, neither. My organ pipe squeaks this morning for want of
    liquoring. Hey down, a-down derry.
LACY: *Forware, Firk, tow best un jolly yongster. Hort, ay, mester ik bid yo cut*   10
    *me un pair vampies vor Mester Jeffries' boots.**
HODGE: Thou shalt, Hans.
FIRK: Master.
HODGE: How now, boy?
FIRK: Pray, now you are in the cutting vein, cut me a pair of   15
    counterfeits,* or else my work will not pass current.* Hey,
    down a-down.
HODGE: Tell me, sirs, are my cousin Mistress Priscilla's shoes done?
FIRK: Your cousin? No, master, one of your aunts.* Hang her, let them
    alone.   20
RAFE: I am in hand with them; she gave charge that none but I should
    do them for her.

FIRK: Thou do for her? Then 'twill be a lame doing, and that she
    loves not. Rafe, thou might'st have sent her to me; in faith, I would
    have yarked and firked* your Priscilla. Hey down, a-down derry;   25
    this gear will not hold.*
HODGE: How sayest thou, Firk? Were we not merry at Old Ford?
FIRK: How, merry? Why, our buttocks went jiggy-joggy like a
    quagmire. Well, Sir Roger Oatmeal, if I thought all meal of that
    nature,* I would eat nothing but bag-puddings.*   30
RAFE: Of all good fortunes, my fellow Hans had the best.
FIRK: 'Tis true, because Mistress Rose drank to him.
HODGE: Well, well: work apace. They say seven of the Aldermen be
    dead, or very sick.
FIRK: I care not; I'll be none.   35
RAFE: No, nor I; but then my Master Eyre will come quickly to be Lord
    Mayor.

               Enter SYBIL.

FIRK: Whoop, yonder comes Sybil.
HODGE: Sybil, welcome, i'faith, and how dost thou, mad wench?
FIRK: Syb-whore,* welcome to London.   40
SYBIL: Godamercy, sweet Firk. Good Lord Hodge, what a delicious shop
    you have got; you tickle it, i'faith.
RAFE: Godamercy, Sybil, for our good cheer at Old Ford.
SYBIL: That you shall have,* Rafe.
FIRK: Nay, by the mass, we had tickling cheer, Sybil. And how the   45
    plague dost thou and Mistress Rose, and my Lord Mayor? I put the
    women in first.
SYBIL: Well, godamercy. But, God's me,* I forgot myself. Where's Hans
    the Fleming?
FIRK: Hark, butter-box, now you must yelp out some spreken.   50
LACY: *Vat begay you, vat vod you, frister.**
SYBIL: Marry, you must come to my young mistress, to pull on* her shoes
    you made last.
LACY: *Vare ben your edle fro, vare ben your mistress?**
SYBIL: Marry, here at our London house in Cornwall.*   55
FIRK: Will nobody serve her turn* but Hans?
SYBIL: No, sir. Come, Hans, I stand upon needles.
HODGE: Why then, Sybil, take heed of pricking.
SYBIL: For that, let me alone; I have a trick in my budget.*
    Come, Hans.   60
LACY: *Yaw, yaw, ik sall meet yo gane.**
HODGE: Go, Hans, make haste again. Come, who lacks work?
                      Exit [LACY as] HANS *and* SYBIL.

FIRK: I, master, for I lack my breakfast; 'tis munching time, and past.
HODGE: Is't so? Why then, leave work, Rafe; to breakfast. Boy,
    look to the tools. Come, Rafe; come, Firk.   *Exeunt.* 65

Scene Fourteen

Enter a SERVINGMAN.

SERVINGMAN: Let me see now, the sign of the Last* in Tower Street.
    Mass, yonder's the house. What ho, who's within?

Enter RAFE.

RAFE: Who calls there? What want you, sir?
SERVINGMAN: Marry, I would have a pair of shoes made for a
    gentlewoman against* tomorrow morning. What, can you do them?   5
RAFE: Yes, sir, you shall have them. But what length's her foot?
SERVINGMAN: Why, you must make them in all parts like this shoe; but at
    any hand* fail not to do them, for the gentlewoman is to be married
    very early in the morning.
RAFE: How? By this shoe must it be made? By this, are you sure, sir,   10
    by this?
SERVINGMAN: How? By this am I sure, by this? Art thou in thy wits? I
    tell thee I must have a pair of shoes, dost thou mark me? A pair of
    shoes, two shoes, made by this very shoe, this same shoe, against
    tomorrow morning by four o'clock. Dost understand me? Canst   15
    thou do't?
RAFE: Yes, sir; yes, ay, ay; I can do't. By this shoe, you say. I should
    know this shoe. Yes, sir, yes. By this shoe, I can do't. Four o'clock,
    well; whither shall I bring them?
SERVINGMAN: To the sign of the Golden Ball* in Watling Street.* Enquire   20
    for one Master Hammon, a gentleman, my master.
RAFE: Yea, sir. By this shoe, you say.
SERVINGMAN: I say: Master Hammon at the Golden Ball. He's the
    bridegroom, and those shoes are for his bride.
RAFE: They shall be done, by this shoe. Well, well, Master Hammon at   25
    the Golden Shoe – I would say the Golden Ball – very well, very well.
    But, I pray you sir, where must Master Hammon be married?
SERVINGMAN: At Saint Faith's Church, under Paul's.* But what's that
    to thee? Prithee, despatch those shoes, and so farewell.   *Exit.*
RAFE: By this shoe, said he. How am I amazed   30
    At this strange accident! Upon my life,
    This was the very shoe I gave my wife
    When I was pressed for France; since when, alas,

I never could hear of her. It is the same,
And Hammon's bride no other but my Jane.   35

Enter FIRK.

FIRK: 'Snails, Rafe, thou hast lost thy part of three pots a countryman*
     of mine gave me to breakfast.
RAFE: I care not. I have found a better thing.*
FIRK: A thing? Away! Is it a man's thing, or a woman's thing?
RAFE: Firk, dost thou know this shoe?   40
FIRK: No, by my troth; neither doth that know me. I have no acquaintance
     with it. 'Tis a mere* stranger to me.
RAFE: Why then, I do. This shoe, I durst be sworn,
     Once covered the instep of my Jane.
     This is her size, her breadth; thus trod my love.   45
     These true love knots I pricked.* I hold my life,
     By this old shoe I shall find out my wife.
FIRK: Ha, ha, old shoe, that wert new! How a murrain* came this ague
     fit of foolishness upon thee?
RAFE: Thus, Firk: even now here came a servingman;   50
     By this shoe would he have a new pair made,
     Against tomorrow morning, for his mistress
     That's to be married to a gentleman.
     And why may not this be my sweet Jane?
FIRK: And why mayest not thou be my sweet ass? Ha, ha!   55
RAFE: Well, laugh and spare not. But the truth is this.
     Against tomorrow morning I'll provide
     A lusty crew of honest shoemakers
     To watch the going of the bride to church.
     If she prove Jane, I'll take her, in despite   60
     Of Hammon and the devil, were he by.
     If it be not my Jane, what remedy?
     Hereof am I sure: I shall live till I die,*
     Although I never with a woman lie.   *Exit.*
FIRK: Thou lie with a woman, to build nothing but Cripplegates!*   65
     Well, God sends fools fortune, and it may be he may light upon
     his matrimony by such a device; for wedding and hanging goes
     by destiny.*   *Exit.*

Scene Fifteen

Enter [LACY *as*] HANS *and* ROSE, *arm in arm.*

LACY: How happy am I by embracing thee!
     O, I did fear such cross* mishaps did reign

That I should never see my Rose again.
ROSE: Sweet Lacy, since fair opportunity
    Offers herself to further our escape,   5
    Let not too over-fond esteem of me
    Hinder that happy hour; invent the means,
    And Rose will follow thee through all the world.
LACY: O, how I surfeit with excess of joy,
    Made happy by thy rich perfection!   10
    But since thou payest sweet interest to my hopes,
    Redoubling love on love, let me once more,
    Like to a bold-faced debtor, crave of thee
    This night to steal abroad; and at Eyre's house
    Who now by death of certain Aldermen   15
    Is Mayor of London, and my master once,
    Meet thou thy Lacy, where, in spite of change,
    Your father's anger, and mine uncle's hate,
    Our happy nuptials will we consummate.

Enter SYBIL.

SYBIL: O God, what will you do, mistress? Shift for yourself: your   20
    father is at hand, he's coming, he's coming! Master Lacy, hide
    yourself in my mistress; for God's sake, shift for yourselves!
LACY: Your father come! Sweet Rose, what shall I do?
    Where shall I hide? How shall I escape?
ROSE: A man, and want* wit in extremity?   25
    Come, come: be Hans still, play the shoemaker.
    Pull on my shoe.

Enter LORD MAYOR.

LACY: Mass, and that's well remembered.
SYBIL: Here comes your father.
LACY: *Forware, Mistress, 'tis un good skow, it sal vel dute, or ye sal neit*   30
    *betallen.**
ROSE: O God, it pincheth me! What will you do?
LACY: Your father's presence pincheth, not the shoe.
LORD MAYOR: Well done; fit* my daughter well, and she shall please
    thee well.   35
LACY: *Yaw, yaw, ik weit dat well; forware, 'tis un good skow, 'tis gi mait van*
    *neit's leather, se ever mine heer.**

Enter a PRENTICE.

LORD MAYOR: I do believe it. What's the news with you?

PRENTICE: Please you, the Earl of Lincoln is at the gate,
    Is newly lighted, and would speak with you.   40
LORD MAYOR: The Earl of Lincoln come to speak* with me?
    Well, well, I know his errand. Daughter Rose,
    Send hence your shoemaker. Despatch, have done.
    Syb, make things handsome. Sir boy, follow me.
                    [*Exeunt* LORD MAYOR, SYBIL *and* PRENTICE].
LACY: Mine uncle come? O, what may this portend?   45
    Sweet Rose, this of our love threatens an end.
ROSE: Be not dismayed at this; what ere befall
    Rose is thine own. To witness I speak truth,
    Where thou appoints the place I'll meet with thee.
    I'll not fix a day to follow thee,   50
    But presently* steal hence. Do not reply:
    Love which gave strength to bear my father's hate
    Shall now add wings to further our escape.   *Exeunt.*

Scene Sixteen

Enter LORD MAYOR *and* LINCOLN.

LORD MAYOR: Believe me, on my credit* I speak truth.
    Since first your nephew Lacy went to France
    I have not seen him. It seemed strange to me
    When Dodger told me that he stayed behind,
    Neglecting the high charge the King imposed.   5
LINCOLN: Trust me, Sir Roger Oatley, I did think
    Your counsel had given head* to this attempt,
    Drawn to it by the love he bears your child.
    Here I did hope to find him in your house,
    But now I see mine error, and confess   10
    My judgement wronged you by conceiving so.
LORD MAYOR: Lodge in my house, say you? Trust me, my lord,
    I love your nephew Lacy too too dearly
    So much to wrong his honour, and he hath done so,
    That first gave him advice to stay from France.   15
    To witness I speak truth, I let you know
    How careful I have been to keep my daughter
    Free from all conference or speech of* him.
    No that I scorn your nephew, but in love
    I bear your honour, lest your noble blood,   20
    Should by my mean worth be dishonoured.
LINCOLN: How far the churl's tongue wanders from his heart.
    Well, well, Sir Roger Oatley, I believe you,

With more than many thanks for the kind love
So much you seem to bear me. But, my lord,   25
Let me request your help to seek my nephew,
Whom, if I find, I'll straight embark for France.
So shall your Rose be free, my thoughts at rest,
And much care die which now lies in my breast.

Enter SYBIL.

SYBIL: O Lord, help, for God's sake! My mistress, O my young mistress!   30
LORD MAYOR: Where is thy mistress? What's become of her?
SYBIL: She's gone, she's fled!
LORD MAYOR: Gone? Whither is she fled?
SYBIL: I know not, forsooth. She's fled out of doors with Hans the
     shoemaker; I saw them scud,* scud, scud, apace, apace.   35
LORD MAYOR: Which way? What, John, where be my men? Which way?
SYBIL: I know not, and it please your worship.
LORD MAYOR: Fled with a shoemaker? Can this be true?
SYBIL: O Lord, sir, as true as God's in heaven.
LINCOLN: Her love turned shoemaker? I am glad of this.   40
LORD MAYOR: A Fleming butter-box, a shoemaker?
     Will she forget her birth? Requite my care
     With such ingratitude? Scorned she young Hammon
     To love a honnikin,* a needy knave?
     Well, let her fly; I'll not fly after her.   45
     Let her starve if she will; she's none of mine.
LINCOLN: Be not so cruel, sir.

Enter FIRK *with shoes.*

SYBIL: I glad she's 'scaped.
LORD MAYOR: I'll not account of her as of my child.
     Was there no better object for her eyes   50
     But a foul drunken lubber,* swill-belly?
     A shoemaker? That's brave!
FIRK: Yea, forsooth, 'tis a a very brave shoe, and as fit as a pudding.*
LORD MAYOR: How now, what knave is this? From whence
     comest thou?   55
FIRK: No knave, sir; I am Firk the shoemaker, lusty Roger's chief lusty
     journeyman, and I come hither to take up the pretty leg of sweet
     Mistress Rose. And thus hoping your worship is in as good health
     as I was at the making hereof, I bid you farewell. Yours, Firk.
LORD MAYOR: Stay, stay, sir knave.   60
LINCOLN: Come hither, shoemaker.

FIRK: 'Tis happy the knave is put before the shoemaker, or else I would not
    have vouchsafed to come back to you. I am moved, for I stir.*

LORD MAYOR: My lord, this villain calls us knaves by craft.

FIRK: Then 'tis by the gentle craft, and to call one knave gently is no   65
    harm. Sit your worship merry.* Sib, your young mistress – I'll so
    bob* them now my master, Master Eyre, is Lord Mayor of London.

LORD MAYOR: Tell me, sirrah, whose man are you?

FIRK: I am glad to see your worship so merry. I have no maw to
    this gear,* no stomach as yet to a red petticoat.   70

Pointing to SYBIL.

LINCOLN: He means not, sir, to woo you to his maid,
    But only demand whose man you are.

FIRK: I sing now to the tune of Rogero;* Roger my fellow is now
    my master.

LINCOLN: Sirrah, knowest thou one Hans, a shoemaker?   75

FIRK: Hans, shoemaker – O yes, stay; yes, I have him.* I tell you what –
    I speak it in secret – Mistress Rose and he are by this time – no, not
    so, but shortly are to come over one another with – 'can you dance
    the shaking of the sheets?*' It is that Hans – I'll so gull these diggers.*

LORD MAYOR: Knowest thou, then, where he is?   80

FIRK: Yes, forsooth; yea, marry.

LINCOLN: Canst thou in sadness?*

FIRK: No forsooth; no, marry.

LORD MAYOR: Tell me, good honest fellow, where he is,
    And thou shalt see what I'll bestow of* thee.   85

FIRK: Honest fellow, no, sir; not so, sir. My profession is the gentle craft;
    I care not for seeing, I love feeling.* Let me feel it here, *aurium tenus*,
    ten pieces of gold, *genuum tenus*,* ten pieces of silver, and then
    Firk is your man in a new pair of stretchers.*

LORD MAYOR: Here is an angel, part of thy reward,   90
    Which I will give thee. Tell me where he is.

FIRK: No point.* Shall I betray my brother? No. Shall I prove Judas to
    Hans? No. Shall I cry treason to my corporation?* No. I shall be
    firked and yarked, then, but give me your angel; your angel shall
    tell you.   95

LINCOLN: Do so, good fellow; 'tis no hurt to thee.

FIRK: Send simpering Sib away.

LORD MAYOR: Huswife,* get you in.   *Exit* SYBIL.

FIRK: Pitchers have ears, and maids have wide mouths.* But for
    Hauns Prauns, upon my word, he and young Mistress Rose go   100
    to this gear;* they shall be married together, by this rush,* or else
    turn Firk to a firkin* of butter to tan leather withall.

LORD MAYOR: But art thou sure of this?

FIRK: Am I sure that Paul's steeple is a handful higher than London
    Stone?* Or that the pissing conduit* leaks nothing but pure Mother   105
    Bunch?* Am I sure I am lusty Firk? God's nails, do you think I am
    so base to gull you?

LINCOLN: Where are they to be married? Dost thou know the church?

FIRK: I never go to church, but I know the name of it. It is a swearing
    church.* Stay a while, 'tis 'Ay, by the mass' – no, no, 'tis 'Ay, by my   110
    troth' – no, nor that, 'tis 'Ay, by my faith'– that, that; 'tis Ay, by my
    Faith's Church under Paul's Cross; there shall they be knit like a
    pair of stockings in matrimony. There they'll be incony.*

LINCOLN: Upon my life, my nephew Lacy walks
    In the disguise of this Dutch shoemaker!   115

FIRK: Yes, forsooth.

LINCOLN: Doth he not, honest fellow?

FIRK: No, forsooth; I think Hans is nobody but Hans, no spirit.

LORD MAYOR: My mind misgives me now; 'tis so indeed.

LINCOLN: My cousin speaks the language, knows the trade.   120

LORD MAYOR: Let me request your company, my lord,
    Your honourable presence may, no doubt,
    Refrain* their headstrong rashness, when myself
    Going alone perchance may be o'erborne.
    Shall I request this favour?

LINCOLN: This, or what else.*   125

FIRK: Then you must rise betimes,* for they mean to fall to their 'hey,
    pass and repass,* pindy-pandy,* which hand will you have'
    very early.

LORD MAYOR: My care shall every way equal their haste.
    This night accept your lodging in my house;   130
    The earlier shall we stir, and at Saint Faith's
    Prevent this giddy hare-brained nuptial.
    This traffic of hot love shall yield cold gains;
    They ban our loves, and we'll forbid their banns.   *Exit.*

LINCOLN: At Saint Faith's Church, thou sayest.   135

FIRK: Yes, by their troth.

LINCOLN: Be secret, on thy life.   *Exit.*

FIRK: Yes, when I kiss your wife. Ha, ha! Here's no craft in the gentle
    craft; I came hither of purpose with shoes to Sir Roger's worship,
    whilst Rose his daughter be coney-catched* by Hans. Soft now;   140
    these two gulls will be at Saint Faith's Church tomorrow morning
    to take Master Bridegroom and Mistress Bride napping, and they
    in the meantime shall chop up* the matter at the Savoy.* But the
    best sport is, Sir Roger Oatley will find my fellow lame Rafe's
    wife going to marry a gentleman, and then he'll stop her instead   145

of his daughter. O brave! There will be fine tickling sport. Soft
now, what have I to do? O, I know now: a mess* of shoemakers
meet at the Woolsack* in Ivy Lane, to cozen* my gentleman of
lame Rafe's wife, that's true.

> Alack, alack,   150
> Girls, hold out tack;*
> For now smocks* for this jumbling*
> Shall go to wrack.   *Exit.*

Scene Seventeen

Enter EYRE, *his* WIFE, [LACY *as*] HANS *and* ROSE.

EYRE: This is the morning, then. Stay, my bully,* my honest Hans,
 is it not?
LACY: This is the morning that must make us two
 Happy or miserable, therefore if you –
EYRE: Away with these ifs and ands, Hans, and these etceteras! By   5
 mine honour, Roland Lacy, none but the King shall wrong thee.
 Come, fear nothing; am not I Simon Eyre? Is not Simon Eyre Lord
 Mayor of London? Fear nothing, Rose, let them all say what they
 can. 'Dainty, come thou to me'* – laughest thou?
WIFE: Good my lord, stand* her friend in what thing you may.   10
EYRE: Why, my sweet Lady Madgy, think you Simon Eyre can forget
 his fine Dutch journeyman? No, vah! Fie, I scorn it; it shall never
 be cast in my teeth* that I was unthankful. Lady Madgy, thou
 hadst never covered thy Saracen's head* with this French flap,
 nor loaden thy bum with this farthingale; 'tis trash, trumpery,   15
 vanity. Simon Eyre had never walked in a red petticoat, nor wore
 a chain of gold, but for my fine journeyman's portagues, and
 shall I leave him? No. Prince am I none, yet bear a princely mind.
LACY: My lord, 'tis time for us to part from hence.
EYRE: Lady Madgy, Lady Madgy, take two or three of my piecrust   20
 eaters, my buff-jerkin varlets* that do walk in black gowns at
 Simon Eyre's heels; take them, good Lady Madgy, trip and go, my
 brown Queen of Periwigs, with my delicate Rose and my jolly
 Roland to the Savoy. See them linked, countenance* the marriage
 and, when it is done, cling, cling together, you Hamborrow*   25
 turtle-doves. I'll bear you out: come to Simon Eyre, come dwell
 with me, Hans; thou shalt eat minced-pies* and marchpane.*
 Rose, away, cricket; trip and go, my Lady Madgy, to the Savoy.
 Hans, wed and to bed; kiss and away; go, vanish.
WIFE: Farewell, my lord.   30

ROSE: Make haste, sweet love.

WIFE: She'd fain the deed were done.

LACY: Come, my sweet Rose, faster than deer we'll run.   *They go out.*

EYRE: Go, vanish, vanish. Avaunt,* I say. By the Lord of Ludgate, it's a
  mad life to be a Lord Mayor. It's a stirring life, a fine life, a velvet   35
  life, a careful* life. Well, Simon Eyre, yet set a good face on it, in
  the honour of Saint Hugh. Soft, the King this day comes to dine
  with me, to see my new buildings.* His majesty is welcome; he
  shall have good cheer, delicate cheer, princely cheer. This day my
  fellow prentices of London come to dine with me too; they shall   40
  have fine cheer, gentlemanlike cheer. I promised the mad
  Cappadocians,* when we all served at the conduit together, that if
  ever I came to be Mayor of London, I would feast them all, and
  I'll do't, I'll do't, by the life of Pharoah; by this beard, Simon Eyre
  will be no flincher. Besides, I have procured that upon every   45
  Shrove Tuesday, at the sound of the pancake bell,* my fine dapper
  Assyrian* lads shall clap up their shop windows, and, away, this
  is the day; and this day they shall do't, they shall do't!
     Boys, that day are you free, let masters care,
     And prentices shall pray for Simon Eyre.   *Exit.*   50

Scene Eighteen

Enter HODGE, FIRK, RAFE *and five or six* SHOEMAKERS,
all with cudgels, or such weapons.

HODGE: Come, Rafe; stand to it, Firk. My masters, as we are the brave
  bloods* of the shoemakers, heirs apparent to Saint Hugh, and
  perpetual benefactors to all good fellows, thou shalt have no
  wrong; were Hammon a king of spades, he should not delve in
  thy close* without thy sufferance.* But tell me, Rafe, art thou sure   5
  'tis thy wife?

RAFE: Am I sure this is Firk? This morning when I stroked on her
  shoes, I looked upon her, and she upon me, and sighed, and
  asked me if ever I knew one Rafe. Yes, said I; for his sake, said
  she, tears standing in her eyes, and for thou art something like   10
  him, spend this piece of gold. I took it; my lame leg, and my travel
  beyond sea, made me unknown. All is one for that; I know
  she's mine.

FIRK: Did she give thee this gold? O glorious, glittering gold! She's
  thine own: 'tis thy wife, and she loves thee, for, I'll stand to't,   15
  there's no woman will give gold to any man but she thinks better
  of him than she thinks of them she gives silver to. And, for

Hammon, neither Hammon nor hangman* shall wrong thee in
London. Is not our old Master Eyre Lord Mayor? Speak, my hearts.
ALL: Yes, and Hammon shall know it to his cost.   20

Enter HAMMON, *his man*, JANE *and others.*

HODGE: Peace, my bullies, here they come.
RAFE: Stand to't, my hearts. Firk, let me speak first.
HODGE: No, Rafe, let me – Hammon, whither away so early?
HAMMON: Unmannerly rude* slave, what's that to thee?
FIRK: To him, sir? Yes, sir, and to me, and others. Good morrow, Jane,   25
   how dost thou? Good Lord, how the world is changed with you,
   God be thanked.
HAMMON: Villains, hands off. How dare you touch my love?
ALL: Villains? Down with them, cry clubs for prentices!
HODGE: Hold, my hearts. Touch her, Hammon? Yea, and more than that;   30
   we'll carry her away with us. My masters and gentlemen, never draw
   your bird-spits;* shoemakers are steel to the back, men every inch of
   them, all spirit.
ALL OF HAMMON'S SIDE: Well, and what of all this?
HODGE: I'll show you. Jane, dost thou know this man? 'Tis Rafe, I can   35
   tell,thee. Nay, 'tis he, in faith, though he be lamed by the wars –
   yet look not strange,* but run to him, fold him about the neck and
   kiss him.
JANE: Lives then my husband? O God, let me go,
   Let me embrace my Rafe.
HAMMON: What means my Jane?   40
JANE: Nay, what meant you to tell me he was slain?
HAMMON: Pardon me, dear love, for being misled;
   'Twas rumoured here in London thou wert dead.
FIRK: Thou seest he lives. Lass, go pack* home with him. Now, Master
   Hammon, where's your mistress your wife?   45
SERVANT: 'Swounds,* master, fight for her! Will you thus lose her?
ALL: Down with that creature! Clubs, down with him!
HODGE: Hold, hold!
HAMMON: Hold, fool; sirs, he shall do no wrong.
   Will my Jane leave me thus, and break her faith?   50
FIRK: Yea, sir, she must, sir; she shall, sir. What then? Mend it.
HODGE: Hark, fellow Rafe: follow my counsel. Set the wench in the midst,
   and let her choose her man, and let her be his woman.
JANE: Whom should I choose? Whom should my thoughts affect*
   But him whom heaven hath made to be my love?   55
   Thou art my husband, and these humble weeds*
   Makes thee more beautiful than all his wealth.

Therefore I will but put off his attire,
Returning it into the owner's hand,
And ever after be thy constant wife.   60
HODGE: Not a rag, Jane; the law's on our side. He that sows in another
   man's ground forfeits his harvest. Get thee home, Rafe; follow him,
   Jane; he shall not have so much as a busk point* from thee.
FIRK: Stand to that, Rafe; the appurtenances* are thine own. Hammon,
   look not at her.   65
SERVANT: O 'Swounds, no!
FIRK: Bluecoat,* be quiet; we'll give you a new livery else. We'll make
   Shrove Tuesday Saint George's day* for you. Look not, Hammon;
   leer not, I'll firk you, for* thy head now. One glance, one sheep's
   eye,* anything at her; touch not a rag, lest I and my brethren beat   70
   you to clouts.*
SERVANT: Come, Master Hammon,; there's no striving* here.
HAMMON: Good fellows, hear me speak and, honest Rafe,
   Whom I have injured most by loving Jane,
   Mark what I offer thee. Here in fair gold   75
   Is twenty pound; I'll give it for thy Jane.
   If this content thee not, thou shalt have more.
HODGE: Sell not thy wife, Rafe, make her not a whore.
HAMMON: Say, wilt thou freely cease thy claim in her,
   And let her be my wife?   80
ALL: No, do not, Rafe!
RAFE: Sirrah* Hammon, Hammon, dost thou think a shoemaker is so
   base to be a bawd to his own wife for commodity?* Take thy gold,
   choke with it. Were I not lame, I would make thee eat thy words.
FIRK: A shoemaker sell his flesh and blood? O indignity!   85
HODGE: Sirrah, take up your pelf* and be packing.
HAMMON: I will not touch one penny, but in lieu
   Of that great wrong I offered thy Jane,
   To Jane and thee I give that twenty pound.
   Since I have failed of her, during my life   90
   I vow no woman else shall be my wife.
   Farewell, good fellows of the gentle trade;
   Your morning's mirth my mourning day hath made.
                                   Exeunt [HAMMON *and* SERVANTS].
FIRK: Touch the gold, creature, if you dare; y'are best be trudging. Here,
   Jane, take thou it. Now, let's home, my hearts.   95
HODGE: Stay: who comes here? Jane, on again with thy mask.*

                 Enter LINCOLN, LORD MAYOR, *and* SERVANTS.

LINCOLN: Yonder's the lying varlet mocked us so.

LORD MAYOR: Come hither, sirrah.

FIRK: Ay, sir; I am sirrah: you mean me, do you not?

LINCOLN: Where is my nephew married?   100

FIRK: Is he married? God give him joy, I am glad of it. They have a fair
  day, and the sign is in a good planet: Mars in Venus.*

LORD MAYOR: Villain, thou told'st me that my daughter Rose
  This morning should be married at Saint Faith's.
  We have watched there these three hours at the least,   105
  Yet we see no such thing.

FIRK: Truly, I am sorry for't; a bride's a pretty thing.

HODGE: Come, to the purpose: yonder's the bride and bridegroom
  you look for, I hope. Though you be lords, you are not to bar, by
  your authority, men from women, are you?   110

LORD MAYOR: See, see: my daughter's masked.

LINCOLN: True, and my nephew,
  To hide his guilt, counterfeits him lame.

FIRK: Yea, truly; God help the poor couple, they are lame and blind.

LORD MAYOR: I'll ease her blindness.

LINCOLN: I'll his lameness cure.

FIRK: Lie down, sirs, and laugh: my fellow Rafe is taken for Roland Lacy, 115
  and Jane for Mistress Damask* Rose. This is all my knavery.

LORD MAYOR: What, have I found you, minion?

LINCOLN: O base wretch!
  Nay, hide thy face; the horror of thy guilt
  Can hardly be washed off. Where are thy powers?*
  What battles have you made? O yes, I see: 120
  Thou fought'st with shame, and shame hath conquered thee.
  This lameness will not serve.

LORD MAYOR: Unmask yourself.

LINCOLN: Lead home your daughter.

LORD MAYOR: Take your nephew hence.

RAFE: Hence! 'Swounds, what mean you? Are you mad? I hope you
  cannot enforce my wife from me. Where's Hammon?   125

LORD MAYOR: Your wife?

LINCOLN: What Hammon?

RAFE: Yea, my wife; and therefore the proudest of you that lays hands
  on her first, I'll lay my crutch cross his pate.

FIRK: To him, brave Rafe! Here's brave sport.   130

RAFE: Rose call you her? Why, her name is Jane. Look here else; do you
  know her now?

LINCOLN: Is this your daughter?

LORD MAYOR: No, nor this your nephew.
  My Lord of Lincoln, we are both abused
  By this base crafty varlet.   135

FIRK: Yea, forsooth, no varlet; forsooth, no base; forsooth, I am but
    mean; no crafty neither, but of the gentle craft.
LORD MAYOR: Where is my daughter Rose? Where is my child?
LINCOLN: Where is my nephew Lacy married?
FIRK: Why, here is good laced mutton,* as I promised you.   140
LINCOLN: Villain, I'll have thee punished for this wrong.
FIRK: Punish the journeyman villain,* but not the journeyman shoemaker.

Enter DODGER.

DODGER: My lord, I come to bring unwelcome news.
    Your nephew Lacy, and your daughter Rose,
    Early this morning wedded at the Savoy,   145
    None being present but the Lady Mayoress.
    Besides, I learnt among the officers*
    The Lord Mayor vows to stand in their defence
    'Gainst any that shall seek to cross the match.
LINCOLN: Dares Eyre the shoemaker uphold the deed?   150
FIRK: Yes, sir; shoemakers dare stand in a woman's quarrel, I warrant
    you, as deep as another, and deeper too.
DODGER: Besides, his Grace* today dines with the Mayor,
    Who on his knees humbly intends to fall
    And beg a pardon for your nephew's fault.   155
LINCOLN: But I'll prevent him. Come, Sir Roger Oatley;
    The King will do us justice in this cause.
    Howe'er their hands have made them man and wife,
    I will disjoin the match, or lose my life.
                            Exeunt [LORD MAYOR *and* LINCOLN].
FIRK: Adieu, Monsieur Dodger; farewell, fools, ha, ha! O, if they had   160
    stayed I would have so lammed them with flouts!* O heart, my
    codpiece point* is ready to fly in pieces every time I think upon
    Mistress Rose – but let that pass, as my Lady Mistress says.
HODGE: This matter is answered.* Come, Rafe, home with thy wife.
    Come, my fine shoemakers, let's to our master's, the new Lord   165
    Mayor, and there swagger this Shrove Tuesday. I'll promise you
    wine enough, for Madge keeps the cellar.
ALL: O rare! Madge is a good wench.
FIRK: And I'll promise you meat enough, for simpering Susan keeps the
    larder. I'll lead you to victuals, my brave soldiers; follow your   170
    captain. O brave! Hark, hark!
                            Bell rings.
ALL: The pancake bell rings! The pancake bell! Trill-lill,* my hearts!
FIRK: O brave! O sweet bell! O delicate pancakes! Open the doors, my
    hearts, and shut up the windows; keep in* the house, and let out

the pancakes! O rare, my hearts! Let's march together, for the 175
honour of Saint Hugh, to the new Great Hall in Gracious Street
Corner, which our master the new Lord Mayor hath built.

RAFE: O the crew of good fellows that will dine at my Lord Mayor's
cost today!

HODGE: By the Lord, my Lord Mayor is a most brave man! How shall 180
prentices be bound to pray for him and the honour of the gentleman
shoemakers? Let's feed and be fat with my lord's bounty.

FIRK: O musical bell still! O Hodge! O my brethren! There's cheer for
the heavens! Venison pasties walk up and down, piping hot, like
sergeants; beef and brewis* comes marching in dry fats;* fritters 185
and pancakes comes trowelling in in wheelbarrows; hens and
oranges hopping in porters' baskets; collops* and eggs in scuttles;*
and tarts and custards comes quavering in in malt shovels.*

Enter more PRENTICES.

ALL: Whoop, look here, look here!

HODGE: How now, mad lads, whither away so fast? 190

FIRST PRENTICE: Whither? Why, to the great new hall! Know you
not why? The Lord Mayor hath bidden all the prentices in London
to breakfast this morning.

ALL: O brave shoemaker! O brave lord of incomprehensible* good
fellowship! Woo, hark you – the pancake bell rings! *Cast up caps.* 195

FIRK: Nay, more, my hearts; every Shrove Tuesday is our year of
jubilee,* and when the pancake bell rings, we are as free as my
Lord Mayor. We may shut up our shops and make holiday. I'll
have it called Saint Hugh's Holiday.

ALL: Agreed, agreed! Saint Hugh's Holiday! 200

HODGE: And this shall continue forever.

ALL: O brave! Come, come, my hearts; away, away.

FIRK: O eternal credit to us of the Gentle Craft! March, fair my
hearts. O rare!

Exeunt.

Scene Nineteen

Enter KING *and his train over the stage.*

KING: Is our Lord Mayor of London such a gallant?

NOBLEMAN: One of the merriest madcaps in your land.
Your Grace will think, when you behold the man,
He's rather a wild ruffian than a Mayor.

Yet thus I'll ensure* your Majesty: 5
In all his actions that concern his state*
He is as serious, provident and wise,
As full of gravity amongst the grave,
As any Mayor hath been these many years.
KING: I am with child* till I behold this huff-cap.*   10
But all my doubt* is, when we come in presence,
His madness will be dashed clean out of countenance.
NOBLEMAN: It may be so, my liege.
KING: Which to prevent,
Let someone give him notice 'tis our pleasure
That he put on his wonted merriment.   15
Set forward.
ALL: On, afore.   *Exeunt.*

Scene Twenty

Enter EYRE, HODGE, FIRK, RAFE *and other* SHOEMAKERS,
all with napkins on their shoulders.

EYRE: Come, my fine Hodge, my jolly gentlemen shoemakers. Soft,
where be these cannibals,* these varlets, my officers? Let them all
walk and wait upon my brethren; for my meaning is that none but
shoemakers, none but the livery* of my company, shall in their
satin hoods* wait upon the trencher of my sovereign.   5
FIRK: O, my lord, it will be rare.
EYRE: No more, Firk. Come lively, let your fellow prentices want no
cheer; let wine be as plentiful as beer, and beer as water. Hang
these penny-pinching fathers, that cram wealth in innocent
lambskins!* Rip,* knaves! Avaunt, look to my guests.   10
HODGE: My lord, we are at our wit's end for room; those hundred tables
will not feast the fourth part of them.
EYRE: Then cover me those hundred tables again, and again, till all my
jolly prentices be feasted. Avoid,* Hodge; run, Rafe; frisk about, my
nimble Firk. Carouse me fathom healths* to the honour of the   15
shoemakers! Do they drink lively, Hodge? Do they tickle it, Firk?
FIRK: Tickle it? Some of them have taken their liquor standing so long
that they can stand no longer. But for meat, they would eat it, and
they had it.
EYRE: Want they meat? Where's this swag-belly, this greasy   20
kitchen-stuff cook? Call the varlet to me. Want meat! Firk, Hodge,
lame Rafe: run, my tall* men, beleaguer* the shambles,* beggar all
Eastcheap,* serve me whole oxen in chargers,* and let sheep

whine upon the tables like pigs for want of good fellows to eat them.
Want meat! Vanish, Firk! Avaunt, Hodge! 25
HODGE: Your lordship mistakes my man Firk; he means their bellies
want meat, not the boards, for they have drunk so much they can
eat nothing.

Enter [LACY *as*] HANS, ROSE *and* WIFE.

WIFE: Where is my lord?
EYRE: How now, Lady Madgy? 30
WIFE: The King's most excellent Majesty is new* come. He sends me
for thy honour. One of his most worshipful peers bade me tell thou
must be merry, and so forth – but let that pass.
EYRE: Is my sovereign come? Vanish, my tall shoemakers, my nimble
brethren; look to my guests the prentices. Yet stay a little – how 35
now, Hans? How looks my little Rose?
LACY: Let me request you to remember me.
I know your honour easily may obtain
Free pardon of the King for me and Rose
And reconcile me to my uncle's grace. 40
EYRE: Have done,* my good Hans, my honest journeyman. Look
cheerly; I'll fall upon both my knees till they be as hard as horn,
but I'll get thy pardon.
WIFE: Good my lord, have a care what you speak to his Grace.
EYRE: Away, you Islington white-pot;* hence, you hopper-arse;* you 45
barley-pudding* full of maggots; you broiled carbonado,* avaunt!
Avaunt, Mephistophilus!* Shall Sim Eyre learn to speak of you,
Lady Madgy? Vanish, Mother Miniver-Cap;* go, trip and go,
meddle with your partlets* and your pishery-pashery, your flews*
and your whirligigs.* Go, rub, out of mine alley.* Sim Eyre knows 50
how to speak to a Pope, to Sultan Solomon, to Tamburlaine* and he
were here. And shall I melt? Shall I droop before my sovereign?
No, come, my Lady Madgy; follow me, Hans; about your business,
my frolic* freebooters.* Firk, frisk about, and about, and about, for
the honour of mad Simon Eyre, Lord Mayor of London. 55
FIRK: Hey for the honour of the shoemakers! *Exeunt.*

Scene Twenty One

A long flourish or two; enter KING, NOBLES, EYRE, *his* WIFE, LACY, ROSE.
LACY *and* ROSE *kneel.*

KING: Well, Lacy, though the fact* was very foul

Of your revolting from our kingly love
And your own duty, yet we pardon you.
Rise, both; and, Mistress Lacy, thank my Lord Mayor
For your young bridegroom here.   5

EYRE: So, my dear liege, Sim Eyre and my brethren the gentlemen
   shoemakers shall set your sweet Majesty's image cheek by jowl
   by Saint Hugh, for this honour you have done poor Simon Eyre.
   I beseech your Grace, pardon my rude behaviour: I am a
   handicrafts-man, yet my heart is without craft.* I would be sorry   10
   at my soul that my boldness should offend my king.

KING: Nay, I pray thee, good Lord Mayor, be even as merry
   As if thou wert among thy shoemakers;
   It does me good to see thee in this humour.

EYRE: Sayest thou me so, my sweet Dioclesian?* Then hump!* Prince   15
   am I none, yet am I princely born. By the Lord of Ludgate, my
   liege, I'll be as merry as a pie.*

KING: Tell me, in faith, mad Eyre, how old thou art.

EYRE: My liege, a very boy, a stripling, a yonker;* you see not a white
   hair on my head, not a grey in this beard. Every hair, I assure thy   20
   Majesty, that sticks in this beard Sim Eyre values at the King of
   Babylon's* ransom; Tamar Cham's beard* was a rubbing-brush*
   to't. Yet I'll shave it off and stuff tennis balls with it to please my
   bully King.

KING: But all this while I do not know your age.   25

EYRE: My liege, I am six and fifty year old, yet I can cry 'hump' with a
   sound heart, for the honour of Saint Hugh. Mark this old wench,
   my King; I danced the shaking of the sheets with her six and thirty
   years ago, and yet I hope to get two or three young Lord Mayors
   ere I die. I am lusty still, Sim Eyre still: care and cold lodging brings 30
   white hairs.* My sweet Majesty, let care vanish; cast it upon thy
   nobles, it will make thee look always young like Apollo,* and cry
   'hump'. Prince am I none, yet am I princely born.

KING: Ha, ha! Say, Cornwall, didst thou ever see his like?

NOBLEMAN: Not I, my Lord.

Enter LINCOLN *and* LORD MAYOR.

KING: Lincoln, what news with you?   35

LINCOLN: My gracious Lord, have care unto your self,
   For there are traitors here.

ALL: Traitors? Where? Who?

EYRE: Traitors in my house? God forbid! Where be my officers? I'll spend*
   my soul ere my King feel harm.

KING: Where is the traitor, Lincoln?

LINCOLN: Here he stands.   40
KING: Cornwall, lay hold on Lacy. Lincoln, speak:
    What canst thou lay unto thy nephew's charge?
LINCOLN: This, my dear liege. Your Grace, to do me honour,
    Heaped on the head of this degenerous* boy
    Desertless favours; you made choice of him   45
    To be commander over powers in France.
    But he –
KING: Good Lincoln, prithee pause a while.
    Even in thine eyes I read what thou wouldst speak.
    I know this Lacy did neglect our love,
    Ran himself deeply, in the highest degree,   50
    Into vile treason.
LINCOLN: Is he not a traitor?
KING: Lincoln, he was; now we have pardoned him.
    'Twas not a base want of true valour's fire
    That held him out of France, but love's desire.
LINCOLN: I will not bear his shame upon my back.   55
KING: Nor shalt thou, Lincoln; I forgive you both.
LINCOLN: Then, good my liege, forbid the boy to wed
    One whose mean birth will much disgrace his bed.
KING: Are they not married?
LINCOLN: No, my liege.
BOTH: We are.
KING: Shall I divorce them then? O, be it far   60
    That any hand on earth should dare untie
    The sacred knot knit by God's Majesty.
    I would not for my crown disjoin their hands
    That are conjoined in holy nuptial bands.
    How sayest thou, Lacy? Wouldst thou lose thy Rose?   65
LACY: Not for all India's wealth, my sovereign.
KING: But Rose, I am sure, her Lacy would forego.
ROSE: If Rose were asked that question, she'd say no.
KING: You hear them, Lincoln.
LINCOLN: Yea, my liege, I do.
KING: Yet canst thou find i'th'heart to part these two?   70
    Who seeks, besides you, to divorce these lovers?
LORD MAYOR: I do, my gracious Lord; I am her father.
KING: Sir Roger Oatley; our last Mayor, I think?
NOBLEMAN: The same, my liege.
KING: Would you offend* love's laws?
    Well, you shall have your wills. You sue to me   75
    To prohibit the match; soft, let me see.
    You both are married, Lacy, are you not?

LACY: I am, dread sovereign.
KING: Then, upon thy life,
    I charge thee not to call this woman wife.
LORD MAYOR: I thank your Grace.
ROSE: O my most gracious Lord!   *Kneel.*   80
KING: Nay, Rose, never woo me; I tell you true,
    Although as yet I am a bachelor,
    Yet I believe I shall not marry you.
ROSE: Can you divide the body from the soul,
    Yet make the body live?
KING: Yea, so profound?   85
    I cannot, Rose, but you I must divide.
    Fair maid, this bridegroom cannot be your bride.*
    Are you pleased, Lincoln? Oatley, are you pleased?
BOTH: Yes, my Lord.
KING: Then must my heart be eased.
    For, credit me, my conscience lives in pain   90
    Till these whom I have divorced be joined again.
    Lacy, give me your hand; Rose, lend me thine.
    Be what you would be: kiss now; that's fine.
    At night, lovers, to bed. Now, let me see:
    Which of you all mislike this harmony?   95
LORD MAYOR: Will you then take from me my child perforce?
KING: Why, tell me, Oatley, shines not Lacy's name
    As bright in the world's eye as the gay beams
    Of any citizen?
LINCOLN: Yes, but my gracious Lord,
    I do mislike the match far more than he;   100
    Her blood is too base.
KING: Lincoln, no more.
    Dost thou not know that love respects no blood?
    Cares not for difference of birth or state?
    The maid is young, well born, fair, virtuous;
    A worthy bride for any gentleman.   105
    Besides, your nephew for her sake did stoop
    To bare necessity; and, as I hear,
    Forgetting honours and all courtly pleasures,
    To gain her love became a shoemaker.
    As for the honour which he lost in France,   110
    Thus I redeem it. Lacy, kneel thee down.
    Arise, Sir Roland Lacy. Tell me now;
    Tell me in earnest, Oatley, canst thou chide,
    Seeing thy Rose a lady and bride?
LORD MAYOR: I am content with what your Grace hath done.   115

LINCOLN: And I, my liege, since there's no remedy.
KING: Come on then, all shake hands; I'll have you friends.
Where there is much love, all discord ends.
What says my Lord Mayor to all this love?
EYRE: O my liege, this honour you have done to my fine journeyman   120
here, Roland Lacy, and all these favours which you have shown to
me this day in my poor house, will make Simon Eyre live longer by
one dozen of warm summers than he should.
KING: Nay, my mad Lord Mayor – that shall be thy name –
If any grace of mine can length thy life,   125
One honour more I'll do thee: that new building
Which at thy cost in Cornhill is erected
Shall take a name from us. We'll have it called
The Leadenhall, because in digging it
You found the lead that covereth the same.   130
EYRE: I thank your Majesty.
WIFE: God bless your Grace.
KING: Lincoln, a word with you.

Enter HODGE, FIRK, RAFE *and more* SHOEMAKERS.

EYRE: How now, my mad knaves? Peace, speak softly; yonder is the King.
KING: With the old troop which there we keep in pay   135
We will incorporate a new supply.
Before one summer more pass o'er my head
France shall repent England was injured.
What are all those?
LACY: All shoemakers, my liege,
Sometimes* my fellows. In their companies   140
I lived as merry as an emperor.*
KING: My mad Lord Mayor, are all these shoemakers?
EYRE: All shoemakers, my liege; all gentlemen of the gentle craft,
true Trojans, courageous cordwainers. They all kneel to the shrine
of holy Saint Hugh.   145
ALL: God save your Majesty!   *All shoemakers.*
KING: Mad Simon, would they anything with us?
EYRE: Mum, mad knaves; not a word! I'll do't, I warrant you. They are
all beggars, my liege, all for themselves; and I for them all, on both
my knees do entreat that for the honour of poor Simon Eyre, and   150
the good of his brethren these mad knaves, your Grace would
vouchsafe some privilege to my new Leadenhall, that it may be
lawful for us to buy and sell leather there two days a week.
KING: Mad Sim, I grant your suit. You shall have patent
To hold two market days in Leadenhall.   155

Mondays and Fridays: those shall be the times.
Will this content you?
ALL: Jesus bless your Grace.
EYRE: In the name of these my poor brethren shoemakers, I most humbly
	thank your Grace. But before I rise, seeing you are in the giving vein 160
	and we in the begging, grant Simon Eyre one boon more.
KING: What is it, my Lord Mayor?
EYRE: Vouchsafe to taste of a poor banquet* that stands sweetly waiting
	for your sweet presence.
KING: I shall undo thee, Eyre, only with feasts.	165
	Already have I been too troublesome;
	Say, have I not?
EYRE: O my dear King, Sim Eyre was taken unawares upon a day of
	shroving* which I promised long ago to the prentices of London.
	For, and't please your Highness, in time past	170
	I bare the water-tankard, and my coat
	Sits not a whit the worse upon my back;
	And then upon a morning some mad boys –
	It was Shrove Tuesday even as 'tis now –
	gave me my breakfast, and I swore then, by the stopple of my	175
	tankard, if ever I came to be Lord Mayor of London, I would feast
	all the prentices. This day, my liege, I did it, and the slaves had an
	hundred tables five times covered. They are gone home and vanished.
	Yet add more honour to the Gentle Trade:
	Taste of Eyre's banquet; Simon's happy made.	180
KING: Eyre, I will taste of thy banquet, and will say
	I have not met more pleasure on a day.
	Friends of the gentle craft, thanks to you all.
	Thanks, my Lady Mayoress, for our cheer.
	Come, lords, a while let's revel it at home;	185
	When all our sports and banqueting are done,
	Wars must right wrongs which Frenchmen have begun.

Exeunt.

Finis

Notes to the Play

Parts in the Play (Not in Q)

Simon EYRE: was elected Lord
Mayor of London in 1445; died
1458
KING: historically speaking, this
should be Henry VI, although
he is not named as such in
the play

To All Good Fellows …

14 three men's songs: songs for a
trio of performers

The First Three-Man's Song

8 breast … briar: proverbially, the
song of the nightingale was
caused by the pain of a thorn
in its breast
9 cuckoo: associated with
cuckoldry

The Second Three-Man's Song

2 Saint Hugh: patron saint of
shoemakers
5 troll: pass round
12 ring … joy: let joy inhabit the
full range

Prologue

4 goddess: i.e. Elizabeth I
8 strike: lower
10 hap: circumstance

Scene One

5 cousin: kinsman
6 affected: attracted
15 doubt: mistrust
21 bills of exchange: promissory
notes
27 embezzled: squandered

38 fox … subtlety: proverbial
46 his Grace: the King
49 wars of France: England was at
war with France from 1413
onwards
53 powers: forces
56 forwardness: readiness
58–61 Mile End … Finsbury: military
training grounds in and
around London
63 imprest: pay
furniture: military equipment
65 Guildhall: London's
administrative centre
66 brethren: fellow aldermen
67 approve: prove
77 painted: i.e. with cosmetics
85 start … bias: deviate from the
natural course (a bowling
image)
90 portagues: Portuguese gold
coins
99 o'er-reach his policies: outwit
his schemes
110 higher consequence: more
important activities
114 jealous: watchful
116 piece: gun
118 puling: whining
122 cavaliers and the colonels:
horsemen and colonels,
i.e. officers
124 pishery-pashery: nonsense
124 best presence: greatest dignity
127 mad: madcap
130 firking: lively, sporting; here
and throughout, has overtones
of 'fucking'
136 cormorant: malapropism for
'colonel'; invokes a predatory
bird
139–40 prick … awl: tools of the
shoemaker's trade, but also
suggesting 'penis' and 'hole'
141 undone: i.e. fucked
143 occupied: used for sex
145 pressed: conscripted
150 within … marriage: cf.
Deuteronomy 24.5: 'when a
man taketh a new wife, he shall
not go to warfare … but shall be

151   free at home one year, and rejoice with his wife which he hath taken'

151   melancholy: reflective
       Grammercy: many thanks

152–3   stand so stiffly: act so harshly (also punning on erection)

153   case: also suggests the vagina

156   polls … edipolls: nonsense talk

157   Cicely Bumtrinket: derogatory nickname for Eyre's wife

158   horns: sign of cuckoldry

162   dankish: soggy

163   hackney: hired drudge

163   Termagant: an imagined Muslim deity in the medieval drama, depicted as ruthlessly violent

164   lord of Ludgate: refers to the legendary origins of one of the entrances to the City of London, reputedly built by its founder, King Lud

164   tall: brave

165   dapper: smart

169   gull: fool

179   gimlet: shoemaker's boring tool; penis

179   weak vessels: i.e. women

182   Stays: waits

186   parasite: servant

187   arrant'st: most shameless

189   pickthank: sycophantic

194   hie … colours: join your regiment

201   cracked … tokens: worthless coinage

207   bombast … quean: a combination of sexist badinage and compliment, indicating that Jane would be best advised to stick to spinning in Rafe's absence

210   cordwainers: leather-workers

210–11   Saint Martin's … Whitechapel: areas where shoemakers were to be found

212   crowns: heads. A 'French crown' (i.e. baldness) was also the sign of sexually-transmitted disease

215   sorrow is dry: proverbial

216   *basa mon cues*: cod-French for *baisez mon culs*: (kiss my arse)

217   heavy: sad

218   slops: baggy breeches
       French crowns: gold coins

232   moe: more

Scene Two

4   gilliflowers: wallflowers

9   loured: frowned

18   against: in preparation for when

18–19   Lady of the Harvest: an honorary role given to a young woman at harvesttime

23   Doctors' Commons: lodgings for Doctors at the College of Law in the area of St Paul's

26   Out of cry: beyond all measure

27   scarf: worn as a favour from a lover

29   Old Ford: a village three miles from London, north-east of St Paul's

31   Cornhill: location of Oatley's town house

32   Marry … wanion: expression of impatience: 'Marry' means 'by Mary'; 'with a wanion' means 'with a vengeance'

33   humorous: temperamental

38   stamped crabs: crushed crab-apples

39   verjuice: juice of unripe fruit

40   much … netherstocks: possibly proverbial; suggesting superficial acquaintance

42   go … by: quoted from Kyd, *Spanish Tragedy*, 3.12.31

43   driblets: small amounts of money

50   snick-up: hang

54   cambric: fine linen
       Romish: Italian leather

55   stomacher: ornamental covering for the chest

57   at whose suit: i.e. need you ask?

59   sweat in purple: undergo physical labour in the clothes of an aristocrat

60   'a God's name: for nothing

61	up-tails all: i.e. let's move it
61	jiggy-joggy: with a jolting movement

Scene Three

6	only happy presence: only presence in which I am happy
11	bareness: poverty
22	sprites: spirits

Scene Four

2	brewis: broth
4	powder-beef queans: 'powder beef' is beef salted for preservation; 'queans' are prostitutes
4	Madge Mumblecrust: featured in Udall's *Ralph Roister Doister*
9	speak ... bedlam: speak like a mad dog and madman
13	Wash ... blessed: possibly proverbial
15	souse-wife: a woman who pickled pigs' offal for eating
20	brave: fine
	towards: to come
30	yawling: yelling
35–40	*Der ... mannekin*: There was a boor from Gelderland/Merry they are/He was so drunk he could not stand/Drunk they all are/Fill up the cannikin/Drink, my fine manikin.
42	Saint Hugh's bones: shoemakers' tools
43	uplandish: foreign
44	gibble-gabble: nonsense talk
46	enow: enough
49	butterbox: derogatory term for a Dutchman, since the Dutch were believed to consume inordinate quantities of butter
59–60	prick ... walls: down tools
62	pudding-broth: water in which pudding or sausage has been boiled
63	gallimaufry: hotch-potch
65	*Goeden ... auch*: Good day, master, and you, mistress, also

66	Nails: God's nails (invoking the nails used in the crucifixion)
68	*Yaw ... skomaker*: Yes, yes, I am a shoemaker
70–2	rubbing-pin ... thumb-leathers: shoemakers' tools
74–5	*Yaw ... clean*: Yes, yes, do not be afraid. I have all the things to make shoes large and small
78	mystery: craft
79	*Ik ... niet*: I know not what you say. I understand you not
81	*Yaw ... done*: Yes, yes, yes; I can do that well
83	double: extra-strength
90	trullibubs: literally, entrails; suggesting obesity
93	Gargantua: voracious giant of French folklore
96–7	*O ... freelick*: O, I understand you. I must pay for half a dozen cans. Here, boy, take this shilling, fill up merrily
98	snipper-snapper: whipper-snapper
99	last of the fives: last for small-sized shoes
100	Have to thee: cheers
101	mad ... Trojans: proverbial expressions for hard-drinking, hard-working companions
106	Clapper Dudgeon: beggar
107	soused conger: pickled conger eel
108	Hyperboreans: according to Greek legend, a people who lived beyond the reach of the North wind

Scene Five

1	brake: thicket
6	take soil: hide in a muddy pool, for refuge
7	embossed: exhausted

Scene Six

1	prove: become
2	Upon some: by no means

4	go by: get away with you wot: know	35	meddle with: interfere with; sexually molest
11	have … you: have a word with you	36	Queen of Clubs: troublemaker; rioting apprentices would traditionally
12	O gross: how stupid		shout 'clubs' as a rallying-cry
16	Wounds: God's wounds	39	use: deal with; fuck
21	horns: associated with cuckoldry	44	kitchen-stuff: kitchen waste
		46	sort: group
27	Come up: get lost	48	venentory: malapropism for
	honeysops: bread pieces soaked in honey		'inventory'
25	Impale me: fence me in; fuck me	51	more … Malkin: proverbial: i.e. there are plenty more where they came from
40	Sith: since	53–4	guts … shoe-thread: proverbial

Scene Seven

		55–6	Turk … Finsbury: proverbial for a change of character;
1–5	*Ik … Hans*: I'll tell you what, Hans: this ship that came from Candy [Crete] is full, by God's sacrament, of sugar, civet [perfume], almonds, cambric, and all things, a thousand, thousand things. Take it, Hans, take it for your master; there are the bills of lading [paperwork]. Your master Simon Eyre shall have a good bargain. What say you, Hans?		images of Turks were used for archery target practice in the fields at Finsbury
		59	Rip: run
		59–60	brown bread tannikin: brown bread was less refined than white; tannikin was a diminutive of Anne or Anna
		61	Eastcheap: known for its butchers
		66	chitterling: pig's offal
7–9	*Mine … Hodge*: My dear brother Firk, bring Master Eyre to the Sign of the Swan; there shall you find this skipper and me. What say you, brother Firk? Do it, Hodge	66–7	Boar's Head: a number of London inns had this name
		71	Mesopotamians: the phrase has no particular significance other than its mock-heroic quality
11	worth … of: whose cargo is worth	76	deal with: (with sexual connotation)
11	two … pounds: a fantastically inflated figure in Elizabethan terms	80	Yark: stitch
		82	from the bias: off the point
		84	give earnest: make a deposit
20	porpentines: porcupines (malapropism for 'portagues')	89	cypress: fabric
		92–3	seal-ring … cassock: accoutrements of an Alderman; 'guarded': embroidered
20	earnest penny: deposit		
22	Saint Mary Overy's: a church in Southwark	94	mad Philistines: again, a phrase with no special significance
25	Monday's … holiday: the shoemakers' traditional day off	96	as … doublet: proverbial for misguided vanity
26	beshrew: curse	97	beaten: embroidered
29	take down: rebuke (also implies 'fuck')	98	for rearing of: in order not to raise
32	take … lower: proverbial: 'take her down a peg'	102	give … wall: let you pass away from the centre of the street

103	right worshipful: appropriate form of address to an Alderman
105	dressed: decorated
107	brisk: smart
110	but only for: but only in
113–14	*Godden … it*: Good day, master; this is the skipper that has the ship of merchandise; the commodity is good: take it, master, take it.
115	Godamercy: thank you
117–19	*De … copen*: The ship is in the river; there are sugar, civet, almonds, cambric, and a thousand thousand things. By God's sacrament, take it, master: you shall have a good bargain
121	brave fatting meat: fine fattening food
125	*Yaw … drunck*: Yes, yes, I have drunk well
127	countenance: favour
128	quoth 'a: says he
129	veal: mishearing of 'veale'
129	thick: extra-strength
132	rising … flesh: i.e. erection
136	pull him down: humiliate him; cause him to lose his erection

Scene Eight

9	name: noble birth
10	Hyam … Ardington: fictional, not historical, personages
19	advised: sure
29	Since … estimate: since he regards my love as worthless
42	credit: finances; reputation
44	to his: for his

Scene Nine

15	If … frail: proverbial
19	sport: joke
20	Square: quarrel
22	strange in fancying: reluctant to fancy
24	fond: foolish
25	quit: requite
34–5	If … wife: cf. Corinthians 7.8

39	end: purpose
40	pule: whine
44	spoil: adventure
51	the Old 'Change: the Old Exchange, near St Paul's
56	mammet: doll (a term of abuse directed at young women)
57	coyness: reluctance
59	strait: strictly
88	keeps: lives
95	start him: drive him out
97	angels: gold coins
106	stay: await

Scene Ten

6	forswear: leave
8	compendious: concise
9–10	like … cartwheel: with high-pitched squeaking, that is, affectedly
11	scalding: cleansing. Ale bottles were made of leather
15	dame – mistress: the correction signals her new status
19	*Mee … vro*: I thank you, madam
21	perdie: by God
23	back friend: false friend
25	*Yaw … vro*: Yes, I will, madam length … foot: both literal and proverbial, as in 'you know how to please me'
28	cork … heel: fashionable means of adding height
30	farthingale: a hooped petticoat
31	French-hood: a pleated hood
33	cat … pillory: prostitute undergoing the punishment of being pilloried
34	all … grass: proverbial
35	hair: hair-piece
36	Gracious Street: Gracechurch Street, also called 'Grass Street'
41	fan … mask: fashionable accessories
47	*Ik … so*: I am happy, let's see you so
48	drink: smoke
50	idle: useless
50	baubles: worthless things; also suggests penis
54	tall: courageous

55	broder: brother
60	impotent: disabled
61	sunburnt: also suggests infection by sexually-transmitted disease
63	France: syphilis was known as the French disease
78	stately: haughty
80	ka me, ka thee: proverbial: I'll help you as you help me
84	opened her case: confided ('case' also means vagina)
87	*Yaw ... vro*: Yes, I shall, madam
89–90	naked ... return: cf. Job 1.21
91–2	pull ... heart: take heart
93	brave: fine
97	worshipful: honourable
102	smug: smarten
104	cry of the country: popular vote
106	voices: votes
107	presently: immediately
110	Shrieve: Sheriff
111	*Yaw ... shrieve*: Yes, my master is the great man, the Sheriff
117	rose: roses were embossed upon threepences to distinguish them from lower-denomination coins
118	pulingly: affectedly
122	cry twang: make a twanging sound indicating satisfaction
128	flap ... mutton: the flap of the French hood
131	hundred for twenty: Lacy's loan is to be returned fivefold
141	crotchets: entertainments

Scene Eleven

12	A fig for: so much for
13	scarlet gown: ceremonial gown worn by the Lord Mayor and Aldermen
16	flip-flap: nonsense talk
16	gulleries: tricks
21–2	pound ... debt: proverbial
22–3	sack and sugar: sweetened wine, associated with the aged
31	ape: fool
34	fine cockney: impudent child
35	coxcomb: fool
39	Wash: kitchen waste, urine
39	pishery-pashery: fripperies

41	marry me: you ought to marry
45	pack: leave
46	*tabor*: a small drum
60	*Ik ... frister*: I thank you, good maid
62	properest: best
63	done their parts: performed (with a sexual innuendo)
67	Stratford Bow: Stratford-le-Bow, a village five miles from St Paul's
69	tickle it: go for it
79	policies: schemes

Scene Twelve

1	*muffled*: disguised *aloof*: to one side
7	still love one: always am in love with someone
10	curious: cautious, choosy
14	happy work: lucky needlework (to be handled by Jane)
23	bands: decorative trimmings
25	How do you sell: how much for
34	wound this cloth: i.e. with the needle
46	fray: timidity, wrangling
64	very trade: full-time occupation
71	fruit ... fall: alludes to the story of Tantalus
75	by wanting: because lacking
85	place: high rank
95	bill: letter
110	rude: rough

Scene Thirteen

0	*at his shop board*: presumably a sign is brought on to indicate Eyre's workplace
1	Hey ... derry: possibly one of the Three-Man's songs is sung here
7	*Yaw, mester*: Yes, master
10–11	*Forware ... boots*: For sure, Firk, you are a jolly youngster. Hey you, master, I bid you cut me a pair of vamps [part of the shoe] for Master Jeffrey's boots

16	counterfeits: copies
	pass current: come up to
	standard; appear genuine
19	aunts: whores
25	yarked and firked: stitched; fucked
26	this ... hold: this (the shoe, Rafe's sexual capacity, Firk's singing voice) won't do
30	of that nature: oatmeal was thought of particularly high quality
30	bag-puddings: skins filled with meat and oatmeal
40	Syb-whore: friendly abuse
44	That ... have: there's more where that came from
48	God's me: God save me
51	*Vat ... frister*: What do you want, what would you, maiden?
52	pull on: try on
54	Vare ... mistress: Where is your noble lady, where is your mistress?
55	Cornwall: Cornhill
56	serve her turn: do as well; sexually satisfy her
59	trick ... budget: something in my bag; also suggests a sexual 'trick', while 'budget' is another term for 'vagina'
61	*Yaw ... gane*: Yes, yes, I'll go with you

Scene Fourteen

1	sign of the Last: indicating a shoemaker's business
5	against: in time for
7–8	at any hand: whatever you do
20	Golden Ball: the name of an inn Watling Street: known for its drapers, near St Paul's
28	Saint ... Paul's: a chapel in the crypt of St Paul's
36	countryman: neighbour
38	thing: sexual organ
42	mere: complete
46	pricked: pierced
48	murrain: plague
63	I ... die: proverbial
65	Cripplegates: one of the gates in the City of London walls
67–8	wedding ... destiny: proverbial

Scene Fifteen

2	cross: adverse
25	want: deficient in
30–1	*Forware ... betallen*: Indeed, mistress, 'tis a good shoe, it will do well, or you shall not pay for it
34	fit: also suggests 'fuck', presumably unintentionally
36–7	*Yaw ... heer*: Yes, yes, I know that well. Indeed, 'tis a good shoe, 'tis made of neat's [cow's] leather, just look, my lord
41	come to speak:Q has 'come speake'
51	presently: immediately

Scene Sixteen

1	credit: reputation
7	given head: authorised; encouraged
18	conference ... of: contact with
35	scud: scurry
44	honnikin: obscure; possibly a derogatory term for a Dutchman
51	lubber: lout
53	as fit ... pudding: from the proverbial 'as fit as a pudding for a friar's mouth'
63	moved ... stir: implies anger as well as movement
66	Sit ... merry: farewell
66	bob: fool
69–70	maw ... gear: taste for this business
73	Rogero: a popular tune
76	have him: know him
79	shaking ... sheets: a song title, suggesting vigorous action in bed
79	diggers: interrogators
82	in sadness: seriously
85	of: upon
87	feeling: i.e. money in his hand
87–8	*aurium ... genuum tenus*: up to the ears ... up to the knees, i.e. how much of the truth will be revealed for successive payments of gold and silver
89	stretchers: shoe stretchers; lies

92	No point: by no means		14	Saracen's head: familiar from
93	corporation: guild			inn signs; also used for target
98	Huswife: hussy			practice
99	Pitchers ... mouths:		21	buff-jerkin varlets: sheriff's
	proverbial			officers
101	gear: business		24	countenance: witness
101	rush: a worthless thing; rushes		25	Hamborrow: Hamburg (the
	were strewn on floors and on			allusion has no obvious
	stage platforms			significance)
102	firkin: small keg		27	minced-pies: pies filled with
104–5	London Stone: large stone close			minced meat
	by St Swithin's Church in		27	marchpane: marzipan
	Candlewick (now Cannon)		34	Avaunt: be gone
	Street, and a well-known		36	careful: full of cares
	landmark		39	my new buildings: Leadenhall
105	pissing conduit: a leaky water-		41–2	mad Cappadocians: a
	conduit at the corner of			nonsensical appellation
	Cornhill, Threadneedle Street		46	pancake bell: church bell tolled
	and Lombard Street			on Shrove Tuesday
105–6	pure Mother Bunch: weak beer		47	Assyrian: another nonsense
	supplied by a well-known			term for Eyre's staff
	alehouse hostess			

Scene Eighteen

109–10	swearing church: a church			
	whose name could be used as		2	bloods: brotherhood
	an oath		4–5	delve ... close: dig your patch,
113	incony: fine			with a sexual innuendo
123	Refrain: restrain		5	sufferance: consent
125	what else: anything else		18	Hammon nor hangman:
126	betimes: early			alludes to the book of Esther's
126–7	hey ... repass: sleight of hand			Hamon, who was hanged on
	pindy-pandy: handy-dandy,			the gallows he built himself
	the game of hiding an object in		24	rude: rough
	one hand and then inviting the		32	bird-spits: rapiers
	other player to choose		37	strange: as if he were a stranger
140	coney-catched: tricked		44	pack: go
143	chop up: finalise		46	'Swounds: by God's wounds
143	the Savoy: pauper's hospital		54	affect: love
	with a chapel		56	weeds: clothes
147	mess: group		63	busk point: lace for tying the
148	the Woolsack: a tavern			bodice
148	cozen: trick		64	appurtenances: belongings
151	hold out tack: hold your own			(a legal term)
152	smocks: maidenheads		67	Bluecoat: servants wore blue
	for this jumbling: as a result of			livery
	this chaos		68	Shrove ... day: St George's
				day (23 April) was when
				servants were dismissed

Scene Seventeen

				to search for new
1	bully: friend			employment
9	Dainty ... me: opening line of a		69	for: for the sake of
	popular song		69–70	sheep's eye: amorous glance
10	stand: act as; get an erection		71	clouts: rags
13	cast ... teeth: thrown in my face			

72	no striving: nothing to be achieved
82	Sirrah: contemptuous form of address
83	commodity: gain
86	pelf: money
96	mask: worn by women to prevent sunburn
102	Mars … Venus: alludes to the liaison between Mars and Venus in classical mythology; also mock-astrological
116	Damask: a variety of rose
119	powers: soldiers
140	laced mutton: prostitute
142	journeyman villain: itinerant labourer, liable to prosecution for vagrancy
147	officers: liverymen
153	his Grace: the King
161	lammed … flouts: wacked them with insults
162	codpiece point: lacework holding the codpiece together
164	answered: resolved
172	Trill-lill: a drinking call
174	keep in: shut up
185	brewis: broth
185	dry fats: vats for storing dry goods
187	collops: bacon
187	scuttles: dishes
188	malt shovels: large shovels used for malt
194	incomprehensible: infinite
196–7	year of jubilee: annual holiday

Scene Nineteen

5	ensure: assure
6	state: position
10	with child: all expectation huff-cap: swaggerer
11	doubt: concern

Scene Twenty

2	cannibals: a grandiose reference to the shoemakers' meat-eating appetites
4	livery: liverymen

5	satin hoods: worn on ceremonial occasions
10	lambskins: purses
10	Rip: quickly
14	Avoid: move
15	Carouse … healths: drink deeply
22	tall: fine
22	beleaguer: besiege
22	shambles: meat stalls
23	Eastcheap: London's main meat market
23	chargers: serving dishes
31	new: just
41	Have done: enough
43	Islington white-pot: a pudding made from milk and eggs, associated with the dairies of Islington, then still a village, favoured for excursions by Londoners
45	hopper-arse: fat-arse
46	barley-pudding: a variety of sausage
46	broiled carbonado: grilled meat or fish
47	Mephistophilus: the devil, as depicted in Marlowe's *Doctor Faustus* (1592)
48	Mother Miniver-Cap: the Wife's cap is presumably edged with ermine
49	partlets: collars
49	flews: skirt-flaps
50	whirligigs: spinning tops
50	rub … alley: out of my way
51	Sultan … Tamburlaine: Eastern warlords, as depicted in Marlowe's *Tamburlaine the Great* (1587) and Kyd's *Solomon and Perseda* (1589–92)
54	frolic: merry freebooters: pirates

Scene Twenty One

1	fact: deed, i.e. of desertion, usually punishable by death
10	craft: guile

15	Dioclesian: a despotic Roman emperor	22	rubbing-brush: short-bristled brush
15	hump: obscure; possibly a version of 'harrumph' or 'ahem'	30–1	care … hairs: proverbial
		32	Apollo: icon of youthful male beauty
17	merry … pie: (proverbial) pie: magpie	38	spend: sacrifice
19	yonker: young man	44	degenerous: degenerate
21–2	King of Babylon: legendarily wealthy	74	offend: offend against
		87	bride: spouse (used of both genders)
22	Tamar Cham's beard: legendary oriental ruler, the subject of a lost play recorded by Henslowe in 1596, possibly represented with a prodigious property beard	140	Sometimes: previously
		141	as … emperor: proverbial
		163	banquet: dessert course at the end of a feast
		169	shroving: festivity

The Alchemist
A Comedy

BEN JONSON

When Ben Jonson wrote in one of the commendatory verses to the Shakespeare First Folio that the works of his former colleague were 'not just for an age, but for all time', he not only provided posterity with the universalising formula which would resonate throughout cultural history, but also unwittingly and, for his own reputation, more damagingly, implicitly supplied the terms of reference within which his own work would subsequently be judged (more often than not, against Shakespeare's). Jonson, unlike his literary colleague and rival, has generally been viewed as a writer whose immersion in his own age has prevented his plays (with a few partial exceptions) from transcending it: not only is his work steeped in socially and historically specific manners and beliefs, and organised according to a classical model of comic dramaturgy that Shakespeare, for one, largely chose to disregard, it is also explicitly and precisely localised in terms of its geographical setting and cultural milieu. *The Alchemist* was first published in quarto in 1612; as in the majority of Jonson's comedies written during the Jacobean period, this setting is the city of London, a locale which is imagined in the kind of vivid detail that hovers perpetually on the edge of the baroque: asserting that 'Our scene is London, 'cause we would make known/ No country's mirth is better than our own' (Prologue, 5–6), the play evokes that scene as an urban topography of roof-tiles and shop-signs, water-conduits and dungheap-choked alleyways, eating-houses, brothels and taverns, in which the steam from pie-shops mingles with the smoke of tobacco-vendors: each detail voraciously observed, itemised and ordered within the overall intellectual and poetic scheme. This hyper-real abundance of detail nonetheless operates within a rigid neoclassical framework: the action is confined to a single day and a tightly delimited space, inhabited by a trio of tricksters acing as a magnet for succession of knaves and fools; while the precise alignment of plot, dramatis personae and thematics is captured, in the play's Argument, in an acrostic which spells out its title. Not for Jonson the fantasy geography deplored by Sir Philip Sidney (see Introduction, pp. xi–xii): beyond the walls of the Blackfriars house which defines the action's sole location, offstage events occur within walking distance, in the streets and meeting-places of the city, the sites of customs, transactions and liaisons which range from the morally questionable to the quasi-legal to the downright criminal.

Jonson's perception of the city as a culture driven by the simultaneously dangerous, horrifying and thrilling energies of expansion and capital accumulation is realised in the motif of alchemy itself, which operates both as a literal practice of chicanery and as a metaphor for the multiple varieties of transformation with which the play is preoccupied. Unlike some of his less sceptical contemporaries, Jonson clearly regards alchemy, the ancient art of transforming base metals into gold, as no more than a confidence trick, albeit one which, in the hands of Face and Subtle, is executed with immense panache. Dazzling their willing victims with an arcane alchemical and astrological jargon which is as technically elaborate as it is utterly bogus, the tricksters play upon dreams of wisdom, wealth and sexual potency, promising to transform and transcend the base matter and circumstance of the everyday civic world; but the talk of furnaces and sand-baths is mere hot air, part of a virtuoso performance which eventually becomes the victim of its own ambition and ingenuity. One by one the dupes – Dapper, Drugger, Sir Epicure Mammon and Surly, Kastril and Dame Pliant, Ananias and Tribulation Wholesome – are drawn in, and kept in motion until the return of the absent master in the fifth act causes the elaborate juggling act to collapse. Face, Subtle and Doll's art is, in essence, that of performance; their capacity for mirroring, magnifying and manipulating the desires of their clients is implicitly paralleled with the practices of the medium in which the play operates, the theatre itself. The play's localisation is, in this respect, exact: the house in which the events of a single day in 1610 transpire is the venue of its first perform-ance, the Blackfriars playhouse, a space of illusions, dreams and trickery, where paying customers gather to be willingly fooled.

If there is a degree of ambivalence towards (or even distrust of) playhouse practice on Jonson's part, it is an aspect of his generally sceptical and pessimistic outlook, in that the theatre's penchant for duplicity and shape-shifting is seen as part of a more general cultural malaise, characterised by the erosion and unsettling of traditional boundaries and hierarchies. As a satirist, Jonson is con-servative: his perception that early modern capitalism's machinery of desire is fuelled by qualities of viciousness, greed and folly that are innate in human nature suggests that his stated faith in the comedy's potential to reform its spectators is, at best, nominal. The conservatism of Jonson's satire is most evident in his treat-ment of the Anabaptists: although in historical reality this was a radical sect which experimented with communitarian ideas, advocating the abolition of private property and challenging social and ecclesiastical hierarchies, Jonson represents them as hypocritical fundamentalists, no less venal than the rest. Nor does Lovewit's return in the final act restore any kind of moral equi-librium or poetic justice: Doll and Subtle have absconded to the far outskirts of London; the hapless victims of their roguery are left impotently demanding restitution; while the chief architect of the scam, Face, remains unpunished in the household, ready once again 'to feast you often, and invite new guests' (5.5.165).

Following its first staging at the Blackfriars by the King's Men in 1610, *The Alchemist* was performed at Court in 1612–13, and again in 1621; there were performances in 1631 and 1639. After the Restoration it proved immediately popular: there were at least three performances on London stage in 1661 (Pepys wrote in his diary that it was 'a most incomparable play'), and from then on it remained a staple of the repertoire until towards the end of the eighteenth century (the part of Drugger was one of Garrick's celebrated roles). In 1770 Francis Gentleman published his redaction, *The Tobacconist*, and then the play was not seen again until the amateur revival by the Elizabethan Stage Society at the Apothecaries' Hall in 1899, which opted to present the play in facsimile Elizabethan performance conditions. *The Alchemist* was regularly revived throughout the twentieth century, notably in 1932 at the Malvern Festival, at the Old Vic in 1947 (and again,

in Tyrone Guthrie's modern dress production in 1962), and by
the Royal Shakespeare Company in 1977 and 1991.

Further reading

Barton, Ann, *Ben Jonson, Dramatist* (Cambridge: Cambridge University
    Press, 1984).
Burt, Richard, *Licensed by Authority: Ben Jonson and the Discourses of
    Censorship* (Ithaca: Cornell University Press, 1993).
Cave, Richard, *Ben Jonson*, English Dramatists (Basingstoke: Macmillan,
    1991).
Cave, Richard, Elizabeth Schafer and Brian Woolland (eds), *Ben Jonson
    and Theatre: Performance, Practice and Theory* (London: Routledge,
    1999).
Chedzgoy, Kate, Julie Sanders and Sue Wiseman (eds), *Refashioning Ben
    Jonson: Gender, Politics and the Jonsonian Canon* (Basingstoke:
    Macmillan, 1998).
Cook, Elizabeth (ed.), *The Alchemist*, Second Edition, New Mermaids
    (London: Ernest Benn, 1991).
Dutton, Richard, *Ben Jonson: Authority: Criticism* (Basingstoke:
    Macmillan, 1996).
Harp, Richard and Stanley Stewart (eds), *The Cambridge Companion to
    Ben Jonson* (Cambridge: Cambridge University Press, 2000).
Herford, C. H., Percy and Evelyn Simpson (eds), *Ben Jonson*, 11 vols
    (Oxford: Oxford University Press, 1925–52).
Jensen, Ejner J., *Ben Jonson's Comedies on the Modern Stage* (Ann Arbor:
    UMI Research Press, 1985).
Kay, W. D., *Ben Jonson: A Literary Life* (Basingstoke: Macmillan, 1995).
Mares, F. H. (ed.), *The Alchemist*, The Revels Plays (Manchester:
    Manchester University Press, 1967).
Sanders, Julie, *Ben Jonson's Theatrical Republics* (Basingstoke: Macmillan,
    1998).
Peter Womack, *Ben Jonson*, Rereading Literature (Oxford: Blackwell,
    1986).

TO THE LADY, MOST DESERVING HER NAME, AND
BLOOD: MARY, LADY WROTH.*

MADAM,

In the age of sacrifices, the truth of religion was not in the greatness and fat of
the offerings, but in the devotion and zeal of the sacrificers; else, what could
a handful of gums* have done in the sight of a hecatomb?* Or how might I
appear at this altar, except with those affections that no less love the light
and witness than they have the conscience* of your virtue? If what I offer 5
bear an acceptable odour, and hold the first strength, it is your value of it,
which remembers where, when, and to whom it was kindled. Otherwise, as
the times are, there comes rarely forth such a thing, so full of authority or
example, but by assiduity and custom grows less, and loses. This, yet, safe
in your judgement (which is a Sidney's) is forbidden to speak more; lest it 10
talk, or look like one of the ambitious faces of the time; who, the more they
paint,* are less themselves.

Your Ladyship's true honourer,

BEN JONSON.

TO THE READER

If thou beest more, thou art an understander, and then I trust thee. If thou art one that takest up, and but a pretender, beware at what hands thou receivest thy commodity; for thou wert never more fair in the way to be cozened (than in this age) in poetry, especially in plays: wherein, now, the concupiscence of jigs and dances so reigneth, as to run away from nature, and be afraid of her, is the only point of art that tickles the spectators. But how out of purpose, and place, do I name art? When the professors* are grown so obstinate contemners of it, and presumers on their own naturals,* as they are deriders of all diligence that way, and, by simple mocking at the terms, when they understand not the things, think to get off wittily with their ignorance. Nay, they are esteemed the more learned, and sufficient for this, by the multitude, through their excellent vice of judgment. For they commend writers as they do fencers or wrestlers; who if they come in robustiously, and put for it with a great deal of violence, are received for the braver fellows: when many times their own rudeness is the cause of their disgrace, and a little touch of their adversary gives all that boisterous force the foil.* I deny not, but that these men, who always seek to do more than enough, may some time happen on something that is good, and great; but very seldom: and when it comes it doth not recompense the rest of their ill.* It sticks out, perhaps, and is more eminent, because all is sordid, and vile about it: as lights are more discerned in a thick darkness than a faint shadow. I speak not this out of a hope to do good on any man against his will; for I know if it were put to the question of theirs and mine, the worse would find more suffrages: because the most favour common errors. But I give thee this warning, that there is a great difference between those that (to gain the opinion of copie*) utter all they can, however unfitly; and those that use election, and a mean.* For it is only the disease of the unskilful to think rude things greater than polished, or scattered more numerous than composed.

The Persons of the Play

SUBTLE, *the Alchemist*
FACE, *the Housekeeper*
DOLL, *their colleague*
DAPPER, *a clerk*
DRUGGER, *a Tobacco-man*   5
LOVEWIT, *master of the House*
EPICURE MAMMON, *a Knight*
SURLY, *a Gamester*
TRIBULATION, *a Pastor of Amsterdam*
ANANIAS, *a Deacon There*   10
KASTRIL,* *the Angry Boy*
DAME PLIANT, *his Sister, a Widow*
NEIGHBOURS
OFFICERS
MUTES   15

Scene: *London*

The Argument

T he sickness* hot, a master quit, for fear,
H is house in town, and left one servant there.
E ase him corrupted, and gave means to know
A cheater and his punk,* who, now brought low,
L eaving their common practice, were become   5
C ozeners* at large; and, only wanting some
H ouse to set up, with him they here contract
E ach for a share, and all begin to act.
M uch company they draw, and much abuse,
I ncanting figures,* telling fortunes, news,   10
S elling of flies,* flat bawdry, with the Stone;*
T ill it, and they, and all in fume* are gone.

Prologue

Fortune, that favours fools, these two short hours
We wish away; both for your sakes, and ours,
Judging spectators: and desire in place
To th'author justice, to ourselves but grace.
Our scene is London, 'cause we would make known   5
No country's mirth is better than our own.
No clime breeds better matter, for your whore
Bawd, squire,* impostor, many persons more,
Whose manners, now called humours,* feed the stage;
And which have still been subject for the rage   10
Or spleen of comic writers. Though this pen
Did never aim to grieve, but better* men;
Howe'er the age he lives in doth endure
The vices that she breeds, above their cure.
But when the wholesome remedies are sweet,   15
And, in their working, gain and profit meet,
He hopes to find no spirit so much diseased,
But will, with such fair correctives,* be pleased.
For here, he doth not fear who can apply.*
If there be any that will sit so nigh   20
Unto the stream, to look what it doth run,
They shall find things they'd think, or wish, were done;
They are so natural follies, but so shown,
As even the doers may see, and yet not own.

Act One, Scene One

[*Enter*] FACE, SUBTLE, DOLL.

FACE: Believe it, I will.
SUBTLE: Thy worst. I fart at thee.
DOLL: Ha' you your wits? Why, gentlemen! For love –
FACE: Sirrah, I'll strip you –
SUBTLE: What to do? Lick figs*
    Out at my –
FACE: Rogue, rogue, out of all your sleights!
DOLL: Nay, look ye! Sovereign, General, are you madmen?   5
SUBTLE: O let the wild sheep loose. I'll gum your silks
    With good strong water, an you come.
DOLL: Will you have
    The neighbours hear you? Will you betray all?
    Hark, I hear somebody.
FACE: Sirrah –
SUBTLE: I shall mar
    All that the tailor has made* if you approach.   10
FACE: You most notorious whelp! You insolent slave,
    Dare you do this?
SUBTLE: Yes, faith; yes, faith.
FACE: Why, who
    Am I, my mongrel? Who am I?
SUBTLE: I'll tell you,
    Since you know not yourself –
FACE: Speak lower, rogue.
SUBTLE: Yes. You were once (time's not long past) the good,   15
    Honest, plain, livery-three-pound-thrum;* that kept
    Your master's worship's house, here in the Friars*
    For the vacations –
FACE: Will you be so loud?
SUBTLE: Since, by my means, translated suburb-captain –
FACE: By your means, Doctor Dog?
SUBTLE: Within man's memory,   20
    All this, I speak of.
FACE: Why, I pray you, have I
    Been countenanced by you? Or you, by me?
    Do but collect, sir, where I met you first.
SUBTLE: I do not hear well.
FACE: Not of this, I think.
    But I shall put you in mind, sir, at Pie Corner.*   25

Taking your meal of steam in from cooks' stalls,
Where, like the father of hunger, you did walk
Piteously costive,* with your pinched-horn nose,
And your complexion of the Roman wash,*
Stuck full of black and melancholic worms,   30
Like powder corns, shot, at th'artillery yard.*
SUBTLE: I wish you could advance your voice a little.
FACE: When you went pinned up, in the several rags
You had raked and picked from dunghills before day,
Your feet in mouldy slippers for your kibes,*   35
A felt of rug,* and a thin threaden cloak
That scarce would cover your no-buttocks –
SUBTLE: So, sir!
FACE: When all your alchemy, and your algebra,
Your minerals, vegetals,* and animals,
Your conjuring, coz'ning, and your dozen of trades,   40
Could not relieve your corpse with so much linen
Would make you tinder, but to see a fire;
I ga'you count'nance, credit for your coals,
Your stills, your glasses, your materials;
Built you a furnace, drew you customers,   45
Advanced all your black arts; lent you, beside,
A house to practice in –
SUBTLE: Your master's house?
FACE: Where you have studied the more thriving skill
Of bawdry* since.
SUBTLE: Yes, in your master's house.
You, and the rats here, kept possession.   50
Make it not strange. I know, y'were one could keep
The buttery-hatch* still locked, and save the chippings,
Sell the dole-beer* to aqua-vitae men,*
The which, together with your Christmas vails*
At post-and-pair,* your letting out of counters   55
Made you a pretty stock, some twenty marks,
And gave you credit, to converse with cobwebs,
Here, since your mistress' death hath broke up house.
FACE: You might talk softlier, rascal.
SUBTLE: No, you scarab;*
I'll thunder you, in pieces. I will teach you   60
How to beware to tempt a fury again
That carries tempest in his hand and voice.
FACE: This place has made you valiant.
SUBTLE: No, your clothes.
Thou vermin, have I ta'en thee out of dung,
So poor, so wretched, when no living thing   65

Would keep thee company but a spider, or worse?
Raised thee from brooms, and dust, and wat'ring pots?
Sublimed thee, and exalted* thee, and fixed thee
I' the third region, called our state of grace?
Wrought thee to spirit, to quintessence, with pains   70
Would twice have won me the philosopher's work?
Put thee in words and fashion? Made thee fit
For more than ordinary fellowships?
Given thee thy oaths, thy quarrelling dimensions?*
Thy rules, to cheat at horse-race, cockpit, cards,   75
Dice, or whatever gallant tincture else?
Made thee a second in mine own great art?
And have I this for thank? Do you rebel?
Do you fly out, i'the projection?*
Would you be gone now?
DOLL: Gentlemen, what mean you?   80
    Will you mar all?
SUBTLE: Slave, thou hadst no name –
DOLL: Will you undo yourselves with civil war?
SUBTLE: Never been known, past *equi clibanum,**
    The heat of horse-dung, under ground, in cellars,
    Or an alehouse, darker than deaf John's: been lost   85
    To all mankind, but laundresses and tapsters,
    Had I not been.
DOLL: Do you know who hears you, Sovereign?
FACE: Sirrah –
DOLL: Nay, General, I thought you were civil –
FACE: I shall turn desperate, if you grow thus loud.
SUBTLE: And hang thyself, I care not.
FACE: Hang thee, collier,   90
    And all thy pots and pans, in picture I will,
    Since thou hast moved me –
DOLL: (O, this'll o'erthrow all.)
FACE: Write thee up bawd, in Paul's;* have all thy tricks
    Of coz'ning with a hollow coal,* dust, scrapings,
    Searching for things lost, with a sieve, and shears;   95
    Erecting figures in your rows of houses,
    And taking in of shadows with a glass,*
    Told in red letters: and a face, cut for thee,
    Worse than Gamaliel Ratsey's.*
DOLL: Are you sound?
    Ha' you your senses, masters?
FACE: I will have   100
    A book, but barely reckoning thy impostures
    Shall prove a true philosopher's stone to printers.

SUBTLE: Away, you trencher-rascal.*
FACE: Out, you dog-leech,
    The vomit of all prisons –
DOLL: Will you be
    Your own destructions, gentlemen?
FACE: Still spewed out   105
    For lying too heavy o' the basket.*
SUBTLE: Cheater.
FACE: Bawd.
SUBTLE: Cow-herd.
FACE: Conjurer.
SUBTLE: Cutpurse.
FACE: Witch.
DOLL: O me!
    We are ruined! Lost! Ha' you no more regard
    To your reputations? Where's your judgement? 'Slight,
    Have yet some care of me, o' your republic* –   110
FACE: Away this brach.* I'll bring thee, rogue, within
    The statute of sorcery, *tricesimo tertio*,
    Of Harry the eight,* ay, and (perhaps) thy neck
    Within a noose, for laund'ring gold, and barbing* it.
DOLL: You'll bring your head within a coxcomb, will you?
    She catcheth out FACE *his sword, and breaks* SUBTLE'S *glass*
    And you, sir, with your menstrue,* gather it up.
    'Sdeath, you abominable pair of stinkards,
    Leave off your barking, and grow one again,
    Or, by the light that shines, I'll cut your throats.
    I'll not be made a prey unto the marshal*   120
    For ne'er a snarling dog-bolt o' you both.
    Ha' you together cozened all this while
    And all the world, and shall it now be said
    Y' have made most courteous shift to cozen yourselves?
    You will accuse him? You will bring him in   125
    Within the statute? Who shall take your word?
    A whoreson, upstart, apocryphal* captain,
    Whom not a puritan in Blackfriars will trust
    So much as for a feather! And you, too,
    Will give the cause, forsooth? You will insult,   130
    And claim a primacy in the divisions?
    You must be chief? As if you only had
    The powder to project with?* And the work
    Were not begun out of equality?
    The venture tripartite? All things in common?   135
    Without priority? 'Sdeath, you perpetual curs,
    Fall to your couples* again, and cozen kindly,

And heartily, and lovingly, as you should,
And lose not the beginning of a term,*
Or, by this hand, I shall grow factious too, 140
And take my part, and quit you.
FACE: 'Tis his fault.
He ever murmurs, and objects his pains,
And says the weight of all lies upon him.
SUBTLE: Why, so it does.
DOLL: does it? Do not we
Sustain our parts?*
SUBTLE: Yes, but they are not equal. 145
DOLL: Why, if your part exceed today, I hope
Ours may tomorrow match it.
SUBTLE: Ay, they may.
DOLL: May, murmuring mastiff? Ay, and do. Death on me!
Help me to throttle him.
SUBTLE: Dorothy, Mistress Dorothy,
'Od's precious, I'll do anything. What do you mean? 150
DOLL: Because o' your fermentation and cibation?*
SUBTLE: Not I, by heaven –
DOLL: Your Sol, and Luna* – help me.
SUBTLE: Would I were hanged then. I'll conform myself.
DOLL: Will you, sir? Do so, then, and quickly: swear.
SUBTLE: What should I swear?
DOLL: To leave your faction,* sir. 155
labour kindly in the common work.
SUBTLE: Let me not breathe if I meant ought beside.
I only used those speeches as a spur
To him.
DOLL: I hope we need no spurs, sir. Do we?
FACE: 'Slid,* prove today who shall bark best.
SUBTLE: Agreed. 160
DOLL: Yes, and work close, and friendly.
SUBTLE: 'Slight,* the knot
Shall grow the stronger, for this breach, with me.
DOLL: Why so, my good baboons! Shall we go make
A sort* of sober, scurvy, precise* neighbours
(That scarce have smiled twice sin' the King came in*) 165
A feast of laughter at our follies? Rascals,
Would run themselves from* breath, to see me ride,*
Or you t' have but a hole* to thrust your heads in,
For which you should pay ear-rent?* No, agree.
And may Don Provost* ride a-feasting, long, 170
In his old velvet jerkin and stained scarves
(My noble Sovereign and worthy General)

Ere we contribute a new crewel* garter
To his most worsted* worship.
SUBTLE: Royal Doll!
    Spoken like Claridiana,* and thyself!   175
FACE: For which, at supper, thou shalt sit in triumph
    And not be styled Doll, but Doll Proper,
    Doll Singular; the longest cut,* at night,
    Shall draw thee for his Doll Particular.
SUBTLE: Who's that? One rings. To the window.
DOLL: Pray heav'n   180
    The master does not trouble us this quarter.
FACE: O, fear not him. While there dies one a week
    O' the plague, he's safe from thinking toward London.
    Beside, he's busy at his hop-yards now;
    I had a letter from him. If he do,   185
    He'll send such word for airing o' the house
    As you shall have sufficient time to quit it;
    Though we break up* a fortnight, 'tis no matter.
SUBTLE: Who is it, Doll?
DOLL: A fine young quodling.*
FACE: O,
    My lawyer's clerk I lighted on last night,   190
    In Holborn, at the Dagger.* He would have
    (I told you of him) a familiar*
    To rifle* with at horses, and win cups.
DOLL: O, let him in.
SUBTLE: Stay, who shall do't?
FACE: Get you
    Your robes on. I will meet him, as going out.   195
DOLL: And what shall I do?
FACE: Not be seen, away.   [*Exit* DOLL.]
    Seem you very reserved.
SUBTLE: Enough.
FACE: God be wi' you, sir.
    I pray you, let him know that I was here.
    His name is Dapper. I would gladly have stayed, but –

Act One, Scene Two

[*Enter* DAPPER.]

DAPPER: Captain, I am here.
FACE: Who's that? He's come, I think, Doctor.
    Good faith, sir, I was going away.

DAPPER: In truth,
  I'm very sorry, Captain.
FACE: But I thought
  Sure, I should meet you.
DAPPER: Ay, I am very glad.
  I had a scurvy writ or two to make, 5
  And that I had lent my watch last night, to one
  That dines today at the Sheriff's; and so was robbed
  Of my pastime. Is this the cunning man?
FACE: This is his worship.
DAPPER: Is he a doctor?
FACE: Yes.
DAPPER: And ha' you broke* with him, Captain?
FACE: Ay.
DAPPER: And how? 10
FACE: Faith, he does make the matter, sir, so dainty,*
  I know not what to say –
DAPPER: Not so, good Captain.
FACE: Would I were fairly rid on't, believe me.
DAPPER: Nay, now you grieve me, sir. Why should you wish so?
  I dare assure you I'll not be ungrateful. 15
FACE: I cannot think you will, sir. But the law
  I such a thing – and then, he says, Reade's* matter
  Falling so lately –
DAPPER: Reade? He was an ass,
  And dealt, sir, with a fool.
FACE: It was a clerk, sir.
DAPPER: A clerk?
FACE: Nay, hear me, sir: you know the law 20
  Better, I think –
DAPPER: I should, sir, and the danger.
  You know I showed the statute to you?
FACE: You did so.
DAPPER: And will I tell, then? By this hand of flesh,
  Would it might never write good court-hand* more
  If I discover. What do you think of me, 25
  That I am a *Chiaus*?*
FACE: What's that?
DAPPER: The Turk was here;
  As one would say, do you think I am a Turk?
FACE: I'll tell the Doctor so.
DAPPER: Do, good sweet Captain.
FACE: Come, noble Doctor; pray thee, let's prevail:
  This is the gentleman, and he is no *Chiaus*. 30
SUBTLE: Captain, I have returned you all my answer.

I would do much, sir, for your love – but this
In neither may, nor can.
FACE: Tut, do not say so.
    You deal, now, with a noble fellow, Doctor,
    One that will thank you richly, and he's no *Chiaus*.   35
    Let that, sir, move you.
SUBTLE: Pray you, forbear –
FACE: He has
    Four angels* here –
SUBTLE: You do me wrong, good sir.
FACE: Doctor, wherein? To tempt you with these spirits?
SUBTLE: To tempt my art, and love, sir, to my peril.
    'Fore heaven, I scarce can think you are my friend   40
    That so would draw me to apparent danger.
FACE: I draw you? A horse draw you, and a halter,*
    You and your flies* together –
DAPPER: Nay, good Captain.
FACE: That know no difference of men.
SUBTLE: Good words, sir.
FACE: Good deeds, sir, Doctor Dog's-meat. 'Slight, I bring you   45
    No cheating Clim o' the Cloughs or Claribels,*
    That look as big as five and fifty and flush,*
    And spit out secrets like hot custard –
DAPPER: Captain.
FACE: Nor any melancholic under-scribe
    Shall tell the Vicar;* but a special gentle   50
    That is the heir to forty marks* a year,
    Consorts with the small poets of the time,
    Is the sole hope of his old grandmother,
    That knows the law, and writes you six fair hands,
    Is a fine clerk, and has his cyph'ring perfect,   55
    Will take his oath, o' the Greek god Xenophon,*
    If need be, in his pocket; and can court
    His mistress out of Ovid.*
DAPPER: Nay, dear Captain.
FACE: Did you not tell me so?
DAPPER: Yes, but I'd ha' you
    Use Master Doctor with some more respect.   60
FACE: Hang him, proud stag, with his broad velvet head.*
    But for your sake I'd choke ere I would change
    An article of breath with such a puck-fist* –
    Come, let's be gone.
SUBTLE: Pray you, let me speak with you.
DAPPER: His worship calls you, Captain.

FACE: I am sorry   65
   I e'er embarked myself in such a business.
DAPPER: Nay, good sir. He did call you.
FACE: Will he take* then?
SUBTLE: First, hear me –
FACE: Not a syllable, 'less you take.
SUBTLE: Pray ye, sir –
FACE: Upon no terms but an *assumpsit*.*
SUBTLE: Your humour must be law.   *He takes the money.*
FACE: Why now, sir, talk.   70
   Now, I dare hear you with mine honour. Speak.
   So may this gentleman too.
SUBTLE: Why, sir –
FACE: No whisp'ring.
SUBTLE: 'Fore heav'n, you do not apprehend the loss
   You do yourself in this.
FACE: Wherein? For what?
SUBTLE: Marry, to be so importunate for one   75
   That, when he has it, will undo you all;
   He'll win up all the money in the town.
FACE: How!
SUBTLE: Yes. And blow up* gamester after gamester,
   As they do crackers* in a puppet-play.
   If I do give him a familiar,   80
   Give you him all you play for; never set* him,
   For he will have it.
FACE: Y'are mistaken, Doctor.
   Why, he does ask one but for cups, and horses,
   A rifling fly;* none o' your great familiars.
DAPPER: Yes, Captain; I would have it, for all games.   85
SUBTLE: I told you so.
FACE: 'Slight, that's a new business!
   I understood you, a tame bird, to fly
   Twice in a term or so; on Friday nights
   When you had left the office, for a nag
   Of forty or fifty shillings.
DAPPER: Ay, 'tis true, sir;   90
   But I do think, now, I shall leave the law,
   And therefore –
FACE: Why, this changes quite the case!
   Do you think that I dare move him?
DAPPER: If you please, sir,
   All's one to him, I see.
FACE: What! For that money?

I cannot with my conscience. Nor should you   95
  Make the request, methinks.
DAPPER: No, sir; I mean
  To add consideration.*
FACE: Why then, sir,
  I'll try. Say that it were for all games, Doctor?
SUBTLE: I say, then, not a mouth shall eat for him
  At any ordinary, but o' the score.*   100
  That is a gaming mouth, conceive me.
FACE: Indeed!
SUBTLE: He'll draw you all the treasure of the realm
  If it be set him.
FACE: Speak you this from art?*
SUBTLE: Ay, sir, and reason too; the ground of art.
  He's o' the only best complexion   105
  The Queen of Fairy loves.
FACE: What! Is he!
SUBTLE: Peace.
  He'll overhear you. Sir, should she but see him –
FACE: What?
SUBTLE: Do not you tell him.
FACE: Will he win at cards too?
SUBTLE: The spirits of dead Holland, living Isaac,*
  You'd swear were in him; such a vigorous luck   110
  As cannot be resisted. 'Slight, he'll put
  Six o' your gallants to a cloak,* indeed.
FACE: A strange success, that some man shall be born to!
SUBTLE: He hears you, man –
DAPPER: Sir, I'll not be ingrateful.
FACE: Faith, I have a confidence in his good nature;   115
  You hear, he says he will not be ingrateful.
SUBTLE: Why, as you please; my venture follows yours.*
FACE: Troth, do it, Doctor. Think him trusty, and make him.
  He may make us both happy* in an hour:
  Win some five thousand pound, and send us two on't.   120
DAPPER: Believe it, and I will, sir.
FACE: And you shall, sir.

                                               FACE *takes him aside.*
  You have heard all?
DAPPER: No, what was't? Nothing, I, sir.
FACE: Nothing?
DAPPER: A little, sir.
FACE: Well, a rare star
  Reigned at your birth.

DAPPER: At mine, sir? No.
FACE: The Doctor
    Swears that you are –
SUBTLE: Nay, Captain, you'll tell all now.   125
FACE: Allied to the Queen of Fairy.
DAPPER: Who? That I am?
    Believe it, no such matter –
FACE: Yes, and that
    You were born with a caul* o' your head.
DAPPER: Who says so?
FACE: Come,
    You know it well enough, though you dissemble it.
DAPPER: I'fac,* I do not. You are mistaken.
FACE: How!   130
    Swear by your fac? And in a thing so known
    Unto the Doctor? How shall we, sir, trust you
    I'the other matter? Can we ever think,
    When you have won five or six thousand pound,
    You'll send us shares in't, by this rate?
DAPPER: By Jove, sir,   135
    I'll win ten thousand pound, and send you half.
    I'fac's no oath.
SUBTLE: No, no; he did but jest.
FACE: Go to. Go, thank the Doctor. He's your friend
    To take it so.
DAPPER: I thank his worship.
FACE: So?
    Another angel.
DAPPER: Must I?
FACE: Must you? 'Slight,   140
    What else is thanks? Will you be trivial?* Doctor,
    When must he come for his familiar?
DAPPER: Shall I not ha' it with me?
SUBTLE: O, good sir!
    There must be a world of ceremonies pass,
    You must be bathed arid fumigated first;   145
    Besides, the Queen of Fairy does not rise
    Till it be noon.
FACE: Not if she danced tonight.
SUBTLE: And she must bless it.
FACE: Did you never see
    Her royal Grace yet?
DAPPER: Whom?
FACE: Your aunt of Fairy?

SUBTLE: Not since she kissed him in the cradle, Captain,   150
    I can resolve* you that.
FACE: Well, see her Grace,
    Whate'er it cost you, for* a thing that I know!
    It will be somewhat hard to compass, but,
    However, see her. You are made, believe it,
    If you can see her. Her Grace is a lone woman,   155
    And very rich, and if she take a fancy,
    She will do strange things. See her, at any hand.
    'Slid, she may hap to leave you all she has!
    It is the Doctor's fear.
DAPPER: How will it be done, then?
FACE: Let you alone, take you no thought. Do you   160
    But say to me: Captain, I'll see her Grace.
DAPPER: Captain, I'll see her Grace.
FACE: Enough.   *One knocks without.*
SUBTLE: Who's there?
    Anon. (Conduct him forth, by the back way.)
    Sir, against one o'clock prepare yourself.
    Till when you must be fasting: only take   165
    Three drops of vinegar in at your nose,
    Two at your mouth, and one at either ear;
    Then, bathe your fingers' ends, and wash your eyes
    To sharpen your five senses; and cry hum
    Thrice, and then buzz as often; and then come.   170
FACE: Can you remember this?
DAPPER: I warrant you.
FACE: Well then, away. 'Tis but your bestowing
    Some twenty nobles 'mong her Grace's servants;
    And put on a clean shirt:* you do not know
    What grace her Grace may do you in clean linen.   175
                     [*Exeunt* FACE *and* DAPPER.]

Act One, Scene Three

[*Enter* DRUGGER.]

SUBTLE: Come in. (Good wives, I pray you, forbear me now;
    Troth, I can do you no good till afternoon.)
    What is your name, say you, Abel Drugger?
DRUGGER: Yes, sir.
SUBTLE: A seller of tobacco?
DRUGGER: Yes, sir.

SUBTLE: 'Umh.
    Free of the Grocers?*
DRUGGER: Ay, and't please you.
SUBTLE: Well –   5
    Your business, Abel?
DRUGGER: This, and 't please your worship:
    I am a young beginner, and am building
    Of a new shop, and't like your worship, just
    At corner of a street. (Here's the plot* on't.)
    And I would know, by art, sir, of your worship,   10
    Which way I should make my door, by necromancy,
    And where my shelves. And which should be for boxes.
    And which for pots. I would be glad to thrive, sir.
    And I was wished* to your worship by a gentleman,
    One Captain Face, that says you know men's planets,*   15
    And their good angels, and their bad.
SUBTLE: I do.
    If I do see 'em –

[*Enter* FACE.]

FACE: What! My honest Abel?
    Thou are well met here!
DRUGGER: Troth, sir, I was speaking,
    Just as your worship came here, of your worship.
    I pray you, speak for me to master Doctor.   20
FACE: He shall do anything, Doctor, do you hear?
    This is my friend Abel, an honest fellow;
    He lets me have good tobacco, and he does not
    Sophisticate it with sack-lees* or oil,*
    Nor washes it in muscadel and grains,*   25
    Nor buries it in gravel underground,
    Wrapped up in greasy leather, or pissed clouts;*
    But keeps it in fine lily-pots,* that opened
    Smell like conserve of roses or French beans.
    He has his maple block, his silver tongs,   30
    Winchester pipes, and fire of juniper;*
    A neat, spruce-honest fellow, and no goldsmith.*
SUBTLE: He's a fortunate fellow, that I am sure on –
FACE: Already, sir, ha' you found it? Lo thee Abel!
SUBTLE: And in right way toward riches –
FACE: Sir.
SUBTLE: This summer   35
    He will be of the clothing* of his company,

And next spring called to the scarlet.* Spend what he can.
FACE: What, and so little beard?*
SUBTLE: Sir, you must think
   He may have a receipt, to make hair come.
   But he'll be wise, preserve his youth, and fine for't;   40
   His fortune looks for him another way.
FACE: 'Slid, Doctor, how canst thou know this so soon?
   I'm amused* at that!
SUBTLE: By a rule, Captain,
   In metoposcopy,* which I do work by;
   A certain star i' the forehead which you see not.   45
   Your chestnut or your olive-coloured face
   Does never fail, and your long ear doth promise.
   I knew't by certain spots, too, in his teeth,
   And on the nail of his mercurial finger.*
FACE: Which finger's that?
SUBTLE: His little finger. Look.   50
   Y'were born upon a Wednesday?
DRUGGER: Yes indeed, sir.
SUBTLE: The thumb, in chiromanty,* we give Venus;
   The forefinger to Jove, the midst to Saturn,
   The ring to Sol; the least, to Mercury,
   Who was the lord, sir, of his horoscope,   55
   His house of life being Libra, which foreshadowed
   He should be a merchant, and should trade with balance.*
FACE: Why, this is strange! Is't not, honest Nab?
SUBTLE: There is a ship now, coming from Ormus,*
   That shall yield him such a commodity   60
   Of drugs – this is the west, and this the south?
DRUGGER: Yes, sir.
SUBTLE: And those are your two sides?
DRUGGER: Ay, sir.
SUBTLE: Make me your door, then, south; your broad side west;
   And on the east side of your shop, aloft,
   Write *Mathlai*, *Tarmiel*, and *Baraborat*;   65
   On the north part, *Rael, Velel, Thiel*.*
   They are the names of those mercurial spirits
   That do fright flies from boxes.
DRUGGER: Yes, sir.
SUBTLE: And
   Beneath your threshold bury me a lodestone*
   To draw in gallants that wear spurs. The rest,   70
   They'll seem to follow.
FACE: That's a secret, Nab!

SUBTLE: And, on your stall, a puppet with a vice,*
    And a court-fucus,* to call city-dames.
    You shall deal much with minerals.
DRUGGER: Sir, I have
    At home, already –
SUBTLE: Ay, I know: you have arsenic,   75
    Vitriol,* sal-tartar,* argaile,* alkali,*
    Cinoper;* I know all. This fellow, Captain,
    Will come, in time, to be a great distiller,
    And give a say* (I will not say directly,
    But very fair) at the philosopher's stone.   80
FACE: Why, how now, Abel! Is this true?
DRUGGER: Good Captain,
    What must I give?
FACE: Nay, I'll not counsel thee.
    Thou hear'st what wealth (he says spend what thou canst)
    Th'art like to come to.
DRUGGER: I would gi' him a crown.
FACE: A crown! And toward such a fortune? Heart,   85
    Thou shalt rather gi' him thy shop. No gold about thee?
DRUGGER: Yes, I have a portague* I ha' kept this half year.
FACE: Out on thee, Nab. 'Slight, there was such an offer –
    'Shalt keep 't no longer; I'll gi' it him for thee?
    Doctor, Nab prays your worship to drink this, and swears   90
    He will appear more grateful, as your skill
    Does raise him in the world.
DRUGGER: I would entreat
    Another favour of his worship.
FACE: What is 't, Nab?
DRUGGER: But to look over, sir, my almanac,
    And cross out my ill* days, that I may neither   95
    Bargain nor trust* upon them.
FACE: That he shall, Nab.
    Leave it; it shall be done 'gainst* afternoon.
SUBTLE: And a direction for his shelves.
FACE: Now, Nab?
    Are you well pleased, Nab?
DRUGGER: Thank you, sir; both your worships.
FACE: Away.
                                    [*Exit* DRUGGER.]
    Why now, you smoky persecutor of nature!   100
    Now, do you see, that something's to be done
    Beside your beech-coal* and your cor'sive* waters,
    Your crosslets,* crucibles, and cucurbites?*

You must have stuff brought home to you to work on!
And yet you think I am at no expense   105
In searching out these veins, then following 'em,
Then trying 'em out. 'Fore God, my intelligence*
Costs me more money than my share oft comes to
In these rare works.
SUBTLE: You are pleasant, sir. How now?

Act One, Scene Four

[*Enter* DOLL.]

SUBTLE: What says my dainty Dollkin?
DOLL: Yonder fishwife
    Will not away. And there's your giantess,
    The bawd of Lambeth.*
SUBTLE: Heart, I cannot speak with 'em.
DOLL: Not afore night, I have told 'em, in a voice
    Thorough the trunk,* like one of your familiars.   5
    But I have spied Sir Epicure Mammon –
SUBTLE: Where?
DOLL: Coming along, at far end the lane,
    Slow of his feet, but earnest of his tongue,
    To one that's with him.
SUBTLE: Face, go you and shift.*   [*Exit* FACE.]
    Doll, you must presently* make ready too.   10
DOLL: Why, what's the matter?
SUBTLE: O, I did look for him
    With the sun's rising; marvel, he could sleep!
    This is the day I am to perfect for him
    The *magisterium*,* our great work, the stone;
    And yield it, made, into his hands, of which   15
    He has this month talked as he were possessed.
    And now he's dealing pieces on't away.*
    Methinks I see him entering ordinaries,
    Dispensing for the pox, and plaguey houses,
    Reaching his dose; walking Moorfields* for lepers;   20
    And offering citizens' wives pomander-bracelets*
    As his preservative, made of the elixir;
    Searching the 'spital,* to make old bawds young;
    And the highways for beggars to make rich;
    I see no end of his labours. He will make   25
    Nature ashamed of her long sleep; when art,

Who's but a stepdame, shall do more than she
In her best love to mankind ever could.
If his dream last, he'll turn the age to gold.   [*Exeunt.*]

Act Two, Scene One

[*Enter*] MAMMON, SURLY.

MAMMON: Come on, sir. Now, you set you foot on shore
    In *novo orbe*;* here's the rich Peru,
    And there within, sir, are the golden mines,
    Great Solomon's Ophir!* He was sailing to't
    Three years, but we have reached it in ten months.   5
    This is the day wherein to all my friends
    I will pronounce the happy word: be rich.
    This day you shall be *spectatissimi*.*
    You shall no more deal with the hollow die*
    Or the frail* card. No more be at charge of keeping   10
    The livery-punk for the young heir, that must
    Seal at all hours in his shirt. No more
    If he deny, ha' him beaten to't, as he is
    That brings him the commodity.* No more
    Shall thirst of satin, or the covetous hunger   15
    Of velvet entrails,* for a rude-spun cloak
    To be displayed at Madam Augusta's,* make
    The sons of sword and hazard* fall before
    The golden calf* and, on their knees, whole nights
    Commit idolatry with wine and trumpets;   20
    Or go a-feasting, after drum and ensign.
    No more of this. You shall start up* young viceroys,
    And have your punks and punketees,* my Surly.
    And unto thee I speak it first: be rich.
    Where is my Subtle, there? Within, ho!   25
FACE [*Within*]:   Sir,
    He'll come to you by and by.
MAMMON: That's his fire-drake,*
    His lungs,* his Zephyrus;* he that puffs his coals
    Till he firk* nature up, in her own centre.
    You are not faithful,* sir. This night I'll change
    All that is metal in my house to gold.   30
    And early in the morning will I send
    To all the plumbers and the pewterers,
    And buy their tin and lead up; and to Lothbury*

For all the copper.
SURLY: What, and turn that too?
MAMMON: Yes, and I'll purchase Devonshire and Cornwall,*   35
And make them perfect Indies!* You admire* now?
SURLY: No, faith.
MAMMON: But when you see th'effects of the great med'cine,*
Of which one part projected on a hundred
Of Mercury or Venus, or the Moon,
Shall turn it to as many of the Sun;*   40
Nay, to a thousand, so *ad infinitum*;
You will believe me.
SURLY: Yes, when I see't, I will.
But if my eyes do cozen me so (and I
Giving 'em no occasion), sure, I'll have
A whore shall piss 'em out next day.
MAMMON: Ha! Why?   45
Do you think I fable with you? I assure you,
He that has once the flower of the sun,
The perfect ruby, which we call elixir,*
Not only can do that, but by its virtue
Can confer honour, love, respect, long life;   50
Give safety, valour, yea, and victory
To whom he will. In eight and twenty days
I'll make an old man of fourscore a child.
SURLY: No doubt he's that already.
MAMMON: Nay, I mean
Restore his years, renew him like an eagle*   55
To the fifth age;* make him get sons and daughters,
Young giants; as our philosophers have done
(The ancient patriarchs* afore the flood)
But taking, once a week on knife's point,
The quantity of a grain of mustard of it;   60
Become stout Marses and beget young Cupids.
SURLY: The decayed Vestals of Pict-Hatch* would thank you,
That keep the fire alive there.
MAMMON: 'Tis the secret
Of nature naturised 'gainst all infections,
Cures all diseases, coming of all causes,   65
A month's grief in a day, a year's in twelve;
And of what age soever, in a month,
Past all the doses of your drugging doctors.
I'll undertake withal to fright the plague
Out o' the kingdom in three months.

SURLY: And I'll   70
  Be bound the players shall sing your praises, then,
  Without their poets.*
MAMMON: Sir, I'll do't. Meantime,
  I'll give away so much unto my man
  Shall serve the whole city with preservative,   75
  Weekly, each house his dose, and at the rate –
SURLY: As he that built the waterwork* does with water?
MAMMON: You are incredulous.
SURLY: Faith, I have a humour;
  I would not willingly be gulled. Your stone
  Cannot transmute me.
MAMMON: Pertinax, Surly: 80
  Will you believe antiquity? Records?
  I'll show you a book where Moses and his sister
  And Solomon have written of the art;
  Ay, and a treatise penned by Adam* –
SURLY: How!
MAMMON: O' the philosopher's stone, and in High Dutch.*
SURLY: Did Adam, sir, write in High Dutch?
MAMMON: He did,   85
  Which proves it was the primitive tongue.
SURLY: What paper?
MAMMON: On cedar board.
SURLY: O that indeed (they say)
  Will last 'gainst worms.
MAMMON: 'Tis like your Irish wood*
  'Gainst cobwebs. I have a piece of Jason's fleece too,
  Which was no other than a book of alchemy   90
  Writ in large sheepskin, a good fat ram-vellum.*
  Such was Pythagoras' thigh,* Pandora's tub,*
  And all that fable of Medea's charms,
  The manner of our work: the bulls, our furnace
  Still breathing fire; our *argent-vive*,* the dragon;   95
  The dragon's* teeth, mercury sublimate,*
  That keeps the whiteness, hardness, and the biting;
  And they are gathered into Jason's helm*
  (Th'alembic*) and then sowed in Mars* his field,
  And thence sublimed so often, till they are fixed.*   100
  Both this, th'Hesperian garden,* Cadmus' story,
  Jove's shower,* the boon of Midas,* Argus' eyes,*
  Boccace his Demogorgon,* thousands more,
  All abstract riddles of our stone.* How now?

Act Two, Scene Two

[*Enter*] FACE.

[MAMMON:] Do we succeed? Is our day come? And holds it?
FACE: The evening will set red upon you, sir;
    You have colour for it, crimson: the red ferment*
    Has done his office. Three hours hence, prepare you
    To see projection.*
MAMMON: Pertinax, my Surly,   5
    Again I say to thee aloud: be rich.
    This day thou shalt have ingots, and tomorrow
    Give lords th'affront.* Is it, my Zephyrus, right?
    Blushes the bolt's head?*
FACE: Like a wench with child, sir,
    That were but now discovered to her master.   10
MAMMON: Excellent, my witty Lungs! My only care is
    Where to get stuff enough now to project on;
    This town will not half serve me.
FACE: No, sir? Buy
    The coverings off o' churches.
MAMMON: That's true.
FACE: Yes.
    Let 'em stand bare, as do their auditory.*   15
    Or cap 'em new with shingles.*
MAMMON: No, good thatch:
    Thatch will lie upo' the rafters, Lungs.
    Lungs, I will manumit* thee from the furnace;
    I will restore thee thy complexion, Puff,
    Lost in the embers; and repair this brain,   20
    Hurt wi' the fume o' the metals.
FACE: I have blown, sir,
    Hard, for your worship; thrown by many a coal
    When 'twas not beech; weighed those I put in, just,
    To keep your heat still even; these bleared eyes
    Have waked to read your several colours, sir,   25
    Of the pale citron, the green lion, the crow,
    The peacock's tail, the plumed swan.*
MAMMON: And, lastly,
    Thou has descried the flower, the *sanguis agni*?*
FACE: Yes, sir.
MAMMON: Where's master?
FACE: At 's prayers; sir, he,

Good man, he's doing his devotions,   30
For the success.
MAMMON: Lungs, I will set a period*
To all thy labours: thou shalt be the master
Of my seraglio.*
FACE: Good, sir.
MAMMON: But do you hear?
I'll geld* you, Lungs.
FACE: Yes, sir.
MAMMON: For I do mean
To have a list of wives and concubines   35
Equal with Solomon, who had the stone
Alike, with me; and I will make me a back
With the elixir that shall be as tough
As Hercules, to encounter* fifty a night.
Th' art sure thou saw'st it blood?
FACE: Both blood and spirit, sir.   40
MAMMON: I will have all my beds blown up, not stuffed:
Down is too hard. And then mine oval room,
Filled with such pictures as Tiberius took
From Elephantis,* and dull Aretine*
But coldly imitated. Then, my glasses,*   45
Cut in more subtle angles, to disperse
And multiply the figures, as I walk
Naked between my *succubae*.* My mists
I'll have of perfume, vapoured 'bout the room,
To lose ourselves in; and my baths, like pits   50
To fall into: from whence we will come forth,
And roll us dry in gossamer and roses.
(Is it arrived at ruby?) – Where I spy
A wealthy citizen, or rich lawyer,
Have a sublimed pure wife, unto that fellow   55
I'll send a thousand pound to be my cuckold.
FACE: And shall I carry it?
MAMMON: No. I'll ha' no bawds
But fathers and mothers. They will do it best.
Best of all others. And my flatterers
Shall be the pure* and gravest of divines   60
That I can get for money. My mere fools,
Eloquent burgesses,* and then my poets,
The same that writ so subtly of the fart,*
Whom I will entertain still for that subject.
The few that would give themselves out to be   65

Court and town stallions and, each where, belie
Ladies who are known most innocent, for them;
Those will I beg to make me eunuchs of,
And they shall fan me with ten ostrich tails
Apiece, made in a plume, to gather wind.   70
We will be brave, Puff, now we ha' the medicine.
My meat shall all come in, in Indian shells,
Dishes of agate, set in gold and studded
With emeralds, sapphires, hyacinths* and rubies.
The tongues of carps,* dormice and camels' heels   75
Boiled i' the spirit of Sol and dissolved pearl,
(Apicius'* diet, 'gainst the epilepsy)
And I will eat these broths with spoons of amber,
Headed with diamant and carbuncle.
My foot-boy shall eat pheasants, calvered* salmons,   80
Knots, godwits, lampreys;* I myself will have
The beards of barbels* served instead of salads;
Oiled mushrooms; and the swelling unctuous paps
Of a fat pregnant sow, newly cut off,
Dressed with an exquisite and poignant* sauce;   85
For which I'll say unto my cook: there's gold,
Go forth, and be a knight.
FACE: Sir, I'll go look
A little, how it heightens.*   [*Exit.*]
MAMMON: Do. My shirts
I'll have of taffeta-sarsnet,* soft and light
As cobwebs; and for all my other raiment,   90
It shall be such as might provoke the Persian,*
Were he to teach the world riot anew.
My gloves of fishes' and birds' skins, perfumed
With gums of paradise,* and eastern air –
SURLY: And do you think to have the stone with this?   95
MAMMON: No, I do think t' have all this with the stone.
SURLY: Why, I have heard he must be *homo frugi*,*
A pious, holy and religious man,
One free from mortal sin, a very virgin.
MAMMON: That makes it, sir; he is so. But I buy it.   100
My venture* brings it me. He, honest wretch,
A notable, superstitious, good soul,
Has worn his knees bare and his slippers bald
With prayer and fasting for it; and, sir, let him
Do it alone for me still. Here he comes.   105
Not a profane word afore him: 'tis poison.

Act Two, Scene Three

[*Enter*] SUBTLE.

MAMMON: Good morrow, father.
SUBTLE: Gentle son, good morrow.
    And to your friend there. What is he, is with you?
MAMMON: An heretic that I did bring along
    In hope, sir, to convert him.
SUBTLE: Son, I doubt*
    Y'are covetous, that thus you meet your time   5
    I' the just point:* prevent* your day at morning.
    This argues something worthy of a fear,
    Of importune and carnal appetite.
    Take heed you do not cause the blessing leave you
    With your ungoverned haste. I should be sorry   10
    To see my labours, now e'en at perfection,
    Got by long watching and large patience,
    Not prosper, where my love and zeal hath placed 'em.
    Which (heaven I call to witness, with yourself,
    To whom I have poured my thoughts) in all my ends   15
    Have looked no way but into public good,
    To pious uses, and dear charity,
    Now grown a prodigy with men. Wherein
    If you, my son, should now prevaricate,*
    And to your own particular lusts employ   20
    So great and catholic* a bliss, be sure
    A curse will follow; yea, and overtake
    Your subtle and most secret ways.
MAMMON: I know, sir;
    You shall not need to fear me. I but come
    To ha' you confute this gentleman.
SURLY: Who is,   25
    Indeed, sir, somewhat costive of belief*
    Toward your stone, would not be gulled.
SUBTLE: Well, son,
    All that I can convince him in is this:
    The work is done; bright Sol is in his robe.*
    We have a med'cine of the triple soul,*   30
    The glorified spirit. Thanks be to heaven,
    And make us worthy of it. Ulen Spiegel.*

[*Enter* FACE.]

FACE: Anon, sir.

SUBTLE: Look well to the register,*
And let your heat still lessen by degrees,
To the aludels.*

FACE: Yes, sir.

SUBTLE: Did you look   35
O' the bolt's head yet?

FACE: Which? On D,* sir?

SUBTLE: Ay.
What's the complexion?

FACE: Whitish.

SUBTLE: Infuse vinegar
To draw his volatile substance and his tincture;
And let the water in glass E be filtered
And put into the gripe's egg.* Lute* him well,   40
And leave him closed in *balneo.**

FACE: I will, sir.   [*Exit.*]

SURLY: What a brave language here is, next to canting!*

SUBTLE: I have another work you never saw, son,
That three days since passed the philosopher's wheel*
In the lent* heat of athanor;* and 's become   45
Sulphur o' nature.*

MAMMON: But 'tis for me?

SUBTLE: What need you?
You have enough in that is perfect.

MAMMON: O, but –

SUBTLE: Why, this is covetise!*

MAMMON: No, I assure you,
I shall employ it all in pious uses,
Founding of colleges and grammar schools,   50
Marrying young virgins, building hospitals,
And now and then a church.

[*Enter* FACE.]

SUBTLE: How now?

FACE: Sir, please you,
Shall I not change the filter?

SUBTLE: Marry, yes.
And bring me the complexion of glass B.   [*Exit* FACE.]

MAMMON: Ha' you another?

SUBTLE: Yes, son; were I assured   55

Your piety were firm, we would not want
The means to glorify it. But I hope the best.
I mean to tinct C in sand-heat* tomorrow,
And give him imbibition.*
MAMMON: Of white oil?
SUBTLE: No, sir, of red. F is come over the helm too,   60
I thank my maker, in St Mary's bath,*
And shows *lac Virginis.** Blessed be heaven.
I sent you of his faeces* there, calcined.*
Out of that calx,* I ha' won the salt* of mercury.
MAMMON: By pouring on your rectified* water?   65
SUBTLE: Yes, and reverberating* in athanor.

                    [*Enter* FACE.]

How now? What colour says it?
FACE: The ground black, sir.
MAMMON: That's your crow's head?*
SURLY: Your coxcomb's, is't not?
SUBTLE: No, 'tis not perfect; would it were the crow.
That work wants something.
SURLY: (O, I looked for this.   70
The hay is a-pitching.)*
SUBTLE: Are you sure you loosed 'em
I' their own menstrue?*
FACE: Yes, sir, and then married 'em,
And put 'em in a bolt's-head, nipped* to digestion,*
According as you bade me; when I set
The liquor of Mars* to circulation   75
In the same heat.
SUBTLE: The process, then, was right.
FACE: Yes, by the token, sir; the retort broke,
And what was saved was put into the pelican,*
And signed with Hermes' seal.*
SUBTLE: I think 'twas so.
We should have a new amalgama.*
SURLY: (O, this ferret   80
Is rank as any polecat.)
SUBTLE: But I care not.
Let him e'en die; we have enough beside
In *embrion.** H has his white shirt on?*
FACE: Yes, sir;
He's ripe for inceration:* he stands warm
In his ash-fire. I would not you should let   85

Any die now, if I might counsel, sir,
For luck's sake to the rest. It is not good.
MAMMON: He says right.
SURLY: Ay, are you bolted?*
FACE: Nay, I know 't, sir;
I have seen th' ill fortune. What is some three ounces
Of fresh materials?
MAMMON: Is 't no more?
FACE: No more, sir,   90
Of gold, t' amalgam with some six of mercury.
MAMMON: Away, here's money. What will serve?
FACE: Ask him sir.
MAMMON: How much?
SUBTLE: Give him nine pound: you may gi' him ten.
SURLY: Yes, twenty, and be cozened: do.
MAMMON: There 'tis.
SUBTLE: This needs not. But that you will have it so,   95
To see conclusions of all. For two
Of our inferior works are at fixation.*
A third is in ascension.* Go your ways.
Ha' you set the oil of Luna* in kemia?*
FACE: Yes, sir.
SUBTLE: And the philosopher's vinegar?*
FACE: Ay. [*Exit.*] 100
SURLY: We shall have a salad.*
MAMMON: When do you make projection?
SUBTLE: Son, be not hasty. I exalt our med'cine
But hanging him in *balneo vaporoso,**
And giving him solution; then congeal him;
And then dissolve him; then again congeal him;   105
For look how oft I iterate the work,
So many times, I add unto his virtue.
As if at first one ounce convert* a hundred,
After his second loose* he'll turn a thousand;
His third solution, ten; his fourth, a hundred;   110
After his fifth, a thousand thousand ounces
Of any imperfect metal into pure
Silver or gold, in all examinations,
As good as any of the natural mine.
Get you your stuff here, against afternoon,   115
Your brass, your pewter, and your andirons.*
MAMMON: Not those of iron?
SUBTLE: Yes, you may bring them too.
We'll change all metals.

SURLY: I believe you in that.
MAMMON: Then I may send my spits?
SUBTLE: Yes, and your racks.
SURLY: And dripping-pans, and pot-hangers, and hooks,   120
   Shall he not?
SUBTLE: If he please.
SURLY: To be an ass.
SUBTLE: How, sir!
MAMMON: This gent'man you must bear withal.
   I told you he had no faith.
SURLY: And little hope, sir,
   But much less charity, should I gull myself.
SUBTLE: Why, what have you observed, sir, in our art   125
   Seems so impossible?
SURLY: But your whole work, no more.
   That you should hatch gold in a furnace, sir,
   As they do eggs in Egypt!*
SUBTLE: Sir, do you
   Believe that eggs are hatched so?
SURLY: If I should?
SUBTLE: Why, I think the greater miracle.   130
   No egg but differs from a chicken more
   Than metals in themselves.
SURLY: That cannot be.
   The egg's ordained by nature to that end,
   And is a chicken in *potentia.*
SUBTLE: The same we say of lead and other metals,   135
   Which would be gold if they had time.
MAMMON: And that
   Our art doth further.
SUBTLE: Ay, for 'twere absurd
   To think that nature, in the earth, bred gold
   Perfect, i' the instant. Something went before.
   There must be remote matter.*
SURLY: Ay, what is that?   140
SUBTLE: Marry, we say –
MAMMON: Ay, now it stands: stand Father.
   Pound him to dust –
SUBTLE: It is, of the one part,
   A humid exhalation, which we call
   *Materia liquida,** or the unctuous* water;
   On th' other part, a certain crass* and viscous   145
   Portion of earth; both which, concorporate,*
   Do make the elementary matter of gold,

Which is not yet *propria material*,*
But common to all metals, and all stones.
For, where it is forsaken of that moisture,   150
And hath more dryness, it becomes a stone;
Where it retains more of the humid fatness,
It turns to sulphur, or to quicksilver,
Who are the parents of all other metals.
Nor can this remote matter suddenly   155
Progress so from extreme unto extreme,
As to grow gold, and leap o'er all the means.*
Nature doth first beget th' imperfect; then
Proceeds she to the perfect. Of that airy
And oily water, mercury is engendered;   160
Sulphur o' the fat and earthy part: the one
(Which is the last) supplying the place of male,
The other of female, in all metals.
Some do believe hermaphrodeity,
That both do act and suffer.* But these two   165
Make the rest ductile, malleable, extensive.*
And even in gold they are; for we do find
Seeds of them, by our fire, and gold in them,
And can produce the species of each metal
More perfect thence than nature doth in earth.   170
Beside, who doth not see, in daily practice,
Art can beget bees, hornets, beetles, wasps,
Out of the carcasses and dung of creatures;
Yea, scorpions, of an herb, being ritely* placed:
And these are living creatures, far more perfect   175
And excellent than metals.
MAMMON: Well said, Father!
Nay, if he take you in hand, sir, with an argument,
He'll bray* you in a mortar.
SURLY: Pray you, sir, stay.
Rather than I'll be brayed, sir, I'll believe
That alchemy is a pretty kind of game,   180
Somewhat like tricks o' the cards, to cheat a man
With charming.
SUBTLE: Sir?
SURLY: What else are all your terms,
Whereon no one o' your writers 'grees with other?
Of your elixir, your *lac Virginis*,
Your stone, your med'cine, and your chrysosperm,*   185
Your sal, your sulphur, and your mercury,
Your oil of height, your tree of life,* your blood,

Your marcasite,* your tutty,* your magnesia,
Your toad, your crow, your dragon, and your panther,*
Your sun, your moon, your firmament, your adrop,*   190
Your lato,* azoch,* zernich,* chibrit, heautarit,*
And then your red man and your white woman,
With all your broths, your menstrues, and materials,
Of piss, and eggshells, women's terms,* man's blood,
Hair o' the head, burnt clouts,* chalk, merds,* and clay,   195
Powder of bones, scaling of iron, glass,
And worlds of other strange ingredients,
Would burst a man to name?

SUBTLE: And all these, named,
Intending but one thing: which art our writers
Used to obscure their art.

MAMMON: Sir, so I told him,   200
Because the simple idiot should not learn it
And make it vulgar.

SUBTLE: Was not all the knowledge
Of the Egyptians writ in mystic symbols?
Speak not the Scriptures oft in parables?
Are not the choicest fables of the poets,   205
That were the fountains and first springs of wisdom,
Wrapped in perplexed allegories?

MAMMON: I urged that,
And cleared to him that Sisyphus* was damned
To roll the ceaseless stone, only because
He would have made ours common.

                    DOLL *is seen.*
                              Who is this?   210

SUBTLE: God's precious – what do you mean? Go in, good lady,
Let me entreat you. Where's this varlet?

                    [*Enter* FACE.]

FACE: Sir?
SUBTLE: You very knave! Do you use me thus?
FACE: Wherein, sir?
SUBTLE: Go in and see, you traitor. Go.   [*Exit* FACE.]
MAMMON: Who is it, sir?
SUBTLE: Nothing, sir. Nothing.
MAMMON: What's the matter? Good sir!   215
I have not seen you thus distempered. Who is't?
SUBTLE: All arts have still had, sir, their adversaries,
But ours the most ignorant.

FACE *returns.*

          What now?

FACE: 'Twas not my fault, sir; she would speak with you.

SUBTLE: Would she, sir? Follow me.   [*Exit.*]

MAMMON: Stay, Lungs.

FACE: I dare not, sir.   220

MAMMON: Stay man, what is she?

FACE: A lord's sister, sir.

MAMMON: How! Pray thee, stay.

FACE: She's mad, sir, and sent hither –

    (He'll be mad too –

MAMMON: I warrant thee.) Why sent hither?

FACE: Sir, to be cured.

SUBTLE [*within*]:   Why, rascal!

FACE: Lo, you. Here, sir!

                                 He goes out.

MAMMON: 'Fore God, a Bradamante,* a brave piece.   225

SURLY: Heart, this is a bawdy-house! I'll be burnt else.

MAMMON: O, by this light, no. Do not wrong him. He's

    Too scrupulous that way. It is his vice.

    No, he's a rare physician, do him right.

    An excellent Paracelsian!* And has done   230

    Strange cures with mineral physic. He deals all

    With spirits, he. He will not hear a word

    Of Galen,* or his tedious recipes.

FACE *again.*

    How now, Lungs!

FACE: Softly, sir, speak softly. I meant

    To ha' told your worship all. This must not hear.   235

MAMMON: No, he will not be gulled; let him alone.

FACE: Y'are very right, sir. She is a most rare scholar,

    And gone mad with studying Broughton's* works.

    If you but name a word, touching the Hebrew,

    She falls into her fit, and will discourse   240

    So learnedly of genealogies*

    As you would run mad, too, to hear her, sir.

MAMMON: How might one do t' have conference with her, Lungs?

FACE: O, divers have run mad upon the conference.

    I do not know, sir: I am sent in haste   245

    To fetch a vial.

SURLY: Be not gulled, Sir Mammon.

MAMMON: Wherein? Pray ye, be patient.
SURLY: Yes, as you are.
    And trust confederate knaves, and bawds, and whores.
MAMMON: You are too foul, believe it. Come here, Ulen,
    One word.
FACE: I dare not, in good faith.
MAMMON: Stay, knave.   250
FACE: He's extreme angry that you saw her, sir.
MAMMON: Drink that. What is she when she's out of her fit?
FACE: O, the most affablest creature, sir! So merry!
    So pleasant! She'll mount you up, like quicksilver,
    Over the helm;* and circulate like oil,   255
    A very vegetal;* discourse of state,
    Of mathematics, bawdry, anything –
MAMMON: Is she no way accessible? No means,
    No trick, to give a man a taste of her – wit –
    Or so?
[SUBTLE *within*:] Ulen!
FACE: I'll come to you again, sir.   [*Exit.*] 260
MAMMON: Surly, I did not think one o' your breeding
    Would traduce personages of worth.
SURLY: Sir Epicure,
    Your friend to use: yet still loth to be gulled.
    I do not like your philosophical bawds.
    Their stone is lechery enough to pay for,   265
    Without this bait.
MAMMON: Heart, you abuse yourself.
    I know the lady and her friends, and means,
    The original* of this disaster. Her brother
    Has told me all.
SURLY: And yet you ne'er saw her
    Till now?
MAMMON: O yes, but I forgot. I have (believe it)   270
    One o' the treacherous'st memories, I do think,
    Of all mankind.
SURLY: What call you her brother?
MAMMON: My lord –
    He wi' not have his name known, now I think on't.
SURLY: A very treacherous memory!
MAMMON: O' my faith –
SURLY: Tut, if you ha' it not about you, pass* it,   275
    Till we meet next.
MAMMON: Nay, by this hand, 'tis true.
    He's one I honour, and my noble friend

And I respect his house.
SURLY: Heart! Can it be
That a grave sir, a rich, that has no need,
A wise sir, too, at other times, should thus   280
With his own oaths and arguments, make hard means
To gull himself? And* this be your elixir,
Your *lapis mineralis,** and your lunary,*
Give me your honest trick, yet, at primero
Or gleek; and take your *lutum sapientis,**   285
Your *menstrum simplex:** I'll have gold before you,
And with less danger of the quicksilver;
Or the hot sulphur.

                         [*Enter* FACE.]

FACE: Here's one from Captain Face, sir, *To* SURLY.
Desires you meet him i' the Temple Church*
Some half hour hence, and upon earnest business.   290
Sir, if you please to quit us now, and come   *He whispers* MAMMON.
Again within two hours, you shall have
My master busy examining o' the works;
And I will steal you in, unto the party.
That you may see her converse. Sir, shall I say   295
You'll meet the Captain's worship?
SURLY: Sir, I will.
But by attorney,* and to a second purpose.
Now, I am sure, it is a bawdy-house;
I'll swear it, were the Marshall here to thank me:
The naming this commander doth confirm it.   300
Don Face! Why, he's the most authentic dealer
I' these commodities! The superintendent*
To all the quainter traffickers* in town.
He is their visitor,* and does appoint
Who lies with whom, and at what hour, what price;   305
Which gown; and in what smock; what fall,* what tire.*
Him will I prove,* by a third person, to find
The subtleties of this dark labyrinth;
Which, if I do discover, dear Sir Mammon,
You'll give your poor friend leave, though no philosopher,   310
To laugh, for you that are, 'tis thought, shall weep.
FACE: Sir. He does pray, you'll not forget.
SURLY: I will not, sir.
Sir Epicure, I shall leave you?
MAMMON: I follow you straight.   [*Exit* SURLY.]

FACE: But do so, good sir, to avoid suspicion.
This gent'man has a parlous* head.
MAMMON: But wilt thou, Ulen,   315
Be constant to thy promise?
FACE: As my life, sir.
MAMMON: And wilt thou insinuate what I am? And praise me?
And say I am a noble fellow?
FACE: O, what else, sir?
And that you'll make her royal with the stone,
An empress; and yourself King of Bantam.*   320
MAMMON: Wilt thou do this?
FACE: Will I, sir?
MAMMON: Lungs, my Lungs!
I love thee.
FACE: Send your stuff, sir, that my master
May busy himself about projection.
MAMMON: Th' hast witched me, rogue: take, go.
FACE: Your jack* and all, sir.
MAMMON: Thou art a villain – I will send my jack;   325
And the weights too. Slave, I could bite thine ear.
Away, thou dost not care for me.
FACE: Not I, sir?
MAMMON: Come, I was born to make thee; my good weasel;
Set thee on a bench and ha' thee twirl a chain*
With the best lord's vermin of 'em all.
FACE: Away, sir.   330
MAMMON: A Count, nay, a Count-Palatine* –
FACE: Good sir, go.
MAMMON: Shall not advance thee better; no, nor faster.   [*Exit.*]

Act Two, Scene Four

[*Enter*] SUBTLE, DOLL.

[SUBTLE:] Has he bit? Has he bit?
FACE: And swallowed too, my Subtle.
I ha' given him line, and now he plays, i' faith.
SUBTLE: And shall we twitch him?
FACE: Thorough both the gills.
A wench is a rare bait, with which a man
No sooner's taken, but he straight firks mad.*   5
SUBTLE: Doll, my Lord Whats'hum's sister, you must now
Bear yourself *statelich.**

DOLL: O, let me alone.
   I'll not forget my race, I warrant you.
   I'll keep my distance, laugh, and talk aloud;
   Have all the tricks of a proud scurvy lady,   10
   And be as rude's her woman
FACE: Well said, sanguine.*
SUBTLE: But will he send his andirons?
FACE: His jack too;
   And's iron shoeing horn: I ha' spoke to him. Well,
   I must not lose my wary gamester yonder.
SUBTLE: O, Monsieur Caution, that will not be gulled?   15
FACE: Ay, if I can strike a fine hook into him now,
   The Temple Church, there I have cast mine angle.
   Well, pray for me. I'll about it.   *One knocks.*
SUBTLE: What, more gudgeons!*
   Doll, scout, scout; stay, Face, you must go to the door.
   Pray God it be my Anabaptist.* Who is't, Doll?   20
DOLL: I know him not. He looks like a gold-end-man.*
SUBTLE: Gods so! 'Tis he, he said he would send. What call you him?
   The sanctified elder,* that should deal
   For Mammon's jack and andirons! Let him in.
   Stay, help me off first with my gown. Away   25
   Madam, to your withdrawing chamber. Now,   [*Exit* DOLL.]
   In a new tune, new gesture, but old language.
   This fellow is sent from one negotiates with me
   About the stone, too; for the holy brethren
   Of Amsterdam, the exiled saints,* that hope   30
   To raise their discipline by it. I must use him
   In some strange fashion now, to make him admire me.

Act Two, Scene Five

[*Enter*] ANANIAS.

[SUBTLE:] Where is my drudge?
FACE: Sir.
SUBTLE: Take away the recipient,*
   And rectify* your menstrue from the phlegma.*
   Then pour it, o' the Sol, in the cucurbite,
   And let 'em macerate* together.
FACE: Yes, sir.
   And save the ground?
SUBTLE: No. *Terra damnata**   5

Must not have entrance in the work. Who are you?
ANANIAS: A faithful brother, if it please you.
SUBTLE: What's that?
  A Lullianist? A Ripley? *Filius Artis*?*
  Can you sublime and dulcify?* Calcine?
  Know you the *sapor pontic*? *Sapor styptic*?*   10
  Or what is the homogene or heterogene?*
ANANIAS: I understand no heathen language, truly.
SUBTLE: Heathen, you Knipperdoling?* Is *Ars sacra*,*
  Or *chrysopoeia*,* or *spagyrica*,*
  Of the pamphysic or panarchic knowledge,*   15
  A heathen language?
ANANIAS: Heathen Greek, I take it.
SUBTLE: How? Heathen Greek?
ANANIAS: All's heathen but the Hebrew.
SUBTLE: Sirrah, my varlet, stand you forth and speak to him
  Like a philosopher: answer i' the language.*
  Name the vexations, and the martyrisations*   20
  Of metals, in the work.
FACE: Sir, putrefaction,*
  Solution, ablution,* sublimation,
  Cohobation,* calcination, ceration and
  Fixation.
SUBTLE: This is heathen Greek to you now?
  And when comes vivification?*
FACE: After mortification.*   25
SUBTLE: What's cohobation?
FACE: 'Tis the pouring on
  Your *Aqua Regis*,* and then drawing him off
  To the trine circle of the seven spheres.*
SUBTLE: What's the proper passion* of metals?
FACE: Malleation.*
SUBTLE: What's your *ultimum supplicium auri*?*
FACE: Antimonium.*   30
SUBTLE: This's heathen Greek to you? And what's your mercury?
FACE: A very fugitive, he will be gone, sir
SUBTLE: How know you him?
FACE: By his viscosity,
  His oleosity,* and his suscitability.*
SUBTLE: How do you sublime him?
FACE: With the calce* of eggshells,   35
  White marble, talc.
SUBTLE: Your *magisterium*,* now?
  What's that?

The Alchemist

FACE: Shifting, sir, your elements,
    Dry into cold, cold into moist, moist into
    Hot, hot into dry.
SUBTLE: This's heathen Greek to you still?
    Your *lapis philosophicus*?
FACE: 'Tis a stone, and not   40
    A stone; a spirit, a soul, and a body:
    Which, if you do dissolve, it is dissolved,
    If you coagulate, it is coagulated,
    If you make it to fly, it flieth.
SUBTLE: Enough.   [*Exit* FACE.]
    This's heathen Greek to you? What are you, sir?   45
ANANIAS: Please you, a servant of the exiled brethren
    That deal with widows and with orphans' goods;
    And make a just account unto the Saints:*
    A deacon.
SUBTLE: O, your are sent from Master Wholesome,
    Your teacher?
ANANIAS: From Tribulation Wholesome,   50
    Our very zealous pastor.
SUBTLE: Good. I have
    Some orphans' goods to come here.
ANANIAS: Of what kind, sir?
SUBTLE: Pewter and brass, andirons and kitchen ware,
    Metals, that we must use our med'cine on:
    Wherein the brethren may have a penn'orth,   55
    For ready money.
ANANIAS: Were the orphans' parents
    Sincere professors?*
SUBTLE: Why do you ask?
ANANIAS: Because
    We then are to deal justly, and give (in truth)
    Their utmost value.
SUBTLE: 'Slid, you'd cozen, else,
    And if their parents were not of the faithful?   60
    I will not trust you, now I think on't,
    Till I ha' talked with your pastor. Ha' you brought money
    To buy more coals?
ANANIAS: No, surely.
SUBTLE: No? How so?
ANANIAS: The brethren bid me say unto you, sir.
    Surely they will not venture any more   65
    Till they see projection.
SUBTLE: How!

ANANIAS: Y'have had
   For the instruments, as bricks, and loam, and glasses,
   Already thirty pound; and for materials
   They say some ninety more; and, they have heard, since
   That one at Heidelberg* made it of an egg   70
   And a small paper of pin-dust.*
SUBTLE: What's your name?
ANANIAS: My name is Ananias.
SUBTLE: Out, the varlet
   That cozened the Apostles!* Hence, away,
   Flee, Mischief; had your holy consistory*
   No name to send me, of another sound,   75
   Than wicked Ananias? Send your elders
   Hither, to make atonement for you quickly.
   And gi' me satisfaction, or out goes
   The fire, and down th' alembics and the furnace,
   *Piger Henricus,** or what not. Thou wretch,   80
   Both *sericon* and *bufo** shall be lost,
   Tell 'em. All hope of rooting out the bishops,
   Or th' antichristian hierarchy, shall perish
   If they stay threescore minutes. The aqueity,
   Terreity and sulphureity*   85
   Shall run together again, and all be annulled,
   Thou wicked Ananias. This will fetch 'em,   [*Exit* ANANIAS]
   And make 'em haste towards their gulling more.
   A man must deal like a rough nurse, and fright
   Those that are froward* to an appetite.   90

Act Two, Scene Six

[*Enter*] FACE, DRUGGER.

[FACE:] He's busy with his spirits, but we'll upon him.
SUBTLE: How now! What mates? What Bayards* ha' we here?
FACE: I told you he would be furious. Sir, here's Nab,
   Has brought you another piece of gold to look on:
   (We must appease him. Give it me) and prays you,
   You would devise – (What is it, Nab?)   5
DRUGGER: A sign, sir.
FACE: Ay, a good lucky one, a thriving sign, Doctor.
SUBTLE: I was devising now.
FACE: ('Slight, do not say so,
   He will repent he ga' you any more.)

What say you to his constellation,* Doctor?   10
    The Balance?*
SUBTLE: No, that way is stale and common.
    A townsman, born in Taurus, gives the bull,
    Or the bull's head; in Aries, the ram.
    A poor device. No, I will have his name
    Formed in some mystic character, whose radii,*   15
    Striking the senses of the passers-by,
    Shall, by a virtual* influence, breed affections*
    That may result upon the party that owns it:
    As thus –
FACE: Nab!
SUBTLE: He first shall have a bell, that's Abel;
    And, by it, standing one whose name is Dee,*   20
    In a rug gown; there's D and Rug, that's Drug;
    And, right anenst him, a dog snarling er;
    There's Drugger, Abel Drugger. That's his sign.
    And here's now mystery and hieroglyphic!
FACE: Abel, thou art made.
DRUGGER: Sir, I do thank his worship.   25
FACE: Six o' thy legs* more will not do it, Nab.
    He has brought you a pipe of tobacco, Doctor.
DRUGGER: Yes, sir:
    I have another thing I would impart –
FACE: Out with it, Nab.
DRUGGER: Sir, there is lodged hard by me
    A rich young widow –
FACE: Good! A *bona roba?**   30
DRUGGER: But nineteen, at the most.
FACE: Very good, Abel.
DRUGGER: Marry, she's not in fashion yet; she wears
    A hood, but 't stands a-cop.*
FACE: No matter, Abel.
DRUGGER: And I do, now and then, give her a fucus* –
FACE: What! Dost thou deal,* Nab?
SUBTLE: I did tell you, Captain.   35
DRUGGER: And physic too, sometime, sir; for which she trusts me
    With all her mind. She's come up here of purpose
    To learn the fashion.
FACE: Good (His match* too!). On, Nab.
DRUGGER: And she does strangely long to know her fortune.
FACE: God's lid, Nab. Send her to the Doctor, hither.   40
DRUGGER: Yes, I have spoken to her of his worship already;
    But she's afraid it will be blown abroad,

And hurt her marriage.
FACE: Hurt it? 'Tis the way
   To heal it, if 'twere hurt; to make it more
   Followed and sought: Nab, thou shalt tell her this.   45
   She'll be more known, more talked of, and your widows
   Are ne'er of any price till they be famous;
   Their honour is their multitude of suitors:
   Send her, it may be thy good fortune. What?
   Thou dost not know.
DRUGGER: No, sir, she'll never marry   50
   Under a knight. Her brother has made a vow.
FACE: What, and dost thou despair, my little Nab,
   Knowing what the Doctor has set down for thee,
   And seeing so many o' the city dubbed?*
   One glass o' thy water, with a Madam I know,   55
   Will have it done, Nab. What's her brother? A knight?
DRUGGER: No, sir, a gentleman, newly warm in* his land, sir,
   Scarce cold in his one and twenty; that does govern
   His sister here, and is a man himself
   Of some three thousand a year, and is come up   60
   To learn to quarrel, and to live by his wits,
   And will go down again and die i' the country.
FACE: How! To quarrel?
DRUGGER: Yes, sir, to carry quarrels,
   As gallants do, and manage 'em by line.*
FACE: 'Slid, Nab! The Doctor is the only man   65
   In Christendom for him. He has made a table*
   With mathematical demonstrations
   Touching the art of quarrels. He will give him
   An instrument to quarrel by. Go, bring 'em both:
   Him, and his sister. And for thee with her   70
   The Doctor haply may persuade. Go to.
   Shalt give his worship a new damask suit
   Upon the premises.
SUBTLE: O, good Captain.
FACE: He shall;
   He is the honestest fellow, Doctor. Stay not,
   No offers; bring the damask, and the parties.   75
DRUGGER: I'll try my power, sir.
FACE: And thy will too, Nab.
SUBTLE: 'Tis good tobacco, this! What is't an ounce?
FACE: He'll send you a pound, Doctor.
SUBTLE: O, no.
FACE: He will do't.

It is the goodest soul. Abel, about it.
(Thou shalt know more anon. Away, be gone.)   [*Exit* DRUGGER.] 80
A miserable rogue, and lives with cheese,
And has the worms. That was the cause indeed
Why he came now. He dealt with me, in private,
To get a med'cine for 'em.
SUBTLE: And shall, sir. This works.
FACE: A wife, a wife for one on* us, my dear Subtle: 85
We'll e'en draw lots, and he that fails shall have
The more in goods, the other has in tail.*
SUBTLE: Rather the less. For she may be so light*
She may want grains.*
FACE: Ay, or be such a burden
A man would scarce endure her for the whole.   90
SUBTLE: Faith, best let's see her first, and then determine.
FACE: Content. But Doll must ha' no breath on't.
SUBTLE: Mum.
Away, you to your Surly yonder, catch him.
FACE: Pray God I ha' not stayed too long.
SUBTLE: I fear it.   [*Exeunt.*]

Act Three, Scene One

[*Enter*] TRIBULATION, ANANIAS.

TRIBULATION: These chastisements are common to the Saints,
And such rebukes we of the Separation*
Must bear, with willing shoulders, as the trials
Sent forth to tempt our frailties.
ANANIAS: In pure zeal,
I do not like the man: he is a heathen.   5
And speaks the language of Canaan,* truly.
TRIBULATION: I think him a profane person, indeed.
ANANIAS: He bears
The visible mark of the Beast* in his forehead.
And for his stone, it is a work of darkness,
And, with philosophy, blinds the eyes of man.   10
TRIBULATION: Good brother, we must bend unto all means
That may give furtherance to the holy cause.
ANANIAS: Which his cannot: the sanctified cause
Should have a sanctified course.
TRIBULATION: Not always necessary.
The children of perdition are oft-times   15

Made instruments even of the greatest works.
Beside, we should give* somewhat to man's nature,
The place he lives in, still* about the fire
And fume of metals, that intoxicate
The brain of man, and make him prone to passion.   20
Where have you greater atheists than your cooks?
Or more profane or choleric than your glassmen?*
More antichristian than your bellfounders?
What makes the Devil so devilish, I would ask you,
Satan, our common enemy, but his being   25
Perpetually about the fire, and boiling
Brimstone and arsenic? We must give, I say,
Unto the motives, and the stirrers up
Of humours in the blood. It may be so.
When as the work is done, the stone is made,   30
This heat of his may turn into a zeal,
And stand up for the beauteous discipline,
Against the menstruous cloth and rag of Rome.*
We must await his calling, and the coming
Of the good spirit. You did fault t' upbraid him   35
With the brethren's blessing of Heidelberg, weighing
What need we have to hasten on the work
For the restoring of the silenced Saints,*
Which will ne'er be, but by the philosopher's stone.
And so a learned elder, one of Scotland,*   40
Assured me: *aurum potabile** being
The only med'cine for the civil magistrate,
T' incline him to a feeling of the cause,
And must be daily used in the disease.
ANANIAS: I have not edified more, truly, by man;   45
Not since the beautiful light first shone on me:
And I am sad my zeal hath so offended.
TRIBULATION: Let us call on him, then.
ANANIAS: The motion's* good,
And of the spirit; I will knock first: peace be within.

Act Three, Scene Two

[Enter] SUBTLE.

[SUBTLE:] O, are you come? 'Twas time. Your threescore minutes
Were at the last thread, you see; and down had gone
*Furnus acediae,** turrus circulatorius:**

Lembic, bolt's-head, retort, and pelican
Had all been cinders. Wicked Ananias!   5
Art thou returned? Nay then, it all goes down, yet.
TRIBULATION: Sir, be appeased, he is come to humble
   Himself in spirit, and to ask your patience,
   If too much zeal hath carried him aside
   From the due path.
SUBTLE: Why, this doth qualify!*   10
TRIBULATION: The brethren had no purpose, verily,
   To give you the least grievance: but are ready
   To lend their willing hands to any project
   The spirit and you direct.
SUBTLE: This qualifies more!
TRIBULATION: And, for the orphans' goods, let them be valued,   15
   Or what is needful else to the holy work,
   It shall be numbered: here, by me, the Saints
   Throw down their purse before you.
SUBTLE: This qualifies most!
   Why, thus it should be, now you understand.
   Have I discoursed to you of our stone?   20
   And of the good that it shall bring your cause?
   Showed you, (beside the main* of hiring forces
   Abroad, drawing the Hollanders, your friends,
   From th' Indies to serve you, with all their fleet)
   That even the med'cinal use shall make you a faction   25
   And party* in the realm? As, put the case,
   That some great man in state, he have the gout,
   Why, you but send three drops of your elixir,
   You help him straight: there you have made a friend.
   Another has the palsy, or the dropsy,   30
   He takes of your incombustible stuff,
   He's young again: there you have made a friend.
   A lady, that is past the feat of body,*
   Though not of mind, and hath her face decayed
   Beyond all cure of paintings,* you restore   35
   With the oil of talc;* there you have made a friend:
   And all her friends. A lord that is a leper,
   A knight that has the bone-ache,* or a squire
   That hath both of these, you make 'em smooth, and sound,
   With a bare fricace* of your med'cine: still,   40
   You increase your friends.
TRIBULATION: Ay, 'tis very pregnant.*
SUBTLE: And then, the turning of this lawyer's pewter
   To plate, at Christmas –

ANANIAS: Christ-tide,* I pray you.
SUBTLE: Yet, Ananias?
ANANIAS: I have done.
SUBTLE: Or changing
  His parcel gilt* to massy* gold. You cannot   45
  But raise you friends. Withal, to be of power
  To pay an army in the field; to buy
  The King of France out of his realms; or Spain
  Out of his Indies: what can you not do
  Against lords spiritual, or temporal,   50
  That shall oppone* you?
TRIBULATION: Verily, 'tis true.
  We may be temporal lords ourselves, I take it.
SUBTLE: You may be anything, and leave off to make
  Long-winded exercises, or suck up
  Your ha and hum in a tune. I not* deny,   55
  But such as are not graced, in a state,
  May, for their ends, be adverse in religion,
  And get a tune to call the flock together:
  For (to say sooth) a tune does much with women,
  And other phlegmatic people; it is your bell.   60
ANANIAS: Bells are profane:* a tune may be religious.
SUBTLE: No warning with you? Then farewell my patience.
  'Slight, it shall down:* I will not be thus tortured.
TRIBULATION: I pray you, sir.
SUBTLE: All shall perish. I have spoke it.
TRIBULATION: Let me find grace, sir, in your eyes; the man   65
  He stands corrected: neither did his zeal
  (But as yourself) allow a tune, somewhere.
  Which now, being toward* the stone, we shall not need.
SUBTLE: No, nor your holy vizard, to win widows
  To give you legacies; or make jealous wives   70
  To rob their husbands for the common cause:
  Nor take the start* of bonds, broke but one day,
  And say they were forfeited by providence.
  Nor shall you need o'ernight to eat huge meals,
  To celebrate your next day's fast the better: 75
  The whilst the brethren and the sisters, humbled,
  Abate the stiffness of the flesh. Nor cast
  Before your hungry hearers scrupulous bones,*
  As whether a Christian may hawk or hunt;
  Or whether matrons of the holy assembly   80
  May lay their hair out or wear doublets,
  Or have that idol, starch, about their linen.

ANANIAS: It is indeed an idol.

TRIBULATION: Mind him not, sir.
   I do command thee, spirit (of zeal, but trouble),
   To peace within him. Pray you, sir, go on.   85

SUBTLE: Nor shall you need to libel 'gainst the prelates,
   And shorten so your ears* against the hearing
   Of the next wire-drawn* grace. Nor, of necessity,
   Rail against plays to please the alderman,*
   Whose daily custard* you devour. Nor lie   90
   With jealous rage till you are hoarse. Not one
   Of these so singular arts. Nor call yourselves
   By names of Tribulation, Persecution,
   Restraint, Long-Patience, and suchlike, affected
   By the whole family or wood* of you,   95
   Only for glory, and to catch the ear
   Of the disciple.

TRIBULATION: Truly, sir, they are
   Ways that the godly brethren have invented
   For propagation of the glorious cause,
   As very notable means, and whereby, also,   100
   Themselves grow soon, and profitably famous.

SUBTLE: O, but the stone, all's idle to it! Nothing!
   The art of angels, nature's miracle,
   The divine secret, that doth fly in clouds
   From east to west, and whose tradition   105
   Is not from men, but spirits.

ANANIAS: I hate traditions:*
   I do not trust them –

TRIBULATION: Peace.

ANANIAS: They are Popish, all.
   I will not peace, I will not –

TRIBULATION: Ananias.

ANANIAS: Please the profane to grieve the godly: I may not.

SUBTLE: Well, Ananias, thou shalt overcome.   110

TRIBULATION: It is an ignorant zeal that haunts him, sir.
   But truly, else, a very faithful brother,
   A botcher:* and a man, by revelation,
   That hath a competent knowledge of the truth.

SUBTLE: Has he a competent sum there i' the bag   115
   To buy the goods within? I am made guardian,
   And must, for charity and conscience sake
   Now, see the most be made for my poor orphan:
   Though I desire the brethren too good gainers.
   There they are, within. When you have viewed, and bought 'em,   120

And ta'en the inventory of what they are,
They are ready for projection; there's no more
To do: cast on the med'cine, so much silver
As there is tin there, so much gold as brass,
I'll gi' it you in, by weight.
TRIBULATION: But how long time,   125
Sir, must the saints expect yet?
SUBTLE: Let me see:
How's the moon now? Eight, nine, ten days hence
He will be silver potate;* then, three days
Before he citronise:* some fifteen days,
The *magisterium* will be perfected.   130
ANANIAS: About the second day of the third week
In the ninth month?
SUBTLE: Yes, my good Ananias.
TRIBULATION: What will the orphans' goods arise to, think you?
SUBTLE: Some hundred marks; as much as filled three cars,*
Unladed now: you'll make six millions of 'em,   135
But I must ha' more coals laid in.
TRIBULATION: How!
SUBTLE: Another load,
And then we ha' finished. We must now increase
Our fire to *ignis ardens,** we are past
*Fimus equinus,** balnei, cineris,*
And all those lenter* heats. If the holy purse   140
Should with this draught fall low, and that the saints
Do need a present sum, I have a trick
To melt the pewter, you shall buy now, instantly,
And with a tincture make you as good Dutch dollars
As any are in Holland.
TRIBULATION: Can you so?   145
SUBTLE: Ay, and shall bide the third examination.
ANANIAS: It will be joyful tidings to the brethren.
SUBTLE: But you must carry it secret.
TRIBULATION: Ay, but stay.
This act of coining: is it lawful?
ANANIAS: Lawful?
We know no magistrate,* or, if we did,   150
This's foreign coin.*
SUBTLE: It is no coining, sir.
It is but casting.
TRIBULATION: Ha? You distinguish well.
Casting of money may be lawful.
ANANIAS: 'Tis, sir.

TRIBULATION: Truly, I take it so.

SUBTLE: There is no scruple,
  Sir, to be made of it; believe it, Ananias: 155
  This case of conscience he is studied in.

TRIBULATION: I'll make a question of it to the brethren.

ANANIAS: The brethren shall approve it lawful, doubt not.
  Where shall 't be done?

SUBTLE: For that we'll talk anon.

                                      Knock without.

  There's some to speak with me. Go in, I pray you,   160
  And view the parcels. That's the inventory.
  I'll come to you straight.

           [*Exeunt* TRIBULATION *and* ANANIAS.]

           Who is it? Face! Appear.

Act Three, Scene Three

           [*Enter*] FACE.

[SUBTLE:] How now? Good prize?

FACE: Good pox! Yond costive cheater
  Never came on.

SUBTLE: How then?

FACE: I ha' walked the round*
  Till now, and no such thing.

SUBTLE: And ha' you quit him?

FACE: Quit him? And hell would quit him too, he were happy.
  'Slight, would you have me stalk like a mill-jade*   5
  All day, for one that will not yield us grains?
  I know him of old.

SUBTLE: O, but to ha' gulled him
  Had been a mastery.

FACE: Let him go, black boy,*
  And turn thee,* that some fresh news may possess thee.
  A noble count, a Don of Spain (my dear   10
  Delicious compeer,* and my party-bawd,*)
  Who is come here, private, for his conscience,
  And brought munition with him, six great slops,*
  Bigger than three Dutch hoys,* beside round trunks,*
  Furnished with pistolets* and pieces of eight,*   15
  Will straight be here, my rogue, to have thy bath

(That is the colour*) and to make his batt'ry
Upon our Doll, our castle, our Cinque Port,*
Our Dover pier, our what thou wilt. Where is she?
She must prepare perfumes, delicate linen,   20
The bath in chief, a banquet, and her wit,
For she must milk his epididimus.*
Where is the doxy?
SUBTLE: I'll send her to thee;
And but despatch my brace of John Leydens,*
And come again myself.
FACE: Are they within then?   25
SUBTLE: Numb'ring the sum.
FACE: How much?
SUBTLE: A hundred marks, boy.   [*Exit.*]
FACE: Why, this's a lucky day! Ten pounds of Mammon!
Three o' my clerk! A portague o' my grocer!
This o' the brethren! Beside reversions,*
And states to come i' the widow, and my count!   30
My share today will not be bought for forty –

[*Enter* DOLL.]

DOLL: What?
FACE: Pounds, dainty Dorothy, art thou so near?
DOLL: Yes, say lord general, how fares our camp?*
FACE: As with the few that had entrenched themselves
Safe, by their discipline, against a world, Doll;   35
And laughed, within those trenches, and grew fat
With thinking on these booties, Doll, brought in
Daily, by their small parties. This dear hour
A doughty don is taken with my Doll;
And thou may'st make his ransom, what thou wilt,   40
My dousabel:* he shall be brought here, fettered
With thy fair looks, before he sees thee; and thrown
In a down-bed as dark as any dungeon;
Where thou shalt keep him waking, with thy drum;*
Thy drum, my Doll, thy drum; till he be tame   45
As the poor blackbirds were i' the great frost,*
Or bees are with a basin;* and so hive him
I' the swanskin coverlid, and cambric sheets,
Till he work honey and wax, my little God's-gift.
DOLL: What is he, General?
FACE: An adalantado,*   50
A grandee, girl. Was not my Dapper here, yet?

DOLL: No.
FACE: Nor my Drugger?
DOLL: Neither.
FACE: A pox on 'em,
  They are so long a-furnishing!* Such stinkards
  Would* not be seen, upon these festival days.

[*Enter* SUBTLE.]

  How now! Ha' you done?
SUBTLE: Done. They are gone. The sum   55
  Is here in bank, my Face. I would we knew
  Another chapman* now, would buy 'em outright.
FACE: 'Slid, Nab shall do 't, against he ha' the widow
  To furnish household.
SUBTLE: Excellent, well thought on.
  Pray God he come.
FACE: I pray he keep away
  Till our new business be o'erpast.   60
SUBTLE: But, Face,
  How camest thou by this secret Don?
FACE: A spirit
  Brought me th' intelligence in a paper here,
  As I was conjuring, yonder, in my circle
  For Surly: I ha' my flies abroad. Your bath   65
  Is famous, Subtle, by my means. Sweet Doll,
  You must go tune your virginal, no losing
  O' the least time. And, do you hear? Good action.
  Firk, like a flounder;* kiss, like a scallop,* close:
  And tickle him with thy mother-tongue. His great   70
  Verdugoship* has not a jot of language:*
  So much the easier to be cozened, my Dolly.
  He will come here in a hired coach, obscure,*
  And our own coachman, whom I have sent as a guide.
  No creature else.   *One knocks.*
              Who's that?
SUBTLE: It i' not he?   75
FACE: O no, not yet this hour.
SUBTLE: Who is't?
DOLL: Dapper,
  Your clerk.
FACE: God's will, then, Queen of Fairy,
  On with your tire; and, Doctor, with your robes.
  Let's despatch him, for God's sake.   [*Exit* DOLL.]

SUBTLE: 'Twill be long.
FACE: I warrant you, take but the cues I give you,   80
    It shall be brief enough. 'Slight, here are more!
    Abel and, I think, the angry boy,* the heir,
    That fain would quarrel.
SUBTLE: And the widow?
FACE: No,
    Not that I see. Away. O sir, you are welcome.   [*Exit* SUBTLE.]

Act Three, Scene Four

[*Enter*] DAPPER, DRUGGER, KASTRIL.

[FACE:] The Doctor is within, a-moving for you
    (I have had the most ado to win him to it);
    He swears you'll be the darling o' the dice:
    He never heard her Highness dote till now (he says).
    Your aunt has given you the most gracious words   5
    That can be thought on.
DAPPER: Shall I see her Grace?
FACE: See her, and kiss her too. What? Honest Nab!
    Hast brought the damask?
DRUGGER: No, sir, here's tobacco.
FACE: 'Tis well done, Nab: thou'lt bring the damask too?
DRUGGER: Yes, here's the gentleman, Captain, Master Kastril,   10
    I have brought to see the Doctor.
FACE: Where's the widow?
DRUGGER: Sir, as he likes, his sister (he says) shall come.
FACE: O, is it so? Good time.* Is your name Kastril, sir?
KASTRIL: Ay, and the best of the Kastrils, I'd be sorry else
    By fifteen hundred a year. Where is this Doctor?   15
    My mad tobacco-boy here tells me of one
    That can do things. Has he any skill?
FACE: Wherein, sir?
KASTRIL: To carry a business, manage a quarrel fairly,
    Upon fit terms.
FACE: It seems, sir, you're but young
    About the town, that can make such a question!   20
KASTRIL: Sir, not so young, but I have heard some speech
    Of the angry boys, and seen 'em take tobacco;
    And in his shop; and I can take it too.
    And I would fain be one of 'em, and go down
    And practise i' the country.

FACE: Sir, for the *duello*,*   25
    The Doctor, I assure you, shall inform you
    To the least shadow of a hair; and show you
    An instrument he has of his own making,
    Wherewith, no sooner shall you make report
    Of any quarrel, but he will take the height on 't   30
    Most instantly; and tell in what degree
    Of safety it lies in, or mortality.*
    And how it may be borne, whether in a straight line
    Or a half circle; or may, else, be cast
    Into an angle blunt, if not acute: 35
    All this he will demonstrate. And then, rules
    To give and take the lie by.
KASTRIL: How? To take it?
FACE: Yes, in oblique, he'll show you, or in circle;
    But never in diameter.* The whole town
    Study his theorems, and dispute them, ordinarily,*   40
    At the eating academies.
KASTRIL: But does he teach
    Living by the wits too?
FACE: Anything, whatever.
    You cannot think that subtlety but he reads* it.
    He made me a captain. I was a stark* pimp,
    Just o' your standing, 'fore I met him: 45
    It i' not two months since. I'll tell you his method.
    First, he will enter you at some ordinary.
KASTRIL: No, I'll not come there. You shall pardon me.
FACE: For why, sir?
KASTRIL: There's gaming there, and tricks.
FACE: Why, would you be
    A gallant, and not game?
KASTRIL: Ay, 'twill spend a man.*   50
FACE: Spend you? It will repair you when you are spent.
    How do they live by their wits there, that have vented
    Six times your fortunes?
KASTRIL: What, three thousand a year!
FACE: Ay, forty thousand.
KASTRIL: Are there such?
FACE: Ay, sir,
    And gallants yet. Here's a young gentleman   55
    Is born to nothing, forty marks a year,
    Which I count nothing. He's to be initiated,
    And have a fly o' the Doctor. He will win you
    By unresistable luck, within this fortnight,

Enough to buy a barony. They will set him   60
Upmost, at the groom-porter's,* all the Christmas!
And, for the whole year through, at every place
Where there is play, present him with the chair;
The best attendance, the best drink, sometimes
Two glasses of canary,* and pay nothing;   65
The purest linen, and the sharpest knife,
The partridge next his trencher; and somewhere
The dainty bed, in private, with the dainty.
You shall ha' your ordinaries bid for him,
As playhouses for a poet; and the master   70
Pray him aloud to name what dish he affects,*
Which must be buttered shrimps; and those that drink
To no mouth else will drink to his, as being
The goodly president mouth of all the board.
KASTRIL: Do you not gull one?
FACE: 'Ods my life! Do you think it?   75
You shall have a cast* commander (can but get
In credit with a glover, or a spurrier,
For some two pair of either's ware aforehand)
Will, by most swift posts,* dealing with him
Arrive at competent means to keep himself,   80
His punk,* and naked boy,* in excellent fashion,
And be admired for't.
KASTRIL: Will the Doctor teach this?
FACE: He will do more, sir, when your land is gone
(As men of spirit hate to keep earth long),
In a vacation, when small money is stirring,   85
And ordinaries suspended till the term,
He'll show a perspective,* where on one side
You shall behold the faces and the persons
Of all sufficient young heirs in town,
Whose bonds are current for commodity;*   90
On th' other side, the merchants' forms, and others,
That, without help of any second broker,
(Who would expect a share) will trust such parcels:
In the third square, the very street and sign
Where the commodity dwells, and does but wait   95
To be delivered, be it pepper, soap,
Hops, or tobacco, oatmeal, woad,* or cheeses.
All which you may so handle, to enjoy
To your own use, and never stand obliged.
KASTRIL: I' faith! Is he such a fellow?
FACE: Why, Nab here knows him.   100

And then for making matches for rich widows,
Young gentlewomen, heirs, the fortunat'st man!
He's sent to, far and near, all over England
To have his counsel, and to know their fortunes.
KASTRIL: God's will, my suster* shall see him.
FACE: I'll tell you, sir,   105
What he tell me of Nab. It's a strange thing!
(By the way, you must eat no cheese, Nab, it breeds melancholy:*
And that same melancholy breeds worms, but pass it.)
He told me honest Nab here was ne'er at tavern,
But once in's life!
DRUGGER: Truth, and no more I was not.   110
FACE: And then he was so sick –
DRUGGER: Could he tell you that too?
FACE: How should I know it?
DRUGGER: In troth we had been a-shooting,
And had a piece of fat ram-mutton to supper,
That lay so heavy o' my stomach –
FACE: And he has no head
To bear any wine; for, what with the noise of the fiddlers,   115
And care of his shop, for he dares keep no servants –
DRUGGER: My head did so ache –
FACE: As he was fain to be brought home,
The Doctor told me. And then, a good old woman –
DRUGGER: (Yes, faith, she dwells in Seacoal Lane*) did cure me
With sodden* ale, and pellitory o' the wall:*   120
Cost me but two pence. I had another sickness,
Was worse than that.
FACE: Ay, and that was with the grief
Thou took'st for being 'sessed* at eighteen pence
For the water-work.*
DRUGGER: In truth, and it was like
T' have cost me almost my life.
FACE: Thy hair went off?   125
DRUGGER: Yes, sir, 'twas done for spite.
FACE: Nay, so says the Doctor.
KASTRIL: Pray thee, tobacco-boy, go fetch my suster;
I'll see this learned boy before I go:
And so shall she.
FACE: Sir, he is busy now;
But if you have a sister to fetch hither   130
Perhaps your own pains may command her sooner;
And he, by that time, will be free.
KASTRIL: I go.   [*Exit.*]

FACE: Drugger, she's thine: the damask. (Subtle and I   [*Exit* DRUGGER.]
    Must wrestle for her.) Come on, master Dapper.
    You see how I turn clients here away   135
    To give your cause despatch. Ha' you performed
    The ceremonies were enjoined you?
DAPPER: Yes, o' the vinegar,
    And the clean shirt.
FACE: 'Tis well: that shirt may do you
    More worship than you think. Your aunt's afire,
    But that she will not show it, t' have a sight on you.   140
    Ha' you provided for her Grace's servants?
DAPPER: Yes, here are six score Edward shillings.
FACE: Good.
DAPPER: And an old Harry's sovereign.*
FACE: Very good.
DAPPER: And three James shillings, and an Elizabeth groat,
    Just twenty nobles.
FACE: O, you are too just.   145
    I would you had had the other nobles in Marys.
DAPPER: I have some Philip and Marys.*
FACE: Ay, those same
    Are best of all. Where are they? Hark, the Doctor.

Act Three, Scene Five

[*Enter*] SUBTLE *disguised like a Priest of Fairy.*

[SUBTLE:] Is yet her Grace's cousin come?
FACE: He is come.
SUBTLE: And is he fasting?
FACE: Yes.
SUBTLE: And hath cried hum?
FACE: Thrice, you must answer.
DAPPER: Thrice.
SUBTLE: And as oft buzz?
FACE: If you have, say.
DAPPER: I have.
SUBTLE: Then, to her coz,
    Hoping that he hath vinegared all his senses   5
    As he was bid, the Fairy Queen dispenses,
    By me, this robe, the petticoat of Fortune;
    Which that he straight put on, she doth importune.

And though to Fortune near be her petticoat,
Yet nearer is her smock, the Queen doth note: 10
And, therefore, even of that a piece she hath sent,
Which, being a child, to wrap him in was rent;
And prays him for a scarf he now will wear it
(With as much love as then her Grace did tear it)
About his eyes, to show he is fortunate.   *They blind him with a rag.* 15
And, trusting unto her to make his state,*
He'll throw away all worldly pelf* about him;
Which that he will perform, she doth not doubt him.
FACE: She need not doubt him, sir. Alas, he has nothing,
But that he will part withal, as willingly,   20
Upon her Grace's word (throw away your purse)
                                    He throws away, as they bid him.
As she would ask it: (handkerchiefs, and all)
She cannot bid that thing, but he'll obey.
(If you have a ring about you, cast it off,
Or a silver seal at your wrist, her Grace will send   25
Her fairies here to search you, therefore deal
Directly with her Highness. If they find
That you conceal a mite, you are undone.)
DAPPER: Truly, there's all.
FACE: All what?
DAPPER: My money, truly.
FACE: Keep nothing that is transitory about you.   30
(Bid Doll play music.)

            DOLL *enters with a cittern:* they pinch him.

Look, the elves are come
To pinch you, if you tell not truth. Advise you.
DAPPER: O, I have a paper with a spur-ryal* in't.
FACE: *Ti, ti.*
They knew 't, they say.
SUBTLE: *Ti, ti, ti, ti,* he has more yet.
FACE: *Ti, ti-ti-ti.* I' the t'other pocket?
SUBTLE: *Titi, titi, titi, titi.*   35
They must pinch him, or he will never confess, they say.
DAPPER: O, O.
FACE: Nay, pray you hold. He is her Grace's nephew.
Ti, ti, ti? What care you? Good faith, you shall care.
Deal plainly, sir, and shame the fairies. Show
You are an innocent.
DAPPER: By this good light, I ha' nothing.   40
SUBTLE: *Ti ti, ti ti to ta.* He does equivocate,* she says:

Ti, ti do ti, ti ti do, ti da. And swears by the light, when he is blinded.
DAPPER: By this good dark, I ha' nothing but a half crown
    Of gold, about my wrist, that my love gave me;
    And a leaden heart I wore, sin' she forsook me.   45
FACE: I thought 'twas something. And would you incur
    Your aunt's displeasure for these trifles? Come,
    I had rather you had thrown away twenty half crowns.
    You may wear your leaden heart still. How now?
SUBTLE: What news, Doll?
DOLL: Yonder's your knight, Sir Mammon.   50
FACE: God's lid, we never thought of him till now.
    Where is he?
DOLL: Here, hard by. He's at the door.
SUBTLE: And you are not ready now? Doll, get his suit.
    He must not be sent back.
FACE: O, by no means.
    What shall we do with this same puffin here,   55
    Now he's o' the spit?*
SUBTLE: Why, lay him back a while
    With some device. *Ti, ti ti, ti ti ti.* Would her Grace speak with me?
    I come. Help, Doll.
FACE: Who's there?
                             He speaks through the keyhole, the other knocking.
                      Sir Epicure;
    My master's i' the way. Please you to walk
    Three or four turns, but till his back be turned,   60
    And I am for you. Quickly, Doll.
SUBTLE: Her Grace
    Commends her kindly to you, master Dapper.
DAPPER: I long to see her Grace.
SUBTLE: She now is set
    At dinner, in her bed; and she has sent you,
    From her own private trencher, a dead mouse,   65
    And a piece of gingerbread, to be merry withal,
    And stay your stomach, lest you faint with fasting;
    Yet, if you could hold out till she saw you (she says)
    It would be better for you.
FACE: Sir, he shall
    Hold out, and 'twere this two hours, for her Highness;   70
    I can assure you that. We will not lose
    All we ha' done –
SUBTLE: He must not see, nor speak
    To anybody, till then.
FACE: For that, we'll put, sir,
    A stay* in his mouth.

SUBTLE: Of what?

FACE: Of gingerbread.   75
    Make you it fit. He that hath pleased her Grace
    Thus far, shall not now crinkle* for a little.
    Gape, sir, and let him fit you.

SUBTLE: Where shall we now
    Bestow him?

DOLL: I' the privy.

SUBTLE: Come along, sir,
    I must now show you Fortune's privy lodgings.

FACE: Are they perfumed? And his bath ready?

SUBTLE: All.   80
    Only the fumigation's somewhat strong.

FACE: Sir Epicure, I am yours, by and by.

[*Exeunt* SUBTLE, DOLL *and* DAPPER.]

Act Four, Scene One

[*Enter*] MAMMON.

[FACE:] O sir, yo' are come i' the only, finest time –

MAMMON: Where's master?

FACE: Now preparing for projection, sir.
    Your stuff will b'all changed shortly.

MAMMON: Into gold?

FACE: To gold, and silver, sir.

MAMMON: Silver I care not for.

FACE: Yes, sir, a little to give beggars.

MAMMON: Where's the lady?   5

FACE: At hand, here. I ha' told her such brave things o' you,
    Touching your bounty and your noble spirit –

MAMMON: Hast thou?

FACE: As she is almost in her fit to see you.
    But, good sir, no divinity* i' your conference,
    For fear of putting her in a rage –

MAMMON: I warrant thee.   10

FACE: Six men will not hold her down. And then,
    If the old man should hear or see you –

MAMMON: Fear not.

FACE: The very house, sir, would run mad. You know it,
    How scrupulous he is, and violent,

'Gainst the least act of sin. Physic, or mathematics,   15
    Poetry, state,* or bawdry (as I told you)
    She will endure, and never startle;* but
    No word of controversy.
MAMMON: I am schooled, good Ulen.
FACE: And you must praise her house, remember that,
    And her nobility.
MAMMON: Let me alone;   20
    No herald, nor no antiquary, Lungs,
    Shall do it better. Go.
FACE: (Why, this is yet
    A kind of modern* happiness, to have
    Doll Common for a great lady.)   [*Exit.*]
MAMMON: Now, Epicure,
    Heighten thyself, talk to her all in gold;   25
    Rain her as many showers as Jove did drops
    Unto his Danae: show the god a miser
    Compared with Mammon. What? The stone will do't.
    She shall feel gold, taste gold, hear gold, sleep gold;
    Nay, we will *concumbere** gold. I will be puissant,*   30
    And mighty in my talk to her! Here she comes.

[*Enter* FACE, DOLL.]

FACE: To him, Doll, suckle him. This is the noble knight
    I told your ladyship –
MAMMON: Madam, with your pardon,
    I kiss your vesture.
DOLL: Sir, I were uncivil
    If I would suffer that; my lip to you, sir.   35
MAMMON: I hope my lord your brother be in health, lady?
DOLL: My lord my brother is, though I no lady, sir.
FACE: (Well said, my guinea-bird.*)
MAMMON: Right noble madam –
FACE: (O, we shall have most fierce idolatry!)
MAMMON: 'Tis your prerogative.
DOLL: Rather your courtesy.   40
FACE: Were there nought else t' enlarge your virtues, to me,
    These answers speak your breeding, and your blood.
DOLL: Blood we boast none, sir, a poor baron's daughter.
MAMMON: Poor! And gat you? Profane not. Had your father
    Slept all the happy remnant of his life   45
    After the act, lain but there still, and panted,
    He'd done enough to make himself, his issue,

And his posterity noble.

DOLL: Sir, although
We may be said to want the gilt and trappings,
The dress of honour, yet we strive to keep   50
The seeds, and the materials.

MAMMON: I do see
The old ingredient, virtue, was not lost,
Nor the drug money, used to make your compound.*
There is a strange nobility i'your eye,
This lip, that chin! Methinks you do resemble   55
One o' the Austraic princes.

FACE: (Very like,
Her father was an Irish costermonger.*)

MAMMON: The House of Valois, just, has such a nose.
And such a forehead, yet, the Medici
Of Florence boast.

DOLL: Troth, and I have been likened   60
To all these princes.

FACE: (I'll be sworn, I heard it.)

MAMMON: I know not how! It is not any one,
But e'en the very choice of all their features.

FACE: (I'll in, and laugh.)   [*Exit.*]

MAMMON: A certain touch, or air,
That sparkles a divinity beyond   65
An earthly beauty!

DOLL: O, you play the courtier.

MAMMON: Good lady, gi' me leave –

DOLL: In faith, I may not,
To mock me, sir.

MAMMON: To burn i' this sweet flame:
The Phoenix never knew a nobler death.

DOLL: Nay, now you court the courtier, and destroy   70
What you would build. This art, sir, i' your words,
Calls your whole faith in question.

FACE: By my soul –

DOLL: Nay, oaths are made o' the same air, sir.

MAMMON: Nature
Never bestowed upon mortality
A more unblamed, a more harmonious feature;*   75
She played the stepdame in all faces, else.
Sweet madam, le' me be particular –

DOLL: Particular, sir? I pray you, know your distance.

MAMMON: In no ill sense, sweet lady, but to ask
How your fair graces pass the hours? I see   80

Y' are lodged here, i' the house of a rare man,
An excellent artist – but what's that to you?
DOLL: Yes, sir. I study here the mathematics,
   And distillation.
MAMMON: O, I cry your pardon.
   He's a divine instructor! Can extract   85
   The souls of all things, by his art; call all
   The virtues, and the miracles of the sun,
   Into a temperate furnace; teach dull nature
   What her own forces are. A man the Emperor
   Has courted, above Kelly;* sent his medals,   90
   And chains,* t' invite him.
DOLL: Ay, and for his physic, sir –
MAMMON: Above the art of Aesculapius,*
   That drew the envy of the Thunderer!
   I know all this, and more.
DOLL: Troth, I am taken, sir,
   Whole, with these studies that contemplate nature.   95
MAMMON: It is a noble humour. But this form
   Was not intended for so dark a use!
   Had you been crooked, foul, of some coarse mould,
   A cloister had done well; but such a feature
   That might stand up the glory of a kingdom,   100
   To live recluse!* – is a mere solecism,
   Though in a nunnery. It must not be.
   I muse my lord your brother will permit it!
   You should spend half my land first, were I he.
   Does not this diamant* better, on my finger,   105
   Than i' the quarry?
DOLL: Yes.
MAMMON: Why, you are like it.
   You were created, lady, for the light!
   Here, you shall wear it; take it, the first pledge
   Of what I speak: to bind you to believe me.
DOLL: In chains of adamant?
MAMMON: Yes, the strongest bands.   110
   And take a secret, too. Here, by your side,
   Doth stand this hour the happiest man in Europe.
DOLL: You are contented, sir?
MAMMON: Nay, in true being:
   The envy of princes and fear of states.
DOLL: Say you so, Sir Epicure!
MAMMON: Yes, and thou shalt prove it, 115
   Daughter of honour. I have cast mine eye

Upon thy form, and I will rear this beauty
Above all styles.
DOLL: You mean no treason, sir?
MAMMON: No, I will take away that jealousy.*
I am the lord of the philosopher's stone,   120
And thou the lady.
DOLL: How, sir! Ha' you that?
MAMMON: I am the master of the mastery.*
This day, the good old wretch, here, o' the house,
Has made it for us. Now he's at projection.
Think therefore thy first wish, now; let me hear it: 125
And it shall rain into thy lap, no shower,
But floods of gold, whole cataracts, a deluge,
To get a nation on thee!
DOLL: You are pleased, sir,
To work on the ambition of our sex.
MAMMON: I am pleased the glory of her sex should know   130
This nook, here, of the Friars,* is no climate
For her to live obscurely in, to learn
Physic and surgery, for the Constable's wife
Of some odd Hundred* in Essex; but come forth,
And taste the air of palaces; eat, drink   135
The toils of emp'rics,* and their boasted practice;
Tincture of pearl, and coral, gold, and amber;
Be seen at feasts, and triumphs; have it asked,
What miracle she is? Set all the eyes
Of court afire, like a burning glass,   140
And work 'em into cinders; when the jewels
Of twenty states adorn thee, and the light
Strikes out the stars; that, when thy name is mentioned,
Queens may look pale: and, we but showing our love,
Nero's Poppaea* may be lost in story!   145
Thus will we have it.
DOLL: I could well consent, sir.
But, in a monarchy, how will this be?
The Prince will soon take notice; and both seize
You, and your stone: it being a wealth unfit
For any private subject.
MAMMON: If he knew it.   150
DOLL: Yourself do boast it, sir.
MAMMON: To thee, my life.
DOLL: O, but beware, sir! You may come to end
The remnant of your days in a loathed prison
By speaking of it.

MAMMON: 'Tis no idle fear!
   We'll therefore go with all, my girl, and live   155
   In a free state; where we will eat our mullets,
   Soused in high-country wines,* sup pheasants' eggs,
   And have our cockles, boiled in silver shells,
   Our shrimps to swim again, as when they lived,
   In a rare butter, made of dolphin's milk,   160
   Whose cream does look like opals; and with these
   Delicate meats, set ourselves high for pleasure,
   And take us down again, and then renew
   Our youth, and strength, with drinking the elixir,
   And so enjoy a perpetuity   165
   Of life, and lust. And thou shalt ha' thy wardrobe,
   Richer than Nature's, still, to change thyself,
   And vary oftener, for thy pride, than she:
   Or Art, her wise and almost equal servant.

[*Enter* FACE]

FACE: Sir, you are too loud. I hear you, every word,   170
   Into the laboratory. Some fitter place.
   The garden, or great chamber above. How like you her?
MAMMON: Excellent, Lungs! There's for thee.
FACE: But do you hear?
   Good sir, no mention of the Rabbins.*
MAMMON: We think not on 'em.   [*Exeunt* DOLL *and* MAMMON]
FACE: O, 'tis well, sir. Subtle!   175

Act Four, Scene Two

[*Enter*] SUBTLE.

FACE: Dost thou not laugh?
SUBTLE: Yes. Are they gone?
FACE: All's clear.
SUBTLE: The widow is come.
FACE: And your quarrelling disciple?
SUBTLE: Ay.
FACE: I must to my Captainship again, then.
SUBTLE: Stay, bring 'em in first.
FACE: So I meant. What is she?
   A bonnibell?*
SUBTLE: I know not.

FACE: We'll draw lots,   5
  You'll stand to that?
SUBTLE: What else?
FACE: O, for a suit
  To fall now, like a curtain flap.*
SUBTLE: To th' door, man.
FACE: You'll ha' the first kiss, 'cause I am not ready.
SUBTLE: Yes, and perhaps hit you through both the nostrils.*

[*Enter* KASTRIL *and* DAME PLIANT.]

FACE: Who would you speak with?
KASTRIL: Where's the Captain?
FACE: Gone, sir,   10
  About some business.
KASTRIL: Gone?
FACE: He'll return straight.
  But master Doctor, his lieutenant, is here.   [*Exit.*]
SUBTLE: Come near, my worshipful boy, my *terrae fili,**
  That is, my boy of land; make thy approaches:
  Welcome, I know thy lusts, and thy desires,   15
  And I will serve, and satisfy 'em. Begin,
  Charge* me from thence, or thence, or in this line;
  Here is my ground; ground thy quarrel.
KASTRIL: You lie.
SUBTLE: How, child of wrath and anger! The loud lie?
  For what, my sudden boy?
KASTRIL: Nay, that look you to,   20
  I am aforehand.
SUBTLE: O, this 's no true grammar,
  And as ill logic! You must render causes, child,
  Your first and second intentions, know your canons,
  And your divisions, moods, degrees, and differences,
  Your predicaments, substance, and accident,   25
  Series extern, and intern, with their causes
  Efficient, material, formal, final,
  And ha' your elements perfect –
KASTRIL: What is this!
  The angry tongue he talks in?
SUBTLE: That false precept,
  Of being aforehand, has deceived a number;   30
  And made 'em enter quarrels, oftentimes,
  Before they were aware, and, afterward,
  Against their wills.

KASTRIL: How must I do then, sir?
SUBTLE: I cry this lady mercy. She should, first,
     Have been saluted. I do call you lady,   35
     Because you are to be one, ere 't be long,
     My soft and buxom widow.   *He kisses her.*
KASTRIL: Is she, i'faith?
SUBTLE: Yes, or my art is an egregious liar.
KASTRIL: How know you?
SUBTLE: By inspection, on her forehead,
     And subtlety of her lip, which must be tasted   40
     Often, to make a judgement.   *He kisses her again.*
                         'Slight, she melts
     Like a myrobalane!* Here is, yet, a line
     *In rivo frontis,** tells me he is no knight.
PLIANT: What is he then, sir?
SUBTLE: Let me see your hand.
     O, your *linea Fortunae** makes it plain;   45
     And *stella*, here, *in monte Veneris;**
     But, most of all, *junctura annularis.**
     He is a soldier, or a man of art, lady:
     But shall have some great honour shortly.
PLIANT: Brother,
     He's a rare man, believe me!
KASTRIL: Hold your peace.   50

                    [*Enter* FACE.]

     Here comes the t'other rare man. Save you, Captain.
FACE: Good master Kastril. Is this your sister?
KASTRIL: Ay, sir.
     Please you to kuss her, and be proud to know her?
FACE: I shall be proud to know you, lady.
PLIANT: Brother,
     He calls me lady, too.
KASTRIL: Ay, peace, I heard it.   55
FACE: The Count is come.
SUBTLE: Where is he?
FACE: At the door.
SUBTLE: Why, you must entertain him.
FACE: What'll you do
     With these the while?
SUBTLE: Why, have 'em up, and show 'em
     Some fustian* book, or the dark glass.*
FACE: 'Fore God,

She is a delicate dabchick! I must have her.   [*Exit.*]   60
SUBTLE: Must you? Ay, if your fortune will, you must.
    Come sir, the Captain will come to us presently.
    I'll ha' you to my chamber of demonstrations,
    Where I'll show you both the grammar, and logic,
    And rhetoric of quarrelling; my whole method   65
    Drawn out in tables;* and my instrument
    That hath the several scale upon't shall make you
    Able to quarrel, at a straw's breadth, by moonlight.
    And, lady, I'll have you look in a glass
    Some half an hour, but to clear your eyesight,   70
    Against* you see your fortune: which is greater
    Than I may judge on the sudden, trust me.

[*Exeunt* SUBTLE, KASTRIL *and* DAME PLIANT]

Act Four, Scene Three

[*Enter*] FACE.

FACE: Where are you, Doctor?
SUBTLE [*Within*]:   I'll come to you presently.
FACE: I will ha' this same widow, now I ha' seen her,
    On any composition.*

[*Enter* SUBTLE]

SUBTLE: What do you say?
FACE: Ha' you disposed of them?
SUBTLE: I ha' sent them up.
FACE: Subtle, in troth, I needs must have this widow.   5
SUBTLE: Is that the matter?
FACE: Nay, but hear me.
SUBTLE: Go to,
    If you rebel once, Doll shall know it all.
    Therefore be quiet, and obey your chance.
FACE: Nay, thou art so violent now – do but conceive –
    Thou art old, and canst not serve* –
SUBTLE: Who cannot? I?   10
    'Slight, I will serve her with thee, for a –
FACE: Nay,
    But understand: I'll gi' you composition.*
SUBTLE: I will not treat* with thee: what, sell my fortune?
    'Tis better than my birthright. Do not murmur.

Win her, and carry her. If you grumble, Doll   15
Knows it directly.
FACE: Well sir, I am silent.
Will you go help to fetch Don in, in state?   [*Exit* FACE]
SUBTLE: I follow you, sir – we must keep Face in awe,
Or he will overlook* us like a tyrant.

                    [*Enter* FACE,] SURLY *like a Spaniard.*

Brain of a tailor! Who comes here? Don John!   20
SURLY: *Señores, beso las manos, á vuestras Mercedes.**
SUBTLE: Would you had stooped a little, and kissed our *anos.**
FACE: Peace, Subtle.
SUBTLE: Stab me; I shall never hold, man.
He looks in that deep ruff like a head in a platter,
Served in by a short cloak upon two trestles!   25
FACE: Or what would you say to a collar of brawn,* cut down
Beneath the souse,* and wriggled with a knife?*
SUBTLE: 'Slud, he does look too fat to be a Spaniard.
FACE: Perhaps some Fleming or some Hollander got him
In d'Alva's* time; Count Egmont's* bastard.
SUBTLE: Don,   30
Your scurvy yellow Madrid face is welcome.
SURLY: *Gratia.**
SUBTLE: He speaks out of a fortification.
Pray God he ha' no squibs* in those deep sets.*
SURLY: *Por Diós, Señores, muy linda casa!**
SUBTLE: What says he?
FACE: Praises the house, I think.   35
I know no more but's action.
SUBTLE: Yes, the *casa,*
My precious Diego, will prove fair enough
To cozen you in. Do you mark? You shall
Be cozened, Diego.
FACE: Cozened, do you see?
My worthy Donzel,* cozened.
SURLY: *Entiendo.**   40
SUBTLE: Do you intend it? So do we, dear Don.
Have you brought pistolets, or portagues?   *He feels his pockets.*
My solemn Don? Dost thou feel any?
FACE: Full.
SUBTLE: You shall be emptied, Don; pumped, and drawn
Dry, as they say.
FACE: Milked, in troth, sweet Don.   45
SUBTLE: See all the monsters; the great lion* of all, Don.

SURLY: *Con licencia, se puede ver á esta señora?**
SUBTLE: What talks he now?
FACE: O' the *señora*.
SUBTLE: O, Don,
   That is the lioness, which you shall see
   Also, my Don.
FACE: 'Slid, Subtle, how shall we do?   50
SUBTLE: For what?
FACE: Why, Doll's employed, you know.
SUBTLE: That's true!
   'Fore heaven, I know not: he must stay, that's all.
FACE: Stay? That he must not, by no means.
SUBTLE: No, why?
FACE: Unless you'll mar all. 'Slight, he'll suspect it.
   And then he will not pay, not half so well.   55
   This is a travelled punk-master, and does know
   All the delays: a notable hot-bed rascal,
   And looks, already, rampant.
SUBTLE: 'Sdeath, and Mammon
   Must not be troubled.
FACE: Mammon, in no case!
SUBTLE: What shall we do then?
FACE: Think: you must be sudden.*   60
SURLY: *Entiendo, que la señora es tan Hermosa, que codicio tan á verla, como la
   bien aventuranza de mi vida.**
FACE: *Mi vida?* 'Slid, Subtle, he puts me in mind of the widow.
   What dost thou say to draw her to't, ha?
   And tell her it is her fortune. All our venture   65
   Now lies upon 't. It is but one man more,
   Which on's chance to have her; and, beside,
   There is no maidenhead to be feared or lost.
   What dost thou think on't, Subtle?
SUBTLE: Who, I? Why –
FACE: The credit of our house too is engaged.
SUBTLE: You made me an offer for my share erewhile.
   What wilt thou gi' me, i'faith?
FACE: O, by that light,
   I'll not buy now. You know your doom to me.
   E'en take your lot, obey your chance, sir; win her,
   And wear her out for me.
SUBTLE: 'Slight, I'll not work her then.   75
FACE: It is the common cause, therefore bethink you.
   Doll else must know it, as you said.
SUBTLE: I care not.

SURLY: *Señores, porqué se tarda tanto?**
SUBTLE: Faith, I am not fit, I am old.
FACE: That's now no reason, sir.
SURLY: *Puede ser de hacer burla de mi amor.** 80
FACE: You hear the Don too? By this air, I call,
   And loose the hinges.* Doll!
SUBTLE: A plague of hell –
FACE: Will you then do?
SUBTLE: Y'are a terrible rogue,
   I'll think of this: will you, sir, call the widow?
FACE: Yes, and I'll take her too, with all her faults, 85
   Now I think on't better.
SUBTLE: With all my heart, sir,
   Am I discharged o' the lot?
FACE: As you please.
SUBTLE: Hands.
FACE: Remember now, that upon any change
   You never claim her.
SUBTLE: Much good joy and health to you, sir.
   Marry a whore? Fate, let me wed a witch first. 90
SURLY: *Por estas honradas barbas** –
SUBTLE: He swears by his beard.
   Dispatch, and call the brother too.   [*Exit* FACE.]
SURLY: *Tengo dúda, Señores,*
   *Que no me hágan alguna tración.**
SUBTLE: How, issue on? Yes, *presto Señor*. Please you
   Enthratha the *chambratha*, worthy Don; 95
   Where, if it please the Fates, in your *bathada*
   You shall be soaked, and stroked, and tubbed, and rubbed;
   And scrubbed, and fubbed,* dear Don, before you go.
   You shall, in faith, my scurvy baboon Don,
   Be curried,* clawed and flawed,* and tawed,* indeed. 100
   I will the heartilier go about it now,
   And make the widow a punk so much the sooner,
   To be revenged on this impetuous Face:
   The quickly doing of it is the grace.   [*Exeunt* SUBTLE *and* SURLY.]

Act Four, Scene Four

[*Enter*] FACE, KASTRIL, DAME PLIANT.

FACE: Come, lady: I knew the Doctor would not leave
   Till he had found the very nick* of her fortune.

KASTRIL: To be a countess, say you?
FACE: A Spanish countess, sir.
PLIANT: Why? Is that better than an English countess?
FACE: Better? 'Slight, make you that a question, lady?   5
KASTRIL: Nay, she is a fool, Captain; you must pardon her.
FACE: Ask from your courtier, to your Inns of Court-man,
    To your mere milliner: they will tell you all,
    Your Spanish jennet* is the best horse. Your Spanish
    Stoop* is the best garb.* Your Spanish beard   10
    Is the best cut. Your Spanish ruffs are the best
    Wear. Your Spanish pavane* the best dance.
    Your Spanish titillation* in a glove
    The best perfume. And, for your Spanish pike,
    And Spanish blade, let your poor Captain speak.   15
    Here comes the Doctor.

                          [*Enter* SUBTLE.]

SUBTLE: My most honoured lady,
    (For so I am now to style you, having found
    By this my scheme,* you are to undergo
    An honourable fortune, very shortly)
    What will you say now, if some –
FACE: I ha' told her all, sir.   20
    And he right worshipful brother, here, that she shall be
    A countess: do not delay 'em, sir. A Spanish countess.
SUBTLE: Still, my scarce worshipful Captain, you can keep
    No secret. Well, since he has told you, madam,
    Do you forgive him, and I do.
KASTRIL: She shall do that, sir.   25
    I'll look to 't, 'tis my charge.
SUBTLE: Well then. Nought rests
    But that she fit her love, now, to her fortune.
PLIANT: Truly, I shall never brook a Spaniard.
SUBTLE: No?
PLIANT: Never sin' eighty-eight* could I abide 'em.
    And that was some three year before I was born, in truth.   30
SUBTLE: Come, you must love him, or be miserable:
    Choose, which you will.
FACE: By this good rush,* persuade her;
    She will cry strawberries* else, within this twelvemonth.
SUBTLE: Nay, shads* and mackerel, which is worse.
FACE: Indeed, sir?
KASTRIL: God's lid, you shall love him, or I'll kick you.

PLIANT: Why?   35
    I'll do as you will ha' me, brother.
KASTRIL: Do,
    Or by this hand, I'll maul you.
FACE: Nay, good sir,
    Be not so fierce.
SUBTLE: No, my enraged child,
    She will be ruled. What, when she comes to taste
    The pleasures of a countess! To be courted –   40
FACE: And kissed, and ruffled!*
SUBTLE: Ay, behind the hangings.*
FACE: And then come forth in pomp!
SUBTLE: And know her state!*
FACE: Of keeping all th' idolators o' the chamber
    Barer* to her than at their prayers!
SUBTLE: Is served
    Upon the knee!
FACE: And has her pages, ushers,   45
    Footmen, and coaches –
SUBTLE: Her six mares –
FACE: Nay, eight!
SUBTLE: To hurry her through London to th' Exchange,*
    Bedlam,* the China-houses* –
FACE: Yes, and have
    The citizens gape at her, and praise her tires!*
    And my lord's goose-turd bands,* that rides with her!   50
KASTRIL: Most brave! By this hand, you are not my suster
    If you refuse.
PLIANT: I will not refuse, brother.

[*Enter* SURLY.]

SURLY: *Qué es esto, Señores, que non se venga?*
    *Esta tardanza me mata!**
FACE: It is the Count come!   55
    The Doctor knew he would be here, by his art.
SUBTLE: *En galanta madama, Don! Galantissima!**
SURLY: *Por todos los dioses, la más acabada*
    *Hermosura, que he visto en mi vida!**
FACE: Is't not a gallant language that they speak?
KASTRIL: An admirable language! Is't not French?   60
FACE: No, Spanish, sir.
KASTRIL: It goes like law-French,*
    And that, they say, is the courtliest language.

FACE: List, sir.
SURLY: *El sol ha perdido su lumbre, con el*
    *Resplandor, que trae esta dama. Válgame Diós!**
FACE: He admires your sister.
KASTRIL: Must not she make curtsy?   65
SUBTLE: 'Ods, will, she must go to him, man, and kiss him!
    It is the Spanish fashion for the women
    To make first court.
FACE: 'Tis true he tells you, sir:
    His art knows all.
SURLY: *Porqué no se acude?**
KASTRIL: He speaks to her, I think?
FACE: That he does, sir.   70
SURLY: *Por el amor de Diós, qué es esto, que se tarda?**
KASTRIL: Nay, see: she will not understand him! Gull.
    Noddy.
PLIANT: What say you, brother?
KASTRIL: Ass, my suster,
    Go kuss him, as the cunning man would ha' you,
    I'll thrust a pin i' your buttocks else.
FACE: O no, sir.   75
SURLY: *Señora mia, mi persona muy indigna está*
    *Allegar á tanta hermosura.**
FACE: Does he not use her bravely?
KASTRIL: Bravely, i' faith!
FACE: Nay, he will use her better.
KASTRIL: Do you think so?
SURLY: *Señora, si sera servida, entremos.**   80
                    [*Exeunt* SURLY *and* DAME PLIANT.]
KASTRIL: Where does he carry her?
FACE: Into the garden, sir;
    Take you no thought: I must interpret for her.
SUBTLE: Give Doll the word.   [*Exit* FACE.]
                    Come, my fierce child, advance,
    We'll to our quarrelling lesson again.
KASTRIL: Agreed.
    I love a Spanish boy, with all my heart.   85
SUBTLE: Nay, and by this means, sir, you shall be brother
    To a great count.
KASTRIL: Ay, I knew that, at first.
    This match will advance the house of the Kastrils.
SUBTLE: Pray God, your sister prove but pliant.
KASTRIL: Why,
    Her name is so, by her other husband.
SUBTLE: How!   90

KASTRIL: The widow Pliant. Knew you not that?
SUBTLE: No, faith, sir.
    Yet, by erection of her figure,* I guessed it.
    Come, let's go practice.
KASTRIL: Yes, but do you think, Doctor,
    I e'er shall quarrel well?
SUBTLE: I warrant you.   [*Exeunt.*]

Act Four, Scene Five

[*Enter*] DOLL, MAMMON.

DOLL: *For, after Alexander's death –*   *In her fit of talking*
MAMMON: Good lady –
DOLL: *That Perdiccas, and Antigonus were slain,*
    The two that stood, Seleuc', and Ptolomy* –
MAMMON: Madam.
DOLL: *Made up the two legs, and the fourth Beast.*
    That was Gog-north, and Egypt-south: which after   5
    Was called Gog Iron-leg, and South Iron-leg –
MAMMON: Lady –
DOLL: *And then Gog-horned. So was Egypt, too.*
    Then Egypt clay-leg, and Gog clay-leg –
MAMMON: Sweet madam.
DOLL: *And last Gog-dust, and Egypt-dust, which fall*
    In the last link of the fourth chain.* And these   10
    Be stars in story, which none see or look at –
MAMMON: What shall I do?
DOLL: *For, as he says, except*
    We call the Rabbins, and the heathen Greeks –
MAMMON: Dear lady.
DOLL: *To come from Salem,* and from Athens,*
    And teach the people of Great Britain –

[*Enter* FACE.]

FACE: What's the matter, sir?   15
DOLL: *To speak the tongue of Eber, and Javan* –*
MAMMON: O,
    She's in her fit.
DOLL: *We shall know nothing –*
FACE: Death, sir,
    We are undone.
DOLL: *Where, then, a learned linguist*

Shall see the ancient used communion
Of vowels and consonants –
FACE: My master will hear!   20
DOLL: *A wisdom, which Pythagoras held most high –*
MAMMON: Sweet honourable lady.
DOLL: *To comprise*
  All sounds of voices, in few marks of letters –
FACE: Nay, you must never hope to lay her now.
                    They speak together.

DOLL: *And so we may arrive*	FACE: How did you put her into 't?
by Talmud skill,	MAMMON: Alas, I talked 25
And profane Greek, to	Of a fifth monarchy*
raise the building up	I would erect,
Of Helen's house, against	With the philosopher's stone
the Ismaelite,	(by chance), and she
King of Thogarma,	Falls upon the other four,* straight.
*And his Habergions**	FACE: Out of Broughton!
Brimstony, blue, and fiery;	I told you so. 'Slid, stop her mouth.
and the force	MAMMON: Is 't best?
Of King Abaddon, and the	FACE: She'll never leave else. If
Beast of Cittim;	the old man hear her, 30
Which Rabbi David	We are but faeces,* ashes.
Kimchi, Onkelos,**	SUBTLE [*within*]: What's to do there?
And Aben-Ezra do interpret*	FACE: O, we are lost. Now she
*Rome**	hears him, she is quiet.

    Upon SUBTLE's *entry they disperse.* [*Exeunt* FACE *and* DOLL.]

MAMMON: Where shall I hide me?
SUBTLE: How! What sight is here!
  Close deeds of darkness, and that shun the light!
  Bring him again.* Who is he? What, my son!   35
  O, I have lived too long.
MAMMON: Nay, good dear father,
  There was no unchaste purpose.
SUBTLE: Not? And flee me
  When I come in?
MAMMON: That was my error.
SUBTLE: Error?
  Guilt, guilt, my son. Give it the right name. No marvel,
  If I found check in our great work within,   40
  When such affairs as these were managing!*
MAMMON: Why, have you so?
SUBTLE: It has stood still this half hour;
  And all the rest of our less works gone back.
  Where is the instrument of wickedness,

My lewd false drudge?
MAMMON: Nay, good sir, blame not him.   45
   Believe me, 'twas against his will or knowledge.
   I saw her by chance.
SUBTLE: Will you commit more sin,
   T' excuse a varlet?
MAMMON: By my hope, 'tis true, sir.
SUBTLE: Nay, then I wonder less if you, for whom
   The blessing was prepared, should so tempt heaven,   50
   And lose your fortunes.
MAMMON: Why, sir?
SUBTLE: This'll retard
   The work, a month at least.
MAMMON: Why, if it do,
   What remedy? But think it not, good father:
   Our purposes were honest.
SUBTLE: As they were,
   So the reward prove.   *A great noise and crack within.*
            How now! Ay me.   55
   God and all saints be good to us. What's that?

[*Enter* FACE.]

FACE: O sir, we are defeated! All the works
   Are flown *in fumo:** every glass is burst.
   Furnace, and all rent down! As if a bolt
   Of thunder had been driven through the house.   60
   Retorts, receivers,* pelicans, bolt-heads,
   All struck in shivers!   SUBTLE *falls down as if in a swoon.*
         Help, good sir! Alas,
   Coldness and death invades him. Nay, Sir Mammon,
   Do the fair offices of a man! You stand,
   As you were readier to depart than he.   *One knocks.*   65
   Who's there? My lord her brother is come.
MAMMON: Ha, Lungs?
FACE: His coach is at the door. Avoid his sight,
   For he's as furious as his sister is mad.
MAMMON: Alas!
FACE: My brain is quite undone with the fume, sir,
   I ne'er must hope to be mine own man* again.   70
MAMMON: Is all lost, Lungs? Will nothing be preserved
   Of all our cost?
FACE: Faith, very little, sir.
   A peck of coals or so, which is cold comfort, sir.
MAMMON: O my voluptuous mind! I am justly punished.

FACE: And so am I, sir.

MAMMON: Cast from all my hopes –   75

FACE: Nay, certainties, sir.

MAMMON: By mine own base affections.

                                        SUBTLE *seems to come to himself.*

SUBTLE: O, the curst fruits of vice and lust!

MAMMON: Good father,
  It was my sin. Forgive it.

SUBTLE: Hangs my roof
  Over us still, and will not fall? O justice
  Upon us for this wicked man!

FACE: Nay, look, sir,   80
  You grieve him, now, with staying in his sight:
  Good sir, the nobleman will come too, and take you,
  And that may breed a tragedy.

MAMMON: I'll go.

FACE: Ay, and repent at home, sir. It may be
  For some good penance you may ha' it yet,   85
  A hundred pound to the box* at Bedlam –

MAMMON: Yes.

FACE: For the restoring such as ha' their wits.

MAMMON: I'll do 't.

FACE: I'll send one to you to receive it.

MAMMON: Do.
  Is no projection left?

FACE: All flown, or stinks, sir.

MAMMON: Will nought be saved that's good for med'cine, thinkst thou?   90

FACE: I cannot tell, sir. There will be, perhaps,
  Something, about the scraping of the shards,
  Will cure the itch: thought not your itch of mind, sir.
  It shall be saved for you, and sent home. Good sir,
  This way: for fear the lord should meet you.   [*Exit* MAMMON.]

SUBTLE: Face.   95

FACE: Ay.

SUBTLE: Is he gone?

FACE: Yes, and as heavily
  As all the gold he hoped for were in his blood.
  Let us be light, though.

SUBTLE: Ay, as balls,* and bound
  And hit our heads against the roof for joy:
  There's so much of our care now cast away.   100

FACE: Now to our Don.

SUBTLE: Yes, your young widow, by this time,
  Is made a countess, Face; she's been in travail
  Of a young heir for you.

FACE:	Good, sir.
SUBTLE:	Off with your case,*

And greet her kindly, as a bridegroom should,
After these common hazards.

FACE:	Very well, sir.	105

Will you go fetch Don Diego off, the while?

SUBTLE: And fetch him over* too, if you'll be pleased, sir:
Would Doll were in her place to pick his pockets now.

FACE: Why, you can do it as well, if you would set to 't.
I pray you prove your virtue.

SUBTLE:	For your sake, sir.	[*Exeunt.*] 110

Act Four, Scene Six

[*Enter*] SURLY, DAME PLIANT.

[SURLY:] Lady, you see into what hands you are fall'n;
'Mongst what a nest of villains! And how near
Your honour was t' have catched a certain clap*
(Through your credulity) had I but been
So punctually forward, as time, place,   5
And other circumstance would ha' made a man:
For y'are a handsome woman; would y' were wise, too.
I am a gentleman, come here disguised,
Only to find the knaveries of this citadel,
And where I might have wronged your honour, and have not,   10
I claim some interest in your love. You are,
They say, a widow, rich; and I am a bachelor,
Worth nought: your fortunes may make me a man,
As mine ha' preferred you a woman. Think upon it,
And whether I have deserved you or no.

DAME PLIANT:	I will, sir.	15

SUBTLE: And for these household-rogues, let me alone
To treat with them.

[*Enter* SUBTLE.]

SUBTLE:	How doth my noble Diego?

And my dear madam countess? Hath the count
Been courteous, lady? Liberal? And open?
Donzel, methinks you look melancholic,   20
After your *coitium*, and scurvy! Truly,
I do not like the dullness of your eye:
It hath a heavy cast, 'tis upsee Dutch,*
And says you are a lumpish* whore-master.

Be lighter, I will make your pockets so.   *He falls to picking of them.* 25
SURLY: Will you, Don bawd, and pickpurse? How now? Reel you?
    Stand up, sir, you shall find since I am so heavy,
    I'll gi' you equal weight.
SUBTLE: Help, murder!
SURLY: No, sir.
    There's no such thing intended. A good cart
    And a clean whip* shall ease you of that fear.   30
    I am the Spanish Don, that should be cozened,
    Do you see? Cozened? Where's your Captain Face?
    That parcel-broker,* and whole-bawd, all rascal.

[*Enter* FACE.]

FACE: How, Surly!
SURLY: O, make your approach, good Captain.
    I have found from whence your copper rings and spoons   35
    Come now, and wherewith you cheat abroad in taverns.
    'Twas here you learned t' anoint your boot with brimstone,
    Then rub men's gold on 't, for a kind of touch,
    And say 'twas naught, when you had changed the colour,*
    That you might ha't for nothing! And this Doctor,   40
    Your sooty, smoky-bearded compeer, he
    Will close you so much gold, in a bolt's head,
    And, on a turn, convey (i' the stead) another
    With sublimed mercury, that shall burst i' the heat,
    And fly out all *in fumo*?* Then weeps Mammon: 45
    Then swoons his worship. Or, he is the Faustus,*   [*Exit* FACE.] 45
    That casteth figures, and can conjure cures,
    Plague, piles, and pox, by the ephemeredes,*
    And holds intelligence with all the bawds
    And midwives of three shires? While you send in –   50
    Captain (what, is he gone?) – damsels with child,
    Wives that are barren, or the waiting-maid
    With the green-sickness?* Nay, sir, you must tarry
    Though he be 'scaped; and answer by the ears,* sir.

Act Four, Scene Seven

[*Enter*] FACE, KASTRIL.

[FACE:] Why, now's the time, if ever you will quarrel
    Well (as they say) and be a true-born child.

The Doctor and your sister both are abused.
KASTRIL: Where is he? Which is he? He is a slave
    Whate'er he is, and the son of a whore. Are you   5
    The man, sir, I would know?
SURLY: I should be loath, sir,
    To confess so much.
KASTRIL: Then you lie, i' your throat.
SURLY: How?
FACE: A very arrant rogue, sir, and a cheater,
    Employed here by another conjurer,
    That does not love the Doctor, and would cross him   10
    If he knew how –
SURLY: Sir, you are abused.
KASTRIL: You lie:
    And 'tis no matter.
FACE: Well said, sir. He is
    The impudentest rascal –
SURLY: You are indeed. Will you hear me, sir?
FACE: By no means: bid him be gone.
KASTRIL: Be gone, sir, quickly.
SURLY: This's strange! Lady, do you inform your brother.   15
FACE: There is not such a foist* in all the town.
    The Doctor had him presently,* and finds, yet,
    The Spanish count will come here. Bear up, Subtle.
SUBTLE: Yes, sir, he must appear within this hour.
FACE: And yet this rogue would come in a disguise,   20
    By the temptation of another spirit,
    To trouble our art, though he could not hurt it.
KASTRIL: Ay,
    I know – away, you talk like a foolish mauther.*
SURLY: Sir, all is truth she says.
FACE: Do not believe him, sir:
    He is the lying'st swabber!* Come your ways, sir.   25
SURLY: You are valiant, out of company.
KASTRIL: Yes, how then, sir?

[*Enter* DRUGGER.]

Nay, here's an honest fellow too, that knows him,
    And all his tricks. (Make good what I say, Abel,
    This cheater would ha' cozened thee o' the widow.)
    He owes this honest Drugger here seven pound   30
    He has had on him, in twopenny'orths of tobacco.
DRUGGER: Yes, sir. And he's damned himself, three terms,* to pay me.

FACE: What does he owe for lotium?*
DRUGGER: Thirty shillings, sir;
    And for six syringes.
SURLY: Hydra* of villainy!
FACE: Nay, sir, you must quarrel him out o' the house.
KASTRIL: I will.   35
    Sir, if you get not out o' doors, you lie:
    And you are a pimp.
SURLY: Why, this is madness, sir,
    Not valour in you: I must laugh at this.
KASTRIL: It is my humour: you are a pimp, and a trig,*
    And an Amadis de Gaul, or a Don Quixote.*   40
DRUGGER: Or a Knight o' the Curious Coxcomb.* Do you see?

                    [*Enter* ANANIAS.]

ANANIAS: Peace to the household.
KASTRIL: I'll keep peace for no man.
ANANIAS: Casting of dollars is concluded lawful.
KASTRIL: Is he the constable?
SUBTLE: Peace, Ananias.
FACE: No, sir.
KASTRIL: Then you are an otter,* and a shad,* a whit,*   45
    A very tim.*
SURLY: You'll hear me, sir?
KASTRIL: I will not.
ANANIAS: What is the motive?
SURLY: Zeal in the young gentleman,
    Against his Spanish slops* –
ANANIAS: They are profane,
    Lewd, superstitious, and idolatrous breeches.
SURLY: New rascals!
KASTRIL: Will you be gone, sir?
ANANIAS: Avoid Satan,   50
    Thou art not of the light. That ruff of pride
    About thy neck betrays thee: and is the same
    With that, which the unclean birds in seventy-seven
    Were seen to prank it with, on divers coasts.*
    Thou look'st like Antichrist in that lewd hat.   55
SURLY: I must give way.
KASTRIL: Begone, sir.
SURLY: But I'll take
    A course with you –
ANANIAS: (Depart, proud Spanish fiend.)

SURLY: Captain, and Doctor –
ANANIAS: (Child of perdition.)
KASTRIL: Hence, sir.   [*Exit* SURLY.]
    Did I not quarrel bravely?
FACE: Yes, indeed, sir.
KASTRIL: Nay, and I give my mind to 't, I shall do 't.   60
FACE: O, you must follow, sir, and threaten him tame.
    He'll turn again else.
KASTRIL: I'll re-turn him, then.   [*Exit.*]
FACE: Drugger, this rogue prevented* us, for thee:
    We had determined that thou shouldst ha' come,
    In a Spanish suit, and ha' carried her so; and he,
    A brokerly slave, goes, puts it on himself.
    Hast brought the damask?
DRUGGER: Yes, sir.
FACE: Thou must borrow
    A Spanish suit. Hast thou no credit with the players?
DRUGGER: Yes, sir; did you never see me play the fool?*
FACE: I know not, Nab: thou shalt, if I can help it.   70
    Hieronymo's* old cloak, ruff, and hat will serve;
    I'll tell thee more when thou bring'st 'em.
ANANIAS: Sir, I know.
                  SUBTLE *hath whispered with him this while.*
    The Spaniard hates the brethren, and hath spies
    Upon their actions; and that this was one
    I make no scruple. But the holy synod*   75
    Have been in prayer and meditation for it.
    And 'tis revealed no less to them than me
    That casting of money is most lawful.
SUBTLE: True.
    But here I cannot do it; if the house
    Should chance to be suspected, all would out,   80
    And we be locked up in the Tower forever,
    To make gold there (for th' state), never come out:
    And then you are defeated.
ANANIAS: I will tell
    This to the elders, and the weaker brethren,
    That the whole company of the Separation   85
    May join in humble prayer again.
SUBTLE: (And fasting.)
ANANIAS: Yea, for some fitter place. The peace of mind
    Rest with these walls.
SUBTLE: Thanks, courteous Ananias.   [*Exit* ANANIAS.]
FACE: What did he come for?

SUBTLE: About casting dollars,
   Presently, out of hand. And so, I told him,   90
   A Spanish minister came here to spy
   Against the faithful –
FACE: I conceive. Come, Subtle,
   Thou art so down upon the least disaster!
   How wouldst th' ha' done, if I had not helped thee out?
SUBTLE: I thank thee, Face, for the angry boy, i' faith.   95
FACE: Who would ha' looked, it should ha' been that rascal?
   Surly? He had dyed his beard, and all. Well, sir,
   Here's damask come, to make you a suit.
SUBTLE: Where's Drugger?
FACE: He is gone to borrow me a Spanish habit,
   I'll be the Count now.
SUBTLE: But where's the widow?   100
FACE: Within, with my lord's sister: Madam Doll
   Is entertaining her.
SUBTLE: By your favour, Face,
   Now she is honest, I will stand again.
FACE: You will not offer it?
SUBTLE: Why?
FACE: Stand to your word,
   Or – here comes Doll. She knows –
SUBTLE: You're tyrannous still.   105

[*Enter* DOLL.]

FACE: Strict for my right. How now, my Doll? Hast told her
   The Spanish count will come?
DOLL: Yes, but another is come
   You little looked for!
FACE: Who's that?
DOLL: Your master:
   The master of the house.
SUBTLE: How, Doll!
FACE: She lies.
   This is some trick. Come, leave your quiblins,* Dorothy.   110
DOLL: Look out, and see.
SUBTLE: Art thou in earnest?
DOLL: 'Slight,
   Forty o' the neighbours are about him, talking.
FACE: 'Tis he, by this good day.
DOLL: 'Twill prove ill day
   For some on us.

FACE: We are undone, and taken.*
DOLL: Lost, I am afraid.
SUBTLE: You said he would not come,   115
    While there died one a week, within the liberties.*
FACE: No, 'twas within the walls.*
SUBTLE: Was't so? Cry you mercy:
    I thought the liberties. What shall we do now, Face?
FACE: Be silent: not a word, if he call or knock.
    I'll into mine old shape* again, and meet him,   120
    Of Jeremy, the butler. I' the meantime,
    Do you two pack up all the goods, and purchase,*
    That we can carry i' the two trunks. I'll keep him
    Off for today, if I cannot longer: and then
    At night I'll ship you both away to Ratcliff,*   125
    Where we'll meet tomorrow, and there we'll share.
    Let Mammon's brass and pewter keep* the cellar:
    We'll have another time for that. But, Doll,
    Pray thee go heat a little water quickly;
    Subtle must shave me. All my Captain's beard   130
    Must off, to make me appear smooth* Jeremy.
    You'll do 't?
SUBTLE: Yes, I'll shave you, as well as I can.
FACE: And not cut my throat, but trim* me?
SUBTLE: You shall see, sir.   [*Exeunt.*]

Act Five, Scene One

[*Enter*] LOVEWIT, NEIGHBOURS.

[LOVEWIT:] Has there been such resort, say you?
NEIGHBOUR 1:   Daily, sir.
NEIGHBOUR 2: And nightly, too.
NEIGHBOUR 3:   Ay, some as brave* as lords.
NEIGHBOUR 4: Ladies, and gentlewomen.
NEIGHBOUR 5:   Citizens' wives.
NEIGHBOUR 1: And knights.
NEIGHBOUR 6:   In coaches.
NEIGHBOUR 2:   Yes, and oyster-women.
NEIGHBOUR 1: Beside other gallants.
NEIGHBOUR 3:   Sailors' wives.
NEIGHBOUR 4:   Tobacco-men.   5
NEIGHBOUR 5: Another Pimlico!*
LOVEWIT: What should my knave advance

To draw this company? He hung out no banners
Of a strange calf, with five legs,* to be seen?
Or a huge lobster, with six claws?
NEIGHBOUR 6:   No, sir.
NEIGHBOUR 3: We had gone in then, sir.
LOVEWIT: He has no gift   10
Of teaching i' the nose* that e'er I knew of!
You saw no bills set up that promised cure
Of agues, or the toothache?
NEIGHBOUR 2:   No such thing, sir.
LOVEWIT: Nor heard a drum struck,* for baboons or puppets?
NEIGHBOUR 5: Neither, sir.
LOVEWIT: What device should he bring forth now!   15
I love a teeming wit, as I love my nourishment.
Pray God he ha' not kept such open house
That he hath sold my hangings, and my bedding:
I left him nothing else. If he have eat 'em,
A plague o' the moth, say I. Sure he has got   20
Some bawdy pictures, to call all this ging;*
The Friar and the Nun;* or the new motion*
Of the knight's courser, covering* the parson's mare;
The boy of six year old, with the great thing:*
Or 't may be he has the fleas that run at tilt   25
Upon a table, or some dog to dance?
When saw you him?
NEIGHBOUR 1:   Who sir, Jeremy?
NEIGHBOUR 2:   Jeremy butler?
We saw him not this month.
LOVEWIT: How!
NEIGHBOUR 4:   Not these five weeks, sir.
NEIGHBOUR 1: These six weeks, at the least.
LOVEWIT: Y' amaze me, neighbours!
NEIGHBOUR 5: Sure, if your worship know not where he is,   30
He's slipped away.
NEIGHBOUR 6:   Pray God he be not made away!
LOVEWIT: Ha? It's no time to question, then.   *He knocks.*
NEIGHBOUR 6:   About
Some three weeks since I heard a doleful cry,
As I sat up, a-mending my wife's stockings.
LOVEWIT: This's strange! That none will answer! Didst thou hear   35
A cry, saist thou?
NEIGHBOUR 6:   Yes, sir, like unto a man
That had been strangled an hour, and could not speak.
NEIGHBOUR 2: I heard it too, just this day three weeks, at two o'clock

Next morning.

LOVEWIT: These be miracles, or you make 'em so!
A man an hour strangled, and could not speak,   40
And both you heard him cry?
NEIGHBOUR 3:   Yes, downward, sir.
LOVEWIT: Thou art a wise fellow: give me thy hand, I pray thee.
What trade art thou on?
NEIGHBOUR 3:   A smith, and 't please your worship.
LOVEWIT: A smith? Then lend me thy help to get this door open.
NEIGHBOUR 3: That I will presently, sir, but fetch my tools –   [*Exit.*] 45
NEIGHBOUR 1: Sir, best to knock again, afore you break it.

Act Five, Scene Two

[*Enter*] FACE.

[LOVEWIT:] I will.
FACE: What mean you, sir?
NEIGHBOURS 1, 2, 4:   O, here's Jeremy!
FACE: Good sir, come from the door.
LOVEWIT: Why! What's the matter?
FACE: Yet farther, you are too near yet.
LOVEWIT: I' the name of wonder!
What means the fellow?
FACE: The house, sir, has been visited.
LOVEWIT: What? With the plague? Stand thou then farther.
FACE: No, sir,   5
I had it not.
LOVEWIT: Who had it then? I left
None else but thee i' the house!
FACE: Yes, sir. My fellow,
The cat that kept the butt'ry, had it on her
A week before I spied it: but I got her
Conveyed away, i' the night. And so I shut   10
The house up for a month –
LOVEWIT: How!
FACE: Purposing then, sir,
T' have burnt rose-water, treacle, and tar,*
And, ha' made it sweet, that you should ne'er ha' known it:
Because I knew the news would but afflict you, sir.
LOVEWIT: Breathe less, and farther off. Why, this is stranger!   15
The neighbours tell me all, here, that the doors
Have still been open –

FACE: How, sir!
LOVEWIT: Gallants, men and women,
    And of all sorts, tag-rag, been seen to flock here
    In threaves,* these ten weeks, as to a second Hogsden,
    In days of Pimlico, and Eye-bright!*
FACE: Sir,   20
    Their wisdoms will not say so!
LOVEWIT: Today they speak
    Of coaches, and gallants; one in a French hood
    Went in, they tell me; and another was seen
    In a velvet gown, at the window! Divers more
    Pass in and out!
FACE: They did pass through the doors then,   25
    Or walls, I assure their eyesights, and their spectacles;
    For here, sir, are the keys, and here have been
    In this my pocket, now, above twenty days!
    And for before, I kept the fort alone there.
    But that 'tis yet not deep i' the afternoon,   30
    I should believe my neighbours had seen double
    Through the black-pot,* and made these apparitions!
    For, on my faith to your worship, for these three weeks
    And upwards, the door has not been opened.
LOVEWIT: Strange!
NEIGHBOUR 1: Good faith, I think I saw a coach!
NEIGHBOUR 2:   And I too,   35
    I'd ha' been sworn!
LOVEWIT: Do you but think it now?
    And but one coach?
NEIGHBOUR 4:   We cannot tell, sir: Jeremy
    Is a very honest fellow.
FACE: Did you see me at all?
NEIGHBOUR 1: No, that we are sure on.
NEIGHBOUR 2:   I'll be sworn o' that.
LOVEWIT: Fine rogues, to have your testimonies built on!   40

                    [*Enter* NEIGHBOUR 3.]

NEIGHBOUR 3: Is Jeremy come?
NEIGHBOUR 1:   O yes, you may leave your tools,
    We were deceived, he says.
NEIGHBOUR 2:   He's had the keys,
    And the door has been shut these three weeks.
NEIGHBOUR 3:   Like enough.
LOVEWIT: Peace, and get hence, you changelings.*

FACE: Surly come!
    And Mammon made acquainted? They'll tell all.   45
    (How shall I beat them off? What shall I do?)
    Nothing's more wretched than a guilty conscience.

Act Five, Scene Three

[*Enter*] SURLY, MAMMON.

[SURLY:] No, sir, he was a great physician. This,
    It was no bawdy-house, but a mere* chancel.
    You knew the lord and his sister.
MAMMON: Nay, good Surly –
SURLY: The happy word, 'be rich' –
MAMMON: Play not the tyrant –
SURLY: Should be today pronounced to all your friends.   5
    And where be your andirons now? And your brass pots?
    That should ha' been golden flagons, and great wedges?*
MAMMON: Let me but breathe. What! They ha' shut their doors,
    Methinks!   MAMMON *and* SURLY *knock*.
SURLY: Ay, now 'tis holiday time with them.
MAMMON: Rogues,
    Cozeners, impostors, bawds!
FACE: What mean you, sir?   10
MAMMON: To enter if we can.
FACE: Another man's house?
    Here is the owner, sir. Turn you to him,
    And speak your business.
MAMMON: Are you, sir, the owner?
LOVEWIT: Yes, sir.
MAMMON: And are those knaves within your cheaters?
LOVEWIT: What knaves? What cheaters?
MAMMON: Subtle and his Lungs.   15
FACE: The gentleman is distracted, sir! No lungs
    Nor lights* ha' been seen here in these three weeks, sir,
    Within these doors, upon my word!
SURLY: Your word,
    Groom arrogant!
FACE: Yes, sir, I am the housekeeper,
    And know the keys ha' not been out o' my hands.   20
SURLY: This's a new Face?
FACE: You do mistake the house, sir!
    What sign* was't at?

SURLY: You rascal! This is one
    O' the confederacy. Come, let's get officers,
    And force the door.
LOVEWIT: Pray you, stay, gentlemen.
SURLY: No, sir, we'll come with warrant.
MAMMON: Ay, and then   25
    We shall ha' your doors open.   [*Exeunt* MAMMON *and* SURLY.]
LOVEWIT: What means this?
FACE: I cannot tell, sir!
NEIGHBOUR 1:   These are two o' the gallants
    That we do think we saw.
FACE: Two o' the fools!
    You talk as idly as they. Good faith, sir,
    I think the moon* has crazed 'em all!

[*Enter* KASTRIL.]

                              (O me,   30
    The angry boy come too? He'll make a noise,
    And ne'er away till he have betrayed us all.)   KASTRIL *knocks.*
KASTRIL: What, rogues, bawds, slaves, you'll open the door, anon!
    Punk, cockatrice,* my suster! By this light
    I'll fetch the marshal to you. You are a whore   35
    To keep your castle –
FACE: Who would you speak with, sir?
KASTRIL: The bawdy Doctor and the cozening Captain,
    And Puss my suster.
LOVEWIT: This is something, sure!
FACE: Upon my trust, these doors were never open, sir.
KASTRIL: I have heard all their tricks, told me twice over,   40
    By the fat knight, and the lean gentleman.*
LOVEWIT: Here comes another.
FACE: Ananias too?

[*Enter* ANANIAS *and* TRIBULATION.]

    And his pastor?
TRIBULATION: The doors are shut against us.
                              They beat, too, at the door.
ANANIAS: Come forth, you seed of sulphur, sons of fire,
    Your stench, it is broke forth: abomination   45
    Is in the house.
KASTRIL: Ay, my suster's there.
ANANIAS: The place,
    It is become a cage of unclean birds.*

KASTRIL: Yes, I will fetch the scavenger,* and the constable.
TRIBULATION: You shall do well.
ANANIAS: We'll join, to weed them out.
KASTRIL: You will not come, then? Punk, device,* my suster!   50
ANANIAS: Call her not sister. She is a harlot, verily.
KASTRIL: I'll raise the street.
LOVEWIT: Good gentlemen, a word.
ANANIAS: Satan, avoid, and hinder not our zeal.
                    [*Exeunt* KASTRIL, ANANIAS *and* TRIBULATION.]
LOVEWIT: The world's turned Bedlam.
FACE: These are all broke loose
    Out of Saint Katherine's,* where they use to keep   55
    The better sort of mad folks.
NEIGHBOUR 1:   All these persons
    We saw go in and out here.
NEIGHBOUR 2:   Yes, indeed, sir.
NEIGHBOUR 3: These were the parties.
FACE: Peace, you drunkards. Sir,
    I wonder at it! Please you, to give me leave
    To touch the door; I'll try, and the lock be changed.   60
LOVEWIT: It mazes me!
FACE: Good faith, sir, I believe
    There's no such thing. 'Tis all *deceptio visus*.*
    (Would I could get him away.)   DAPPER *cries out within.*
DAPPER: Master Captain, master Doctor.
LOVEWIT: Who's that?
FACE: (Our clerk within, that I forgot.) I know not, sir.
DAPPER: For God's sake, when will her Grace be at leisure?
FACE: Ha!   65
    Illusions, some spirit o' the air. (His gag is melted,
    And now he sets out the throat.*)
DAPPER: I am almost stifled –
FACE: (Would you were altogether.)
LOVEWIT: 'Tis i' the house.
    Ha! List.
FACE: Believe it, sir, i' the air!
LOVEWIT: Peace, you –
DAPPER: Mine aunt's Grace does not use me well.
SUBTLE [*within*]:   You fool,   70
    Peace, you'll mar all.
FACE: Or you will else, you rogue.
LOVEWIT: O, is it so? Then you converse with spirits!
    Come, sir. No more o' your tricks, good Jeremy,
    The truth, the shortest way.*
FACE: Dismiss this rabble, sir.

What shall I do? I am catched.
LOVEWIT: Good neighbours,   75
   I thank you all. You may depart.   [*Exeunt* NEIGHBOURS.]
                     Come, sir,
   You know that I am an indulgent master;
   And therefore conceal nothing. What's your med'cine,
   To draw so many different sorts of wild fowl?
FACE: Sir, you were wont to affect mirth, and wit: 80
   (But here's no place to talk on 't i' the street.)
   Give me but leave to make the best of my fortune,
   And only pardon me th' abuse of the house:
   It's all I beg. I'll help you to a widow
   In recompense, that you shall gi' me thanks for,   85
   Will make you seven years younger, and a rich one.
   'Tis but your putting on a Spanish cloak,
   I have her within. You need not fear the house,
   It was not visited.*
LOVEWIT: But by me, who came
   Sooner than you expected.
FACE: It is true, sir.
   Pray you forgive me.
LOVEWIT: Well: let's see your widow.
               [*Exeunt* LOVEWIT *and* FACE.]

Act Five, Scene Four

[*Enter*] SUBTLE, DAPPER.

[SUBTLE:] How! Ha' you eaten your gag?
DAPPER: Yes, faith, it crumbled
   Away i' my mouth.
SUBTLE: You ha' spoiled all then.
DAPPER: No,
   I hope my aunt of Fairy will forgive me.
SUBTLE: Your aunt's a gracious lady; but in troth
   You were to blame.
DAPPER: The fume did overcome me,   5
   And I did do 't to stay my stomach. Pray you
   So satisfy her Grace. Here comes the Captain.

[*Enter* FACE.]

FACE: How now? Is his mouth down?*
SUBTLE: Ay! He has spoken!

FACE: (A pox, I heard him, and you too.) He's undone, then.
   (I have been fain to say, the house is haunted   10
   With spirits, to keep churl* back.
SUBTLE: And hast thou done it?
FACE: Sure, for this night.
SUBTLE: Why, then triumph, and sing
   Of Face so famous, the precious king
   Of present wits.
FACE: Did you not hear the coil*
   About the door?
SUBTLE: Yes, and I dwindled with it.)   15
FACE: Show him his aunt, and let him be dispatched:
   I'll send her to you.   [*Exit.*]
SUBTLE: Well, sir, your aunt her Grace
   Will give you audience presently, on my suit,*
   And the Captain's word, that you did not eat your gag
   In any contempt of her Highness.
DAPPER: Not I, in troth, sir.   20

        [*Enter*] DOLL *like the Queen of Fairy.*

SUBTLE: Here she is come. Down o' your knees, and wriggle:
   She has a stately presence. Good. Yet nearer,
   And bid, God save you.
DAPPER: Madam.
SUBTLE: And your aunt.
DAPPER: And my most gracious aunt, God save your Grace.
DOLL: Nephew, we thought to have been angry with you: 25
   But that sweet face of yours hath turned the tide,
   And made it flow with joy, that ebbed of love.
   Arise, and touch our velvet gown.
SUBTLE: The skirts,
   And kiss 'em. So.
DOLL: Let me now stroke that head.
   Much, nephew, shalt thou win; much shalt thou spend;   30
   Much shalt thou give away; much shalt thou lend.
SUBTLE: (Ay, much indeed.) Why do you not thank her Grace?
DAPPER: I cannot speak, for joy.
SUBTLE: See, the kind* wretch!
   Your Grace's kinsman right.
DOLL: Give me the bird.*
   Here is a fly in your purse, about your neck, cousin,   35
   Wear it, and feed it, about this day se'ennight*
   On your right wrist –
SUBTLE: Open a vein, with a pin,

And let it suck but once a week; till then,
You must not look on 't.
DOLL: No. And, kinsman,
Bear yourself worthy of the blood you come on.*   40
SUBTLE: Her Grace would ha' you eat no more Woolsack pies,
Nor Dagger* frumety.*
DOLL: Nor break his fast,
In Heaven, and Hell.*
SUBTLE: She's with you everywhere!
Nor play with costermongers, at mum-chance, tray-trip,*
God-make-you-rich* (whenas your aunt has done it) but keep   45
The gallantest company, and the best games –
DAPPER: Yes, sir.
SUBTLE: Gleek and primero:* and what you get, be true to us.*
DAPPER: By this hand, I will.
SUBTLE: You may bring 's a thousand pound
Before tomorrow night (if but three thousand
Be stirring*) an you will.
DAPPER: I swear, I will then.   50
SUBTLE: Your fly will learn* you all games.
FACE [*within*]:   Ha' you done there?
SUBTLE: Your Grace will command him no more duties?
DOLL: No:
But come and see me often. I may chance
To leave him three or thousand chests of treasure,
And some twelve thousand acres of Fairyland,   55
If he game well, and comely,* with good gamesters.
SUBTLE: There's a kind aunt! Kiss her departing part.
But you must sell your forty mark a year, now.
DAPPER: Ay, sir, I mean.
SUBTLE: Or gi' t away: pox on 't.
DAPPER: I'll gi' t mine aunt. I'll go and fetch the writings.   [*Exit.*] 60
SUBTLE: 'Tis well, away.

[*Enter* FACE.]

FACE: Where's Subtle?
SUBTLE: Here. What news?
FACE: Drugger is at the door, go take his suit,
And bid him fetch a parson presently:
Say he shall marry the widow. Thou shalt spend*
A hundred pound by the service.   [*Exit* SUBTLE.]
                    Now, queen Doll,   65
Ha' you packed up all?

DOLL: Yes.
FACE: And how do you like
   The Lady Pliant?
DOLL: A good dull innocent.

[*Enter* SUBTLE.]

SUBTLE: Here's your Hieronymo's cloak and hat.
FACE: Give me 'em.
SUBTLE: And the ruff too?
FACE: Yes, I'll come to you presently.   [*Exit.*]
SUBTLE: Now, he is gone about his project, Doll,   70
   I told you of, for the widow.
DOLL: 'Tis direct
   Against our articles.
SUBTLE: Well, we'll fit* him, wench.
   Hast thou gulled her of her jewels, or her bracelets?
DOLL: No, but I will do 't.
SUBTLE: Soon, at night, my Dolly,
   When we are shipped, and all our goods aboard,   75
   Eastward for Ratcliff, we will turn our course
   To Brainford,* westward, if thou saist the word;
   And take our leaves of this o'er-weaning rascal,
   This peremptory Face.
DOLL: Content, I am aweary of him.
SUBTLE: Th' hast cause, when the slave will run a-wiving, Doll,   80
   Against the instrument* that was drawn between us.
DOLL: I'll pluck his bird as bare as I can.
SUBTLE: Yes, tell her
   She must by any means address some present
   To th' cunning man; make him amends for wronging
   His art with her suspicion; send a ring;   85
   Or chain of pearl; she will be tortured else
   Extremely in her sleep, say: and ha' strange things
   Come to her. Wilt thou?
DOLL: Yes.
SUBTLE: My fine flitter-mouse,*
   My bird of the night; we'll tickle it at the Pigeon,*
   When we have all, and may unlock the trunks,
   And say, this's mine, and thine, and thine, and mine –   *They kiss.* 90

[*Enter* FACE.]

FACE: What now, a-billing?

SUBTLE: Yes, a little exalted
      In the good passage of our stock-affairs.*
FACE: Drugger has brought his parson; take him in, Subtle,
      And send Nab back again to wash his face.   95
SUBTLE: I will; and shave himself?
FACE: If you can get him.
DOLL: You are hot upon it, Face, whate'er it is!
FACE: A trick that Doll shall spend ten pound a month by.
      Is he gone?
SUBTLE: The chaplain waits you i' the hall, sir.
FACE: I'll go bestow* him.
DOLL: He'll now marry her, instantly.   100
SUBTLE: He cannot yet, he is not ready. Dear Doll,
      Cozen her of all thou canst. To deceive him
      Is no deceit, but justice, that would break
      Such an inextricable tie as ours was.
DOLL: Let me alone to fit him.
FACE: Come, my venturers,   105
      You ha' all packed up? Where be the trunks? Bring forth.
SUBTLE: Here.
FACE: Let's see 'em. Where's the money?
SUBTLE: Here,
      In this.
FACE: Mammon's ten pound: eight score before.
      The Brethren's money, this. Drugger's, and Dapper's.
      What paper's that?
DOLL: The jewel of the waiting-maids,   110
      That stole it from her lady, to know certain –
FACE: If she should have precedence of her mistress?
DOLL: Yes.
FACE: What box is that?
SUBTLE: The fishwives' rings, I think;
      And th' ale-wives' single money.* Is 't not, Doll?
DOLL: Yes, and the whistle that the sailor's wife   115
      Brought you, to know and* her husband were with Ward.*
FACE: We'll wet it* tomorrow: and our silver beakers,
      And tavern cups. Where be the French petticoats,
      And girdles, and hangers?*
SUBTLE: Here, i' the trunk,
      And the bolts of lawn.*
FACE: Is Drugger's damask there?   120
      And the tobacco?
SUBTLE: Yes.
FACE: Give me the keys.

DOLL: Why you the keys?
SUBTLE: No matter, Doll: because
    We will not open 'em before he comes.
FACE: 'Tis true, you shall not open them, indeed;
    Not have 'em forth. Do you see? Not forth, Doll.
DOLL: No!   125
FACE: No, my smock-rampant.* The right is, my master
    Knows all, has pardoned me, and he will keep 'em;
    Doctor, 'tis true (you look) for all your figures:*
    I sent for him, indeed. Wherefore, good partners,
    Both he and she, be satisfied: for here   130
    Determines* the indenture tripartite
    'Twixt Subtle, Doll and Face. All I can do
    Is to help you over the wall, o' the backside;*
    Or lend you a sheet, to save your velvet gown, Doll.
    Here will be officers presently; bethink you   135
    Of some course suddenly to 'scape the dock:*
    For thither you'll come else.   *Some knock.*
                          Hark you, thunder.
SUBTLE: You are a precious fiend!
OFFICERS [*without*]:   Open the door.
FACE: Doll, I am sorry for thee, i' faith. But hear'st thou?
    It shall go hard, but I will place thee somewhere: 140
    Thou shalt ha' my letter to Mistress Amo.
DOLL: Hang you –
FACE: Or Madam Caesarean.*
DOLL: Pox on you, rogue,
    Would I had but time to beat thee.
FACE: Subtle,
    Let's know where you set up next; I'll send you
    A customer now and then, for old acquaintance:*   145
    What new course ha' you?
SUBTLE: Rogue, I'll hang myself:
    That I may walk a greater devil than thou,
    And haunt thee i' the flock-bed, and the buttery.*   [*Exeunt.*]

Act Five, Scene Five

[*Enter*] LOVEWIT, PARSON.

[LOVEWIT:] What do you mean, my masters?
MAMMON [*without*]:   Open your door,
    Cheaters, bawds, conjurers.

OFFICERS [*without*]:   Or we'll break it open.
LOVEWIT: What warrant have you?
OFFICER [*without*]:   Warrant enough, sir, doubt not,
    If you'll not open it.
LOVEWIT: Is there an officer there?
OFFICER [*without*]: Yes, two or three for failing.*
LOVEWIT: Have but patience,   5
    And I will open it straight.

[*Enter* FACE.]

FACE: Sir, ha' you done?
    Is it a marriage? Perfect?
LOVEWIT: Yes, my brain.
FACE: Off with your ruff and cloak then, be yourself, sir.
SURLY [*without*]: Down with the door.
KASTRIL [*without*]:   'Slight, ding* it open.
LOVEWIT: Hold.
    Hold, gentlemen, what means this violence?   10

[*Enter* MAMMON, SURLY, KASTRIL, ANANIAS, TRIBULATION *and* OFFICERS.]

MAMMON: Where is this collier?
SURLY: And my Captain Face?
MAMMON: These day-owls.
SURLY: That are birding* in men's purses.
MAMMON: Madam Suppository.*
KASTRIL: Doxy, my suster.
ANANIAS: Locusts
    Of the foul pit.
TRIBULATION: Profane as Bel, and the Dragon.*
ANANIAS: Worse than grasshoppers, or the lice of Egypt.*   15
LOVEWIT: Good gentlemen, hear me. Are you officers,
    And cannot stay* this violence?
OFFICER: Keep the peace.
LOVEWIT: Gentlemen, what is the matter? Whom do you seek?
MAMMON: The chemical cozener.
SURLY: And the Captain pandar.
KASTRIL: The nun* my suster.
MAMMON: Madam Rabbi.
ANANIAS: Scorpions   20
    And caterpillars.
LOVEWIT: Fewer at once, I pray you.
OFFICER: One after another, gentlemen, I charge you,

    By virtue of my staff –
ANANIAS: They are the vessels
    Of pride, lust, and the cart.*
LOVEWIT: Good zeal, lie still
    A little while.
TRIBULATION: Peace, Deacon Ananias.   25
LOVEWIT: The house is mine here, and the doors are open:
    If there be any such persons as you seek for,
    Use your authority, search on o' God's name.
    I am but newly come to town, and finding
    This tumult 'bout my door (to tell you true)   30
    It somewhat mazed* me; till my man here (fearing
    My more displeasure) told me he had done
    Somewhat an insolent part, let out my house
    (Belike, presuming on my known aversion
    From any air o' the town, while there was sickness)
    To a Doctor and a Captain; who, what they are,
    Or where they be, he knows not.   *They enter.*
MAMMON: Are they gone?
LOVEWIT: You may go in and search, sir. Here I find
    The empty walls, worse than I left 'em, smoked,
    A few cracked pots, and glasses, and a furnace,   40
    The ceiling filled with poesies of the candle;*
    And MADAM, with a dildo, writ o' the walls.
    Only one gentlewoman I met here,
    That is within, that said she was a widow –
KASTRIL: Ay, that's my suster. I'll go thump her. Where is she?   *[Exit.]* 45
LOVEWIT: And should ha' married a Spanish count, but he,
    When he came to 't, neglected her so grossly
    That I, a widower, am gone through with her.*
SURLY: How! Have I lost her then?
LOVEWIT: Were you the Don, sir?
    Good faith, now, she does blame y' extremely, and says   50
    You swore, and told her you had ta'en the pains
    To dye your beard and umber o'er your face,
    Borrowed a suit and ruff, all for her love;
    And then did nothing. What an oversight
    And want of putting forward, sir, was this!   55
    Well fare an old harquebuzier,* yet,
    Could prime his powder, and give fire, and hit,
    All in a twinkling.   MAMMON *comes forth.*
MAMMON: Whole nest are fled!
LOVEWIT: What sort of birds are they?
MAMMON: A kind of choughs,*

Or thievish daws, sir, that have picked my purse   60
Of eight score and ten pounds within these five weeks,
Beside my first materials, and my goods
That lie i' the cellar, which I am glad they ha' left.
I may come home yet.
LOVEWIT: Think you so, sir?
MAMMON: Ay.
LOVEWIT: By order of law, but not otherwise.   65
MAMMON: Not mine own stuff?
LOVEWIT: Sir, I can take no knowledge
That they are yours, but by public means.*
If you can bring certificate that you were gulled of 'em,
Or any formal writ, out of a court,
That you did cozen yourself, I will not hold them.   70
MAMMON: I'd rather lose 'em.
LOVEWIT: That you shall not, sir,
By me, in troth. Upon these terms they are yours.
What should they ha' been, sir, turned into gold, all?
MAMMON: No.
I cannot tell. It may be they should. What then?
LOVEWIT: What a great loss in hope have you sustained?   75
MAMMON: Not I, the commonwealth has.
FACE: Ay, he would ha' built
The city new; and made a ditch about it
Of silver, should have run with cream from Hogsden;
That every Sunday in Moorfields the younkers*
And tits and tomboys* should have fed on, *gratis*.   80
MAMMON: I will go mount a turnip-cart,* and preach
The end o' the world within these two months. Surly,
What! In a dream?
SURLY: Must I needs cheat myself
With that same foolish vice of honesty!
Come, let us go and harken out* the rogues.   85
That Face I'll mark for mine, if e'er I meet him.
FACE: If I can hear of him, sir, I'll bring you word
Unto your lodging; for in troth, they were strangers
To me; I thought 'em honest as myself, sir.
                                [*Exeunt* MAMMON *and* SURLY.]
TRIBULATION: 'Tis well, the saints shall not lose all yet. Go,   90
                                        They come forth.

And get some carts –
LOVEWIT: For what, my zealous friends?
ANANIAS: To bear away the portion of the righteous,
Out of this den of thieves.

LOVEWIT: What is that portion?
ANANIAS: The goods, sometime the orphans', that the Brethren
  Bought with their silver pence.
LOVEWIT: What, those i' the cellar   95
  The knight Sir Mammon claims?
ANANIAS: I do defy
  The wicked Mammon, so do all the Brethren,
  Thou profane man. I ask thee, with what conscience
  Thou canst advance that idol against us,
  That have the seal?* Were not the shillings numbered   100
  That made the pounds? Were not the pounds told out
  Upon the second day of the fourth week,
  In the eighth month, upon the table dormant,*
  The year, of the last patience of the Saints,*
  Six hundred and ten?*
LOVEWIT: Mine earnest vehement botcher,   105
  And Deacon also, I cannot dispute with you,
  But, if you get you not away the sooner,
  I shall confute you with a cudgel.
ANANIAS: Sir.
TRIBULATION: Be patient, Ananias.
ANANIAS: I am strong,
  And will stand up, well-girt, against an host,   110
  That threaten Gad in exile.*
LOVEWIT: I shall send you
  To Amsterdam, to your cellar.
ANANIAS: I will pray there
  Against thy house: may dogs defile thy walls,
  And wasps and hornets breed beneath thy roof,
  This seat of falsehood, and this cave of cozenage.   115

DRUGGER *enters and he* [LOVEWIT] *beats him away.*

LOVEWIT: Another too?
DRUGGER: Not I, sir, I am no brother.
LOVEWIT: Away, you Harry Nicholas,* do you talk?
FACE: No, this was Abel Drugger. Good sir, go   *To the* PARSON.
  And satisfy him; tell him all is done:
  He stayed too long a-washing of his face.   120
  The Doctor, he shall hear of him at Westchester;*
  And of the Captain, tell him at Yarmouth, or
  Some good port-town else, lying for a wind.   [*Exit* PARSON.]
  If you get off the angry child now, sir –

[*Enter* KASTRIL *and* DAME PLIANT.]

KASTRIL: *To his sister.*
    Come on, you ewe, you have matched most sweetly, ha' you not?   125
    Did I not say I would never ha' you tupped*
    But by a dubbed boy,* to make you a lady-tom?*
    'Slight, you are a mammet!* O, I could touse you now.
    Death, mun'* you marry, with a pox?
LOVEWIT: You lie, boy;
    As sound* as you, and I am aforehand with you.
KASTRIL: Anon?   130
LOVEWIT: Come, will you quarrel? I will feeze* you, sirrah.
    Why do you not buckle to your tools?*
KASTRIL: God's light!
    This is a fine old boy, as e'er I saw!
LOVEWIT: What, do you change your copy* now? Proceed,
    Here stands my dove: stoop at* her if you dare.   135
KASTRIL: 'Slight, I must love him! I cannot choose, i' faith!
    And I should be hanged for 't. Suster, I protest
    I honour thee for this match.
LOVEWIT: O, do you so, sir?
KASTRIL: Yes, and thou canst take tobacco and drink, old boy,
    I'll give her five hundred pound more to her marriage   140
    Than her own state.
LOVEWIT: Fill a pipe-full, Jeremy.
FACE: Yes, but go and take it, sir.
LOVEWIT: We will.
    I will be ruled by thee in anything, Jeremy.
KASTRIL: 'Slight, thou art not hide-bound! Thou art a jovy* boy!
    Come, let's in, I pray thee, and take our whiffs.   145
LOVEWIT: Whiff in with your sister, brother boy.
                     [*Exeunt* KASTRIL *and* DAME PLIANT.]
                       That master
    That had received such happiness by a servant,
    In such a widow, and with so much wealth,
    Were very ungrateful, if he would not be
    A little indulgent to that servant's wit,   150
    And help his fortune, though with some small strain
    Of his own candour.* Therefore, gentlemen
    And kind spectators, if I have outstripped
    An old man's gravity or strict canon,* think
    What a young wife and a good brain may do: 155
    Stretch age's truth sometimes, and crack it too.
    Speak for thyself, knave.

FACE: So I will, sir. Gentlemen,
    My part a little fell in this last scene,
    Yet 'twas decorum.* And though I am clean
    Got off from Subtle, Surly, Mammon, Doll,   160
    Hot Ananias, Dapper, Drugger, all
    With whom I traded, yet I put myself
    On you, that are my country;* and this pelf,*
    Which I have got, if you do quit* me, rests
    To feast you often, and invite new guests.   165

The End.

This Comedy was first
acted in the year
1610

By the King's Majesty's
Servants.

The principal Comedians were:

RIC. BURBAGE	JOH. HEMINGS
JOH. LOWIN	WILL OSTLER
HEN. CONDEL	JOH. UNDERWOOD
ALEX. COOKE	NIC. TOOLY
ROB. ARMIN	WILL. EGLESTONE

With the allowance of the Master of REVELS

Notes to the Play

To the Lady

Mary, LADY WROTH: the
daughter of the first Earl of
Leicester, Robert Sidney, and
niece of Sir Philip Sidney. The
name was also spelt 'worth',
therefore 'most deserving her
name'

3   gums: incense
3   hecatomb: public sacrifice
5   conscience: consciousness
12   paint: employ cosmetics

To the Reader

7   professors: practitioners of
     writing
8   naturals: natural abilities; also
     plays upon 'fools'
16   foil: overthrow
19   ill: bad work
26   copie: copiousness
26–7 election and a mean: selection
     and moderation

The Persons of the Play

KASTRIL: obsolete spelling of
'kestril'

The Argument

1   sickness: plague
4   punk: whore
6   Cozeners: tricksters
10   figures: horoscopes
11   flies: familiar spirits
     Stone: philosopher's stone; also
     slang for 'testicle'
12   fume: smoke

Prologue

8   squire: pimp
9   humours: simplified
     characteristics, defined by the

predominance of one of the
four humours (blood, phlegm,
bile, choler)
12   better: i.e. to make better
18   correctives: medicines
19   apply: read coded references

Act One, Scene One

3   figs: piles (*ficus morbus*); the
     missing word in l. 6 is 'arse'
10   All ... made: proverbial: 'The
     tailor makes the man'
16   livery ... thrum: a poorly-paid
     liveried servant, earning three
     pounds a year
17   Friars: Blackfriars, the location
     of both Lovewit's house and
     the playhouse
25   Pie Corner: near West
     Smithfield, where meat pies
     were sold to be eaten on the
     street
28   costive: constipated
29   Roman wash: flushed and
     angry
31   powder ... yard: traces of
     gunpowder left at the Artillery
     Garden in Teasel Close. It had
     opened in 1610 for shooting
     practice
35   kibes: chilblains
36   felt of rug: coarse woollen hat
39   vegetals: vegetables
49   bawdry: brothel-keeping
52   buttery-hatch: pantry door.
     Face is accused of profiteering
     from the sale of leftovers
     intended to be given to charity
53   dole-beer: stale beer
     aqua-vitae men: distillers and
     spirit vendors
54   vails: tips
55   post-and-pair: a card game
59   scarab: dung-beetle
68   Sublimed ... exalted:
     alchemical terms, suggesting
     that Subtle has worked face up
     from base matter to the highest
     level ('our state of grace')

74	quarrelling dimensions: formalised conventions of argument
79	fly ... projection: alchemical term, referring to the volatile final phase of the gold-making process
83	*equi clibanum*: horse dung, employed in alchemy
93	Paul's: St Paul's, where advertisements and scandal notices would be displayed
94	hollow coal: a classic alchemical trick
97	taking ... glass: consulting a crystal ball
99	Gamaliel Ratsey: a notorious theatrically-inclined highwayman, executed in 1605, who wore a mask to terrorise his victims
103	trencher-rascal: parasite
106	lying ... basket: helping himself to food intended for prisoners
110	republic: common interests
111	brach: bitch
112	statute ... eight: in 1403 an act had been passed which prohibited the multiplication of gold and silver; in 1541, Henry VIII issued a more general edict against sorcery, which was confirmed by James I in 1604
114	laund'ring ... barbing: dissolving the surface of gold in acid; clipping the coinage. These were capital offences
116	menstrue: solvent
120	marshal: prison officer
127	apocryphal: fraudulent
133	powder ... with: powder ground from the philosopher's stone, used in alchemy
137	Fall ... couples: work together
139	term: term of the Law Courts; the busiest periods in London
145	parts: shares in the business; also theatrical parts
151	fermentation ... cibation: sixth and seventh processes in alchemy
152	Sol ... Luna: sun and moon; gold and silver

155	faction: dispute
160	'Slid: God's (eye)lid
161	'Slight: God's light
164	sort: set
	precise: puritanical
165	sin' ... in: i.e. since 1603, the year of the accession of James I
167	from: out of
	ride: displayed on a cart as a whore
168	hole: pillory
169	pay ... rent: pay for by having ears clipped or cut off
170	Don Provost: the Provost-Marshal, as hangman
173	crewel: fine yarn
174	worsted: coarse yarn; also baffled
175	Claridiana: heroine of the popular romance *The Mirror of Knighthood*, published in English translation in 1578
178	cut: Face and Subtle will draw lots to sleep with Doll; 'cut' also means 'cunt'
188	break up: i.e. as business partners
189	quodling: unripe apple; a green boy
191	Dagger: an inn celebrated for its pies
192	familiar: familiar spirit
193	rifle: gamble

Act One, Scene Two

10	broke: broached the subject
11	dainty: difficult, touchy
17	Reade: Dr Simon Read, a physician who had fallen foul of the College of Physicians in 1602 for unlicensed practice, and who in 1608 received a royal pardon for having conjured spirits in 1607 to discover who had stolen money from the 'fool', Toby Matthew
24	court-hand: script used in law courts
26	Chiaus: cheat. In 1607 a Turkish messenger named Mustapha visited England under the

	pretext of being an envoy from the Sultan, and was both entertained by the Levant Company and received at Windsor
37	angels: gold coins worth around ten shillings
42	horse … halter: i.e. be taken in a horse-drawn cart to be hanged
43	flies: demons
46	Clim … Claribels: Legendary outlaw in *The Ballad of Adam Bell*; Sir Claribel features in Spenser's *The Faerie Queene*, Book IV.
47	five … flush: unbeatable hands in the game of primero
50	Vicar: vicar-general, who acted on behalf of the bishop in the ecclesiastical courts
51	marks: worth around fifteen shillings
56	Xenophon: the Q reading here is 'Testament', presumably altered in F as a result of the tightening of the censorship of profanity
58	Ovid: Roman author of the *Amores*, which supplied would-be lovers with a model of seductive eloquence
61	velvet head: Doctor's velvet hat
63	puck-fist: puff-ball fungus
67	take: make the agreement
68	assumpsit: a legal term referring to a voluntary verbal promise
78	blow up: outwit
79	crackers: fireworks
81	set: bet on
84	rifling fly: gambling demon
97	consideration: renumeration
99–100	not … score: obscure; it may mean that Dapper will be so successful that London's gamblers will have to eat at inns (ordinaries) on credit (o' the score), having lost all their cash to Dapper
103	art: necromantic skill
109	dead … Isaac: Isaac and John Isaac Holland, legendary fifteenth-century Dutch alchemists

112	to … cloak: i.e. strip them to their cloaks
117	my … yours: I'm game if you are
119	happy: rich and fortunate (from the Latin *beatus*)
128	caul: membrane encasing the foetus in the womb; to be born with part of it on the head was considered a sign of good luck
130	I'fac: in faith (a mild oath)
141	trivial: mean, petty
151	resolve: confirm
152	for: because of
174	clean shirt: fairies were known to favour cleanliness

Act One, Scene Three

5	Free … Grocers: a Freeman of the Grocers' Company
9	plot: plan
14	wished: recommended
15	planets: horoscopes
24	Sophisticate … oil: See Dr William Barclay: 'Some others have *Tabacco* from *Florida* indeede, but because either it is exhausted of spiritualitie, or the radicall humor is spent, and wasted, or it hath gotten moisture by the way, or it hath been dried for expedition in the Sunne, or carried too negligently, they sophisticate and fared the same in sundrie sorts with black spice, *Galanga, aqua vitae*, Spanish wine, Anise seedes, oyle of Spicke and such like.' (*Nepenthes, or the vertues of Tabacco*, Edinburgh, 1614, sig. A4v–A5) sack-lees: sediment of the white wine sack
25	muscadel and grains: a sweet white wine, spices
27	pissed clouts: cloth soaked in urine
28	lily-pots: ornamental flower pots
30–1	maple … juniper: the maple block is used for shredding tobacco leaf; silver tongs are for

handling the coals; Winchester was known for the manufacture of good tobacco pipes; juniper is a slow-burning wood, supplied to enable the smokers to light their pipes in the shop

32   goldsmith: moneylender

36   clothing: livery

37   called ... scarlet: be elected a sheriff

38   so ... beard: so young

43   amused: puzzled or amazed

44   metoposcopy: the art of interpreting personality by observing the features of the face and forehead

46–9   chestnut ... finger: According to R. Sanders, *Physiognomie and Chiromancie, Metoscopie* (London, 1653, pp. 166–7), 'The colours of the Body, and especially of the face, denote the Humour and inclination of the person ... Those that be chestnut or olive colour are Jovialists and honest people, open without painting or cheating.' Subtle's identification of planetary signs with the digits follows that of J. B. Porta's *Coelestis Physiognomoniae* (Naples, 1603).

52   chiromanty: palm-reading

55–7   lord ... balance: Subtle is playing upon Drugger's gullibility and astrological illiteracy: Libra is ruled by Venus, not Mercury, but Mercury, as the god of business (and thieves), is more appealing to the would-be entrepreneur. Libra is represented by the scales.

59   Ormus: Hormuz, a trading centre on the Persian Gulf, important in the spice trade

65–6   *Mathlai ... Thiel*: Taken from *Heptameron, seu Elementa magica Pietri Abano Philosophi*, appended to Cornelius Agrippa's *De Occulta Philosopha*, possibly published in Paris around 1567

69   lodestone: magnet

72   vice: device for operating the puppet

73   court-fucus: cosmetics made fashionable by ladies at court

76   Vitriol: sulphuric acid
     sal-tartar: carbonate of potash
     argaile: cream of tartar
     alkali: caustic soda

77   Cinoper: cinnabar, or red mercuric sulphide

79   give a say: make an attempt

87   portague: a Portuguese gold coin

95   ill: unlucky

96   trust: extend credit

97   'gainst: by

102   beech-coal: beech-wood, which made the best charcoal
      cor'sive: corrosive

103   crosslets: melting pots
      cucurbites: retorts

107   intelligence: information

Act One, Scene Four

3   Lambeth: the haunt of thieves and prostitutes

5   trunk: speaking tube

9   shift: change clothes

10   presently: immediately

14   magisterium: master work

17   dealing ... away: planning how he will dispense it

20   Moorfields: an area of marshland to the north of the city walls, and within the Liberties (now the site of Finsbury Square), where lepers were licensed to beg

21   pomander-bracelets: bracelets containing a perfumed ball, carried as a protection against infection and noxious odours

23   'spital: hospital, especially for sexually transmitted diseases

Act Two, Scene One

2   *novo orbe*: new world

4   Solomon's Ophir: Solomon was thought by alchemists to have

possessed the philosopher's stone; Ophir, legendarily in Arabian Africa, was the source of his gold, which was delivered every three years

8   *spectatissimi*: (Latin) most respected or regarded

9   hollow die: loaded dice

10   frail: marked

10–14   No … commodity: refers to the moneylenders' practice of forcing debtors to receive part of a loan in the shape of useless goods rather than cash. The 'livery-punk' is a prostitute employed to cajole the client ('young heir') into 'sealing' the bad deal

16   entrails: linings

17   Madam Augusta's: a brothel madam

18   sons … hazard: gamblers and brawlers

19   golden calf: the false idol referred to in Exodus, 32

22   start up: breed

23   punketees: little (child?) prostitutes

26   fire-drake: fiery dragon; meteorite; (figuratively) stoker

27   lungs: bellows; the alchemist's laboratory assistant
Zephyrus: the west wind

28   firk: stir

29   are not faithful: lack faith

33   Lothbury: a London street inhabited by 'Founders, that cast Candlesticks, Chafingdishes, Spice mortars and such like Copper or Laton workes'. (John Stow, *A Survey of London* (1598), ed. C. L. Kingsford, Oxford, 1908, p, 277)

35   Devonshire … Cornwall: known for their copper and tin mines

36   perfect Indies: the West Indies, reputed to be rich in gold and spice
admire: are impressed

37   great med'cine: philosopher's stone

39–40   Mercury … Sun: Mercury refers to quicksilver, Venus to copper,

the Moon to silver, the Sun to gold

47–8   flower … elixir: synonyms for the philosopher's stone

55   renew … eagle: cf. Psalms, 103: 5

56   fifth age: mature manhood, between fifty and sixty-five

58   ancient patriarchs: the longevity of the Patriarchs in Genesis (Noah was reported to have lived six centuries at the time of the Flood) was believed to owe to their alchemical knowledge

62   Vestals … Hatch: Pict-Hatch, near Charterhouse, was well known for prostitutes

71–2   players … poets: players were required to close the playhouses when plague deaths reached forty a week (as occurred in 1610); Mammon's cure would re-open them

76   waterwork: one of the two pump-houses, located at London Bridge and Broken Wharf, that supplied private houses with Thames water

81–3   Moses … Adam: it was frequently claimed that the Patriarchs were alchemists

84   High Dutch: High German, claimed by the Flemish physician Joannes Goropius Becanus as the original pre-Babel language

87–9   cedar … wood: cedar wood had a reputation for durability, while Irish wood was resistant to insects, a consequence of the blessing of Saint Patrick

91   ram-vellum: parchment made from ram's skin

92   Pythagoras' thigh: reported to have been made of gold
tub: box (also believed to be golden)

93–100   fable … fixed: in his quest for the golden fleece, Jason was required to plough a field with a pair of fire-breathing bulls whose feet were made of brass. He then sowed dragon's teeth, which sprouted warriors,

95   *argent-vive*: quicksilver or mercury

96   dragon's teeth: Cadmus, the founder of Thebes, established the city on the site of his defeat of a dragon, whose teeth he planted in the ground, from which grew fighting men. These fought amongst themselves until the five survivors joined with Cadmus to found Thebes
mercury sublimate: chloride of mercury

98   Jason's helm: part of the distilling apparatus

99   Th'alembic: still
Mars: the planet of iron

101   th' Hesperian garden: the place of the golden apples, which were guarded by a dragon.

102   Jove's shower: Jove (Jupiter) visited Danae in a shower of gold while she was imprisoned in a brass tower
boon ... Midas: the gift, or curse, of the golden touch, bestowed by Bacchus
Argus' eyes: Argus was a dog with a hundred eyes, who was employed to guard Jupiter's lover, Io (who had been turned into a heifer) by his wife, Juno.

103   Boccace ... Demogorgon: the Demogorgon was a primeval god mentioned by Boccacio in his *Genealogica Deorum*.

104   abstract ... stone: allegories of the alchemical transformation of metals

Act Two, Scene Two

3   ferment: leaven; red the colour of Mars and Venus, is that of the final stage of alchemy

5   projection: the making of gold

8   Give ... th'affront: confront lords as an equal

9   bolt's head: a long-necked globular flask

15   auditory: congregation, who listen bare-headed

16   shingles: wooden slats, used as roof tiles

18   manumit: release

26–7   pale ... swan: colours and stages in the alchemical process

25–8   colours ... agni: designates stages in the alchemical process. *Sagnis agni* is the blood of the lamb (i.e. Christ)

31   period: time limit

33   seraglio: harem

34   geld: castrate

39   encounter: fuck

43–4   pictures ... Elephantis: Seutonius, the Roman biographer of the emperor Tiberius, gives an account of the pornographic décor of his villa; Elephantis is a Roman pornographer.
Aretine: Pietro Aretino (1492–1550), Italian satirist and poet, notorious for his work of erotica, *Sonnetti Lussuriosi* (1523)

45   glasses: mirrors. Seneca's *Naturales Questiones* (I, xvi) describes Hostius Quadra's auto-erotic use of mirrors, so that he became spectator of his own sexual practices

48   *succubae*: demons who take on female form to have sex with men

60   pure: purest

62   burgesses: members of Parliament

63   writ ... fart: *Musarum Deliciae or the Muses Recreation*, a volume published in 1656, contains the poem 'The Fart Censured in the Parliament House', which documented 'the peculiar manner in which Henry Ludlow said "noe" to a message brought by the Serjeant from the Lords' in 1607

74   hyacinths: a gemstone

75   tongues of carps: an expensive delicacy

77   Apicius: a Roman cookery writer

80	calvered: carved whilst still alive
81	Knots, godwits, lampreys: a species of wild-fowl; marsh-birds; eel-like fish
82	barbels: a species of carp
85	poignant: piquant
88	heightens: proceeds
89	taffeta-sarsnet: fine, soft silk
91	Persian: Sardanapulus, King of Ninevah during the ninth century B.C., legendarily luxurious
94	gums … paradise: incense imported from the Middle East, fabled location of the Garden of Eden
97	*homo frugi*: alchemical manuals instructed the aspirant alchemist to embrace a pure and pious lifestyle in order to achieve success
101	venture: investment

Act Two, Scene Three

4	doubt: suspect
6	I' … point: exactly prevent: anticipate
19	prevaricate: act deceptively (Latin *praevaricari* means to 'walk a crooked path')
21	catholic: universal (opposed to 'particular', l. 20)
26	costive … belief: sceptical ('costive' means constipated)
29	Sol … robe: Sol, the sun, which is the planet of gold, is robed and prepared to officiate
30	triple soul: it was thought that the soul was tripartite, consisting of the vegetable, the animal and the intellectual; and that the soul was also linked to the body through the vital, natural and animal spirits
32	Ulen Speigel: Til Eulen Speigel (Owlglass) was the prankster hero of folklore, popularised in German jest-books which were published in English translation in the early sixteenth century

33	register: damper, used to regulate air and heat
35	aludels: pear-shaped pots open at either end
36	On D: i.e. one of a number of furnaces, identified alphabetically
40	gripe's egg: a large egg-shaped vessel (a 'gripe' is a vulture) Lute: block with clay
41	in balneo: in a bath, of sand or water
42	canting: thieves' and beggars' jargon
44	philosopher's wheel: alchemical cycle
45	lent: (Latin) slow athanor: the 'digesting furnace', which kept the materials at low temperatures for long periods
46	Sulphur o' nature: pure sulphur
48	covetise: greed, covetousness
58	sand-heat: the heat of a sand-bath
59	imbibition: immersion
61	St Mary's bath: a heat-bath
62	*lac Virginis*: (Latin) the milk of the virgin, a name for mercury
63	faeces: sediment calcined: turned to powder through dehydration by heating
64	calx: burnt powder salt: oxide
65	rectified: distilled
66	reverberating: acted upon by reflected heat
68	crow's head: blackness that signifies successful calcination
71	hay … a-pitching: the trap is set. The terms are taken from the art of rabbit (or coney) catching
71–2	loosed … menstrue: dissolved them in the liquid drawn from them
73	nipped: sealed digestion: extraction of solutions through slow cooking
75	liquor of Mars: molten iron

78	pelican: a vessel with a long neck which curves to re-enter the body, resembling the figure of a pelican pecking at its breast
79	signed … seal: hermetically sealed
79	amalgama: compound of mercury and other metals
83	embrion: the early stages
	his … on: turned white
84	inceration: rendered the consistency of wax
88	bolted: i.e. like a rabbit from its burrow
97	fixation: stabilising a volatile substance
98	ascension: distillation
99	oil of Luna: white elixir (Luna: 'the moon')
	kemia: (Greek) alchemy
100	philosopher's vinegar: obscure; possibly mercury
101	salad: i.e. the combination of oil and vinegar provides a salad dressing (the term was used by alchemists without irony)
104	*balneo vaporoso*: a device for hanging vessels over steam
108	convert: convert to
109	loose: solution
116	andirons: metal frames for burning logs in a fireplace
128	eggs in Egypt: Pliny's *Naturalis Historia* (x. lxxv. 153, lxxvi. 154) refers to the Egyptians hatching eggs on dunghills, used as incubators
140	remote matter: some primary matter
144	Materia liquida: liquid matter unctuous: oily
145	crass: dense
146	concorporate: acting as a single body
148	propria material: a specific substance
157	means: intervening stages
165	do act and suffer: are active and passive
166	extensive: extendable
174	ritely: appropriately; according to the rites
178	bray: pound
185	chrysosperm: (Greek) seed of gold
187	tree of life: philosopher's stone
188	marcasite: crystallised iron pyrites
	tutty: impure zinc oxide
189	toad … panther: colours which emerge in progressive stages of the alchemical process
190	adrop: lead
191	lato: latten, a compound similar to brass
	azoch: mercury (Arabic: az-zaug)
	zernich: trisulphide of arsenic (Arabic: zirnikh)
	chibrit: sulphur (Arabic: kibrit)
	heautarit: mercury (Arabic: utarid)
194	women's terms: menstrual blood
195	clouts: rags
	merds: turds
208	Sisyphus: In Greek mythology, Sisyphus was punished for betraying the secrets of the gods by being assigned to the task of pushing a huge rock up a hill in Hades; the rock always rolls down the hill again when the top is reached
225	Bradamante: a formidable female knight in Ariosto's *Orlando Furioso*
230	Paracelsian: adherent to the theories of Paracelsus (1493–1541), who applied alchemical theories to medicine
233	Galen: Roman physician (AD 130–210), the doyen of traditional medicine
238	Broughton: Hugh Broughton (1549–1612), controversial puritan and rabbinical scholar
241	genealogies: in *A Concent of Scripture* (1590), Broughton attempted to rationalise Biblical chronology: this is the source of Doll's 'fit of talking' in Act Four, Scene Five
255	helm: refers both to the alchemical apparatus and to the head of the penis
256	vegetal: lively one
268	original: origin

275	pass: forget
282	And: if
283	*lapis mineralis*: mineral stone
	lunary: common lunary or
	moonwart, a plant achemically
	linked with silver, and now
	known as honesty
285	*lutum sapientis*: a paste made
	from quicklime and eggs, used
	to seal the necks of vessels
	rapidly
286	*menstrum simplex*: simple
	solvent
289	Temple Church: the law
	students' church, a common
	place for meetings
297	by attorney: by proxy; i.e. not
	as myself
302	superintendent: pimp
303	quainter traffickers: prostitutes
	(quaint: cunt)
304	visitor: regulator, inspector
306	fall: collar
	tire: attire
307	prove: test (Latin: *probare*)
315	parlous: perilous
320	Bantam: the legendary capital
	of a Mohammedan empire in
	what now corresponds to
	Indonesia
324	jack: machinery for turning a
	spit
329	chain: the steward's chain of
	office in a lord's household
331	Count-Palatine: a Count who
	has jurisdiction over a
	substantial territory, and
	authority equal to the King's

Act Two, Scene Four

5	firks mad: runs wild, with a
	play on 'fucks'
7	*statelich*: (Dutch) in a stately
	fashion
11	sanguine: i.e. governed by the
	sanguine humour, and thus
	brave,
	optimistic and amorous
18	gudgeons: small freshwater
	fish, used as bait
20	Anabaptist: member of the
	non-conformist Christian sect,
	originating in Germany in the

	early sixteenth century, who
	advocated adult baptism,
	common ownership of goods,
	and adherence to the Scriptures
	as the sole source of authority
21	gold-end-man: itinerant trader
	in gold scraps
23	elder: pastor
29–30	holy ... saints: Anabaptists had
	sought refuge from Dutch
	persecution in England from
	the 1530s onwards

Act Two, Scene Five

1	recipient: collecting vessel
2	rectify: purify
	phlegma: watery product of
	distillation
4	macerate: soften by soaking
5	*Terra damnata*: damned earth
8	Lullianist ... *Artis*: schools of
	alchemy, after Raymond Lull
	(1235–1315), George Ripley
	(died *c*. 1490); and 'the sons
	of art'
9	dulcify: sweeten, by removing
	salts
10	*sapor ... styptic*: alchemists
	distinguished nine tastes
	(sapors): pontic means sour,
	styptic astringent
11	homogene ... heterogene:
	homogeneous or heterogeneous
13	Knipperdoling: Bernard
	Knipperdollinck, Anabaptist
	activist in the Munster rising of
	1534, when John of Leyden
	established a short-lived
	'Kingdom of God'
	Ars sacra: the sacred art
	(alchemy)
14	*chrysopoeia*: (Greek)
	gold-making
	spagyrica: a Paracelsian coinage
	from Greek meaning the
	alchemical technique of
	separation and combination
15	pamphysic ... knowledge:
	all-powerful knowledge
19	language: i.e. of alchemy
20	vexations ... martyrisations:
	alchemical processes
21	putrefaction: disintegration

22	ablution: washing
23	Cohobation: repeated distillation
25	vivification: restoration of a substance to its natural state mortification: alteration of the form of metals
27	*Aqua Regis*: King's Water, made of nitric and hydrochloric acid, and capable of dissolving 'noble' metals
28	trine ... spheres: triple (and thus well-favoured) conjunction of the first five planets, sun and moon
29	passion: predisposition (also alludes to Christ's Passion) Malleation: malleability
30	*ultimum ... auri*: extreme punishment for gold Antimonium: Antimony, which when alloyed with gold makes it lose its malleability
34	oleosity: oiliness suscitability: excitability
35	calce: calx, or powder
36	*magisterium*: master-work
48	Saints: i.e. the Brethren, who confidently anticipate their own salvation
57	professors: i.e. of the Anabaptist faith
70	Heidelberg: the centre of alchemy
71	pin-dust: filings produced in pin manufacture
72–3	Ananias ... Apostles: see Acts, 5, 1–2
74	consistory: assembly of elders, minister and deacons
80	*Piger Henricus*: a 'lazy Henry' or multiple furnace
81	*sericon* and *bufo*: red and black tincture
84–85	aqueity ... sulphureity: water, earth and sulphur
90	froward: obstinate

Act Two, Scene Six

2	Bayards: Bayard was a common horse's name
10	constellation: zodiac sign
11	Balance: Libra

15	radii: rays
17	virtual: virtuous affections: inclinations
20	Dee: Dr John Dee (1527–1608), astrologer and alchemist patronised by Queen Elizabeth
26	legs: bows
30	*bona roba*: high class prostitute
33	a-cop: on the top of the head, like a hat (which would have been more fashionable)
34	fucus: cosmetic (which Face hears as 'fuck', prompting the innuendo in the next line)
35	deal: do business, fuck
38	His match: one just like him
54	dubbed: knighted
57	newly warm in: having just acquired
64	by line: by the book
66	table: diagram
85	on: of
87	in tail: entail, or settlement of the succession of landed estate; 'tail' also means 'cunt'
88	light: promiscuous
89	grains: the smallest unit of weight

Act Three, Scene One

2	Separation: Anabaptists believed that, as the elect, they were separated from the broad mass of sinners
6	language ... Canaan: considered a heathen tongue
8	mark ... Beast: See Revelation, 16, 2; 19, 20
17	give: concede
18	still: always
22	glassmen: glass-blowers
33	menstruous ... Rome: the Roman Catholic Church was equated by Puritans with the scarlet woman of Revelation, 17, sated with the blood of saints and martyrs; here the red surplice is likened to rags stained with menstrual blood. Alchemists also made use of 'menstruum' or solvent
38	silenced Saints: puritan clergy who were excommunicated

for heresy following the 1604 Hampton Court conference

40 one of Scotland: Puritanism was stronger in Scotland than in England

41 *aurum potabile*: drinkable gold; indicates bribery

48 motion: motive

Act Three, Scene Two

3   *Furnus acediae*: furnace of sloth, the 'lazy Henry' referred to earlier
    turrus circulatorius: circulation tower

10 qualify: excuse

22 main: chief use

25–6 make … party: make you powerful, and attract followers

33 feat of body: sexual activity

35 paintings: cosmetics

36 oil of talc: alchemists' white elixir

38 bone-ache: syphilis

40 fricace: application through rubbing

42 pregnant: persuasive

43 Christ-tide: 'mass' was considered 'Popish' by Puritans

45 parcel gilt: partly gilded silverware
    massy: solid

51 oppone: oppose

55 not: do not

61 Bells are profane: bells were also 'Popish'

63 it shall down: refers to the alchemical apparatus

68 toward: close to

72 the start: advantage

78 scrupulous bones: minor points of dispute

87 shorten … ears: have your ears clipped or cut off, the punishment for 'libel 'gainst the prelates'

88 wire-drawn: drawn out

89 alderman: used in the plural sense for city magistrates

90 custard: an open pie

95 wood: used to designate a group, also has the sense of 'mad'

106 I hate traditions: traditions were 'Popish' and Judaic

113 botcher: tailor

128 silver potate: liquid silver

129 citronise: turn yellow

134 cars: carts

138 *ignis ardens*: the hottest fire

139 *Fimus equinus*: heat produced from horse dung
     cineris: heat of ashes

140 lenter: slower

150 We … magistrate: many Puritans refused to recognise civil law on matters of conscience

151 foreign coin: Ananias's sophistry is misguided: counterfeiting foreign coin was still a capital offence

Act Three, Scene Three

2   walked the round: the Temple Church was known as 'the round'

5   mill-jade: a horse on a treadmill

8   black boy: because Subtle's face is blackened with soot

9   turn thee: move on

11 compeer: comrade
    party-bawd: bawdry-partner; part-bawd

13 slops: breeches

14 hoys: small sailing vessels
    trunks: large padded knee breeches

15 pistolets: Spanish gold coins
    pieces of eight: Spanish dollars

17 colour: scheme

18 Cinque Port: the Cinque Ports were five ports on the South-East coast (Dover being among them) afforded special privileges because they occupied key defence positions against continental invasion

22 epididimus: 'a long narrow structure attached to the posterior border of the adjoining outer surface of the testicle' (*OED*)

24   John Leydens: Jan Bockelson of
      Leyden, leader of the Munster
      Anabaptists
29   reversions: future benefits
33   say ... camp: quotes Thomas
      Kyd's well-known *The Spanish
      Tragedy*
41   dousabel: (French) *douce et
      belle*: sweet and beautiful
44   drum: belly
46   the great frost: during the
      winter of 1607–08, when the
      Thames froze over
47   bees ... basin: Virgil's *Georgics*
      (4.64) records that swarming
      bees can be tamed by the
      tapping of a metal basin
50   adalantado: from the Spanish
      adalantar, to advance; literally,
      the governor of a province,
      here signifying a grandee
53   a-furnishing: getting ready
54   Would: should
57   chapman: merchant
69   Firk ... flounder: move
      vigorously, like a fish
      kiss ... scallop: invokes the
      resemblance between the
      vagina and shellfish
71   Verdugoship: (Spanish)
      hangman
      language: English
73   obscure: hidden
82   angry boy: term used to denote
      an aristocratic hooligan

Act Three, Scene Four

13   time: timing
25   *duello*: duel
32   mortality: risk
39   in diameter: directly
40   ordinarily: because eating-
      houses were known as
      'ordinaries'
43   reads: comprehends
44   stark: plain
50   spend a man: waste a man's
      fortune
61   groom-porter's: a member of
      the Lord Chamberlain's office,
      responsible for the licensing
      of gaming

65   canary: canary wine
71   affects: wishes for
76   cast: cashiered
79   by ... posts: swiftly
81   punk: prostitute
      naked boy: catamite
87   perspective: magic mirror
90   commodity: see Act Two, Scene
      One, 10–14
97   woad: blue dye
105   suster: sister; indicates that
      Kastril speaks as a rustic
107   melancholy: thought to be
      produced by milk products
119   Seacoal Lane: joins Farringdon
      Street to Fleet Lane, inhabited
      by fruiterers
120   sodden: boiled
      pellitory o' the wall: lichwort;
      used in remedies for urinary
      dysfunction
123   'sessed: assessed
124   water-work: either the London
      Bridge pump-house or the
      New River, an aqueduct
143   old Harry's sovereign: a
      sovereign from the eras of
      Henry VII or Henry VIII, worth
      ten shillings
147   Philip and Marys: coins which
      showed the heads of the king
      and queen facing each other

Act Three, Scene Five

16   state: fortune
17   pelf: goods
32   cittern: a guitar-like instrument
33   spur-ryal: a noble coined in the
      reign of Edward IV, which was
      backed with the image of a
      blazing sun, similar to the
      rowel of a spur
41   equivocate: attempt to deceive
56   o' the spit: ready to roast
74   stay: gag
76   crinkle: shrink

Act Four, Scene One

9   divinity: theology
16   state: affairs of state

17	startle: be startled
23	modern: commonplace
30	*concumbere*: lie together
	puissant: (French) powerful
38	guinea-bird: slang for
	prostitute
51–3	seeds ... compound: alchemical
	jargon is employed by Face and
	Subtle here
57	Irish costermonger: many
	London fruit peddlers were
	Irish
75	feature: form
77	particular: intimate
90	Kelly: Edward Kelly (1555–95),
	who acted as John Dee's
	medium (or 'scryer')
91	chains: Emperor Rudolph of
	Germany had Kelly
	imprisoned for failing to live
	up to his boast of possession of
	the philosopher's stone
92	Aesculapius: the god of
	medicine, who had the habit of
	restoring men to life until he
	was killed by one of Jove's
	thunderbolts
101	recluse: as a recluse
105	diamant: diamond
119	jealousy: suspicion
122	mastery: the *magisterium*, the
	master-work
131	the Friars: Blackfriars
134	Hundred: a county subdivision
136	emp'rics: experimenters (used
	in the sense of charlatans)
145	Nero's Poppaea; Nero had
	Poppaea's husband killed in
	order to gain her; he
	subsequently kicked her to
	death
157	high-country wines: wine from
	grapes grown at high altitudes
174	Rabbins: rabbis

Act Four, Scene Two

5	bonnibell: (French, *bonne et*
	belle) beautiful woman
6–7	suit ... flap: i.e. a lightning
	costume change
9	hit ... nostrils: lead you by the
	nose

13	*terrae fili*: (Latin) son of the soil
17	Charge: attack
42	myrobalane: a plum-like fruit
	from the East
43	*In rivo frontis*: in the forehead
	vein
45	*linea Fortunae*: line of Fortune
46	*stella ... Veneris*: star on the
	mount of Venus, found at the
	base of the thumb
47	*junctura annularis*: the ring
	finger joint
59	fustian: spuriously jargon-
	ridden
	dark glass: crystal ball
66	tables: diagrams
71	Against: so that

Act Four, Scene Three

3	composition: agreement
10	serve: fuck
12	composition: compensation
13	treat: deal
19	overlook: dominate
21	*Señores ... mercedes*:
	'Gentlemen, I kiss your hands'
22	*anos*: arse
26	collar of brawn: meat from a
	pig's neck
27	souse: ear
	wriggled ... knife: i.e. cut in a
	zigzag pattern like a ruff
30	d'Alva: Fernando Alvarez,
	Duke of Alva, who was
	governor of the Spanish
	Netherlands from 1567 to 1573
	Count Egmont: Flemish patriot
	executed by Alvarez in 1568
32	*Gratia*: Thank you
33	squibs: missiles
	sets: crenellations of a fortress
34	*Por ... casa*: By God,
	gentlemen, such a charming
	house
40	Donzel: little Don
	Entiendo: I understand
46	lion: lions were housed in the
	Tower of London
47	*Con ... señora*: With your
	permission, may one see the
	lady?
60	sudden: quick

61–2   *Entiendo … vida*: I understand
        that the lady is so beautiful that
        I long to see her, as the great
        good fortune of my life
78   *Señores … tanto*: Gentlemen,
        why the delay?
80   *Puede … amor*: Perhaps you
        are making fun of my love
82   loose the hinges: break the
        agreement
91   *Por … barbas*: By this
        honourable beard
92–3   *Tengo … tración*: I suspect,
        gentlemen, that you are
        deceiving me
98   fubbed: tricked
100   curried: rubbed down
        flawed: flayed
        tawed: tanned, beaten
        (like leather)

Act Four, Scene Four

2   nick: turning point; also vagina
9   jennet: small Spanish horse,
        associated with female
        sexuality
10   Stoop: bow
        garb: fashion
12   pavane: stately dance
13   titillation: perfume
18   scheme: horoscope
29   eighty-eight: 1588, year of the
        Spanish Armada
32   rush: possibly refers to the
        rushes which were used to
        cover the stage floor
33   cry strawberries: as a street
        fruit-hawker
34   shads: herring
41   ruffled: fondled
        hangings: tapestries, wall-
        hangings
42   state: status
44   Barer: of hats, and possibly
        more
47   th' Exchange: New Exchange,
        the Strand, which opened in
        1609 as a fashionable meeting
        place
48   Bedlam: Bethlehem Royal
        Hospital for the insane
        China-houses: houses where

        imported porcelain, ivory and
        silk were sold
49   tires: attire, clothes
50   goose-turd bands: collars in
        fashionable yellowish-green
53–4   *Qué … mata*: Why doesn't she
        come, gentlemen? This delay is
        killing me
56   *En … Galantissima*: (mock-
        Spanish) A gallant lady, Don!
        Most gallant!
57–8   *Por … vida*: By all the gods, the
        most perfect beauty that I have
        seen in my life
61   law-French: corrupt
        descendent of Norman French,
        used in the English law courts
        until the seventeenth century
63–4   *El … Diós*: The sun has lost its
        light with the splendour that
        this lady carries. So help me
        God
69   *Porqué … acude*: Why does she
        not come?
71   *Por … tarda*: For the love of
        God, what is she waiting for?
76–7   *Señora … hermosura*: Lady, my
        person is unworthy to
        approach such beauty
80   *Señora … entremos*: Lady, if it
        will serve, let us go in
92   erection … figure: casting her
        horoscope, with a double
        entendre

Act Four, Scene Five

1–32   *For … Rome*: Doll's fit of
        talking mangles Hugh
        Broughton's account of Biblical
        chronology in his *A Concent of
        Scripture* (1590)
2–3   *Perdiccas … Ptolomy*: the four
        generals of Alexander the
        Great, who divided his empire
        between them after his death
10   *fourth chain*: Broughton
        organised history into four
        periods; the 'fourth chain' was
        the last before the apocalypse
14   *Salem*: Jerusalem
16   *Eber and Javan*: Hebrew and
        Greek

26	fifth monarchy: the millennium
27	other four: i.e. the other four monarchies
28	Habergions: sleeveless mail coats
31	David Kimchi: Jewish scholar (1160–1235) who lived at Narbonne
	Onkelos: first century biblical scholar
	faeces: alchemical sediment
32	*Aben-Ezra*: Abraham ben Meir Ibn Ezra (1092–1167), biblical scholar and poet
35	again: back
41	managing: happening
58	*in fumo*: up in smoke
61	receivers: vessels to receive distilled matter
70	mine own man: myself
86	box: collection box
98	balls: bubbles
103	case: disguise
107	fetch him over: get one over on him

Act Four, Scene Six

3	clap: gonorrhea, also misfortune
23	upsee Dutch: from the Dutch *op zijn*; meaning 'in the manner of the Dutch'. Usually used in relation to drinking
24	lumpish: dull and heavy
29–30	cart … whip: pimps and prostitutes were punished by being tied to the back of a cart and whipped through the streets
33	parcel-broker: handler of stolen goods
37–9	boot … colour: a boot was used as a touchstone to test the quality of gold
40–5	Doctor … *in fumo*: describes the trick whereby the alchemist conceals the client's gold and contrives an explosion of mercury sublimate to explain its absence
46	Faustus: Johann Faustus, legendary magician

48	ephemeredes: astrological almanacs
53	green-sickness: chlorosis, anaemic condition affecting pubertal girls
54	by the ears: i.e. by having them clipped; cf. Act One, Scene One, 169

Act Four, Scene Seven

16	foist: dice or card cheat; also a silent fart
17	had him presently: saw through him straight away
23	mauther: young woman
25	swabber: deck-hand
32	three terms: i.e. over three law terms
33	lotium: stale urine, used to dress hair
34	Hydra: the many-headed snake of Lerna, encountered by Hercules, who grew two heads for every one that was cut off
39	trig: dandy, coxcomb, possibly male prostitute
40	Amadis … Quixote: heroes of Spanish romances, which Jonson despised
41	Knight … Coxcomb: a reference to Surly's hat; possibly also an allusion to Beaumont and Fletcher's *The Coxcomb* and Beaumont's *The Knight of the Burning Pestle*
45	otter: i.e. thus neither aquatic nor land animal
	shad: herring
	whit: obscure; possibly a small, insignificant thing, or a bawd
46	tim: an unknown term of abuse
48	slops: baggy breeches
53–4	unclean … coasts: an obscure allusion, for which various explanations have been put forward: 'seventy-seven' may be a slip for 'sixty-seven' (or 1567), the date of the Spanish invasion of the Netherlands; it may be a reference to Revelations, 18, 2 ('the habitation of devils, and the

hold of every foul spirit, and a cage of every unclean and hateful bird'); it may be a contemporary joke whose significance is now lost

54   prank it with: display their plumage
63   prevented: interrupted
69   play the fool: this suggests that Robert Armin, lead clown with the King's Men, took Drugger's part
71   Hieronymo: hero of Kyd's *The Spanish Tragedy*, for which Jonson may have written additional scenes in 1602. Thomas Dekker's *Satiromastix* claims that Jonson played the part of Hieronymo himself in a early touring production
75   synod: ecclesiastical assembly
110   quiblins: tricks, quibbles
114   taken: caught
116   liberties: cf. Act One, Scene Four, 20
117   walls: London wall
120   shape: appearance
122   purchase: winnings
125   Ratcliff: riverside area of East London, known for sailors and prostitutes
127   keep: keep to
131   smooth: clean-shaven
132–3   shave ... trim: with the additional sense of 'trick'

Act Five, Scene One

2   brave: splendid
6   Pimlico: a celebrated tavern in Hoxton (then Hogsden), close by the Fortune, Theatre and Curtain playhouses
8   calf ... legs: the kind of spectacle that would be seen at a fairground freak-show
11   teaching ... nose; refers to the nasal speech of puritan preachers
14   drum struck: to gather spectators for a show
21   ging: gang
22   Friar ... Nun: a popular pornographic caricature

motion: puppet show, also sexual action
23   covering: fucking
24   great thing: swollen penis

Act Five, Scene Two

This scene borrows from Plautus's *Mostellaria*, in which the trickster servant persuades his master that the house is haunted in order to keep him out

12   T' have ... tar: for fumigation
19   threaves: droves; literally, twenty four sheaves of corn
20   Eye-bright: another tavern in Hogsden (see Act Five, Scene One, 1.6)
32   black-pot: beer tankard
44   changelings: persons of fickle opinion; imps left by the fairies in place of stolen babies

Act Five, Scene Three

2   mere: absolute
7   wedges: gold or silver ingots
16–17   lungs ... lights: the lungs of beasts, sold by butchers, were known as lights
22   sign: of a tavern, eating-house or brothel
30   moon: thought to provoke lunacy
34   cockatrice: a mythical serpent, also called a basilisk, that could kill with a glance; slang for 'whore'
41   fat ... gentleman: i.e. Mammon and Surly
47   unclean birds: the fallen in Revelation, 18, 2
48   scavenger: parish officer responsible for street cleaning
50   Punk, device: total whore (plays on 'point device', or perfectly dressed)
55   Saint Katherine's: hospital founded in 1148
62   *deceptio visus*: hallucination
66   sets ... throat: shouts

74	the shortest way: directly	131	Determines: terminates
89	visited: by plague	133	backside: the rear of the house
		136	dock: for prisoners in a law court

Act Five, Scene Four

		141–2	Amo … Caesarean: generic names for brothel keepers
8	mouth down: gag removed	145	old acquaintance: old time's sake
11	churl: countryman		
14	coil: rumpus	148	flock-bed … buttery: i.e. day and night
18	suit: persuasion		
33	kind: showing natural feeling		
34	bird: the 'fly' or familiar spirit	**Act Five, Scene Five**	
36	se'ennight: week (seven night)		
40	come on: come from	5	for failing: to prevent failure
41–2	Woolsack … Dagger: taverns in Cheapside	9	ding: batter
		12	birding: bird-catching
42	frumety: wheat boiled in milk and spiced	13	Madam Suppository: supposed lady; also a prostitute offering both vaginal and anal sex
43	Heaven … Hell: taverns in Westminster, frequented by lawyer's clerks	14	Bel … Dragon: false idols in the Apocrypha
44	mum … trip: dice games	15	grasshoppers … Egypt: punishments visited upon the Egyptians in Exodus, 7–12
45	God-make-you-rich: a version of backgammon		
47	Gleek … primero: high-class card games	17	stay: control
	be … us: remember us	20	nun: slang for prostitute
50	Be stirring: is available to gamble	24	Of the cart: deserving the cart
		31	mazed: amazed
51	learn: teach	41	poesies … candle: smoke and grease stains
56	comely: in a comely manner		
64	spend: gain	48	am … her: have completed the marriage ceremony with her (and consummated it)
72	fit: fix		
77	Brainford: a village in the area now called Brentford, west of London	56	harquebuzier: musketeer armed with a harquebus, a kind of early rifle
81	instrument: agreement	59	choughs: a species of crow
88	flitter-mouse: bat	67	public means: course of law
89	Pigeon: The Three Pigeons, a tavern in Brentford market-place	79	younkers: youths
		80	tits and tomboys: minxes and wild girls
93	stock-affairs: trading capital		
100	bestow: accompany	81	turnip-cart: used by travelling preachers
114	single money: small change		
116	and: if	85	harken out: find out
	Ward: notorious Mediterranean pirate, the subject of pamphlets and plays	100	the seal: the mark of God on their foreheads, marking them as the chosen
117	wet it: drink to it	103	table dormant: permanent table
119	hangers: ornamental belt-loops to take a sword	104	last … saints: the 'last patience' is the final millennium
120	bolts of lawn: rolls of fine linen	105	Six … ten: 1610
126	smock-rampant: unruly whore	111	Gad in exile: refers to Genesis 49, 19; Gad's defeat in battle
128	for … figures: despite your horoscopes		

and subsequent victory

117   Harry Nicholas: Hendrick
Niclaes, Anabaptist mystic and
founder of the Family of Love
during the reign of Edward VI,
a sect proscribed by Elizabeth I
121   Westchester: Chester
126   tupped: mated
127   dubbed boy: knight
lady-tom: knight's wife
128   mammet: doll, puppet
129   mun': must
130   sound: pox-free
131   feeze: settle

132   buckle … tools: get your
weapons ready
134   copy: type
135   stoop at: attack (a term from
falconry)
144   jovy: jovial, merry
152   candour: honour
154   canon: rule
159   decorum: propriety
163   country: countrymen; refers to
a prisoner appealing to be tried
by his peers
pelf: gains
164   quit: acquit

A New Way to Pay Old Debts

A Comedy

PHILIP MASSINGER

A New Way to Pay Old Debts was probably written in the mid-1620s; it was entered in the Stationers' Register on 10 November 1632, and published in quarto in 1633. According to the title page of the first edition, the play 'hath often been acted at the Phoenix in Drury Lane, by the Queen's Majesty's servants': the company was formed following Charles I's marriage to Henrietta Maria of France in 1625, and a plague epidemic in London during the summer of that year brought about the closure of the theatres. Its author, Philip Massinger (born 1583) had been part of Philip Henslowe's stable of playwrights since at least 1613; he had been educated at Salisbury grammar school and Oxford University, but left without completing his degree. Like many of his dramatist colleagues, he spent some of his early career in debtors' prison, scraping a living by collaborating with, amongst others, John Fletcher, Thomas Dekker and Thomas Middleton, and contributing to over fifty plays during a period of thirty years. From 1615 onwards he worked for the King's Men, eventually assuming from John Fletcher the mantle of chief dramatist (which Fletcher had inherited from Shakespeare). The performance of *New Way* by the Queen Majesty's company was something of an exception in terms of the overall pattern of Massinger's career, in that from 1626 to 1634 he wrote exclusively for the King's Men. He died in 1640.

A date of composition of 1625 is also suggested by allusions to the ongoing military campaigns in the Low Countries, which involved English forces in an alliance with the Dutch against Spain, and in possible echoes of the financial misdeeds of the monopolist Sir Giles Mompesson (1584–ca.1651), who has often been seen as the model for Massinger's Sir Giles Overreach. Mompesson was elected as a Member of Parliament in 1614 and knighted in 1616; in 1617 he acquired the rights of a commissioner and licence-holder. Charged with the responsibility of concocting new sources of revenue for the Crown, Mompesson (aided by his associate, Sir Francis Michell the model for Justice Greedy) turned the office to his own advantage, levying arbitrary and punitive fines on landlords (faintly echoed in the play in Sir Giles's manipulation of Tapwell), whilst licensing the activities of brothels. He also profited from the patenting of Crown estates. He was investigated by Parliament in 1621, tried in his absence and stripped of his knighthood.

Whether Mompesson was the source for Sir Giles Overreach is open to debate. Although the dramatic creation shares some of the ruthless and corrupt traits of his historical namesake, his is the generic role of the grasping and abusive landlord, who is also the figure of patriarchal opposition to be outwitted by young lovers (it can be noted here that the main plot of *New Way* is appropriated from Middleton's *A Trick to Catch the Old One* [published 1608], which shows an impoverished nephew duping his uncle into restoring his inheritance through the device of a fake marriage). Massinger's satirical energies are oriented less towards the abuse of office than the violation of class boundaries and hierarchies. The public outrage over Mompesson's extortions, and the sense of *schadenfreude* generated by his subsequent exposure and disgrace, were partly fuelled by the sense that his actions were tolerated and even encouraged amidst the general corruption and decadence of the final Jacobean years; Sir Giles Overreach, however, acts solely on his own behalf, targeting not only the poor but, more importantly for the play's scheme, an increasingly impoverished aristocracy, which he treats with undisguised hatred and contempt. Although he is equipped with a knighthood (probably acquired through corrupt means), Sir Giles is, essentially, a social climber, an aspirant middle-class parvenu who attempts both to expropriate land and to force his daughter into marriage with the aristocratic Lord Lovell. Sir Giles's rapacity is equalled only by his vanity and vulgarity, and his disdain for the traditional privileges of rank is matched by his eagerness to appropriate them for himself. Representing what many in Massinger's audience might have recognised as the social and economic power of new money without honour, Sir Giles is a figure of satire, but the demonic virulence of the caricature is also a way of managing the anxiety that his type provokes. The play recognises, moreover, that the threat which Sir Giles personifies cannot be accommodated or neutralised within its comic conclusion, and it is appropriate, therefore, that his final moments on stage take the shape of a sudden and spectacular descent into madness, as he grotesquely visualises his sins returning to haunt him before being hauled offstage to Bedlam. Lovell is quick to draw a pious moral ('Here is a precedent to teach wicked men/That when they leave religion, and turn atheists / Their own abilities leave 'em' [5.1.379–81]); whether either Massinger or his audience would have been convinced by it is open to speculation.

Villain that he is, Sir Giles is the driving force of the play, a factor that has been recognised in its substantial post-seventeenth-century stage history. Robert Hamilton Ball's detailed and entertaining study, *The Amazing Career of Sir Giles Overreach* (1939), documents hundreds of productions on the British, Irish and American stage, commencing with a handful of Restoration revivals followed by a hiatus of nearly a century, and then a reappearance in the mid-eighteenth century with Garrick's production at Drury Lane (1748). For the rest of the eighteenth century and throughout the nineteenth, up until the 1880s, the play was rarely out of the theatrical repertoire; the part of Sir Giles was played by John Philip Kemble (who published an adaptation of the play in 1810), Edmund Kean, Charles Kean and Samuel Phelps. By the end of the nineteenth century, the play was out of fashion (Henry Irving took the part of Welborne in 1861, but never played Sir Giles, although the part interested him greatly), although it enjoyed reasonably regular revivals during the twentieth century. In 1914 the play was staged by the Birmingham Repertory Theatre in modern dress (anticipating subsequent innovations in the staging of Shakespeare by over a decade), and in 1922 Robert Atkins played Sir Giles in the Old Vic production. In 1950 Donald Wolfit attacked the role of Sir Giles in characteristic barnstorming style. The most recent production of the play in the British Isles was that staged by the Royal Shakespeare Company in 1983.

Further reading

Ball, Robert Hamilton, *The Amazing Career of Sir Giles Overreach* (Princeton: Princeton University Press, 1939).

Butler, Martin, 'The Outsider as Insider', in *The Theatrical City: Culture, Theatre and Politics in London, 1576–1649*, ed. David L. Smith, Richard Strier and David Bevington (Cambridge: Cambridge University Press, 1995).

Craik, T. W. (ed.), *A New Way to Pay Old Debts*, New Mermaids (London: Ernest Benn, 1964).

Edwards, Philip and Colin Gibson (eds), *The Plays and Poems of Philip Massinger*, 5 vols (Oxford: The Clarendon Press, 1976).

Gibson, Colin (ed.), *The Selected Plays of Philip Massinger* (Cambridge: Cambridge University Press, 1978).

Howard, Douglas (ed.), *Philip Massinger: A Critical Reassessment* (Cambridge: Cambridge University Press, 1985).

Lindley, Keith, 'Noble Scarlet vs London Blue', in *The Theatrical City* (ed.) Smith, Strier and Bevington.

Sanders, Julie, *Caroline Drama: The Plays of Massinger, Ford, Shirley and Brome*, Writers and Their Work (Plymouth: Northcote House, 1999).

TO THE RIGHT HONOURABLE ROBERT, EARL OF
CAERNARVON,*

Master Falconer of England

My Good Lord,

Pardon I beseech you my boldness, in presuming to shelter this comedy
under the wings of your Lordship's favour, and protection. I am not ignorant (having never yet deserved you in my service) that it cannot but meet
with a severe construction, if in the clemency of your noble disposition, you 5
fashion not a better defence for me than I can fancy for myself. All I can
allege is that divers Italian Princes, and lords of eminent rank in England,
have not disdained to receive and read poems of this nature, nor am I
wholly lost in my hopes, but that your Honour (who have ever expressed
yourself a favourer, and friend to the Muses) may vouchsafe, in your gra- 10
cious acceptance of this trifle, to give me some encouragement, to present
you with some laboured work, and of a higher strain hereafter. I was born a
devoted servant to the thrice noble family of your incomparable lady, and
am most ambitious, but with a becoming distance, to be known to your
Lordship, which if you please to admit, I shall embrace it as a bounty, that 15
while I live shall oblige me to acknowledge you for my noble patron, and
profess myself to be.

> Your Honour's true servant
> Philip Massinger

TO THE MOST INGENIOUS
AUTHOR MASTER
PHILIP MASSINGER
ON HIS COMEDY
Called *A New Way to Pay Old Debts*

'Tis a rare charity, and thou couldst not
So proper to the time have found a plot;
Yet whilst you teach to pay, you lend: the age
We wretches live in, that to come, the stage;
The thronged audience, that was hither brought   5
Invited by your fame, and to be taught
This lesson. All are grown indebted more,
And when they look for freedom run in score.*
It was a cruel courtesy to call
In hope of liberty, and then enthral.   10
The nobles are your bondmen, gentry, and
All besides those that did not understand.
They were no men of credit, bankrupts born,
Fit to be trusted with no stock but scorn.
You have more wisely credited to such,   15
That though they cannot pay, can value much.
I am your debtor too, but to my shame
Repay you nothing back, but your own fame.

Henry Moody, miles.

To his friend the Author

You may remember how you chid me when
I ranked you equal with those glorious men,
Beaumont and Fletcher; if you love not praise
You must forbear the publishing of plays.
The crafty mazes of the cunning plot;   5
The polished phrase; the sweet expressions; got
Neither by theft, nor violence; the conceit
Fresh, and unsullied; all is of weight,
Able to make the captive reader know
I did but justice when I placed you so.   10
A shamefast* blushing would become the brow
Of some weak virgin writer; we allow
To you a kind of pride; and there, where most
Should blush at commendations, you should boast.
If any think I flatter, let him look   15
Off from my idle trifles on thy book.

Thomas Jay,* miles.

Dramatis Personae

LOVELL, *an English lord*
SIR GILES OVERREACH, *a cruel extortioner*
WELBORNE, *a prodigal*
ALWORTH, *a young gentleman page to Lord* LOVELL
GREEDY, *a hungry Justice of the Peace*
MARRALL, *a term-driver.* A creature of* SIR GILES OVERREACH
ORDER
AMBLE
FURNACE   *servants to the* LADY ALWORTH
WATCHALL
WILL-DO, *a parson*
TAPWELL, *an alehouse keeper*
Three CREDITORS
LADY ALWORTH, *a rich widow*
MARGARET, OVERREACH'S *daughter*
WAITING WOMAN
CHAMBERMAID
FROTH, TAPWELL'S *wife*

Act One, Scene One

[*Enter*] WELBORNE, TAPWELL, FROTH.

WELBORNE: No booze? Nor no tobacco?
TAPWELL: Not a suck, sir.
    Nor the remainder of a single can
    Left by a drunken porter, all night palled* too.
FROTH: Not the dropping of the tap for your morning's draft, sir,
    'Tis verity I assure you.
WELBORNE: Verity, you brach!*   5
    The devil turned precisian?* Rogue, what am I?
TAPWELL: Troth, durst I trust you with a looking glass
    To let you see your trim shape, you would quit me,
    And take the name yourself.
WELBORNE: How, dog?
TAPWELL: Even so, sir.
    And I must tell you if you but advance   10
    Your Plymouth cloak,* you shall be soon instructed
    There dwells, and within call, if it please your worship,
    A potent monarch, called the constable,
    That does command a citadel, called the stocks,
    Whose guards are certain files of rusty billmen,*   15
    Such as with great dexterity will hale
    Your tattered, lousy –
WELBORNE: Rascal, slave!
FROTH: No rage, sir.
TAPWELL: At his own peril; do not put yourself
    In too much heat, there being no water near
    To quench your thirst, and sure for other liquor,   20
    As mighty ale, or beer, they are things I take it
    You must no more remember, not in a dream, sir.
WELBORNE: Why, thou unthankful villain, dar'st thou talk thus?
    Is not thy house and all thou hast my gift?
TAPWELL: I find it not in chalk,* and Timothy Tapwell   25
    Does keep no other register.
WELBORNE: Am I not he
    Whose riots* fed and clothed thee? Wert thou not
    Born on my father's land, and proud to be
    A drudge in his house?
TAPWELL: What I was, sir, it skills* not;
    What you are is apparent. Now for a farewell;   30
    Since you talk of father, in my hope it will torment you,
    I'll briefly tell your story. Your dead father,

My quondam* master, was a man of worship,
Old Sir John Welborne, justice of peace, and *quorum,**
And stood fair to be *custos rotulorum;**   35
Bare the whole sway of the shire; kept a great house,
Relieved the poor, and so forth; but he dying,
And the twelve hundred a year coming to you,
Late Master Francis, but now forlorn Welborne –
WELBORNE: Slave, stop, or I shall lose myself.
FROTH: Very hardly;   40
You cannot out of your way.*
TAPWELL: But to my story.
You were then a lord of acres, the prime gallant,
And I your under-butler; note the change now.
You had a merry time of 't. Hawks, and hounds,
With choice of running horses; mistresses   45
Of all sorts, and all sizes; yet so hot
As their embraces made your lordships* melt;
Which your uncle Sir Giles Overreach observing,
Resolving not to lose a drop of 'em,
On foolish mortgages, statutes,* and bonds,   50
For a while supplied your looseness, and then left you.
WELBORNE: Some curate hath penned this invective, mongrel,
And you have studied it.
TAPWELL: I have not done yet:
Your land gone, and your credit not worth a token,*
You grew the common borrower, no man 'scaped   55
Your paper-pellets,* from the gentleman
To the beggars on highways, that sold you switches
In your gallantry.
WELBORNE: I shall switch your brains out.
TAPWELL: Where* poor Tim Tapwell with a little stock,
Some forty pounds or so, bought a small cottage   60
Humbled myself to marriage with my Froth here,
Gave entertainment.
WELBORNE: Yes, to whores, and canters,*
Clubbers* by night.
TAPWELL: True, but they brought in profit,
And had a gift to pay for what they called for,
And stuck not* like your mastership. The poor income   65
I gleaned from them hath made me in my parish
Thought worthy to be scavenger, and in time
May rise to be overseer of the poor;*
Which if I do, on your petition, Welborne,
I may allow you thirteen pence a quarter,   70
And you shall thank my worship.

WELBORNE: Thus you dogbolt,*
   And thus.   *Beats and kicks him.*
TAPWELL: Cry out for help.
WELBORNE: Stir, and thou diest:
   Your potent prince the constable shall not save you.
   Hear me, ungrateful hellhound; did not I
   Make purses* for you? Then you licked my boots,   75
   And thought your holiday cloak too coarse to clean 'em.
   'Twas I that when I heard thee swear, if ever
   Thou couldst arrive at forty pounds, thou wouldst
   Live like an emperor: 'twas I that gave it,
   In ready gold. Deny this, wretch.
TAPWELL: I must, sir,   80
   For from the tavern to the taphouse, all
   On forfeiture of their licences stand bound,
   Never to remember who their best guests were,
   If they grew poor like you.
WELBORNE: They are well rewarded
   That beggar themselves to make cuckolds rich.   85
   Thou viper, thankless viper; impudent bawd!
   But since you are grown forgetful, I will help
   Your memory, and tread* thee into mortar:
   Not leave one bone unbroken.
TAPWELL: O!
FROTH: Ask mercy.

Enter ALWORTH.

WELBORNE: 'Twill not be granted.
ALWORTH: Hold, for my sake hold.   90
   Deny me, Frank? They are not worth your anger.
WELBORNE: For once thou hast redeemed them from this sceptre
                                       His Cudgel
   But let 'em vanish, creeping on their knees,
   And if they grumble, I revoke my pardon.
FROTH: This comes of your prating, husband, you presumed   95
   On your ambling wit, and must use your glib tongue
   Though you are beaten lame for 't.
TAPWELL: Patience, Froth.
   There's law to cure our bruises.   *They go off on their hands and knees.*
WELBORNE: Sent to your mother?
ALWORTH: My lady, Frank, my patroness! My all!
   She's such a mourner for my father's death,   100
   And in her love to him, so favours me,

That I cannot pay too much observance to her.
There are few such stepdames.
WELBORNE: 'Tis a noble widow,
    And keeps her reputation pure, and clear
    From the least taint of infamy; her life   105
    With the splendour of her actions, leaves no tongue
    To envy, or detraction. Prithee tell me:
    Has she no suitors?
ALWORTH: Even the best of the shire, Frank,
    My lord excepted. Such as sue, and send,
    And send, and sue again, but to no purpose.   110
    Their frequent visits have no gained her presence;
    Yet she's so far from sullenness, and pride,
    That I dare undertake you shall meet from her
    A liberal entertainment. I can give you
    A catalogue of her suitor's names.
WELBORNE: Forbear it,   115
    While I give you good counsel. I am bound to it;
    Thy father was my friend, and that affection
    I bore to him, in right descends to thee;
    Thou art a handsome and a hopeful youth,
    Nor will I have the least affront stick on thee,   120
    If I with any danger can prevent it.
ALWORTH: I thank your noble care, but pray you in what
    Do I run the hazard?
WELBORNE: Art thou not in love?
    Put it not off with wonder.
ALWORTH: In love at my years?
WELBORNE: You think you walk in clouds, but are transparent,   125
    I have heard all, and the choice that you have made;
    And with my finger can point out the north star,
    By which the lodestone* of your folly's guided.
    And to confirm this true, what think you of
    Fair Margaret the only child, and heir   130
    Of cormorant* Overreach? Does it blush? And start,
    To hear her only named? Blush at your want
    Of wit, and reason.
ALWORTH: You are too bitter, sir.
WELBORNE: Wounds of this nature are not to be cured
    With balms, but corrosives. I must be plain: 135
    Art thou scarce manumized* from the porter's lodge
    And yet sworn servant to the pantophle,*
    And dar'st thou dream of marriage? I fear
    'Twill be concluded for impossible,
    That there is now, nor e'er shall be hereafter,   140

A handsome page, or player's boy of fourteen,
But either loves a wench, or drabs* love him;
Court-waiters* be not exempted.
ALWORTH: This is madness.
Howe'er you have discovered my intents,
You know my aims are lawful, and if ever   145
The queen of flowers, the glory of the spring,
The sweetest comfort to our smell, the rose
Sprang from an envious briar, I may infer
There's such disparity in their conditions,
Between the goddess of my soul, the daughter,   150
And the base churl her father.
WELBORNE: Grant this true,
As I believe it; canst thou ever hope
To enjoy a quiet bed with her, whose father
Ruined thy state?
ALWORTH: And yours too.
WELBORNE: I confess it.
True, I must tell you as a friend, and freely,   155
That where impossibilities are apparent,
'Tis indiscretion to nourish hopes.
Canst thou imagine (let not self-love blind thee)
That Sir Giles Overreach, that to make her great
In swelling titles, without touch of conscience,   160
Will cut his neighbour's throat, and I hope his own too,
Will e'er consent to make her thine? Give o'er,
And think of some course suitable to thy rank,
And prosper in it.
ALWORTH: You have well advised me.
But in the meantime, you that are so studious   165
Of my affairs, wholly neglect your own.
Remember yourself, and in what plight you are.
WELBORNE: No matter, no matter.
ALWORTH: Yes, 'tis very much material:
You know my fortune, and my means, yet something
I can spare from myself to help your wants.   170
WELBORNE: How's this?
ALWORTH: Nay, be not angry. There's eight pieces*
To put you in better fashion.
WELBORNE: Money from thee?
From a boy? A stipendiary?* One that lives
At the devotion of a stepmother,
And the uncertain favour of a lord?   175
I'll eat my arms first. Howsoe'er blind fortune
Hath spent the utmost of her malice on me;

Though I am vomited out of an alehouse,
And thus accoutred; know not where to eat,
Or drink, or sleep, but underneath this canopy;*   180
Although I thank thee, I despise thy offer.
And as I in my madness broke my state,
Without th' assistance of another's brain,
In my right wits I'll piece it; at the worst   185
Die thus, and be forgotten.
ALWORTH: A strange humour.*   *Exeunt.*

Act One, Scene Two

[*Enter*] ORDER, AMBLE, FURNACE, WATCHALL.

ORDER: Set all things right, or as my name is Order,
       And by this staff of office that commands you,
       This chain, and double ruff, symbols of power;
       Whoever misses in his function,
       For one whole week makes forfeiture of his breakfast,   5
       And privilege in the wine-cellar.
AMBLE: You are merry,
       Good master steward.
FURNACE: Let him; I'll be angry.
AMBLE: Why, fellow Furnace, 'tis not twelve o'clock yet,
       Nor dinner taking up; then 'tis allowed
       Cooks by their places may be choleric.   10
FURNACE: You think you have spoke wisely, goodman Amble,
       My lady's go-before.*
ORDER: Nay, nay; no wrangling.
FURNACE: Twit me with the authority of the kitchen?
       At all hours, and all places I'll be angry;
       And thus provoked, when I am at my prayers,   15
       I will be angry.
AMBLE: There was no hurt meant.
FURNACE: I am friends with thee, and yet I will be angry.
ORDER: With whom?
FURNACE: No matter whom; yet now I think on 't
       I am angry with my lady.
WATCHALL: Heaven forbid, man.
ORDER: What cause has she given thee?
FURNACE: Cause enough, master steward.   20
       I was entertained by her to please her palate,
       And till she forswore eating I performed it.

Now since our master noble Alworth died,
Though I crack my brains to find out tempting sauces,
And raise fortifications in the pastry,   25
Such as might serve for models in the Low Countries,
Which if they had been practiced at Breda,*
Spinola might have thrown his cap at it, and ne'er took it –
AMBLE: But you had wanted matter there to work on.
FURNACE: Matter? With six eggs, and a strike* of rye-meal   30
   I had kept the town till doomsday, perhaps longer.
ORDER: But what's this to your pet against my lady?
FURNACE: What's this? Marry, this: when I am three parts roasted,
   And the fourth part parboiled, to prepare her viands,
   She keeps her chamber, dines with a panada,*   35
   Or water-gruel; my sweat never thought on.
ORDER: But your art is seen in the dining-room.
FURNACE: By whom?
   By such as pretend to love her, but come
   To feed upon her. Yet of all the harpies
   That do devour her, I am out of charity   40
   With none so much as the thin-gutted squire
   That's stol'n into commission.*
ORDER: Justice Greedy?
FURNACE: The same, the same. Meat's cast away upon him,
   It never thrives. He holds this paradox,
   Who eats not well, can ne'er do justice well: 45
   His stomach's as insatiate* as the grave,
   Or strumpets' ravenous appetites.
WATCHALL: One knocks.

                ALWORTH *knocks and enters.*

ORDER: Our late young master.
AMBLE: Welcome, sir.
FURNACE: Your hand;
   If you have a stomach, a cold bake-meat's ready.
ORDER: His father's picture in little.*
FURNACE: We are all your servants.   50
AMBLE: In you he lives.
ALWORTH: At once, my thanks to all;
   This is yet some comfort. Is my lady stirring?

      Enter the LADY ALWORTH, [WAITING-] WOMAN, CHAMBERMAID.

ORDER: Her presence answer for us.

LADY: Sort these silks well;
  I'll take the air alone.

        Exeunt [WAITING-] WOMAN *and* CHAMBERMAID.

FURNACE: You air, and air,
  But will you never taste but spoonmeat* more?   55
  To what use serve I?
LADY: Prithee be not angry,
  I shall ere long: i' the meantime, there is gold
  To buy thee aprons, and a summer suit.
FURNACE: I am appeased, and Furnace now grows cool.
LADY: And, as I gave direction, if this morning   60
  I am visited by any, entertain 'em
  As heretofore; but say in my excuse
  I am indisposed.
ORDER: I shall, madam.
LADY: Do, and leave me.
  Nay, stay you, Alworth.

       Exeunt ORDER, AMBLE, FURNACE, WATCHALL.

ALWORTH: I shall gladly grow here,
  To wait on your commands.
LADY: So soon turned courtier.   65
ALWORTH: Style not that courtship, madam, which is duty,
  Purchased on your part.
LADY: Well, you shall o'ercome;
  I'll not contend in words. How is it with
  Your noble master?
ALWORTH: Ever like himself;
  No scruple lessened in the full weight of honour;   70
  He did command me (pardon my presumption)
  As his unworthy deputy to kiss
  Your ladyship's fair hands.
LADY: I am honoured in
  His favour to me. Does he hold his purpose
  For the Low Countries?
ALWORTH: Constantly, good madam,   75
  But he will in person first present his service.
LADY: And how approve you of his course? You are yet
  Like virgin parchment, capable of* any
  Inscription, vicious, or honourable;
  I will not force your will, but leave you free   80

To your own election.
ALWORTH: Any form you please
   I will put on: but, might I make my choice,
   With humble emulation I would follow
   The path my lord marks to me.
LADY: 'Tis well answered,
   And I commend your spirit; you had a father   85
   (Blessed be his memory) that some few hours
   Before the will of heaven took him from me,
   Who did commend you, by the dearest ties
   Of perfect love between us, to my charge;
   And therefore what I speak, you are bound to hear   90
   With such respect, as if he lived in me;
   He was my husband, and howe'er you are not
   Son of my womb, you may be of my love,
   Provided you deserve it.
ALWORTH: I have found you
   (Most honoured madam) the best mother to me,   95
   And with my utmost strengths of care and service,
   Will labour that you may never repent
   Your bounties showered upon me.
LADY: I much hope it.
   These were your father's words. If e'er my son
   Follow the war, tell him it is a school   100
   Where all the principles tending to honour
   Are taught if truly followed; but for such
   As repair thither, as a place in which
   They do presume they may with licence practice
   Their lusts and riots, they shall never merit   105
   The noble name of soldiers. To dare boldly
   In a fair cause, and for the country's safety
   To run upon the cannon's mouth undaunted;
   To obey their leaders, and shun mutinies;
   To bear, with patience, the winter's cold,   110
   And summer's scorching heat, and not to faint,
   When plenty of provision fails, with hunger,
   Are the essential parts make up a soldier,
   Not swearing, dice, or drinking.
ALWORTH: There's no syllable
   You speak, but is to me an oracle,   115
   Which but to doubt were impious.
LADY: To conclude:
   Beware ill company, for often men
   Are like to those with whom they do converse,

And from one man I warn you, and that's Welborne:
Not because he's poor, that rather claims your pity,   120
But that he's in his manners so debauched,
And hath to vicious courses sold himself.
'Tis true your father loved him, while he was
Worthy the loving, but if he had lived
To have seen him as he is, he had cast him off   125
As you must do.
ALWORTH: I shall obey in all things.
LADY: Go, follow me to my chamber; you shall have gold
To furnish you like my son, and still supplied,
As I hear from you.
ALWORTH: I am still your creature.   *Exeunt.*

Act One, Scene Three

[*Enter*] OVERREACH, GREEDY, ORDER, AMBLE, FURNACE, WATCHALL, MARRALL.

GREEDY: Not to be seen?
OVERREACH: Still cloistered up? Her reason
I hope assures her, though she make herself
Close prisoner ever for her husband's loss,
'Twill not recover him.
ORDER: Sir, it is her will,
Which we that are her servants ought to serve it,   5
And not dispute. Howe'er, you are nobly welcome,
And if you please to stay, that you may think so,
There came not six days since from Hull* a pipe
Of rich canary, which shall spend itself
For my lady's honour.
GREEDY: Is it of the right race?*   10
ORDER: Yes, Master Greedy.
AMBLE: How his mouth runs o'er!
FURNACE: I'll make it run and run. Save your good worship.
GREEDY: Honest master cook, thy hand again. How I love thee:
Are the good dishes still in being? Speak, boy.
FURNACE: If you have a mind to feed, there is a chine*   15
Of beef, well seasoned.
GREEDY: Good!
FURNACE: A pheasant larded.
GREEDY: That I might now give thanks for 't!
FURNACE: Other kickshaws.*

Besides, there came last night from the forest of Sherwood
The fattest stag I ever cooked.
GREEDY: A stag, man?
FURNACE: A stag, sir, part of it prepared for dinner,   20
And baked in puffpaste.
GREEDY: Puffpaste too, Sir Giles!
A ponderous chine of beef! A pheasant larded!
And red deer too, Sir Giles, and baked in puffpaste!
All business set aside; let us give thanks here.
FURNACE: How the lean skeleton's rapt!
OVERREACH: You know we cannot.   25
MARRALL: Your worships are to sit on a commission,
And if you fail to come, you lose the cause.
GREEDY: Cause me no causes. I'll prove 't, for such a dinner
We may put off a commission: you shall find it
*Henrici decimo quarto.**
OVERREACH: Fie, Master Greedy.   30
Will you lose me a thousand pounds for a dinner?
No more, for shame. We must forget the belly,
When we think of profit.
GREEDY: Well, you shall o'errule me.
I could e'en cry now. Do you hear, master cook,
Send but a corner of that immortal pasty,   35
And I, in thankfulness, will by your boy
Send you a brace of threepences.
FURNACE: Will you be so prodigal?

Enter WELBORNE.

OVERREACH: Remember me to your lady. Who have we here?
WELBORNE: You know me.
OVERREACH: I did once, but now I will not,
Thou art no blood of mine, Avaunt, thou beggar;   40
If ever thou presume to own me more,
I'll have thee caged and whipped.
GREEDY: I'll grant the warrant;
Think of Pie Corner,* Furnace.
                              Exeunt OVERREACH, GREEDY, MARRALL.
WATCHALL: Will you out, sir?
I wonder how you durst creep in.
ORDER: This is rudeness,
And saucy impudence.
AMBLE: Cannot you stay   45
To be served among your fellows from the basket,*
But you must press in to the hall?

FURNACE: Prithee vanish
   Into some outhouse, though it be the pigsty;
   My scullion shall come to thee.

Enter ALWORTH.

WELBORNE: This is rare:
   O here's Tom Alworth. Tom.
ALWORTH: We must be strangers,   50
   Nor would I have you seen here for a million.   *Exit* ALWORTH.
WELBORNE: Better and better. He contemns me too?
   Enter [WAITING-] WOMAN *and* CHAMBERMAID.
WOMAN: Foh, what a smell's here! What thing's this?
CHAMBERMAID: A creature
   Made out of the privy. Let us hence for love's sake,
   Or I shall swoon.
WOMAN: I begin to faint already.   55
                  Exeunt [WAITING-] WOMAN *and* CHAMBERMAID.
WATCHALL: Will know your way?
AMBLE: Or shall we teach it you,
   By the head and shoulders?
WELBORNE: No: I will not stir.
   Do you mark, I will not. Let me see the wretch
   That dares attempt to force me. Why, you slaves,
   Created only to make legs,* and cringe;   60
   To carry in a dish, and shift a trencher;
   That have not souls only to hope a blessing
   Beyond blackjacks,* or flagons; you that were born
   Only to consume meat, and drink, and batten
   Upon reversions:* who advances? Who   65
   Shows me the way?

Enter LADY, [WAITING-] WOMAN, CHAMBERMAID.

ORDER: My lady.
CHAMBERMAID: Here's the monster.
WOMAN: Sweet madam, keep your glove to your nose.
CHAMBERMAID: Or let me
   Fetch some perfumes may be predominant,
   You wrong yourself else.
WELBORNE: Madam, my designs
   Bear me to you.
LADY: To me?
WELBORNE: And though I have met with   70
   But ragged entertainment from your grooms here,

I hope from you to receive that noble usage
As may become the true friend of your husband,
And then I shall forget these.
LADY: I am amazed
    To see and hear this rudeness. Dar'st thou think,   75
    Though sworn, that it can ever find belief
    That I, who to the best men of this country
    Denied my presence since my husband's death,
    Can fall so low, as to change words with thee?
    Thou son of infamy, forbear my house,   80
    And know and keep the distance that's between us,
    Or, though it be against my gentler temper,
    I shall take order* you no more shall be
    An eyesore to me.
WELBORNE: Scorn me not, good lady;
    But as in form you are angelical   85
    Imitate the heavenly natures, and vouchsafe
    At the least awhile to hear me. You will grant
    The blood that runs in this arm is as noble
    As that which fills your veins; those costly jewels,
    And those rich clothes you wear; your men's observance,   90
    And women's flattery, are in you no virtues,
    Not these rags, with my poverty, in me vices.
    You have a fair fame, and I know deserve it;
    Yet, lady, I must say in nothing more
    Than in the pious sorrow you have shown   95
    For your late noble husband.
ORDER: How she starts!
FURNACE: And can hardly keep finger from the eye*
    To hear him named.
LADY: Have you aught else to say?
WELBORNE: That husband, madam, was once in his fortune
    Almost as low as I. Want, debts, and quarrels   100
    Lay heavy on him: let it not be thought
    A boast in me, though I say, I relieved him.
    'Twas I that gave him fashion;* mine the sword
    That did on all occasions second his;
    I brought him on, and off, with honour, lady;   105
    And when in all men's judgements he was sunk,
    And in his own hopes not to be buoyed up,
    I stepped unto him, took him by the hand,
    And set him upright.
FURNACE: Are not we base rogues
    That could forget this?

WELBORNE: I confess you made him   110
     Master of your estate, nor could your friends,
     Though he brought no wealth with him, blame you for 't;
     For he had a shape, and to that shape a mind
     Made up of all parts, either great, or noble,
     So winning a behaviour, not to be   115
     Resisted, madam.
LADY: 'Tis most true. He had.
WELBORNE: For his sake, then, in that I was his friend,
     Do not contemn* me.
LADY: For what's past, excuse me,
     I will redeem it. Order, give the gentleman
     A hundred pounds.
WELBORNE: No, madam, on no terms: 120
     I will nor beg nor borrow six pence of you,
     But be supplied elsewhere, or want thus ever.
     Only one suit I make, which you deny not
     To strangers, and 'tis this.   *Whispers to her.*
LADY: Fie, nothing else?
WELBORNE: Nothing; unless you please to charge your servants
     To throw away a little respect upon me.
LADY: What you demand is yours.
WELBORNE: I thank you, Lady.
     Now what can be wrought out of such a suit
     Is yet in supposition; I have said all,
     When you please you may retire. Nay, all's forgotten,   130
     And for a lucky omen to my project,
     Shake hands, and end all quarrels in the cellar.
ORDER: Agreed, agreed.
FURNACE: Still merry, master Welborne.   *Exeunt.*

Act Two, Scene One

[*Enter*] OVERREACH, MARRALL.

OVERREACH: He's gone, I warrant thee; this commission crushed him.
MARRALL: Your worship have the way on 't, and ne'er miss
     To squeeze these unthrifts into air; and yet
     The chap-fallen* justice did his part, returning
     For your advantage the certificate   5
     Against his conscience, and his knowledge too
     (With your good favour), to the utter ruin
     Of the poor farmer.

OVERREACH: 'Twas for these good ends
    I made him a justice. He that bribes his belly
    Is certain to command his soul.
MARRALL: I wonder   10
    (Still with your licence) why, your worship having
    The power to put this thin-gut in commission,
    You are not in 't yourself?
OVERREACH: Thou art a fool:
    In being out of office I am out of danger;
    Where if I were a justice, besides the trouble,   15
    I might, or out of wilfulness, or error,
    Run myself finely into a *praemunire*,*
    And so become a prey to the informer.
    No, I'll have none of it; 'tis enough I keep
    Greedy at my devotion: so he serve   20
    My purposes, let him hang, or damn, I care not.
    Friendship is but a word.
MARRALL: You are all wisdom.
OVERREACH: I would be worldly wise, for the other wisdom
    That does prescribe us a well-governed life,
    And do right to others, as to ourselves,   25
    I value not an atom.
MARRALL: What course take you,
    With your good patience, to hedge in* the manor
    Of your neighbour Master Frugal? As 'tis said,
    He will nor sell, nor borrow, nor exchange,
    And his land, lying in the midst of your many lordships,   30
    Is a foul blemish.
OVERREACH: I have thought on 't, Marrall,
    And it shall take. I must have all men sellers,
    And I the only purchaser.
MARRALL: 'Tis most fit, sir.
OVERREACH: I'll therefore buy some cottage near his manor,
    Which done, I'll make my men break ope his fences;   35
    Ride o'er his standing corn, and in the night
    Set fire on his barns; or break his cattle's legs.
    These trespasses draw on suits, and suits expenses,
    Which I can spare, but will soon beggar him.
    When I have harried him thus two or three year,   40
    Though he sue *in forma pauperis*,* in spite
    Of all his thrift and care he'll grow behind-hand.
MARRALL: The best I ever heard; I could adore you.
OVERREACH: Then, with the favour of my man of law,
    I will pretend some title:* want will force him   45
    To put it to arbitrement;* then if he sell

For half the value, he shall have ready money
And I possess his land.
MARRALL: 'Tis above wonder!
Welborne was apt to sell, and needed not
These fine arts, sir, to hook him in.
OVERREACH: Well thought on.   50
This varlet, Marrall, lives too long to upbraid me
With my close cheat* put on him. Will nor cold
Nor hunger kill him?
MARRALL: I know not what to think on 't.
I have used all means, and the last night I caused
His host the tapster to turn him out of doors;   55
And have been since with all your friends and tenants,
And on the forfeit of your favour charged 'em,
Though a crust of mouldy bread would keep him from starving,
Yet they should not relieve him. This is done, sir.
OVERREACH: That was something, Marrall, but thou must go further,   60
And suddenly, Marrall.
MARRALL: Where and when you please, sir.
OVERREACH: I would have thee seek him out, and, if thou canst,
Persuade him that 'tis better steal than beg.
Then if I prove he has but robbed a hen-roost,
Not all the world shall save him from the gallows.   65
Do anything to work him to despair,
And 'tis thy masterpiece.
MARRALL: I will do my best, sir.
OVERREACH: I am now on my main work with the Lord Lovell,
The gallant-minded, popular Lord Lovell:
The minion* of the people's love. I hear   70
He's come into the country,* and my aims are
To insinuate myself into his knowledge,
And then invite him to my house.
MARRALL: I have you.
This points at my young mistress.
OVERREACH: She must part with
That humble title, and write honourable,   75
Right honourable, Marrall, my right honourable daughter,
If all I have, or e'er shall get will do it.
I will have her well attended; there are ladies
Of errant* knights decayed, and brought so low,
That for cast-clothes and meat will gladly serve her.   80
And 'tis my glory, though I come from the city,
To have their issue, whom I have undone,
To kneel to mine, as bond-slaves.
MARRALL: 'Tis fit state, sir.

OVERREACH: And, therefore, I'll not have a chambermaid
    That ties her shoes, or any meaner office,   85
    But such whose fathers were right worshipful.
    'Tis a rich man's pride, there having ever been
    More than a feud, a strange antipathy
    Between us and true gentry.

Enter WELBORNE.

MARRALL: See who's here, sir.
OVERREACH: Hence, monster, prodigy!
WELBORNE: Sir, your wife's nephew;   90
    She and my father tumbled in one belly.
OVERREACH: Avoid my sight, thy breath's infectious, rogue.
    I shun thee as a leprosy, or the plague.
    Come hither, Marrall, this is the time to work him.
MARRALL: I warrant you, sir.   *Exit* OVERREACH.
WELBORNE: By this light, I think he's mad.   95
MARRALL: Mad? Had you took compassion on yourself,
    You long since had been mad.
WELBORNE: You have took a course
    Between you and my venerable uncle
    To make me so.
MARRALL: The more pale-spirited you,
    That would not be instructed. I swear deeply.   100
WELBORNE: By what?
MARRALL: By my religion.
WELBORNE: Thy religion!
    The devil's creed, but what would you have done?
MARRALL: Had there been but one tree in all the shire,
    Nor any hope to compass a penny halter,
    Before, like you, I had outlived my fortunes,   105
    A withe* had served my turn to hang myself.
    I am zealous in your cause: pray you hang yourself,
    And presently,* as you love your credit.*
WELBORNE: I thank you.
MARRALL: Will you stay till you die in a ditch? Or lice devour you?
    Or if you dare not do the feat yourself,   110
    But that you'll put the state to charge and trouble,
    Is there no purse to be cut? House to be broken?
    Or market women with eggs that you may murder,
    And so despatch the business?
WELBORNE: Here's variety,
    I must confess; but I'll accept of none   115
    Of all your gentle offers, I assure you.

MARRALL: Why, have you hope ever to eat again?
   Or drink? Or be the master of three farthings?
   If you like not hanging, drown yourself, take some course
   For your reputation.
WELBORNE: 'Twill not do, dear tempter,   120
   With all the rhetoric the fiend hath taught you.
   I am as far as thou art from despair;
   Nay, I have confidence, which is more than hope,
   To live, and suddenly, better than ever.
MARRALL: Ha, ha! These castles you build in the air   125
   Will not persuade me or to give or lend
   A token to you.
WELBORNE: I'll be more kind to thee.
   Come, thou shalt dine with me.
MARRALL: With you!
WELBORNE: Nay, more, dine gratis.*
MARRALL: Under what hedge, I pray you? Or at whose cost?
   Are they padders or abram-men* that are your consorts?   130
WELBORNE: Thou art incredulous, but thou shalt dine,
   Not alone at her house, but with a gallant lady,
   With me, and with a lady.
MARRALL: Lady! What lady?
   With the Lady of the Lake,* or Queen of Fairies?
   For I know it must be an enchanted dinner.   135
WELBORNE: With the Lady Alworth, knave.
MARRALL: Nay, now there's hope
   Thy brain is cracked.
WELBORNE: Mark there with what respect
   I am entertained.
MARRALL: With choice no doubt of dog-whips.
   Why, dost thou ever hope to pass her porter?
WELBORNE: 'Tis not far off. Go with me: trust thine own eyes.   140
MARRALL: Troth, in my hope, or my assurance rather
   To see thou curvet,* and mount like a dog in a blanket,
   If ever thou presume to pass her threshold,
   I will endure thy company.
WELBORNE: Come along, then.   *Exeunt.*

Act Two, Scene Two

[*Enter*] ALWORTH, [WAITING-] WOMAN, CHAMBERMAID, ORDER,
AMBLE, FURNACE, WATCHALL.

WOMAN: Could you not command your leisure one hour longer?

CHAMBERMAID: Or half an hour?
ALWORTH: I have told you what my haste is:
  Besides being now another's, not mine own,
  Howe'er I much desire to enjoy you longer,
  My duty suffers, if to please myself   5
  I should neglect my lord.
WOMAN: Pray you do me the favour
  To put these few quince-cakes into your pocket;
  They are of mine own preserving.
CHAMBERMAID: And this marmalade;
  'Tis comfortable for your stomach.
WOMAN: And at parting
  Excuse me if I beg a farewell from you.   10
CHAMBERMAID: You are still before me. I move the same suit, sir.
                            Kisses 'em severally.
FURNACE: How greedy these chamberers* are of a beardless chin!
  I think the tits* will ravish him.
ALWORTH: My service
  To both.
WOMAN: Ours waits on you.
CHAMBERMAID: And shall do ever.
ORDER: You are my lady's charge, be therefore careful   15
  That you sustain your parts.
WOMAN: We can bear, I warrant you.
            Exeunt [WAITING-] WOMAN *and* CHAMBERMAID.
FURNACE: Here, drink it off: the ingredients are cordial,
  And this the true elixir;* it hath boiled
  Since midnight for you. 'Tis the quintessence
  Of five cocks of the game, ten dozen of sparrows,   20
  Knuckles of veal, potato roots,* and marrow;
  Coral, and ambergris: were you two years elder,
  And I had a wife, or gamesome mistress,
  I durst trust you with neither. You need not bait*
  After this, I warrant you; though your journey's long,   25
  You may ride on the strength of this till tomorrow morning.
ALWORTH: Your courtesies overwhelm me: I much grieve
  To part from such true friends, and yet find comfort;
  My attendance on my honourable lord
  (Whose resolution holds to visit my lady)   30
  Will speedily bring me back.
        Knocking at the gate; MARRALL *and* WELBORNE *within.*
MARRALL: Dar'st thou venture further?
WELBORNE: Yes, yes, and knock again.
ORDER: 'Tis he; disperse.

AMBLE: Perform it bravely.
FURNACE: I know my cue, ne'er doubt me.
                         They go off several ways.
WATCHALL: Beast that I was to make you stay: most welcome,
    You were long since expected.
WELBORNE: Say so much   35
    To my friend, I pray you.
WATCHALL: For your sake I will, sir.
MARRALL: For his sake!
WELBORNE: Mum; this is nothing.
MARRALL: More than ever
    I would have believed, though I had found it in my primer.*
ALWORTH: When I have giv'n you reasons for my late harshness,
    You'll pardon and excuse me: for, believe me,   40
    Though now I part abruptly, in my service
    I will deserve it.
MARRALL: Service! With a vengeance!
WELBORNE: I am satisfied: farewell, Tom.
ALWORTH: All joy stay with you. *Exit.*

Enter AMBLE.

AMBLE: You are happily encountered: I never
    Presented one so welcome, as I know   45
    You will be to my lady.
MARRALL: This is some vision;
    Or sure these men are mad, to worship a dunghill;
    It cannot be a truth.
WELBORNE: Be still a pagan,
    And unbelieving infidel; be so, miscreant,
    And meditate on blankets, and on dog-whips.   50

Enter FURNACE.

FURNACE: I am glad you are come; until I know your pleasure,
    I knew not how to serve up my lady's dinner.
MARRALL: His pleasure; is it possible?
WELBORNE: What's thy will?
FURNACE: Marry, sir, I have some grouse, and turkey chicken,*
    Some rails,* and quails, and my lady willed me ask you   55
    What kind of sauces best affect* your palate,
    That I may use my utmost skill to please it.

MARRALL: The devil's entered this cook: sauce for his palate!
    That on my knowledge, for almost this twelve month,
    Durst wish but cheese-parings, and brown bread on Sundays.   60
WELBORNE: That way I like 'em best.
FURNACE: It shall be done, sir.
                                                  Exit.
WELBORNE: What think you of the hedge we shall dine under?
    Shall we feed gratis?
MARRALL: I know not what to think;
    Pray you make me not mad.

                    Enter ORDER.

ORDER: This place becomes you not;
    Pray you walk, sir, to the dining room.
WELBORNE: I am well here   65
    Till her ladyship quits her chamber.
MARRALL: Well here, say you?
    'Tis a rare change! But yesterday you thought
    Yourself well in a barn, wrapped up in pease-straw.

            Enter [WAITING-] WOMAN *and* CHAMBERMAID.

WOMAN: O sir, you are wished for.
CHAMBERMAID: My lady dreamt, sir, of you.
WOMAN: And the first command she gave after she rose   70
    Was (her devotions done) to give her notice
    When you approached here.
CHAMBERMAID: Which is done, on my virtue.
MARRALL: I shall be converted, I begin to grow
    Into a new belief, which saints nor angels
    Could have won me to have faith in.

                    Enter LADY.

WOMAN: Sir, my lady.   75
LADY: I come to meet you, and languished till I saw you.
    The first kiss is for form; I allow a second
    To such a friend.
MARRALL: To such a friend! Heaven bless me!
WELBORNE: I am wholly yours; yet, madam, if you please
    To grace this gentleman with a salute –   80
MARRALL: Salute me at his bidding!
WELBORNE: – I shall receive it
    As a most high favour.

LADY: Sir, you may command me.
WELBORNE: Run backward from a lady? And such a lady?
MARRALL: To kiss her foot is, to poor me, a favour
    I am unworthy of –   *Offers to kiss her foot.*
LADY: Nay, pray you rise,   85
    And since you are so humble, I'll exalt you;
    You shall dine with me today, at mine own table.
MARRALL: Your ladyship's table? I am not good enough
    To sit at your steward's board.
LADY: You are too modest:
    I'll not be denied.

               Enter FURNACE.

FURNACE: Will you still be babbling,   90
    Till your meat freeze on the table? The old trick still.
    My art ne'er thought on.
LADY: You arm, Master Welborne:
    Nay, keep us company.
MARRALL: I was never so graced.
               Exeunt WELBORNE, LADY, ALWORTH,
        AMBLE, MARRALL, [WAITING-] WOMAN, [CHAMBERMAID].
ORDER: So we have played our parts, and are come off well.
    But if I know the mystery, why my lady   95
    Consented to it, or why master Welborne
    Desired it, may I perish.
FURNACE: Would I had him
    The roasting of his heart, that cheated him,
    And forces the poor gentleman to these shifts.
    By fire (for cooks are Persians,* and swear by it)   100
    Of all the griping and extorting tyrants
    I ever heard or read of, I ne'er met
    A match to Sir Giles Overreach.
WATCHALL: What will you take
    To tell him so, fellow Furnace?
FURNACE: Just as much
    As my throat is worth, for that would be the price on 't.   105
    To have a usurer that starves himself,
    And wears a cloak of one and twenty years
    On a suit of fourteen groats, bought of the hangman,*
    To grow rich, and then purchase, is too common;
    But this Sir Giles feeds high, keeps many servants,   110
    Who must at his command do any outrage;
    Rich in his habit; vast in his expenses;

Yet he to admiration* still increases
In wealth, and lordships.
ORDER: He frights men out of their estates,
   And breaks through all law-nets made to curb ill men,   115
   As they were cobwebs. No man dares reprove him.
   Such a spirit to dare, and power to do, were never
   Lodged so unluckily.

Enter AMBLE.

AMBLE: Ha, ha: I shall burst.
ORDER: Contain thyself, man.
FURNACE: Or make us partakers
   Of your sudden mirth.
AMBLE: Ha, ha, my lady has got   120
   Such a guest at her table, this term-driver Marrall,
   This snip of an attorney.
FURNACE: What of him, man?
AMBLE: The knave thinks still he's at the cook's shop in Ram Alley,*
   Where the clerks divide,* and the elder is to choose;
   And feeds so slovenly.
FURNACE: Is this all?
AMBLE: My lady   125
   Drank to him for fashion sake, or to please Master Welborne.
   As I live, he rises, and takes up a dish,
   In which there were some remnants of a boiled capon,
   And pledges her in whitebroth.*
FURNACE: Nay, 'tis like
   The rest of his tribe.
AMBLE: And when I brought him wine,   130
   He leaves his stool, and after a leg* or two
   Most humbly thanks my worship.
ORDER: Rose already!
AMBLE: I shall be chid.*

Enter LADY, WELBORNE, MARRALL.

FURNACE: My lady frowns.
LADY: You wait well.
   Let me have no more of this, I observed your jeering.
   Sirrah, I'll have you know whom I think worthy   135
   To sit at my table, be he ne'er so mean,
   When I am present, is not your companion.*

ORDER: Nay, she'll preserve what's due to her.

FURNACE: This refreshing
  Follows your flux of laughter.

LADY: You are master
  Of your own will. I know so much of manners   140
  As not to enquire your purposes, in a word
  To me you are ever welcome, as to a house
  That is your own.

WELBORNE: Mark that.

MARRALL: With reverence, sir,
  And it like your worship.

WELBORNE: Trouble yourself no farther,
  Dear madam; my heart's full of zeal and service,   145
  However in my language I am sparing.
  Come, Master Marrall.

MARRALL: I attend your worship.
                                      Exeunt WELBORNE, MARRALL.

LADY: I see in your looks you are sorry, and you know me
  An easy mistress: be merry; I have forgot all.
  Order and Furnace, come with me, I must give you   150
  Further directions.

ORDER: What you please.

FURNACE: We are ready.   *Exeunt.*

Act Two, Scene Three

[*Enter*] WELBORNE, MARRALL.

WELBORNE: I think I am in a good way.

MARRALL: Good sir, the best way;
  The certain best way.

WELBORNE: These are casualties
  That men are subject to.

MARRALL: You are above 'em.
  And as you are already worshipful,
  I hope ere long you will increase in worship,   5
  And be right worshipful.

WELBORNE: Prithee do not flout* me.
  What I shall be, I shall be. Is 't for your ease
  You keep your hat off?

MARRALL: Ease, and it like your worship?
  I hope Jack Marrall shall not live so long
  To prove himself such an unmannerly beast,   10

Though it hail hazelnuts, as to be covered
When your worship's present.

WELBORNE: Is not this a true rogue?   *Aside.*
That out of mere hope of a future coz'nage*
Can turn thus suddenly: 'tis rank already.

MARRALL: I know your worship's wise, and needs no counsel;   15
Yet if in my desire to do you service
I humbly offer my advice (but still
Under correction), I hope I shall not
Incur your high displeasure.

WELBORNE: No; speak freely.

MARRALL: Then in my judgement, sir, my simple judgement   20
(Still with your worship's favour), I could wish you
A better habit,* for this cannot be
But much distasteful to the noble lady
(I say no more) that loves you, for this morning
To me (and I am but a swine to her*)   25
Before th' assurance of her wealth perfumed you,
You savoured not of amber.

WELBORNE: I do now then?

MARRALL: This your baton hath got a touch of it.

                                        Kisses the end of his cudgel.

Yet if you please for change* I have twenty pounds here
Which out of my true love I presently   30
Lay down at your worship's feet: 'twill serve to buy you
A riding suit.

WELBORNE: But where's the horse?

MARRALL: My gelding
Is at your service; nay, you shall ride me
Before your worship shall be put to the trouble
To walk afoot. Alas, when you are lord   35
Of this lady's manor (as I know you will be),
You may, with the lease of glebe land* called Knave's Acre,
A place I would manure,* requite your vassal.

WELBORNE: I thank your love; but must make no use of it.
What's twenty pounds?

MARRALL: 'Tis all I can make,* sir.   40

WELBORNE: Dost thou think though I want clothes I could not have 'em
For one word to my lady?

MARRALL: As I know not that!

WELBORNE: Come, I'll tell thee a secret, and so leave thee.
I'll not give her the advantage, though she be
A gallant-minded lady, after we are married   45
(There being no woman but is sometimes froward*)

To hit me in the teeth, and say she was forced
To buy my wedding clothes, and took me on
With a plain riding suit, and an ambling nag.
No, I'll be furnished something like myself.   50
And so farewell; for thy suit touching Knave's Acre,
When it is mine, 'tis thine.
MARRALL: I thank your worship.   *Exit* WELBORNE.
How was I cozened in the calculation
Of this man's fortune, my master cozened too,
Whose pupil I am in the art of undoing men,   55
For that is our profession; well, well, Master Welborne,
You are of a sweet nature, and fit again to be cheated:
Which, if the fates please, when you are possessed
Of the land, and lady, you sans question shall be.
I'll presently think of the means.   *Walk by musing.*

                  Enter OVERREACH.

OVERREACH: Sirrah, take my horse.   60
I'll walk to get me an appetite; 'tis but a mile,
And exercise will keep me from being pursy.*
Ha! Marrall! Is he conjuring? Perhaps
The knave has wrought the prodigal to do
Some outrage on himself, and now he feels   65
Compunction in his conscience for 't: no matter,
So it be done. Marrall.
MARRALL: Sir.
OVERREACH: How succeed we
In our plot on Welborne?
MARRALL: Never better, sir.
OVERREACH: Has he hanged or drowned himself?
MARRALL: No, sir, he lives.
Lives once more to be made a prey to you,   70
A greater prey than ever.
OVERREACH: Art thou in thy wits?
If thou art, reveal this miracle, and briefly.
MARRALL: A lady, sir, is fall'n in love with him.
OVERREACH: With him? What lady?
MARRALL: The rich Lady Alworth.
OVERREACH: Thou dolt: how dar'st thou speak this?
MARRALL: I speak truth;   75
And* I do so but once a year, unless
It be to you, sir. We dined with her ladyship,
I thank his worship.

OVERREACH: His worship!
MARRALL: As I live, sir,
    I dined with him at the great lady's table,
    Simple* as I stand here, and saw when she kissed him,   80
    And would at his request have kissed me too,
    But I was not so audacious as some youths are,
    And dare do anything, be it ne'er so absurd,
    And sad* after performance.
OVERREACH: Why, thou rascal,
    To tell me these impossibilities: 85
    Dine at her table? And kiss him? Or thee?
    Impudent varlet! Have not I myself,
    To whom great countesses' doors have oft flew open,
    Ten times attempted, since her husband's death,
    In vain to see her, though I came a suitor;   90
    And yet your good solicitorship and rogue, Welborne,
    Were brought into her presence, feasted with her.
    But that I know thee a dog, that cannot blush,
    This most incredible lie would call up one
    On thy buttermilk cheeks.
MARRALL: Shall I not trust my eyes, sir?
    Or taste? I feel her good cheer in my belly.
OVERREACH: You shall feel me, if you give not over, sirrah;
    Recover your brains again, and be no more gulled
    With a beggar's plot assisted by the aides
    Of serving men and chambermaids, for beyond these   100
    Thou never saw'st a woman, or I'll quit you
    From my employments.
MARRALL: Will you credit this yet?
    On my confidence of their marriage I offered Welborne
    (I would give a crown now, I durst say his worship)   *Aside.*
    My nag, and twenty pounds.
OVERREACH: Did you so, idiot?   *Strikes him down.*
    Was this the way to work him to despair,
    Or rather to cross* me?
MARRALL: Will your worship kill me?
OVERREACH: No, no; but drive the lying spirit out of you.
MARRALL: He's gone.
OVERREACH: I have done, then. Now, forgetting
    Your late imaginary feast, and lady,   110
    Know my Lord Lovell dines with me tomorrow.
    Be careful nought be wanting to receive him,
    And bid my daughter's women trim her up.
    Though they paint her so she catch the lord, I'll thank 'em;

There's a piece for my late blows.

MARRALL:　　　　　　　　　　I must yet suffer;　　　　　115
　But there may be a time –　　　　　　　　　　*Aside.*

OVERREACH:　　　　　　Do you grumble?

MARRALL:　　　　　　　　　　No, sir.　　　　　[*Exeunt.*]

Act Three, Scene One

[*Enter*] LOVELL, ALWORTH, SERVANTS.

LOVELL: Walk the horses down the hill: something in private
　I must impart to Alworth.　　　　　*Exeunt* SERVANTS.

ALWORTH:　　　　　　　　O my lord,
　What sacrifice of reverence, duty, watching;
　Although I could put off the use of sleep,
　And ever wait on your commands to serve 'em;　　　5
　What dangers, though in ne'er so horrid shapes,
　Nay, death itself, though I should run to meet it,
　Can I, and with a thankful willingness suffer;
　But still the retribution will fall short
　Of your bounties showered upon me.

LOVELL:　　　　　　　　　　Loving youth,　　　10
　Till what I purpose be put into act,
　Do not o'erprize it. Since you have trusted me
　With your soul's nearest, nay, her dearest secret,
　Rest confident 'tis in a cabinet locked,
　Treachery shall never open. I have found you　　15
　(For so much to your face I must profess,
　Howe'er you guard* your modesty with a blush for 't)
　More zealous in your love and service to me
　Than I have been in my rewards.

ALWORTH:　　　　　　　　Still great ones
　Above my merit.

LOVELL:　　　　　　Such your gratitude calls 'em:　　20
　Nor am I of that harsh and rugged temper
　As some great men are taxed with, who imagine
　They part from the respect due to their honours
　If they use not all such as follow 'em
　Without distinction of their births, like slaves.　　25
　I am not so conditioned:* I can make
　A fitting difference between my foot-boy
　And a gentleman by want compelled to serve me.

ALWORTH:'Tis thankfully acknowledged: you have been

More like a father to me than a master.   30
Pray you pardon the comparison.
LOVELL: I allow it;
    And to give you assurance I am pleased in it,
    My carriage and demeanour to* your mistress,
    Fair Margaret, shall truly witness for me
    I can command my passions.
ALWORTH: 'Tis a conquest   35
    Few lords can boast of when they are tempted. O!
LOVELL: Why do you sigh? Can you be doubtful of me?
    By that fair name I in the wars have purchased,
    And all my actions hitherto untainted,
    I will not be more true to mine own honour   40
    Than to my Alworth.
ALWORTH: As you are the brave Lord Lovell,
    Your bare word only given is an assurance
    Of more validity and weight to me
    Than all the others bound up with imprecations,
    Which when they would deceive, most courtiers practice;   45
    Yet being a man (for sure to style you more
    Would relish of gross flattery), I am forced,
    Against my confidence of your worth and virtues,
    To doubt, nay more, to fear.
LOVELL: So young, and jealous?
ALWORTH: Were you to encounter with a single foe,   50
    The victory were certain; but to stand
    The charge of two such potent enemies
    At once assaulting you, as wealth and beauty,
    And those too seconded with power, is odds
    Too great for Hercules.
LOVELL: Speak your doubts and fears,   55
    Since you will nourish 'em, in plainer language,
    That I may understand 'em.
ALWORTH: What's your will,
    Though I lend arms against myself (provided
    They may advantage you), must be obeyed.
    My much loved lord, were Margaret only fair,   60
    The cannon of her more than earthly form,
    Though mounted high, commanding all beneath it,
    And rammed with bullets of her sparkling eyes,
    Of all the bulwarks that defend your senses
    Could batter none, but that which guards your sight.   65
    But when the well tuned accents of her tongue

Make music to you, and with numerous* sounds
Assault your hearing (such as if Ulysses
Now lived again, howe'er he stood the Sirens
Could not resist), the combat must grow doubtful   70
Between your reason and rebellious passions.
Add this too: when you feel her touch and breath,
Like a soft western wind when it glides o'er
Arabia, creating gums and spices,
And in the van,* the nectar of her lips,   75
Which you must taste, bring the battalia* on,
Well armed, and strongly lined* with her discourse,
And knowing manners, to give entertainment;
Hippolytus* himself would leave Diana
To follow such a Venus.

LOVELL: Love hath made you   80
Poetical, Alworth.

ALWORTH: Grant all these beat off,
Which if it be in man to do, you'll do it;
Mammon in Sir Giles Overreach steps in
With heaps of ill-got gold, and so much land
To make her more remarkable, as would tire   85
A falcon's wings in one day to fly over.
O my good lord, these powerful aids, which would
Make a misshapen Negro beautiful
(Yet are but ornaments to give her lustre,
That in herself is perfection), must   90
Prevail for her. I here release your trust.
'Tis happiness enough for me to serve you,
And sometimes with chaste eyes to look upon her.

LOVELL: Why, shall I swear?

ALWORTH: O, by no means, my lord;
And wrong not so your judgement to the world   95
As from your fond indulgence to a boy,
Your page, your servant, to refuse a blessing
Divers great men are rivals for.

LOVELL: Suspend
Your judgement till the trial. How far is it
T' Overreach's house?

ALWORTH: At the most some half hour's riding; 100
You'll soon be there.

LOVELL: And you the sooner freed
From your jealous fears.

ALWORTH: O that I durst but hope it.   *Exeunt.*

Act Three, Scene Two

[*Enter*] OVERREACH, GREEDY, MARRALL.

OVERREACH: Spare for no cost, let my dressers crack with the weight
    Of curious viands.
GREEDY: Store indeed's no sore,* sir.
OVERREACH: That proverb fits your stomach, Master Greedy.
    And let not plate be seen but what's pure gold,
    Or such whose workmanship exceeds the matter   5
    That it is made of; let my choicest linen
    Perfume the room, and when we wash, the water
    With precious powders mixed, so please my lord,
    That he may with envy wish to bathe so ever.
MARRALL: 'Twill be very chargeable.*
OVERREACH: Avaunt, you drudge: 10
    Now all my laboured ends are at the stake,
    Is't a time to think of thrift? Call in my daughter,   [*Exit* MARRALL.]
    And, Master Justice, since you love choice dishes,
    And plenty of 'em –
GREEDY: As I do indeed, sir,
    Almost as much as to give thanks for 'em.   15
OVERREACH: I do confer that providence,* with my power
    Of absolute command, to have abundance
    To your best care.
GREEDY: I'll punctually discharge it
    And give the best directions. Now am I
    In mine own conceit* a monarch, at the least   20
    Arch-president of the boiled, the roast, the baked,
    For which I will eat often, and give thanks,
    When my belly is braced up like a drum, and that's pure justice.   *Exit.*
OVERREACH: It must be so: should the foolish girl prove modest,
    She may spoil all. She had it not from me,   25
    But from her mother; I was ever forward,
    As she must be, and therefore I'll prepare her.

[*Enter*] MARGARET.

Alone, and let your women wait without.
MARGARET: Your pleasure, sir?
OVERREACH: Ha, this is a neat dressing!
    These orient pearls, and diamonds well placed too!   30
    The gown affects* me not, it should have been

Embroidered o'er and o'er with flowers of gold,
But these rich jewels and quaint* fashion help it.
And how below? Since oft the wanton eye, 35
The face observed, descends unto the foot;
Which being well proportioned, as yours is,
Invites as much as perfect white and red,
Though without art. How like you your new woman,
The Lady Downfal'n?

MARGARET:　　　　　　 Well, for a companion;
　　Not as a servant.

OVERREACH:　　　　　　 Is she humble, Meg? 40
　　And careful, too; her ladyship forgotten?

MARGARET: I pity her fortune.

OVERREACH:　　　　　　 Pity her? Trample on her.
　　I took her up in an old tamin* gown
　　(Even starved of for want of twopenny chops), to serve thee:
　　And if I understand she but repines 45
　　To do thee any duty, though ne'er so servile,
　　I'll pack her to her knight, where I have lodged him
　　Into the Counter,* and there let 'em howl together.

MARGARET: You know your own ways, but for me I blush
　　When I command her, that was once attended 50
　　With persons not inferior to myself
　　In birth.

OVERREACH: In birth? Why, art thou not my daughter?
　　The blest child of my industry and wealth?
　　Why, foolish girl, was 't not to make thee great
　　That I have ran, and still pursue those ways 55
　　That hale down curses on me, which I mind not.
　　Part with these humble thoughts, and apt thyself
　　To the noble state I labour to advance thee,
　　Or by my hopes to see thee set honourable,
　　I will adopt a stranger to* my heir, 60
　　And throw thee from my care; do not provoke me.

MARGARET: I will not, sir; mould me which way you please.

Enter GREEDY.

OVERREACH: How, interrupted?

GREEDY:　　　　　　 'Tis a matter of importance.
　　The cook is self-willed, and will not learn
　　From my experience; there's a fawn brought in, sir, 65
　　And for my life I cannot make him roast it

With a Norfolk dumpling in the belly of it.
And sir, we wisemen know without the dumpling
'Tis not worth threepence.
OVERREACH: Would it were whole in thy belly
To stuff it out; cook it any way, prithee leave me.   70
GREEDY: Without order for the dumpling?
OVERREACH: Let it be dumpled
Which way thou wilt, or tell him I will scald him
In his own cauldron.
GREEDY: I had lost my stomach,
Had I lost my mistress dumpling, I'll give thanks for 't.   *Exit.*
OVERREACH: But to our business, Meg. You have heard who dines here?   75
MARGARET: I have, sir.
OVERREACH: 'Tis an honourable man,
A lord, Meg, and commands a regiment
Of soldiers, and what's rare, is one himself;
A bold and understanding one; and to be
A lord and a good leader in one volume*   80
Is granted unto few, but such as rise up
The kingdom's glory.

Enter GREEDY.

GREEDY: I'll resign my office
If I be not better obeyed.
OVERREACH: 'Slight, art thou frantic?
GREEDY: Frantic, 'twould make me a frantic, and stark-mad,
Were I not a justice of peace, and coram* too,   85
Which this rebellious cook cares not a straw for.
There are a dozen of woodcocks.*
OVERREACH: Make thyself
Thirteen, the baker's dozen.
GREEDY: I am contented
So they may be dressed to my mind; he has found out
A new device for sauce, and will not dish 'em   90
With toasts and butter. My father was a tailor,
And my name, though a justice, Greedy Woodcock,
And ere I'll see my lineage so abused,
I'll give up my commission.
OVERREACH: Cook, rogue, obey him.
I have given the word, pray you now remove yourself   95
To a collar of brawn, and trouble me no farther.
GREEDY: I will, and meditate what to eat at dinner.   *Exit.*
OVEREACH: And as I said, Meg, when this gull disturbed us;

This honourable lord, this colonel
I would have thy husband.
MARGARET: There's too much disparity   100
  Between his quality* and mine to hope it.
OVERREACH: I more than hope 't, and doubt not to effect it.
  Be thou no enemy to thyself; my wealth
  Shall weigh his titles down, and make you equals.
  Now for the means to assure him thine, observe me;   105
  Remember he's a courtier and a soldier,
  And not to be trifled with, and therefore when
  He comes to woo you, see you do not coy it.
  This mincing modesty hath spoiled many a match
  By a first refusal, in vain after hoped for.   110
MARGARET: You'll have me, sir, preserve the distance that
  Confines a virgin?
OVERREACH: Virgin me no virgins.
  I must have you lose that name, or you shall lose me.
  I will have you private;* start not, I say private;
  If thou art my true daughter, not a bastard,   115
  Thou wilt venture alone with one man, though he came
  Like Jupiter to Semele,* and come off too.
  And therefore when he kisses you, kiss close.
MARGARET: I have heard this is the strumpet's fashion, sir,
  Which I must never learn.
OVERREACH: Learn anything,   120
  And from any creature that may make thee great;
  From the devil himself.
MARGARET: This is but devilish doctrine.
OVERREACH: Or if his blood grow hot, suppose he offer
  Beyond this, do not you stay till it cool
  But meet his ardour: if a couch be near,   125
  Sit down on 't, and invite him.
MARGARET: In your house?
  Your own house, sir, for heaven's sake, what are you then?
  Or what shall I be, sir?
OVERREACH: Stand not on form;
  Words are no substances.
MARGARET: Though you could dispense
  With your own honour, cast aside religion,   130
  The hope of heaven or fear of hell, excuse me;
  In worldly policy,* this is not the way
  To make me his wife; his whore I grant it may do.
  My maiden honour so soon yielded up,
  Nay, prostituted, cannot but assure him   135

I that am light to him will not hold weight
When his, tempted, by others; so in judgment
When to his lust I have given up my honour
He must and will forsake me.
OVERREACH: How? Forsake thee?
Do I wear a sword for fashion? Or is this arm   140
Shrunk up? Or withered? Does there live a man
Of that large list I have encountered with
Can truly say I e'er gave inch of ground,
Not purchased with his blood, that did oppose me?
Forsake thee when the thing is done? He dares not.   145
Give me but proof he has enjoyed thy person,
Though all his captains, echoes to his will,
Stood armed by his side to justify the wrong,
And he himself in the head of his bold troupe,
Spite of his lordship, and his colonelship,   150
Or the judge's favour, I will make him render
A bloody and a strict accompt, and force him
By marrying thee, to cure thy wounded honour;
I have said it.

Enter MARRALL.

MARRALL: Sir, the man of honour's come,
Newly alighted.
OVERREACH: In; without reply,   155
And do as I command, or thou art lost.   *Exit* MARGARET.
Is the loud music I gave order for
Ready to receive him?
MARRALL: 'Tis, sir.
OVERREACH: Let 'em sound
A princely welcome.   [*Exit* MARRALL.]
                           Roughness a while leave me,
For fawning now, a stranger to my nature   160
Must make way for me.

Loud music. Enter LOVELL, GREEDY, ALWORTH, MARRALL.

LOVELL: Sir, you meet your trouble.
OVERREACH: What you are pleased to style so is an honour
Above my worth and fortunes.
ALWORTH: Strange, so humble.
OVERREACH: A justice of peace, my lord.   *Presents* GREEDY *to him.*
LOVELL: Your hand, good sir.

GREEDY: This is a lord, and some think this a favour;   165
    But I had rather have my hand in my dumpling.
OVERREACH: Room for my lord.
LOVELL: I miss, sir, your fair daughter
    To crown my welcome.
OVERREACH: May it please my lord
    To taste a glass of Greek wine first, and suddenly*
    She shall attend, my lord.
LOVELL: You'll be obeyed, sir.   170
                       Exeunt omnes. Praeter OVERREACH.
OVERREACH: 'Tis to my wish; as soon as come ask for her!
    Why, Meg! Meg Overreach.

                [*Enter* MARGARET.]

                  How! Tears in your eyes!
    Ha! Dry 'em quickly, or I'll dig 'em out.
    Is this a time to whimper? Meet that greatness
    That flies to thy bosom, think what 'tis   175
    For me to say, my honourable daughter,
    And thou, when I stand bare,* to say put on,
    Or father, you forget yourself, no more,
    But be instructed, or expect – he comes.

        Enter LOVELL, GREEDY, ALWORTH, MARRALL.

    A black-browed girl, my lord.
LOVELL: As I live, a rare one.   *They salute.*   180
ALWORTH: He's took already: I am lost.
OVERREACH: That kiss
    Came twanging off, I like it; quit the room.   *The rest off.*
    A little bashful, my good lord, but you
    I hope will teach her boldness.
LOVELL: I am happy
    In such a scholar; but –
OVERREACH: I am past learning,   185
    And therefore leave you to yourselves; remember –   *To his daughter.*
                            Exit OVERREACH.

LOVELL: You see, fair lady, your father is solicitous
    To have you change the barren name of virgin
    Into a hopeful wife.
MARGARET: His haste, my lord,
    Holds no power o'er my will.
LOVELL: But o'er your duty.   190

MARGARET: Which forced too much may break.
LOVELL: Bend rather, sweetest:
    Think of your years.
MARGARET: Too few to match with yours:
    And choicest fruits too soon plucked rot and wither.
LOVELL: Do you think I am old?
MARGARET: I am sure I am too young.
LOVELL: I can advance you.
MARGARET: To a hill of sorrow,   195
    Where every hour I may expect to fall,
    But never hope firm footing. You are noble,
    I of a low descent, however rich;
    And tissues matched with scarlet suit but ill.
    O my good lord, I could say more, but that   200
    I dare not trust these walls.
LOVELL: Pray you trust my ear then.

Enter OVERREACH *listening.*

OVERREACH: Close at it! Whispering! This is excellent!
    And, by their postures, a consent on both parts.

Enter GREEDY.

GREEDY: Sir Giles, Sir Giles.
OVERREACH: The great fiend stop that clapper.
GREEDY: It must ring out, sir, when my belly rings none.   205
    The baked meats are run out, the roast turned powder.*
OVERREACH: I shall powder you.
GREEDY: Beat me to dust, I care not.
    In such a cause as this I'll die a martyr.
OVERREACH: Marry, and shall: you Barathrum of the shambles.*   *Strikes him.*
GREEDY: How! Strike a justice of the peace? 'Tis petty treason,   210
    Edwardi quinto, but that you are my friend
    I could commit you without bail or main-prise.*
OVERREACH: Leave your bawling, sir, or I shall commit you
    Where you shall not dine today; disturb my lord
    When he is in discourse?
GREEDY: Is 't a time to talk   215
    When we should be munching?
LOVELL: Ha! I heard some noise.
OVERREACH: Mum, villain, vanish: shall we break a bargain
    Almost made up?   *Thrust* GREEDY *off.*
LOVELL: Lady, I understand you,

And rest most happy in your choice; believe it,
    I'll be a careful pilot to direct   220
    Your yet uncertain bark to a port of safety.
MARGARET: So shall your honour save two lives, and bind us
    Your slaves for ever.
LOVELL: I am in the act rewarded,
    Since it is good; howe'er, you must put on
    An amorous carriage towards me, to delude   225
    Your subtle father.
MARGARET: I am prone to that.
LOVELL: Now break we off our conference. Sir Giles.
    Where is Sir Giles?

Enter OVERREACH *and the rest.*

OVERREACH: My noble lord; and how
    Does your lordship find her?
LOVELL: Apt, Sir Giles, and coming,*
    And I like her the better.
OVERREACH: So do I too.   230
LOVELL: Yet should we take forts at the first assault,
    'Twere poor in the defendant, I must confirm her
    With a love letter or two, which I must have
    Delivered by my page, and* you give way to 't.
OVERREACH: With all my soul, a towardly* gentleman;   235
    Your hand, good master Alworth, know my house
    Is ever open to you.
ALWORTH: 'Twas shut till now.   *Aside.*
OVERREACH: Well done, well done, my honourable daughter:
    Th' art so already; know this gentle youth,
    And cherish him, my honourable daughter.   240
MARGARET: I shall with my best care.   *Noise within as of a coach.*
OVERREACH: A coach.
GREEDY: More stops
    Before we go to dinner! O my guts!

Enter LADY, *and* WELBORNE.

LADY: If I find welcome
    You share in it; if not I'll back again.
    Now I know your ends, for I come armed for all   245
    Can be objected.
LOVELL: How! The Lady Alworth!
OVERREACH: And thus attended!

MARRALL: No, I am a dolt;

LOVELL *salutes the* LADY, *the* LADY *salutes* MARGARET.

   The spirit of lies had entered me.

OVERREACH: Peace, patch,*
   'Tis more than wonder! An astonishment
   That does possess me wholly!

LOVELL: Noble lady, 250
   This is a favour, to prevent my visit,
   The service of my life can never equal.

LADY: My lord, I laid wait for you, and much hoped
   You would have made my poor house your first inn;
   And therefore doubting that you might forget me, 255
   Or too long dwell here, having such ample cause
   In this unequalled beauty for your stay;
   And fearing to trust any but myself
   With the relation of my service to you,
   I borrowed so much from my long restraint, 260
   And took the air in person in invite you.

LOVELL: Your bounties are so great they rob me, madam,
   Of words to give you thanks.

LADY: Good Sir Giles Overreach. *Salutes him.*
   How dost thou, Marrall? Liked you my meat so ill
   You'll dine no more with me? 265

MARRALL: I will when you please,
   And it like your ladyship.

LADY: When you please, Master Greedy;
   If meat can do it, you shall be satisfied.
   And now, my lord, pray take into your knowledge
   This gentleman; howe'er his outside's coarse, *Presents* WELBORNE.
   His inward linings are as fine, and fair, 270
   As any man's: wonder not how I speak at large,*
   And howsoe'er his humour* carries him
   To be thus accoutred, or what taint soever
   For his wild life hath stuck upon his fame.
   He may ere long, with boldness, rank himself 275
   With some that have contemned him. Sir Giles Overreach,
   If I am welcome, bid him so.

OVERREACH: My nephew.
   He has been too long a stranger; faith, you have:
   Pray let it be mended. LOVELL *conferring with* WELBORNE.

MARRALL: Why sir, what do you mean?
   This is rogue Welborne, monster, prodigy. 280
   That should hang or drown himself, no man of worship,
   Much less your nephew.

OVERREACH: Well, sirrah, we shall reckon
   For this hereafter.
MARRALL: I'll not lose my jeer
   Though I'll be beaten dead for 't.
WELBORNE: Let my silence plead
   In my excuse, my lord, till better leisure   285
   Offer itself to hear a full relation
   Of my poor fortunes.
LOVELL: I would hear, and help 'em.
OVERREACH: Your dinner waits you.
LOVELL: Pray you lead, we follow.
LADY: Nay, you are my guest, come here, dear Master Welborne.
                                 Exeunt. Manet GREEDY.
GREEDY: Dear Master Welborne! So she said; heaven! Heaven!   290
   If my belly would give me leave I could ruminate
   All day on this: I have granted twenty warrants
   To have him committed, from all prisons in the shire,
   To Nottingham jail; and now dear Master Welborne!
   And my good nephew! But I play the fool   295
   To stand here prating, and forget my dinner.

Enter MARRALL.

   Are they set,* Marrall?
MARRALL: Long since. Pray you a word, sir.
GREEDY: No wording now.
MARRALL: In troth, I must; my master,
   Knowing you are his good friend, makes bold with you,
   And does entreat you, more guests being come in   300
   Than he expected, especially his nephew,
   The table being full too, you would excuse him
   And sup with him on the cold meat.
GREEDY: How! No dinner
   After all my care?
MARRALL: 'Tis but a penance for
   A meal; besides, you broke your fast.
GREEDY: That was   305
   But a bit to stay my stomach: a man in commission
   Give place to a tatterdemalion?*
MARRALL: No bug* words, sir,
   Should his worship hear you –
GREEDY: Lose my dumpling too?
   And buttered toasts, and woodcocks?

MARRALL: Come, have patience.
   If you will dispense a little with your worship,*   310
   And sit with the waiting-women, you'll have dumpling,
   Woodcock, and buttered toasts too.
GREEDY: This revives me,
   I will gorge there sufficiently.
MARRALL: This is the way, sir.   *Exeunt.*

Act Three, Scene Three

[Enter] OVERREACH *as from dinner.*

OVERREACH: She's caught! O women! She neglects my lord,
   And all her compliments applied to Welborne!
   The garments of her widowhood laid by,
   She now appears as glorious as the spring.
   Her eyes fixed on him; in the wine she drinks,   5
   He being her pledge, she sends him burning kisses,
   And sits on thorns, till she be private with him.
   She leaves my meat to feed upon his looks;
   And if in our discourse he be but named
   From her a deep sigh follows; but why grieve I   10
   At this? It makes for me, if she prove his,
   All that is hers is mine, as I will work him.

Enter MARRALL.

MARRALL: Sir, the whole board is troubled at your rising.
OVERREACH: No matter, I'll excuse it. Prithee Marrall,
   Watch an occasion to invite my nephew   15
   To speak with me in private.
MARRALL: Who? The rogue
   The lady scorned to look on?
OVERREACH: You are a wag.

Enter LADY *and* WELBORNE.

MARRALL: See sir, she's come, and cannot be without him.
LADY: With your favour, sir, after a plenteous dinner,
   I shall make bold to walk a turn or two   20
   In your rare garden.
WELBORNE: There's an arbour too,
   If your ladyship please to use it.

LADY: Come, Master Welborne.
                              Exeunt LADY *and* WELBORNE.
OVERREACH: Grosser and grosser; now I believe the poet
    Feigned not but was historical when he wrote
    Pasiphae was enamoured of a bull:*   25
    This lady's lust's more monstrous.

                    Enter LOVELL, MARGARET *and the rest.*

                              My good lord,
    Excuse my manners.*
LOVELL: There needs none, Sir Giles,
    I may ere long say father, when it pleases
    My dearest mistress to give warrant to it.
OVERREACH: She shall seal to it, my lord, and make me happy.   30
MARGARET: My lady is returned.

                    Enter WELBORNE *and the* LADY.

LADY: Provide my coach,
    I'll instantly away: my thanks, Sir Giles,
    For my entertainment.
OVERREACH: 'Tis your nobleness
    To think it such.
LADY: I must do you a further wrong
    In taking away your honourable guest.   35
LOVELL: I wait on you, madam; farewell, good Sir Giles.
LADY: Good Mistress Margaret; nay come, Master Welborne,
    I must not leave you behind, in sooth I must not.
OVERREACH: Rob me not, madam, of all joys at once;
    Let my nephew stay behind: he shall have my coach   40
    And (after some small conference between us)
    Soon overtake your ladyship.
LADY: Stay not long, sir.
LOVELL: This parting kiss: you shall every day hear from me
    By my faithful page.
ALWORTH: 'Tis a service I am proud of.

                    Exeunt LOVELL, LADY, ALWORTH, MARRALL.

OVERREACH: Daughter to your chamber.   [*Exit* MARGARET.]
                              You may wonder, nephew,   45
    After so long an enmity between us
    I should desire your friendship?
WELBORNE: So I do, sir.

'Tis strange to me.

OVERREACH: But I'll make it wonder,
And what is more unfold my nature to you.
We worldly men, when we see friends and kinsmen
Past hope sunk in their fortunes, lend no hand   50
To lift 'em up, but rather set our feet
Upon their heads, to press 'em to the bottom;
As I must yield,* with you I practiced it.
But now I see you in a way to rise,   55
I can and will assist you. This rich lady
(And I am glad of 't) is enamoured of you;
'Tis too apparent, nephew.

WELBORNE: No such thing:
Compassion rather, sir.

OVERREACH: Well, in a word,
Because your stay is short, I'll have you seen   60
No more in this base shape;* nor shall she say
She married you like a beggar, or in debt.

WELBORNE: He'll run into the noose, and save my labour.   *Aside.*

OVERREACH: You have a trunk of rich clothes not far hence
In pawn, I will redeem 'em, and that no clamour   65
May taint your credit for your petty debts,
You shall have a thousand pounds to cut 'em off,
And go a freeman to the wealthy lady.

WELBORNE: This done, sir, out of love, and no ends else –

OVERREACH: As it is, nephew.

WELBORNE: Binds me still your servant.   70

OVERREACH: No compliments; you are stayed for; ere you have supped
You shall hear from me. My coach, knave, for my nephew:
Tomorrow I will visit you.

WELBORNE: Here's an uncle
In a man's extremes!* How much they do belie you
That say you are hard-hearted.

OVERREACH: My deeds, nephew,
Shall speak my love, what men report I weigh not.   *Exeunt.*
                  Finis Actus tertii.

Act Four, Scene One

[*Enter*] LOVELL, ALWORTH.

LOVELL: 'Tis well: give me my cloak. I now discharge you

From further service. Mind your own affairs,
I hope they will prove successful.
ALWORTH: What is blest
With your good wish, my lord, cannot but prosper.
Let after-times report, and to your honour,   5
How much I stand engaged, for I want language
To speak my debt; yet if a tear or two
Of joy for your much goodness can supply
My tongue's defects, I could –
LOVELL: Nay, do not melt:
This ceremonial thanks to me's superfluous.   10
OVERREACH: Is my lord stirring?   *Within.*
LOVELL: 'Tis he; O, here's your letter: let him in.

Enter OVERREACH, GREEDY, MARRALL.

OVERREACH: A good day to my lord.
LOVELL: You are an early riser,
    Sir Giles.
OVERREACH: And reason, to attend your lordship.
LOVELL: And you, Master Greedy, up so soon?   15
GREEDY: In troth, my lord, after the sun is up
    I cannot sleep, for I have a foolish stomach
    That croaks for breakfast. With your lordship's favour,
    I have a serious question to demand
    Of my worthy friend Sir Giles.
LOVELL: Pray you use your pleasure.   20
GREEDY: How far, Sir Giles, and pray you answer me
    Upon your credit, hold you it to be
    From your manor house to this of my Lady Alworth?
OVERREACH: Why, some four mile.
GREEDY: How! Four mile? Good Sir Giles,
    Upon your reputation think better,   25
    For if you do abate but one half quarter
    Of five you do yourself the greatest wrong
    That can be in the world: for four miles riding
    Could not have raised so huge an appetite
    As I feel gnawing in me.
MARRALL: Whether you ride   30
    Or go afoot, you are that way still provided
    And it please your worship.
OVERREACH: How now, sirrah? Prating
    Before my lord: no difference?* Go to my nephew;
    See all his debts discharged, and help his worship

To fit on his rich suit.

MARRALL: I may fit you* too;   35
Tossed like a dog still.   *Exit.*

LOVELL: I have writ this morning
A few lines to my mistress your fair daughter.

OVERREACH: 'Twill fire her, for she's wholly yours already:
Sweet Master Alworth, take my ring, 'twill carry you
To her presence, I dare warrant you, and there plead   40
For my good lord, if you shall find occasion.
That done, pray ride to Nottingham, get a licence,
Still by this token, I'll have it dispatched,
And suddenly, my lord, that I may say
My honourable, nay, right honourable daughter.   45

GREEDY: Take my advice, young gentleman: get your breakfast.
'Tis unwholesome to ride fasting, I'll eat with you
And eat to purpose.

OVERREACH: Some fury's in that gut:
Hungry again! Did you not devour this morning
A shield of brawn,* and a barrel of Colchester* oysters?   50

GREEDY: Why, that was, sir, only to scour my stomach,*
A kind of preparative. Come, gentleman,
I will not have you feed the hangman of Flushing*
Alone, while I am here.

LOVELL: Haste your return.

ALWORTH: I will not fail, my lord.

GREEDY: Nor I to line   55
My Christmas coffer.*   *Exeunt* GREEDY *and* ALWORTH.

OVERREACH: To my wish, we are private.
I come not to make offer with my daughter
A certain portion, that were poor and trivial:
In one word I pronounce all that is mine,
In lands, leases, ready coin, or goods,   60
With her, my lord, comes to you; nor shall you have
One motive to induce you to believe
I live too long, since every year I'll add
Something to the heap, which shall be yours too.

LOVELL: You are a right kind father.

OVERREACH: You shall have reason   65
To think me such; how do you like this seat?
It is well wooded, and well watered, the acres
Fertile and rich; would it not serve for change
To entertain your friends in a summer progress?*
What thinks my noble lord?

LOVELL: 'Tis a wholesome air,   70

And well built pile, and she that's mistress of it
Worthy the large revenue.
OVERREACH: She the mistress?
  It may be so for a time, but let my lord
  Say only that he likes it, and would have it,
  I say ere long 'tis his.
LOVELL: Impossible.   75
OVERREACH: You do conclude too fast, not knowing me,
  Nor the engines* that I work by; 'tis not alone
  The Lady Alworth's lands, for those once Welborne's
  (As by her dotage on him, I know they will be)
  Shall soon be mine; but point out any manse   80
  In all the shire, and say they lie convenient
  And useful to your lordship, and once more
  I say aloud, they are yours.
LOVELL: I dare not own
  What's by unjust and cruel means extorted:
  My fame and credit are more dear to me   85
  Than so to expose 'em to be censured by
  The public voice.
OVERREACH: You run, my lord, no hazard.
  Your reputation shall stand as fair
  In all good men's opinions as now:
  Nor can my actions, though condemned for ill,   90
  Cast any foul aspersion upon yours;
  For though I do contemn report myself
  As a mere sound, I still will be so tender
  Of what concerns you in all points of honour,
  That the immaculate whiteness of your fame   95
  Nor your unquestioned integrity
  Shall e'er be sullied with one taint or spot
  That may take from your innocence and candour.
  All my ambition is to have my daughter
  Right honourable, which my lord can make her.   100
  And might I live to dance upon my knee
  A young Lord Lovell, borne by her unto you,
  I write *nil ultra** to my proudest hopes.
  As for possessions, and annual rents
  Equivalent to maintain you in the port*   105
  Your noble birth and present state requires,
  I do remove that burden from your shoulders
  And take it on mine own; for though I ruin
  The country to supply your riotous waste,
  The scourge of prodigals, want, shall never find you.   110

LOVELL: Are you not frighted with the imprecations
      And curses of whole families made wretched
      By your sinister* practices?
OVERREACH: Yes, as rocks are
      When foamy billows split themselves against
      Their flinty ribs; or as the moon is moved   115
      When wolves with hunger pined howl at her brightness.
      I am of a solid temper, and like these
      Steer on a constant course: with mine own sword
      If called into the field, I can make that right,
      Which fearful enemies murmured at as wrong.   120
      Now, for these other piddling complaints
      Breathed out in bitterness, as when they call me
      Extortioner, tyrant, cormorant, or intruder
      On my poor neighbour's right, or grand encloser
      Of what was common to my private use;
      Nay, when my ears are pierced with widows' cries,
      And undone orphans wash with tears my threshold,
      I only think what 'tis to have my daughter
      Right honourable; and 'tis a powerful charm
      Makes me insensible of remorse or pity,   130
      Or the least sting of conscience.
LOVELL: I admire*
      The toughness of your nature.
OVERREACH: 'Tis for you,
      My lord, and for my daughter, I am marble;
      Nay more, more, if you will have my character
      In little, I enjoy more true delight   135
      In my arrival to my wealth, these dark
      And crooked ways, than you shall e'er take pleasure
      In spending what my industry hath compassed.
      My haste commands me hence. In one word, therefore,
      Is it a match?
LOVELL: I hope that is past doubt now.   140
OVERREACH: The rest secure, not the hate of all mankind here,
      Nor fear of what can fall on me hereafter,
      Shall make me study aught but your advancement
      One storey higher. An earl! If gold can do it.
      Dispute not my religion, nor my faith,   145
      Though I am borne thus headlong by my will;
      You may make choice of what belief you please,
      To me they are all equal; so my good lord, good morrow.   *Exit.*
LOVELL: He's gone. I wonder how the earth can bear
      Such a portent!* I, that have lived a soldier,   150
      And stood the enemy's violent charge undaunted,

To hear this blasphemous beast, am bathed all over
In a cold sweat; yet like a mountain he,
Confirmed in atheistical assertions,
Is no more shaken than Olympus* is   155
When angry Boreas* loads his double head
With sudden drifts of snow.

             Enter AMBLE, LADY, [WAITING-] WOMAN.

LADY: Save you, my lord.
  Disturb I now your privacy?
LOVELL: No, good madam;
  For your own sake I am glad you cam no sooner.
  Since this bold, bad man, Sir Giles Overreach,
  Made such a plain discovery of himself,   160
  And read this morning such a devilish matins
  That I should think it a sin next to his
  But to repeat it.
LADY: I ne'er pressed, my lord,
  On others' privacies, yet against my will,   165
  Walking, for health sake, into the gallery
  Adjoining your lodgings, I was made
  (So vehement and loud he was) partaker
  Of his tempting offers.
LOVELL: Please you to command
  Your servants hence, and I shall gladly hear   170
  Your wiser counsel.
LADY: 'Tis, my lord, a woman's,
  But true, and hearty; wait in the next room,
  But be within call, yet not so near to force me
  To whisper my intents.
AMBLE: We are taught better
  By you, good madam.
WOMAN: And know well our distance.   175
LADY: Do so, and talk not; 'twill become your breeding.
                  Exeunt AMBLE *and* [WAITING-] WOMAN
  Now, my good lord, if I may use my freedom
  As to an honoured friend?
LOVELL: You lessen else
  Your favour to me.
LADY: I dare then say thus:
  As you are noble (howe'er common men   180
  Make sordid wealth the object and sole end
  Of their industrious aims), 'twill not agree

With those of eminent blood (who are engaged
More to prefer* their honours than to increase
The state* left to 'em by their ancestors)   185
To study large additions to their fortunes
And quite neglect their births; though I must grant
Riches well got to be a useful servant,
But a bad master.

LOVELL: Madam, 'tis confessed;
But what infer you from it?

LADY: This, my lord: 190
That as all wrongs, though thrust into one scale
Slide themselves off, when right fills the other,
And cannot abide the trial; so all wealth
(I mean if ill acquired) cemented to honour
By virtuous ways achieved and bravely purchased,   195
Is but as rubbish poured into a river
(Howe'er intended to make good the bank)
Rendering the water that was pure before
Polluted and unwholesome. I allow*
The heir of Sir Giles Overreach, Margaret,   200
A maid well qualified, and the richest match
Our north part can make boast of, yet she cannot
With all that she brings with her fill their mouths,*
That never will forget who was her father;
Or that my husband Alworth's land, and Welborne's   205
(How wrung from both needs now no repetition)
Were real motive, that more worked your lordship
To join your families than her form and virtues.
You may conceive* the rest.

LOVELL: I do, sweet madam;
And long since have considered it. I know   210
The sum of all that makes a just man happy
Consists in the well choosing of his wife;
And there, well to discharge it, does require
Equality of years, of birth, of fortune,
For beauty being poor, and not cried up*   215
By birth or wealth, can truly mix with neither.
And wealth, where there's such difference in years
And fair descent, must make the yoke uneasy:
But I come nearer.*

LADY: Pray you do, my lord.

LOVELL: Were Overreach's states thrice centupled, his daughter   220
Millions of degrees much fairer than she is
(Howe'er I might urge precedents to excuse me),
I would not so adulterate my blood

By marrying Margaret, and so leave my issue
Made up of several pieces, one part scarlet 225
And the other London blue.* In my own tomb
I will inter my name first.
LADY: I am glad to hear this: *Aside.*
  Why then my lord pretend you marriage to her?
  Dissimulation but ties false knots
  On that straight line by which you hitherto 230
  Have measured all your actions.
LOVELL: I make answer
  And aptly, with a question. Wherefore have you,
  That since your husband's death have lived a strict
  And chaste nun's life, on the sudden given yourself
  To visits and entertainments? Think you, madam, 235
  'Tis not grown public conference?* Or the favours
  Which you too prodigally have thrown on Welborne,
  Being too reserved before, incur not censure?
LADY: I am innocent here, and on my life I swear
  My ends are good.
LOVELL: On my soul, so are mine 240
  To Margaret: but leave both to the event;
  And since this friendly privacy does serve
  But as an offered means unto ourselves
  To search each other farther, you having shown
  Your care of me, I, my respect to you, 245
  Deny me not, but still in chaste words, madam,
  And afternoon's discourse.
LADY: So I shall hear you.   *Exeunt.*

Act Four, Scene Two

[*Enter*] TAPWELL, FROTH.

TAPWELL: Undone, undone! This was your counsel, Froth.
FROTH: Mine! I defy thee, did not Master Marrall
  (He has marred all, I am sure) strictly command us
  (On pain of Sir Giles Overreach displeasure)
  To turn the gentleman out of doors?
TAPWELL: 'Tis true, 5
  But now he's his uncle's darling, and has got
  Master Justice Greedy (since he filled his belly)
  At his commandment, to do anything;
  Woe, woe to us.

FROTH: He may prove merciful.
TAPWELL: Troth, we do not deserve it at his hands: 10
    Though he knew all the passages* of our house,
    As the receiving of stolen goods, and bawdry,
    When he was rogue Welborne, no man would believe him,
    And then his information could not hurt us.
    But now he is right worshipful again,   15
    Who dares but doubt his testimony? Methinks
    I see thee Froth already in a cart*
    For a close* bawd, thine eyes e'en pelted out
    With dirt and rotten eggs, and my hand hissing
    (If I scape the halter) with the letter R*   20
    Printed on it.
FROTH: Would that were the worst:
    That were but nine day's wonder, as for credit*
    We have none to lose; but we shall lose the money
    He owes us and his custom, there's the hell on 't.
TAPWELL: He has summoned all his creditors by the drum,   25
    And they swarm about him like so many soldiers
    On the pay day, and has found out such a new way
    To pay his old debts, as 'tis very likely
    He shall be chronicled for it.
FROTH: He deserves it
    More than ten pageants.* But are you sure his worship   30
    Comes this way to my ladies?
                        A cry within, 'Brave Master Welborne'.
TAPWELL: Yes, I hear him.
FROTH: Be ready with your petition and present it
    To his good grace.

Enter WELBORNE *in a rich habit,* GREEDY, [MARRALL], ORDER, FURNACE,
    three CREDITORS. TAPWELL *kneeling delivers his bill of debt.*

WELBORNE: How's this! Petitioned too?
    But note what miracles the payment of
    A little trash and a rich suit of clothes   35
    Can work upon these rascals. I shall be,
    I think, Prince Welborne.
MARRALL: When your worship's married
    You may be, I know what I hope to see you.
WELBORNE: Then look thou for advancement.
MARRALL: To be known
    Your worship's bailiff is the mark I shoot at.   40
WELBORNE: And thou shall hit it.

MARRALL: Pray you, sir, despatch
   These needy followers, and for my admittance,
   Provided you'll defend me from Sir Giles,
     This interim, TAPWELL *and* FROTH *flattering and bribing Justice* GREEDY.
   Whose service I am weary of. I'll say something
   You shall give thanks for.
WELBORNE: Fear me not,* Sir Giles.   45
GREEDY: Who? Tapwell? I remember thy wife brought me
   Last new year's tide a couple of fat turkeys.
TAPWELL: And shall do every Christmas, let your worship
   But stand my friend now.
GREEDY: How? With Master Welborne?
   I can do anything with him, on such terms;   50
   See you this honest couple: they are good souls
   As ever drew out fosset,* have they not
   A pair of honest faces?
WELBORNE: I o'erheard you,
   And the bribe he promised; you are cozened in 'em,
   For of all the scum that grew rich by my riots   55
   This is a most unthankful knave, and this
   For a base bawd and whore, have worst deserved me,*
   And therefore speak not for 'em. By your place
   You are rather to do me justice; lend me your ear,
   Forget his turkeys, and call in his licence,   60
   And at the next fair I'll give you a yoke of oxen
   Worth all his poultry.
GREEDY: I am changed on the sudden
   In my opinion! Come near; nearer, rascal.
   And now I view him better; did you e'er see
   One look so like an arch-knave? His very countenance,   65
   Should an understanding judge but look on him,
   Would hang him, though he were innocent.
TAPWELL, FROTH: Worshipful sir.
GREEDY: No, though the great Turk came instead of turkeys,
   To beg my favour. I am inexorable:
   Thou hast an ill name; besides thy musty ale   70
   That hath destroyed many of the King's liege people
   Thou never hadst in thy house to stay men's stomachs
   A piece of Suffolk cheese, or gammon of bacon,
   Or any esculent,* as the learned call it,
   For their emolument,* but sheer drink only.   75
   For which gross fault, I here do damn thy licence,
   Forbidding thee ever to tap or draw.
   For instantly I will in my own person

Command the constable to pull down thy sign;
And do it before I eat.
FROTH: No mercy?
GREEDY: Vanish.   80
   If I show any, may my promised oxen gore me.
TAPWELL: Unthankful knaves are ever so rewarded.

                         Exeunt GREEDY, TAPWELL, FROTH.

WELBORNE: Speak: what are you?
1 CREDITOR: A decayed vintner, sir,
   That might have thrived, but that your worship broke me
   With trusting you with muscadine* and eggs,   85
   And five pound suppers, with your after drinkings,
   When you lodged upon the Bankside.*
WELBORNE: I remember.
1 CREDITOR: I have not been hasty, nor e'er laid* to arrest you.
   And therefore sir –
WELBORNE: Thou art an honest fellow:
   I'll set thee up again; see his bill paid.   90
   What are you?
2 CREDITOR: A tailor once, but now mere botcher.*
   I gave you credit for a suit of clothes,
   Which was all my stock, but you failing in payment
   I was removed from the shop-board, and confined
   Under a stall.
WELBORNE: See him paid, and botch no more.   95
2 CREDITOR: I ask no interest, sir.
WELBORNE: Such tailors need not;
   If their bills are paid in one and twenty year
   They are seldom losers. O, I know thy face:
   Thou wert my surgeon;* you must tell no tales.
   Those days are done. I will pay you in private.   100
ORDER: A royal gentleman.
FURNACE: Royal as an emperor!
   He'll prove a brave master, my good lady knew
   To choose a man.
WELBORNE: See all men else discharged,
   And since old debts are cleared by a new way,
   A little bounty will not misbecome me;   105
   There's something, honest cook, for thy good breakfasts,
   And this for your respect, take 't, 'tis good gold
   And I able to spare it.
ORDER: You are too munificent.
FURNACE: He was ever so.
WELBORNE: Pray you, on before.

3 CREDITOR:　　　　　　　　　　Heaven bless you.

MARRALL: At four o' clock the rest know where to meet me.　　　110

　　　　　　　　　　Exeunt ORDER, FURNACE, CREDITORS.

WELBORNE: Now, Master Marrall, what's the weighty secret
　　You promised to impart?

MARRALL:　　　　　　　　Sir, time nor place
　　Allow me to relate each circumstance;
　　This only in a word: I know Sir Giles
　　Will come upon you for security　　　　　　　　115
　　For his thousand pounds, which you must not consent to.
　　As he grows in heat, as I am sure he will,
　　Be you but rough, and say he's in your debt
　　Ten times the sum, upon sale of your land;
　　I had a hand in 't (I speak it to my shame)　　　120
　　When you were defeated* of it.

WELBORNE:　　　　　　　　That's forgiven.

MARRALL: I shall deserve 't; then urge him to produce
　　The deed in which you passed it over to him,
　　Which I know he'll have about him to deliver
　　To the Lord Lovell, with many other writings,　　　125
　　And present monies; I'll instruct you further
　　As I wait upon your worship; if I play not my prize*
　　To your full content, and your uncle's much vexation,
　　Hang up Jack Marrall.

WELBORNE:　　　　　　I rely upon thee.　　　　　*Exeunt.*

Act Four, Scene Three

[*Enter*] ALWORTH, MARGARET.

ALWORTH: Whether to yield the first praise to my lord's
　　Unequalled temperance, or your constant sweetness,
　　That I yet live, my weak hands fastened on
　　Hope's anchor, spite of all storms of despair,
　　I yet rest doubtful.

MARGARET:　　　　　　Give it to Lord Lovell.　　　5
　　For what in him was bounty, in me's duty.
　　I make but payment of a debt, to which
　　My vows in that high office* registered
　　Are faithful witnesses.

ALWORTH:　　　　　　'Tis true, my dearest,
　　Yet when I call to mind how many fair ones　　　10
　　Make wilful shipwreck of their faiths, and oaths

To God and Man, to fill the arms of greatness,
And you rise up no less than a glorious star
To the amazement of the world, that hold out
Against the stern authority of a father,   15
And spurn at honour when it comes to court you,
I am so tender of your good that faintly
With your wrong I can wish myself that right
You yet are pleased to do me.
MARGARET: Yet, and ever.
To me what's title, when content is wanting?   20
Or wealth raked up together with much care,
And to be kept with more, when the heart pines,
In being dispossessed of what it longs for,
Beyond the Indian mines; or the smooth brow
Of a pleased sire, that slaves me to his will?   25
And so his ravenous humour may be feasted
By my obedience, and he see me great,
Leaves to my soul nor faculties nor power
To make her own election.
ALWORTH: But the dangers
That follow the repulse.
MARGARET: To me they are nothing;   30
Let Alworth love, I cannot be unhappy.
Suppose the worst, that in his rage he kill me;
A tear or two by you dropped on my hearse
In sorrow for my fate will call back life
So far, as but to say that I die yours,   35
I then shall rest in peace; or should he prove
So cruel, as one death would not suffice
His thirst of vengeance, but with ling'ring torments
In mind and body I must waste to air,
In poverty, joined with banishment, so* you share   40
In my afflictions (which I dare not wish you,
So high I prize you), I could undergo 'em
With such a patience as should look down
With scorn on his worst malice.
ALWORTH: Heaven alert
Such trials of your true affection to me,   45
Nor will it unto you that are all mercy
Show so much rigour; but since we must run
Such desperate hazards, let us do our best
To steer between 'em.
MARGARET: Your lord's ours,* and sure,
And though but a young actor, second me   50
In doing to the life what he has plotted.

Enter OVERREACH.

The end may yet prove happy; now, my Alworth.
ALWORTH: To your letter, and put on a seeming anger.
MARGARET: I'll pay my lord all debts due to his title,
    And when with terms, not taking from his honour,   55
    He does solicit me, I shall gladly hear him.
    But in this peremptory, nay, commanding, way
    T' appoint a meeting, and without my knowledge,
    A priest to tie the knot can ne'er be undone
    Till death unloose it, is a confidence   60
    In his lordship will deceive him.
ALWORTH: I hope better,
    Good lady.
MARGARET: Hope, sir, what you please; for me,
    I must take a safe and secure course; I have
    A father, and without his full consent,
    Though all lords of the land kneeled for my favour,   65
    I can grant nothing.
OVERREACH: I like this obedience.
    But whatsoever my lord writes must and shall be
    Accepted and embraced. Sweet Master Alworth,
    You show yourself a true and faithful servant
    To your good lord, he has a jewel of you.   70
    How? Frowning, Meg? Are these looks to receive
    A messenger from my lord? What's this? Give it me.
MARGARET: A piece of arrogant paper like th' inscriptions.
                            OVERREACH *read the letter.*
OVERREACH: Fair mistress, from your servant learn all joys
    That we can hope for, if deferred, prove toys;*   75
    Therefore this instant and in private meet
    A husband that will gladly at your feet
    Lay down his honours, tend'ring them to you
    With all content, the church being paid her due.
    Is this the arrogant piece of paper? Fool,   80
    Will you still be one? In the name of madness, what
    Could his good honour write more to content you?
    Is there aught else to be wished after these two
    That are already offered? Marriage first,
    And lawful pleasure after: what would you more?   85
MARGARET: Why sir, I would be married like your daughter;
    Not hurried away i' th' night I know not wither,
    Without all ceremony; no friends invited
    To honour the solemnity.
ALWORTH: An 't please your honour,

For so before tomorrow I must style you,   90
My lord desires this privacy in respect*
His honourable kinsmen are far off,
And his desires to have it done brook not
So long delay as to expect* their coming;
And yet he stands resolved, with all due pomp,   95
As running at the ring,* plays, masques, and tilting,
To have his marriage at court celebrated
When he has brought your honour up to London.
OVERREACH: He tells you true; 'tis the fashion on my knowledge,
Yet the good lord to please your peevishness   100
Must put it off forsooth, and lose a night
In which perhaps he might get two boys on thee.
Tempt me no farther; if you do, this goad*
Shall prick you to him.
MARGARET: I should be contented,
Were you but by to do a father's part,   105
And give me in the church.
OVERREACH: So my lord have you:
What do I care who gives you? Since my lord
Does purpose to be private, I'll not cross him.
I know not, Master Alworth, how my lord
May be provided, and therefore there's a purse   110
Of gold, 'twill serve this night's expense; tomorrow
I'll furnish him with any sums: in the meantime
Use my ring to my chaplain; he is beneficed
At my manor of Gotham, and called Parson Will-do.
'Tis no matter for a licence, I'll bear him out in 't.   115
MARGARET: With your favour, sir, what warrant is your ring?
He may suppose I got that twenty ways
Without your knowledge, and then to be refused
Were such a stain upon me; if you pleased, sir,
Your presence would do better.
OVERREACH: Still perverse?   120
I say again I will not cross my lord,
Yet I'll prevent you* too. Paper and ink there!
ALWORTH: I can furnish you.
OVERREACH: I thank you, I can write then.
                                                      Writes on his book.
ALWORTH: You may, if you please, put the name of my lord,
In respect he comes disguised, and only write: 125
Marry her to this gentleman.
OVERREACH: Well advised.   MARGARET *kneels.*
'Tis done, away! My blessing, girl? Thou hast it.

Nay, no reply; begone, Master Alworth:
This shall be the best night's work you ever made.
ALWORTH: I hope so, sir.   *Exeunt* ALWORTH *and* MARGARET.
OVERREACH: Farewell; now all's cock-sure:*   130
Methinks I hear already knights and ladies
Say: Sir Giles Overreach, how is it with
Your honourable daughter? Has her honour
Slept well tonight? Or will her honour please
To accept this monkey? Dog? Or paraquit?*   135
(This is state* in ladies) Or my eldest son
To be her page, and wait upon her trencher?
My ends! My ends are compassed! Then for Welborne
And the lands; were he once married to the widow,
I have him here, I can scarce contain myself,   140
I am so full of joy; nay, joy all over.   *Exit.*

The end of the fourth Act

Act Five, Scene One

[*Enter*] LOVELL, LADY, AMBLE.

LADY: By this you know how strong the motives were
That did, my lord, induce me to dispense
A little with my gravity, to advance
(In personating* some few favours to him)
The plots and projects of the down-trod Welborne.   5
Nor shall I e'er repent (although I suffer
In some few men's opinions for 't) the action.
For he that ventured all for my dear husband
Might justly claim an obligation from me
To pay him such a courtesy: which had I   10
Coyly or over-curiously* denied,
It might have argued me of little love
To the deceased.
LOVELL: What you intended, madam,
For the poor gentleman hath found good success,
For, as I understand, his debts are paid,   15
And he once more furnished for fair employment.
But all the arts that I have used to raise
The fortunes of your joy, and mine, young Alworth,
Stand yet in supposition; though I hope well,

For the young lovers are in wit more pregnant   20
Than their years can promise; and, for their desires,
On my knowledge they are equal.
LADY: As my wishes
Are with yours, my lord; yet give me leave to fear
The building, though well grounded: to deceive
Sir Giles, that's both a lion and a fox   25
In his proceedings, were a work beyond
The strongest undertakers, not the trial
Of two weak innocents.
LOVELL: Despair not, madam:
Hard things are compassed oft by easy means,
And judgment, being a gift derived from heaven,   30
Though sometimes lodged i'th' hearts of worldly men
(That ne'er consider from whom they receive it)
Forsakes such as abuse the giver of it.
Which is the reason that the politic*
And cunning statesman, that believes he fathoms   35
The counsels of all kingdoms on the earth,
Is by simplicity oft overreached.
LADY: May he be so, yet in his name to express it
Is a good omen.
LOVELL: May it to myself
Prove so, good lady, in my suit to you: 40
What think you of the motion?*
LADY: Troth, my lord,
My own unworthiness may answer for me;
For had you, when I was in my prime,
My virgin-flower uncropped, presented me
With this great favour, looking on my lowness   45
Not in a glass of self-love, but of truth,
I could not but have thought it as a blessing
Far, far beyond my merit.
LOVELL: You are too modest,
And undervalue that which is above
My title, or whatever I call mine.   50
I grant, were I a Spaniard to marry
A widow might disparage me, but being
A true-born Englishman, I cannot find
How it can taint my honour; nay, what's more,
That which you think a blemish is to me   55
The fairest lustre. You already madam
Have given sure proofs how dearly you can cherish
A husband that deserves you, which confirms me

That if I am not wanting in my care
To do you service, you'll still be the same   60
That you were to your Alworth; in a word,
Our years, our states, our births are not unequal,
You being descended nobly, and allied so;
If then you may be won to make me happy,
But join your lips to mine, and that shall be   65
A solemn contract.
LADY: I were blind to my own good
    Should I refuse it, yet my lord receive me
    As such a one, the study of whose whole life
    Shall know no other object but to please you.
LOVELL: If I return not with all tenderness,   70
    Equal respect to you, may I die wretched.
LADY: There needs no protestation, my lord,
    To her that cannot doubt.

Enter WELBORNE.

                              You are welcome, sir.
    Now you look like yourself.
WELBORNE: And will continue
    Such in my free acknowledgement that I am   75
    Your creature, madam, and will never hold
    My life mine own, when you please to command it.
LOVELL: It is a thankfulness that well becomes you;
    You could not make choice of a better shape
    To dress your mind in.
LADY: For me, I am happy   80
    That my endeavours prospered; saw you of late
    Sir Giles, your uncle?
WELBORNE: I heard of him, madam,
    By his minister, Marrall; he's grown into strange passions
    About his daughter, this last night he looked for
    Your lordship at his house, but, missing you,   85
    And she not yet appearing, his wise head
    Is much perplexed and troubled.
LOVELL: It may be,
    Sweetheart, my project took.*
LADY: I strongly hope.
Enter OVERREACH *with distracted looks, driving in* MARRALL *before him.*
OVERREACH: Ha! Find her, booby, thou huge lump of nothing;
    I'll bore thine eyes out else.
WELBORNE: May it please your lordship   90

For some ends of mine own but to withdraw
A little out of sight, though not of hearing,
You may perhaps have sport.
LOVELL: You shall direct me.   *Steps aside.*
OVERREACH: I shall sol fa* you, rogue.
MARRALL: Sir, for what cause
  Do you use me thus?
OVERREACH: Cause, slave? Why, I am angry,   95
  And thou a subject only fit for beating,
  And so to cool my choler; look to the writing,
  Let but the seal be broke upon the box,
  That has slept in my cabinet these three years,
  I'll rack thy soul for 't.
MARRALL: I may yet cry quittance,   100
  Though now I suffer, and dare not resist.   *Aside.*
OVERREACH: Lady, by your leave, did you see my daughter, lady?
  And the lord her husband? Are they in your house?
  If they are, discover, that I may bid 'em joy;
  And as an entrance to her place of honour,   105
  Set your ladyship on her left hand, and make curtsies
  When she nods on you; which you must receive
  As a special favour.
LADY: When I know, Sir Giles,
  Her state* requires such ceremony, I shall pay it,
  But not in the meantime, as I am myself,   110
  I give you to understand that I neither know
  Nor care where her honour is.
OVERREACH: When you once see her
  Supported and led by the lord her husband,
  You'll be taught better. Nephew.
WELBORNE: Sir.
OVERREACH: No more?
WELBORNE: 'Tis all I owe you.
OVERREACH: Have your redeemed rags   115
  Made you thus insolent?
WELBORNE: Insolent to you?   *In scorn.*
  Why, what are you, sir, unless in your years,
  At the best, more than myself?
OVERREACH: His fortune swells him,
  'Tis rank* he's married.
LADY: This is excellent!
OVERREACH: Sir, in calm language (though I seldom use it)   120
  I am familiar with the cause that makes you
  Bear up thus bravely, there's a certain buzz*

Of a stol'n marriage, do you hear? Of a stol'n marriage,
In which 'tis said there's somebody hath been cozened.
I name no parties.
WELBORNE: Well, sir, and what follows?   125
OVERREACH: Marry, this, since you are peremptory: remember,
      Upon mere hope of your great match, I lent you
      A thousand pounds; put me in good security,
      And suddenly, by mortgage or by statute,
      Of some of your new possessions, or I'll have you   130
      Dragged in your lavender robes* to the jail; you know me,
      And therefore do not trifle.
WELBORNE: Can you be
      So cruel to your nephew, now he's in
      The way to rise? Was this the courtesy
      You did me in pure love, and no ends else?   135
OVERREACH: End me no ends: engage the whole estate,
      And force your spouse to sign it; you shall have
      Three or four thousand more to roar and swagger,
      And revel in bawdy taverns.
WELBORNE: And beg after:
      Mean you not so?
OVERREACH: My thoughts are mine, and free.   140
      Shall I have security?
WELBORNE: No, indeed, you shall not:
      Nor bond, nor bill, nor bare acknowledgement,
      Your great looks fright not me.
OVERREACH: But my deeds shall:
      Outbraced?   *They both draw, the* SERVANTS *enter.*
LADY: Help, murder, murder.
WELBORNE: Let him come on,
      With all his wrongs and injuries about him,   145
      Armed with his cut-throat practices to guard him;
      The right that I bring with me will defend me,
      And punish his extortion.
OVERREACH: That I had thee
      But single in the field.
LADY: You may, but make not
      My house my quarrelling scene.
OVERREACH: Were 't in a church,   150
      By heaven and hell, I'll do 't.
MARRALL: Now put him to
      The showing of the deed.
WELBORNE: This rage is vain, sir,
      For fighting, fear not, you shall have your hands full,

Upon the least incitement; and whereas
You charge me with a debt of a thousand pounds,   155
If there be law (howe'er you have no conscience)
Either restore my land, or I'll recover
A debt that's truly due to me from you,
In value ten times more than what you challenge.*
OVERREACH: I in thy debt! O impudence! Did I not purchase   160
The land left by thy father? That rich land,
That had continued in Welborne's name
Twenty descents; which like a riotous fool
Thou didst make sale of? Is not here enclosed
The deed that does confirm it mine?
MARRALL: Now, now!   165
WELBORNE: I do acknowledge none; I ne'er passed o'er
Any such land. I grant for a year or two
You had it in trust, which, if you do discharge,
Surrendering the possession, you shall ease
Yourself, and me, of chargeable* suits in law,   170
Which if you prove not honest (as I doubt it)
Must of necessity follow.
LADY: In my judgement
He does advise you well.
OVERREACH: Good! Good! Conspire
With your new husband, lady; second him
In his dishonest practices; but when   175
This manor is extended* to my use
You'll speak in an humbler key, and sue for favour.
LADY: Never: do not hope it.
WELBORNE: Let despair first seize me.
OVERREACH: Yet to shut up thy mouth and make thee give
Thyself the lie, the loud lie: I draw out   180
The precious evidence; if thou canst forswear
Thy hand and seal, and make a forfeit of   *Opens the box.*
Thy ears to the pillory, see here's that will make
My interest clear. Ha!
LADY: A fair skin of parchment!
WELBORNE: Indented,* I confess, and labels* too,   185
But neither wax nor words. How! Thunderstruck?
Not a syllable to insult with? My wise uncle,
Is this your precious evidence? Is this that makes
Your interest* clear?
OVERREACH: I am o'er whelmed with wonder!
What prodigy is this? What subtle devil   190
Hath razed out the inscription? The wax

Turned into dust! The rest of my deeds whole,
As when they were delivered! And this only
Made nothing! Do you deal with witches, rascal?
There is a statute for you, which will bring   195
Your neck in a hempen circle,* yes there is.
And now 'tis better thought for, cheater, know
This juggling shall not save you.
WELBORNE: To save thee
   Would beggar the stock of mercy.
OVERREACH: Marrall.
MARRALL: Sir.
OVERREACH: Though the witnesses are dead, your testimony   200
   Help with an oath or two, and for thy master,   *Flattering him.*
   Thy liberal master, my good honest servant,
   I know you will swear anything to dash
   This cunning sleight; besides, I know thou art
   A public notary, and such stand in law   205
   For a dozen witnesses; the deed being drawn too
   By thee, my careful Marrall, and delivered
   When thou wert present, will make good my title;
   Wilt thou not swear this?
MARRALL: I? No, I assure you.
   I have a conscience, not seared up like yours,   210
   I know no deeds.
OVERREACH: Wilt thou betray me?
MARRALL: Keep him
   From using of his hands, I'll use my tongue
   To his no little torment.
OVERREACH: Mine own varlet
   Rebel against me?
MARRALL: Yes, and uncase* you too.
   The idiot, the patch, the slave, the booby;   215
   The property fit only to be beaten
   For your morning exercise; your football, or
   Th' unprofitable lump of flesh; your drudge
   Can now anatomise you, and lay open
   All your black plots; and level with the earth   220
   Your hill of pride; and with these gabions* guarded,
   Unload my great artillery, and shake,
   Nay pulverise, the walls you think defend you.
LADY: How he foams at the mouth with rage.
WELBORNE: To him again.
OVERREACH: O that I had thee in my grip, I would tear thee   225
   Joint after joint.

MARRALL: I know you are a tearer,
    But I'll have your fangs pared off, and then
    Come nearer to you, when I have discovered,
    And made it good before the judge, what ways
    And devilish practices you used to cozen   230
    With an army of whole families, who yet live,
    And but enrolled for soldiers were able
    To take in* Dunkirk.
WELBORNE: All will come out.
LADY: The better.
OVERREACH: But that I will live, rogue, to torture thee,
    And make thee wish and kneel in vain to die,   235
    These swords that keep thee from me should fix here,
    Although they made my body but one wound,
    But I would reach thee.
LOVELL: Heaven's hand is in this,
    One bandog* worry the other.   *Aside.*
OVERREACH: I play the fool,
    And make my anger but ridiculous.   240
    There will be a time and place, there will be, cowards,
    When you shall feel what I dare do.
WELBORNE: I think so:
    You dare do any ill, yet want true valour
    To be honest, and repent.
OVERREACH: They are words I know not,
    Nor e'er will learn. Patience, the beggar's virtue,   245
    Shall find no harbour here.

                    Enter GREEDY *and* PARSON WILL-DO.

                        After these storms
    At length a calm appears. Welcome, most welcome:
    There's comfort in thy looks; is the deed done?
    Is my daughter married? Say but so, my chaplain,
    And I am tame.
WILL-DO: Married? Yes, I assure you.   250
OVERREACH: Then vanish all sad thoughts; there's more gold for thee.
    My doubts and fears are in the titles drowned
    Of my honourable, my right honourable daughter.
GREEDY: Here will I be feasting; at least for a month
    I am provided: empty guts, croak no more,   255
    You shall be stuffed like bagpipes, not with wind
    But bearing* dishes.
OVERREACH: Instantly be here?   *Whispering to* WILL-DO.

To my wish, to my wish, now you that plot against me
And hoped to trip my heels up; that contemned me; *Loud music.*
Think on 't, and tremble, they come, I hear the music.   260
A lane* there for my lord.

WELBORNE: This sudden heat
May yet be cooled, sir.

OVERREACH: Make way there for my lord.

Enter ALWORTH *and* MARGARET.

MARGARET: Sir, first your pardon, then your blessing, with
Your full allowance of the choice I have made.   *Kneeling.*
As ever you could make use of your reason,   265
Grow not in passion; since you may as well
Call back the day that's past, as untie the knot
Which is too strongly fastened, not to dwell
Too long on words, this's my husband.

OVERREACH: How!

ALWORTH: So I assure you: all the rites of marriage   270
With every circumstance are past; alas, sir,
Although I am no lord, but a lord's page,
Your daughter, and my loved wife, mourns not for it,
And for right honourable son-in-law, you may say
Your dutiful daughter.

OVERREACH: Devil: are they married?   275

WILL-DO: Do a father's part, and say heaven give 'em joy.

OVERREACH: Confusion and ruin, speak, and speak quickly,
Or thou art dead.

WILL-DO: They are married.

OVERREACH: Thou hadst better
Have made a contract with the king of fiends
Than these; my brain turns!

WILL-DO: Why this rage to me?   280
Is not this your letter, sir? And these the words?
'Marry her to this gentleman.'

OVERREACH: It cannot:
Nor will I e'er believe it, 'sdeath, I will not,
That I, that in all passages I touched,
At worldly profit, have not left a print   285
Where I have trod for the most curious* search
To trace my footsteps, should be gulled by children,
Baffled* and fooled, and all my hopes and labours
Defeated and made void.

WELBORNE: As it appears,

You are so, my grave uncle.

OVERREACH: Village nurses   290
    Revenge their wrongs with curses; I'll not waste
    A syllable, but thus I take the life
    Which wretched I gave to thee.   *Offers to kill* MARGARET.

LOVELL: Hold, for your own sake!
    Though charity to your daughter hath quite left you,
    Will you do an act, though in your hopes lost here,   295
    Can leave no hope for peace or rest hereafter?
    Consider: at the best you are but a man,
    And cannot so create your aims, but that
    They may be crossed.

OVERREACH: Lord, thus I spit at thee,
    And at thy counsel; and again desire thee   300
    And as thou art a soldier, if thy valour
    Dares show itself where multitude and example
    Lead not the way, let's quit the house, and change
    Six words in private.

LOVELL: I am ready.

LADY: Stay, sir,
    Contest with one distracted?

WELBORNE: You'll grow like him   305
    Should you answer his vain challenge.

OVERREACH: Are you pale?
    Borrow his help, though Hercules call it odds,
    I'll stand against both, as I am hemmed in thus.
    Since like the Libyan lion in the toil*
    My fury cannot reach the coward hunters   310
    And only spends itself, I'll quit the place;
    Alone I can do nothing, but I have servants
    And friends to second me, and if I make not
    This house a heap of ashes (by my wrongs,
    What I have spoke I will make good), or leave   315
    One throat uncut, if it be possible,
    Hell add to my afflictions.   *Exit.*

MARRALL: Is 't not brave sport?

GREEDY: Brave sport? I am sure it has ta'en away my stomach;
    I do not like the sauce.

ALWORTH: Nay, weep not, dearest;
    Though it express your pity, what's decreed   320
    Above, we cannot alter.

LADY: His threats move me
    No scruple, madam.

MARRALL: Was it not a rare trick
    (And it please your worship) to make the deed nothing?

I can do twenty neater, if you please
To purchase, and grow rich, for I will be   325
Such a solicitor and steward for you,
As never worshipful had.
MARRALL: I do believe thee.
But first discover the quaint* means you used
To raze out the conveyance.
MARRALL: They are mysteries
Not to be spoke in public; certain minerals   330
Incorporated in the ink and wax.
Besides, he gave me nothing, but still fed me
With hopes, and blows; and that was the inducement
To this conundrum. If it please your worship
To call to memory, this mad beast once caused me   335
To urge you or to drown or hang yourself;
I'll do the like to him if you command me.
WELBORNE: You are a rascal: he that dares be false
To a master, though unjust, will ne'er be true
To any other; look not for reward   340
Or favour from me, I will shun thy sight
As I would do a basilisk's.* Thank my pity
If thou keep thy ears, howe'er I will take order,
Your practice shall be silenced.
GREEDY: I'll commit him
If you'll have me, sir?
WELBORNE: That were to little purpose;   345
His conscience be his prison, not a word,
But instantly be gone.
ORDER: Take this kick with you.
AMBLE: And this.
FURNACE: If that I had my cleaver here
I would divide your knave's head.
MARRALL: This is the haven
False servants still arrive at.   *Exit.*

Enter OVERREACH.

LADY: Come again!   350
LOVELL: Fear not, I am your guard.
WELBORNE: His looks are ghastly.
WILL-DO: Some little time I have spent, under your favours,
In physical studies,* and, if my judgement err not,
He's mad beyond recovery: but observe him,
And look to yourselves.

OVERREACH: Why is not the whole world   355
    Included in myself? To what use then
    Are friends and servants? Say there were a squadron
    Of pikes, lined through with shot,* when I am mounted
    Upon my injuries, shall I fear to charge 'em?
    No: I'll through the battalia, and that routed,   360
                     Flourishing his sword ensheathed.
    I'll fall to execution. Ha! I am feeble:
    Some undone widow sits upon mine arm,
    And takes away the use of 't; and my sword,
    Glued to my scabbard with wronged orphans' tears,
    Will not be drawn. Ha! What are these? Sure hangmen,   365
    That come to bind my hands, and then to drag me
    Before the judgement seat! Now they are new shapes
    And do appear like furies with steel whips
    To scourge my ulcerous soul! Shall I then fall
    Ingloriously and yield? No, spite of fate,   370
    I will be forced to hell like to myself;
    Though you were legion of accursed spirits,
    Thus I would fly among you.
WELBORNE: There's no help;
    Disarm him first, then bind him.
GREEDY: Take a mittimus*
    And carry him to Bedlam.*
LOVELL: How he foams!   375
WELBORNE: And bites the earth.
WILL-DO: Carry him to some dark room;
    There try what art can do for his recovery.
MARGARET: O my dear father!   *They force* OVERREACH *off.*
ALWORTH: You must be patient, mistress.
LOVELL: Here is a precedent to teach wicked men
    That when they leave religion, and turn atheists,   380
    Their own abilities leave 'em. Pray you, take comfort,
    I will endeavour you shall be his guardians
    In his distractions; and for your land, Master Welborne,
    Be it good or ill in law, I'll be an umpire
    Between you and this, the undoubted heir   385
    Of Sir Giles Overreach; for me, here's the anchor
    That I must fix on.
ALWORTH: What you shall determine,
    My lord, I will allow of.*
WELBORNE: 'Tis the language
    That I speak too; but there is something else
    Beside the repossession of my land,   390

And payment of my debts, that I must practice.
I had a reputation, but 'twas lost
In my loose courses; and till I redeem it
Some noble way, I am but half made up.
It is a time of action: if your lordship   395
Will please to confer a company upon me
In your command, I doubt not, in my service
To my king and country, but I shall do something
That may make me right again.
LOVELL: Your suit is granted,
And you loved for the motion.*   400
WELBORNE: Nothing wants, then,
But your allowance.*

The Epilogue

But your allowance, and, in that, our all
Is comprehended; it being known, nor we,
Nor he that wrote the comedy, can be free
Without your manumission,* which if you
Grant willingly, as a fair favour due   5
To the poet's and our labours (as you may,
For we despair not, gentlemen, of the play),
We jointly shall profess your grace hath might
To teach us action, and him how to write.

Finis

Notes to the Play

Dedication

ROBERT, EARL OF
CAERNARVON: Robert Dormer
(1610–43), who inherited the title
of Baron Dormer of Wyng and
Master Falconer of England at
the age of six.

Verses

To ... *Debts*

8   run in score: continue to
      accumulate debts

To ... Author

11   shamefast: shameful
      Thomas Jay: associate and
      patron of Massinger

Dramatis Personae

6   term-driver: obscure; probably a
      term for a corrupt lawyer

Act One, Scene One

3   palled: stale, flat
5   brach: bitch
6   precisian: puritan
11   Plymouth cloak: cudgel
15   rusty billmen: officers equipped
      with rusty bills (halberds)
25   in chalk: on the slate
27   riots: indulgences
29   skills: matters
33   quondam: former
34   *quorum*: a key Justice of the
      Peace, required to make a bench
      quorate
35   *custos rotulorum*: custodian of
      the rolls and Chief Justice

40–1 Very ... way: i.e. hardly; you are
      lost (destitute) already
47   lordships: estates
50   statutes: bonds specifying
      forteiture of land for default
54   token: unofficial small-
      denomination currency issued
      by shopkeepers
56   paper-pellets: promissory notes
59   Where: whereas
62   canters: literally, speakers of
      cant; jargon-spouting rogues
63   Clubbers: obscure; possibly
      'associates'
65   stuck not: were not resistant
68   overseer ... poor: an office
      instituted in the reign of
      Elizabeth I: the Overseer was
      responsible for levying the poor
      rate and ensuring that it was
      distributed
71   dogbolt: blunt arrow
75   make purses: secure deals
88   tread: grind
128   lodestone: magnet
131   cormorant: devouring,
      extortionate
136   manumized: released by hand
137   sworn ... pantophle: subject to a
      lady ('pantophle': slipper)
142   drabs: whores
143   Court-waiters: pages at court
171   pieces: i.e. of gold or silver
173   stipendiary: one on a stipend
182   canopy: sky
187   humour: whim

Act One, Scene Two

12   go-before: gentleman usher
27   Breda: Dutch town under siege
      from 1624 to 1625 from forces
      commanded by the Marquis of
      Spinola
30   strike: bushel
35   panada: boiled bread pudding
43   stol'n into commission: arrived
      at his position through fraud
46   insatiate: insatiable
49   in little: in miniature

55	spoonmeat: invalids' food		134	Lady … Lake: mistress of Merlin the enchanter in Malory's *Morte d'Arthur*
78	capable of: susceptible to		142	curvet: leap

Act One, Scene Three

Act Two, Scene Two

8	Hull: key port for the wine trade
10	race: variety
15	Chine: backbone and rib
17	kickshaws: delicacies
30	Henrici … quarto: according to a statute issued in the fourteenth year of the reign of Henry (i.e. Henry VIII). Intended to be nonsensical
43	Pie Corner: the junction of Giltspur Street and Cock Lane, known for its pie-shops
46	basket: filled with leftovers for beggars at the gate
60	make legs: bow
63	blackjacks: leather beer tankards
65	reversions: leftovers
84	take order: ensure that
97	keep … eye: stop herself weeping
103	gave him fashion: introduced him to fashionable society
118	contemn: scorn

12	chamberers: waiting-women
13	tits: women (derogatory)
18	true elixir: water of life
21	potato roots: sweet potato, considered an aphrodisiac
24	bait: break the journey for refreshment
38	primer: child's prayer book
54	turkey chicken: young turkey
55	rails: corn-crakes
56	affect: appeal to
100	Persians: i.e. fire-worshippers
108	bought … hangman: the clothes of the victim went to the executioner
113	to admiration: astonishingly
123	Ram Alley: off Fleet Street, a place of sanctuary for pimps, cooks, tobacconists and ale-house keepers
124	divide: i.e. divide a meal between them
129	whitebroth: white sauce
131	leg: bow
133	chid: scolded
137	companion: equal (to be jeered at)

Act Two, Scene One

Act Two, Scene Three

4	chap-fallen: open-mouthed
17	*praemunire*: predicament; liability to prosecution
27	hedge in: enclose
41	in … pauperis: as a pauper, and thus not liable for legal costs
45	pretend some title: advance a claim
46	put … arbitrement: make a settlement
52	close cheat: secret fraud
70	minion: favourite
71	country: county
79	errant: arrant; genuine
106	withe: willow branch
108	presently: immediately credit: reputation
128	gratis: for free
130	padders: footpads abram-men: beggars masquerading as madmen

6	flout: tease
13	coz'nage: opportunity for cheating
22	a better habit: better dressed
25	to her: compared to her
29	for change: i.e. of clothes
37	glebe land: farm land
38	manure: cultivate; occupy as tenant
40	make: afford
46	froward: assertive
62	pursy: unfit
76	And: if
80	Simple: as true

84 sad: serious
107 cross: obstruct

Act Three, Scene One

17 guard: adorn; preserve
26 so conditioned: of that character
33 carriage ... to: bearing towards
67 numerous: by numbers, musically speaking
75 in the van: i.e. in the vanguard, in the front rank
76 battalia: army in battledress
77 lined: reinforced
79 Hippolytus: Son of Theseus, lusted after by Phaedra, his stepmother

Act Three, Scene Two

2 Store ... sore: there's no harm in excess (proverbial)
10 chargeable: costly
16 providence: capacity to bestow
20 conceit: imagination
31 affects: pleases
33 quaint: intricate
43 tamin: thin woollen
48 Counter: a London debtors' prison
61 to: as
80 in one volume: at the same time
85 coram: (Latin) coram populo; publicly
87 woodcocks: synonymous with 'fools'
101 quality: rank
114 private: intimate
117 Jupiter to Semele: according to classical mythology, Jove approached Semele in his full godlike status, which caused her to be consumed by fire
132 worldly policy: common sense
169 suddenly: soon
177 bare: bare-headed
206 turned powder: gone dry
209 Barathrum ... shambles: taken from Horace, *Epistles*, I, xv, 31: a gulf to devour the contents of the abbatoir

212 main-prise: surety
229 coming: susceptible
234 and: if
235 towardly: promising
248 patch: fool
271 speak at large: speak freely
272 humour: whim
297 set: i.e. for dinner
307 tatterdemalian: wretched beggar bug: threatening
310 worship: dignity

Act Three, Scene Three

25 *Pasiphae ... bull*: mother of Phaedra and wife of Minos, the king of Crete; as reported in Ovid, *Metamorphoses*, XV, the Minotaur was the result of her breeding with a bull
27 excuse my manners: i.e. for quitting the table prematurely
54 yield: admit
61 shape: costume
74 extremes: time of need

Act Four, Scene One

33 difference: deference
35 fit you: sort you out; get back at you
50 shield of brawn: jellied brawn cooked in a pigskin Colchester: renowned for its oysters
51 scour my stomach: provide a starter
53 hangman of Flushing: obscure (Q has 'Vllushing'): possibly refers to the Dutch town which was the site of English landings in 1625
56 Christmas coffer: stomach
69 progress: tour of the country
77 engines: stratagems
103 *nil ultra*: (Latin) nothing beyond this
105 port: position
113 sinister: literally, left-handed
131 admire: am amazed by
150 portent: personification of evil

155 Olympus: the seat of the gods, mistakenly substituted for Parnassus
156 Boreas: the North Wind
184 prefer: promote
185 state: estate
199 allow: grant
203 fill their mouths: shut them up
209 conceive: imagine
215 cried up: exaggerated
219 come nearer: speak frankly
226 London blue: the colour of servants' livery
236 public conference: common knowledge

Act Four, Scene Two

11 passages: activities
17 cart: i.e. carted through the streets as a form of public humiliation
18 close: covert
20 the letter R: for rogue or receiver of stolen goods
22 credit: reputation
30 pageants: triumphal processions
45 fear me not: fear not
52 drew out fosset: drew from a barrel
57 deserved me: deserved from me
74 esculent: edible substances
75 emolument: benefit
85 muscadine: sweet Muscatel wine
87 Bankside: Southwark, on the South bank of the Thames
88 laid: arranged
91 botcher: mender
99 surgeon: who presumably dealt with Welborne's sexually-transmitted afflictions
121 defeated: deprived
127 play … prize: conduct my part well, as in a fencing tournament

Act Four, Scene Three

8 that high office: heaven
40 so: on condition that
49 ours: on our side
75 toys: inconsequentialities

91 in respect: because
94 expect: await
96 running … ring: thrusting a lance through a ring while on horseback
103 goad: i.e. Overreach's sword
122 prevent you: forestall your objections
130 cock-sure: certain; safe
135 paraquit: parakeet
136 state: a sign of dignity

Act Five, Scene One

4 personating: pretending
11 over-curiously: too scrupulously
34 politic: devious
41 motion: proposal
88 project took: scheme succeeded
94 sol fa: literally, syllables of the musical scale; in this context, refers to the noises provoked by beating
109 state: rank
119 'tis rank: it's obvious; it is for the sake of the title
122 buzz: rumour
131 lavender robes: recently stored in lavender, or pawned
159 challenge: allege
170 chargeable: expensive
176 extended: legally appropriated
185 Indented: a legal contract could be split between its two parties; the indentations would mark the act of tearing
    labels: tags attaching the seals of the parties to the contract
189 interest: legal claim
196 neck … circle: involvement in witchcraft was punished by hanging
214 uncase: expose
221 gabions: baskets filled with earth to strengthen fortifications
233 take in: capture
239 ban-dog: fierce dog
257 bearing: weighty
261 lane: passageway
286 curious: exacting
288 Baffled: publicly humiliated
309 toil: trap

328   quaint: clever
342   basilisk: mythical serpent able to
       kill by a glance
353   physical studies: medicine
358   pikes ... shot: pikemen backed
       with muskets
374   mittimus: warrant for committal
       to an asylum
375   Bedlam: Bethlehem Hospital, an
       insane asylum

288   allow of: endorse
400   motion: proposal
401   allowance: indulgence; approval

Epilogue

4   manumission: setting free
       (by applause)

Further Reading

Bakhtin, Mikhail, *Rabelais and His World*, trans. Hélène Iswolsky (Cambridge, MA: MIT Press, 1968).

Bradbrook, M. C., *The Growth and Structure of Elizabethan Comedy* (Harmondsworth: Penguin, 1963).

Braunmuller, A. R. and Michael Hattaway (eds), *The Cambridge Companion to English Renaissance Drama* (Cambridge: Cambridge University Press, 1990).

Bristol, Michael D., *Carnival and Theater: Plebeian Culture and the Structure of Authority in Renaissance England* (London: Methuen, 1985).

Bruster, Douglas, *Drama and the Market in the Age of Shakespeare* (Cambridge: Cambridge University Press, 1992).

Butler, Martin, *Theatre and Crisis 1632–1642* (Cambridge: Cambridge University Press, 1984).

Cordner, Michael, Peter Holland and John Kerrigan (eds), *English Comedy* (Cambridge: Cambridge University Press, 1994).

Cox, John D. and David Scott Kastan (eds), *A New History of Early English Drama* (New York: Columbia University Press, 1997).

Esche, Edward J. (ed.), *Shakespeare and His Contemporaries in Performance* (Aldershot: Ashgate, 2000).

Gibbons, Brian, *Jacobean City Comedy* (London: Methuen, 1980).

Griswold, Wendy, *Renaissance Revivals: City Comedy and Revenge Tragedy in the London Theatre, 1576–1980* (Chicago and London: University of Chicago Press, 1986).

Gurr, Andrew, *The Shakespearean Stage 1574–1642*, 3rd edition (Cambridge: Cambridge University Press, 1992).

Gurr, Andrew, *Playgoing in Shakespeare's London* (Cambridge: Cambridge University Press, 1987).

Gurr, Andrew, *The Shakespearean Playing Companies* (Oxford: Clarendon Press, 1996).

Hattaway, Michael, *Elizabethan Popular Theatre: Plays in Performance* (London: Routledge, 1982).

Heinemann, Margot, *Puritanism and Theatre: Thomas Middleton and Opposition Drama under the Early Stuarts* (Cambridge: Cambridge University Press, 1980).

Howard, Jean E., *The Stage and Social Struggle in Early Modern England* (London and New York: Routledge, 1994).

Kastan, David Scott, *Shakespeare After Theory* (London: Routledge, 1999).

Kastan, David Scott (ed.), *A Companion to Shakespeare* (Oxford: Blackwell, 1999).

Kastan, David Scott and Peter Stallybrass (eds), *Staging the Renaissance: Reinterpretations of Elizabethan and Jacobean Drama* (London and New York: Routledge, 1991).

Kinney, Arthur F. (ed.), *A Companion to English Renaissance Drama* (Oxford: Blackwell, 2002).

Leggatt, Alexander, *English Stage Comedy 1490–1990* (London: Routledge, 1998).

Leggatt, Alexander, *Introduction to English Renaissance Comedy* (Manchester: Manchester University Press, 1999).

Leinwand, Theodore B., *The City Staged: Jacobean Comedy 1603–1613* (Madison, Wisconsin, 1986).

McLuskie, Kathleen, *Renaissance Dramatists* (Hemel Hempstead: Harvester Wheatsheaf, 1989).

Masten, Jeffrey, *Textual Intercourse: Collaboration, Authorship, and Sexualities in Renaissance Drama* (Cambridge: Cambridge University Press, 1996).

Scott, Michael, *Renaissance Drama and a Modern Audience* (Basingstoke: Macmillan, 1982).

Shaughnessy, Robert (ed.), *Shakespeare in Performance: Contemporary Critical Essays* (Basingstoke: Macmillan, 2000).

Shepherd, Simon and Peter Womack, *English Drama: A Cultural History* (Oxford: Blackwell, 1996).

Smith, David L., Richard Strier and David Bevington (eds), *The Theatrical City: Culture, Theatre and Politics in London, 1576–1649* (Cambridge: Cambridge University Press, 1995).

Weimann, Robert, *Shakespeare and the Popular Tradition in the Theater*, trans. Robert Schwartz (Baltimore: Johns Hopkins University Press, 1978).

Weimann, Robert, *Author's Pen and Actor's Voice* (Cambridge: Cambridge University Press, 2000).

Thomson, Peter, *Shakespeare's Theatre*, 2nd edition (London: Routledge, 1992).

White, Martin, *Renaissance Drama in Action* (London: Routledge, 1998).

Wiggins, Martin, *Shakespeare and the Drama of His Time* (Oxford: Oxford University Press, 2000).

Wiles, David, *Shakespeare's Clown: Actor and Text in the Elizabethan Playhouse* (Cambridge: Cambridge University Press, 1987).

Zimmerman, Susan (ed.), *Erotic Politics: Desire on the Renaissance Stage* (London and New York: Routledge, 1992).

AQA

AS/A LEVEL YEAR 1

WORKBOOK

Physics

Mechanics and materials
Electricity

Jeremy Pollard

HODDER EDUCATION
LEARN MORE

Contents

WORKBOOK

Section 4 Mechanics and materials

Topic 1 Force, energy and momentum 3
    Scalars and vectors. 3
    Moments 5
    Motion along a straight line 7
    Projectile motion 10
    Newton's laws of motion 12
    Momentum 13
    Work, energy and power 15
    Conservation of energy 17

Topic 2 Materials 21
    Bulk properties of solids 21
    The Young modulus 24

Section 5 Electricity

Topic 1 Current electricity 29
    Basics of electricity 29
    Current–voltage characteristics 30
    Resistivity 32
    Circuits 33
    Potential divider 34
    Electromotive force and internal resistance 36

① **This workbook will help you** to prepare for the following exams:

- AQA Physics AS Paper 1: the exam is 1 hour 30 minutes long, worth 70 marks and 50% of your AS. There is a range of questions split by topic.
- AQA Physics AS Paper 2: the exam is 1 hour 30 minutes long, worth 70 marks and 50% of your AS. There are three sections to the exam: Section A covers practical skills and data analysis, Section B tests all areas of AS content, and Section C contains multiple-choice questions.
- AQA Physics A-level Paper 1: the exam is 2 hours long, worth 34% of your A-level and includes a range of questions. The exam is divided into two sections. In Section A you will answer short- and long-answer questions worth 60 marks. In Section B you will answer 25 multiple-choice questions worth 1 mark each.

② **For each topic** there are:

- stimulus materials, including key terms and concepts
- short-answer questions
- long-answer questions
- multiple-choice questions
- questions that test your mathematical skills
- space for you to write your answers

③ **Answering the questions** will help you to build your skills and meet the three assessment objectives, AO1 (knowledge and understanding), AO2 (application) and AO3 (analysis, interpretation and evaluation).

④ **You still need** to read your textbook and refer to your revision guides and lesson notes.

⑤ **Marks available** are indicated for all questions so that you can gauge the level of detail required in your answers.

⑥ **Timings** are given for the exam-style questions to make your practice as realistic as possible.

⑦ **Answers** are available at:
www.hoddereducation.co.uk/workbookanswers